M000035931

HARRY HOPKINS

The Franklin and Eleanor Roosevelt Institute Series on
Diplomatic and Economic History

General Editors: Arthur M. Schlesinger, Jr., William vanden Heuvel, and Douglas Brinkley

**FDR AND HIS
CONTEMPORARIES**
FOREIGN PERCEPTIONS OF AN AMERICAN
PRESIDENT
Edited by Cornelis A. van Minnen
and John F. Sears

**NATO: THE FOUNDING OF THE
ATLANTIC ALLIANCE
AND THE INTEGRATION OF
EUROPE**
Edited by Francis H. Heller and
John R. Gillingham

AMERICA UNBOUND
WORLD WAR II AND THE MAKING
OF A SUPERPOWER
Edited by Warren F. Kimball

**THE ORIGINS OF U.S. NUCLEAR
STRATEGY, 1945-1953**
Samuel R. Williamson, Jr. and
Steven L. Rearden

**AMERICAN DIPLOMATS IN THE
NETHERLANDS, 1815-50**
Cornelis A. van Minnen

**EISENHOWER, KENNEDY, AND
THE UNITED STATES OF EUROPE**
Pascaline Winand

ALLIES AT WAR
THE SOVIET, AMERICAN, AND BRITISH
EXPERIENCE, 1939-1945
Edited by David Reynolds, Warren F. Kimball,
and A. O. Chubarian

THE ATLANTIC CHARTER
Edited by Douglas Brinkley and
David R. Facey-Crowther

PEARL HARBOR REVISITED
Edited by Robert W. Love, Jr.

FDR AND THE HOLOCAUST
Edited by Verne W. Newton

**THE UNITED STATES AND THE
INTEGRATION OF EUROPE**
LEGACIES OF THE POSTWAR ERA
Edited by Francis H. Heller and John R.
Gillingham

ADENAUER AND KENNEDY
A STUDY IN GERMAN-AMERICAN
RELATIONS
Frank A. Mayer

**THEODORE ROOSEVELT AND
THE BRITISH EMPIRE**
A STUDY IN PRESIDENTIAL STATECRAFT
William N. Tilchin

**TARIFFS, TRADE AND EUROPEAN
INTEGRATION, 1947-1957**
FROM STUDY GROUP TO COMMON
MARKET
Wendy Asbeek Brusse

SUMNER WELLES
FDR'S GLOBAL STRATEGIST
A Biography by Benjamin Welles

**THE NEW DEAL AND PUBLIC
POLICY**
Edited by Byron W. Daynes, William D.
Pederson, and Michael P. Riccards

WORLD WAR II IN EUROPE
Edited by Charles F. Brower

FDR AND THE U.S. NAVY
Edward J. Marolda

**THE SECOND QUEBEC
CONFERENCE REVISITED**
Edited by David B. Woolner

HARRY HOPKINS
SUDDEN HERO, BRASH REFORMER
June Hopkins

HARRY HOPKINS

SUDDEN HERO, BRASH REFORMER

June Hopkins

St. Martin's Press
New York

HARRY HOPKINS: SUDDEN HERO, BRASH REFORMER

©June Hopkins 1999. All rights reserved. Printed in the United States of America. No part of this book may be used or reproduced in any manner whatsoever without written permission except in the case of brief quotations embodied in critical articles or reviews. For information, address St. Martin's Press, 175 Fifth Avenue, New York, N.Y. 10010.

ISBN 0-312-21206-2

Library of Congress Cataloging-in-Publication Data

Hopkins, June, 1940-
    Harry Hopkins: sudden hero, brash reformer / June Hopkins
    p. cm.
  Includes bibliographical references and index
  ISBN 0-312-21206-2
  1. Hopkins, Harry Lloyd, 1890-1946. 2. Social reformers—United
States—Biography. 3. Public welfare—United States—History—20th
century. 4. United States—Social policy. 5. New Deal, 1933-1939.
  I. Title.
  HV28.H66 H66 1999
  361.2'4'092—dc21
  [B]   98-37963
                                                  CIP

First published in hardcover in the United States of America in 1999

10 9 8 7 6 5 4 3 2 1

To Dennis K. Bradley

Contents

Six pages of photographs appear between pages 124 and 125.

Abbreviations

AALL	American Association for Labor Legislations
AASW	American Association of Social Workers
ADC	Aid to Dependent Children
AFDC	Aid to Families with Dependent Children
AFL	American Federation of Labor
AICP	Association for Improving the Condition of the Poor
APH	Anna Pickett Hopkins
ARC	American Red Cross
BCW	Bureau of Child Welfare
CES	Committee on Economic Security
COS	Charity Organization Society
CSS	Community Service Society
CWA	Civil Works Administration
DAH	David Aldona Hopkins
EFS	Equal Franchise Society
EGH	Ethel Gross Hopkins
EWB	Emergency Work Bureau
FERA	Federal Emergency Relief Administration
FTP	Federal Theatre Project
HLH	Harry L. Hopkins
MLH	Municipal Lodging House
NCL	National Consumers League
NCLC	National Child Labor Committee
NIRA	National Industrial Relations Administration
NYHA	New York Health Association
NYTBA	New York Tuberculosis Association
NYTBHA	New York Tuberculosis and Health Association
OAA	Old Age Assistance
PWA	Public Works Administration
RFC	Reconstruction Finance Corporation
SCAA	State Charities Aid Association
SSL	Social Service League
TERA	Temporary Emergency Relief Administration
WPA	Work Progress Administration
WPU	Women's Political Union
WTUL	Women's Trade Union League

Acknowledgments

There are a great many people to thank for their help over the past years while I was writing this book. Georgetown University's History Department has been generous in the support they have given me. I am particularly grateful to Richard Duncan, Ronald Johnson, and Emmett Curren for their advice and encouragement. Edward Berkowitz at George Washington University was most helpful in pointing me in new directions during the writing process.

From the very beginning, Dorothy Brown has been a gentle critic, an enthusiastic mentor, and, most of all, an inspiring model of what a scholar should be. My colleagues at Georgetown, Joseph Slater, Peter Cole, and Daniel Byrne, all took the time out of their hectic schedules to read various drafts of my manuscript, and they all made valuable suggestions. Their moral support was even more appreciated. Allida Black has been a constant friend and booster. She has shared with me her considerable scholarly expertise and, on occasion, made lunch. Lynne Luciano, who was present when this all started, has given me unbounded encouragement and really good movie tips.

I am beholden to the staff at the various archives I visited for their expertise and guidance. The Franklin and Eleanor Roosevelt Institute provided me with a generous grant which allowed me to conduct my research at the Franklin Delano Roosevelt Library at Hyde Park. I thank Vernon Newton and the staff there, especially Bob Parks and Nancy Snedeker. I am also grateful to Anne Kintner at the Grinnell College Archives, Ingrid Hopkins at Christodora, Inc., and Nicholas Scheetz at Georgetown University's Special Collections. They all provided me with indispensable help. In addition, I am grateful to my aunt, Diana Hopkins Halsted, who generously shared information with me.

My very good friends in New York City eased the rigors of research for me in so many ways. Harriette Delsener, Anna and Irving Straus, and Penny Miller provided me with their loving hospitality while I was struggling through masses of material. Mary Brosnahan's wisdom and insight enabled me to relate the history I was writing to the present. Talking to Gail Jaffe on the phone or having tea with her in her rose garden calmed me down and geared me up. They will all have my eternal gratitude.

I thank with all my heart my sisters, Cherry Bandler, Jo Ann Hopkins, Stephanie Harris, Barbara Cleveland, Kit Raeder, Jill Hopkins, and Sarah Hopkins and my brothers, Harry Hopkins and John Hopkins. I owe so much to them for their fierce loyalty and dedication to family. My niece and Down Under journalist, Cerentha Harris, read parts of the manuscript and used her considerable intellect to help me center my arguments. Individually they are remarkable. Collectively they are my ballast.

Ethel Gross Hopkins Conant, my grandmother and my inspiration, kept everything—letters, diaries, photos, and even notes on books she read. I am indebted to her for that and for the memories she left me. I never asked her all the questions, but I know she would have wanted me to tell this story.

My partner, Dennis Bradley, saw me through this six-year project with remarkable stamina and equanimity. He is also an ace proofreader. More than anything, his loving presence has given me the courage to try a new path.

Finally, my daughter, Allison Giffen, and my son, David Giffen, have given me not only brilliant ideas and constant emotional support but a reason to write this book.

CHAPTER ONE

INTRODUCTION

ONE HOT SUMMER DAY IN 1935, federal relief administrator Harry Hopkins presented his plan for alleviating the effects of the Great Depression to a group of shirt-sleeved Iowa farmers, not noted for their liberal ideas. As Hopkins began to describe how government-sponsored jobs on public projects would provide both wages for the unemployed and a stimulus for foundering businesses, a voice shouted out the question that was on everyone's mind: "Who's going to pay for all that?" Hopkins, with his characteristic flair for the dramatic, slowly took off his coat and tie, rolled up his sleeves, and looked out at the now-fascinated audience sitting outside on the Iowa University campus. Everyone knew the extent of Hopkins' influence in Washington. He spoke for the president. "You are," Hopkins shouted, "and who better? Who can better afford to pay for it? Look at this great university. Look at these fields, these forests and rivers. This is America, the richest country in the world. We can afford to pay for anything we want. And we want a decent life for all the people in this country. And we are going to pay for it."[1] Ever optimistic as to the future of America, even during the dark days of the Great Depression, Hopkins was convinced that there was no good reason "for any American to be destitute, to be illiterate, to be reduced by the bondage of [unemployment and poverty] into either political or economic impotence."[2]

Harry Hopkins, President Franklin Roosevelt's outspoken and often caustic relief administrator, seemed to have reached the pinnacle of his social work career after only two intense, crisis-filled years in Washington. Dedicated to democracy, capitalism, and government responsibility for families in need, he had brought to Washington some very distinct ideas about the relief of poverty. He impatiently rejected the concept that "the respectable rich have rammed down the throats of Americans [—the idea that] those who cannot make a living are in some way reprehensible, in some way morally corrupt; and must not be helped because they are worthless, shiftless and always will remain so."[3] Hopkins took a positive view of human nature, believing that the unemployed poor wanted only the dignity of work. He was committed to the American capitalist system. While he recognized that American business and industry certainly had a "predatory" side, he knew that the profit motive provided the ballast for the ship of state.

Hopkins' methods and his ideals seemed to strike a common note with those of his boss, and the two men, despite their different backgrounds, forged a mutual trust and a deep friendship that endured through the long years of depression and war. John Adams Kingsbury, a prominent New York social worker and Hopkins' long-time friend, wrote that Hopkins had "that rare quality of boldness of mind combined with vigorous and courageous action." This, Kingsbury guessed, was the key to the bond between Roosevelt and Hopkins.[4] Whatever the nature of that bond, Roosevelt trusted Hopkins implicitly—trusted his instincts and trusted his loyalty. Hopkins likewise had tremendous admiration for the president and generally followed his lead in the setting of policy. He had the president's ear, and this gave him enormous power during Roosevelt's four terms of office. From 1933 through 1945 most Washington insiders knew that if something needed to be done, Hopkins was the man to see. No president had ever placed such confidence in another man; no president had given another man such power and influence. Yet the Iowa farm boy who made a career of spending other people's money, the man who became indispensable to one of America's most effective presidents, died with virtually no money to his name. He left a much richer endowment.

In a 1946 memorial on the occasion of Harry Hopkins' death, novelist John Steinbeck wrote that Hopkins, who had served his country in peace and war, left an idea as his most important legacy to the American people—the idea that "human welfare is the first and final task of government. It has no other."[5] During the 1930s Hopkins had no other task but the welfare of Americans made destitute and hopeless because of the economic crisis. For Hopkins, the task of national economic recovery had to begin with jobs for the unemployed. This formed the core of his social policy. By the time he arrived in Washington in May 1933, it had become the driving force behind everything he did. But Hopkins' social policies had deep roots.

Gwendolyn Mink, in her recently published study of government policy toward poor women, notes that "the initiatives of the Progressive Era became the reflexes of the New Deal."[6] An investigation into Harry Hopkins' career before 1933 can shed light on the connectives between these initiatives and the resultant New Deal reflexes, and looking at this history in light of New Deal policies can clarify the evolution of America's welfare system. The social philosophy that informed the New Deal programs Hopkins formulated and directed from 1933 to 1939 had been developing over two decades, drawing from his education at Grinnell College, his experiences at Christodora Settlement House, his work with the New York Association for Improving the Conditions of the Poor (AICP), his administration of widows' pensions in New York City, his wartime activities with the Red Cross, his involvement with public health issues during the 1920s as head of the New York Tuberculosis Association, and his work as head of New York State relief from 1931 to 1933. In 1933 President Roosevelt made Hopkins his federal relief administrator, giving him responsibility for both direct- and work-relief programs. As federal relief administrator, Hopkins sat on the president's cabinet-level Committee on Economic Security that wrote the Social Security Act of 1935, the revolutionary legislation that established federal responsibility for the economic well-being of Americans.

Hopkins' policies developed in crucial ways during his formative years as a New York City social worker. There, from 1912 to 1917, he developed a credo influenced by a city rife with social and economic problems, political upheavals, and social dissension. He became convinced that work was eminently better than the dole both for the morale of the welfare recipient and the economic health of the nation, and that the state should provide public funds for women with dependent children in amounts sufficient to allow mothers to stay home and care for their children. His dedication to full employment and counter-cyclical public works as a way to ensure economic stability for the American worker took root during the severe recession of 1915, when he devised one of the first work-relief programs in New York City. As secretary of the New York City Board of Child Welfare from 1915 to 1917, Hopkins came to recognize both the logic and the pitfalls of mothers' pensions.

During the Great Depression twenty years later, Hopkins' emphasis on work-relief and federal jobs programs drew from this early experience. Dedicated to jobs as an antidote to poverty caused by unemployment, he was convinced that the vast army of idle American workers wanted nothing more than the opportunity to earn a decent living. Therefore, he committed himself to ensuring that jobs would be available, even if he had to create them himself. The economic crisis of the 1930s reinforced his belief that employment assurance resulting from rationally planned public works programs could be used during times of economic depression as an alternate form of unemployment insurance.

From 1933 to 1935 these two previously distinct policies, work-relief and mothers' pensions, merged during Hopkins' management of the Federal Emergency Relief Administration (FERA), the Civil Works Administration (CWA), and the Works Progress Administration (WPA). This merger resulted in the American system of social security. Hopkins continuously and vociferously defended the government-sponsored work-relief and jobs programs he directed by placing them well within the American tradition. He argued that federal help for the deserving needy was but an extension of our national heritage: "From the very first years of Washington's administration the national government intervened with all its resources frequently and aggressively in order to develop commerce, agriculture and industry." He listed free land for war veterans, railroad companies, and settlers; internal improvements; protective tariffs; public utility franchises; and bank credit—all ways that the national government had not only enlarged American industry but "put men to work [and] created buying power."[7] It should do no less for American workers in the midst of a national depression. Government jobs programs employing previously idle workers not only ameliorated the miseries of unemployment but also helped stabilize business by increasing consumerism. Hopkins' commitment to this solution to poverty emerged from his firm belief that merely providing cash or in-kind relief degraded the recipient, wasted his or her work potential, and returned little to the community.

Hopkins recognized full well that the work programs would not be a solution for poor women with dependent children. He had campaigned for and then administered the widows' pension program in New York City during the Progressive Era,[8] and he remained committed to public assistance for families without a breadwinner, not as charity but as an entitlement. In 1914 and again in 1934, Hopkins supported public funding for needy mothers as a way to ensure that no child would be removed from the home merely because the family was poor. Further, such assistance would ensure that fatherless children would have the benefit of maternal guidance and nurturance. The state-funded mothers' pension programs served as a model for Title IV of the Social Security Act, Aid to Dependent Children (ADC, later AFDC). In 1935 Hopkins made clear his adherence to the prevailing assumptions as to women's role in society when he declared that it would be "unthinkable" that any social security program would not encompass support for the fatherless families, not only because waged work for mothers threatened the well-being of children but also because women looking for work to support their families were competing with men on relief who were also seeking work.[9]

Hopkins lost his fight for a permanent job assurance program, and his particular plan for ADC was not adopted. Yet he retained his position as FDR's confidential advisor, a position of immense power in Washington during the crisis years of the Great Depression and World War II. He himself wondered how this had come about. In 1912 he was just a "hick" from Iowa, no different from hundreds of other college graduates who traveled to New York City with high hopes. In July of 1941 when he flew to Moscow at Roosevelt's behest to confer with Joseph Stalin, he remembered thinking: "I couldn't believe it. There I was, walking up the staircase, going to talk to a man who ruled 180 million people. And I asked myself—what are you doing here, Hopkins, you—the son of a harness maker from Sioux City?" A friend, responding to this statement, said to Hopkins, "Can't you ever stop boasting about your humble origins? It's the only sign of pretentiousness I've ever seen in you."[10] The echo of Hopkins publicly reveling in his Midwestern roots must be taken as a cue by any historian to look more deeply into the man's past.

There can be no doubt that his Iowa roots defined a good part of his social policies and political ideology. His family was well aware of this. In a 1964 taped interview Ethel Gross Hopkins Conant, who was married to Hopkins when he was a social worker in New York and the South, made reference to one of Hopkins' biographers who wrote: "A native of Iowa, Hopkins left Grinnell upon graduation for New York City where he became a prominent social worker." Conant remarked to the interviewer, "Well, it wasn't quite that quick. I don't wonder that people wondered what right he had to be doing all those things; and what right, what background did he have for being put in such a responsible spot with so much money at his disposal? And I think for that reason, more needs to be told about his background."[11] Yet Hopkins' career before 1933, a period during which he formulated his single-minded perspective on how to provide economic security for Americans, has been largely ignored by historians. While scholars have examined Hopkins' work during the New Deal as relief administrator, none have drawn the important connection between the policies developed in the 1930s and his experience with work-relief and mothers' pensions during the Progressive Era in New York City.

Two of the best sources for overall information on Harry Hopkins are Robert E. Sherwood's *Roosevelt and Hopkins: An Intimate History* (1948) and George McJimsey's *Harry Hopkins: Ally of the Poor, Defender of Democracy* (1987). Sherwood's widely acclaimed book, although written fifty years ago, provides a rich source of data on Hopkins' life, but the emphasis is on his relationship to Franklin Roosevelt and most of the book deals with the war years. In the late 1940s Sherwood wrote a letter to Hopkins' old friend John Kingsbury, in which he admitted that he was emphasizing Hopkins' role as Roosevelt's wartime emissary and would give little attention to his social work career. Sherwood suggested that Kingsbury write a supplementary volume about that experience. Kingsbury never did.[12]

George McJimsey's meticulously researched and insightful biography of Hopkins, written in 1987, paid more attention to the Depression era but devoted only thirteen pages to his family and his Grinnell experiences and fewer than twenty pages to his social work in New York City. Moreover, it was McJimsey's intention to emphasize Hopkins' development as a professional social worker rather than to draw connections between his social policy and the emerging American welfare state.

Additional biographers include Henry Adams, Searle F. Charles, and Paul A. Kurzman.[13] Adams skims over Hopkins' early years and draws no connection between his social work career and his later achievements. Charles provides a very good, in-depth account of the New Deal work-relief programs but very little of Hopkins' life before 1933. The Kurzman book presents an especially interesting analysis of Hopkins' personality and innovative administrative style. Although he does note that Hopkins was instrumental in establishing the citizen's right to a workable economic system, he does not discuss this in connection with the Social Security Act. Because these biographies were written over twenty years ago, they lack the perspective added by the exciting new research into the history of welfare in America.[14]

In 1956, ten years after Hopkins died, Donald Howard of the Russell Sage Foundation, dean of the School of Social Welfare at UCLA and author of *The WPA and Federal Relief Policy,* also suggested to John Kingsbury that someone should write a book about Hopkins' social work career, stating "for a long time I have had the impression that the work of Harry Hopkins as a social worker and as a man deeply interested in social welfare has to date been very inadequately documented."[15] There is no doubt that a more complete understanding of this phase of Hopkins' career can help to decipher the man and his motives and can provide new insight into the American welfare system. Yet the story begins even earlier.

Hopkins' contribution to the American welfare system cannot be understood without first examining his family background and education in Grinnell, Iowa, a town smack in the middle of the United States that provided a substructure for the way he thought about American society. In this small farming community young Harry stumbled a bit, finally found his footing, and used the training he received at home and the direction he received at college as a springboard for his unique form of practical idealism. By 1933, when Harry Hopkins burst upon the public scene with a suddenness that took even his contemporaries by surprise, he had been preparing for his role as hero of the unemployed and minister of relief for many years. The story begins with Hopkins as a product of genteel Midwest poverty, of a religious upbringing rooted in Methodism, of an education steeped in the Social Gospel, and of a large and rather boisterous family.

CHAPTER TWO

FROM THE DAKOTAS TO GRINNELL, IOWA

What men say and think about the operations of oxygen and hydrogen makes no difference to the phenomena; but what men say and think about the relations of capitalists and employees does make a difference.

—Professor Jesse Macy, Grinnell College

HARRY HOPKINS GREW UP IN A LARGE, CLOSELY-KNIT HOUSEHOLD that contained three generations. The family was bound together by moral lessons taught by his parents, David Aldona and Anna Pickett Hopkins, lessons that were drawn from the experiences of their forebears. Although the Hopkins and Picketts originally came from Scotland, England, and Canada, it was the American Midwest that molded Hopkins into an urban social worker and federal relief administrator. From his Iowa roots, Hopkins absorbed some of his mother's Methodist teachings, his father's cynicism, his sister's commitment to social service, and his college's Social Gospel message that rallied Christians to the cause of reform, and combined them with his own idealism and ambition.

Hopkins learned a great deal from his father. Not all of these lessons, especially a tendency toward excessive frankness, had a positive effect on his public career. Yet there can be no doubt that David Aldona (Al) Hopkins exerted a strong influence on his son's early development. Al's complicated personality can be better understood in light of his experiences as a young man on the American frontier in the wake of the Panic of 1873. Then eighteen years of age, Al had the vitality of youth, a yearning for adventure, and a need to make some money in hard times. Al's father, Lewis Hopkins, was no stranger to adventure and the pioneer spirit. He had fought for the Union Army for four years and survived. At the end of the Civil War, the lure of a better life in the West brought Lewis to Sioux City, Iowa. He left his family in Bangor, Maine, and, too eager to wait until the railroad was completed, made the difficult journey overland. Lewis had married Mary Ann Emery in Bangor, where his father held the position of police chief for a time. David Aldona, born May 26, 1856, was their only surviving child. Two months after Lewis left, his wife and child followed—more comfortably and certainly more quickly on the newly completed railroad.[1]

In the late 1860s Sioux City was "an unpretentious looking place, with a motley array of one and two story frame buildings." Lewis Hopkins started a business digging water wells. Al entered the local grammar school and got a job with the local newspaper, a job that required him to rise at three-thirty every morning and perform a wide variety of jobs—everything from turning the wheel for printing to delivering the paper. Yet despite hard work the family had little money. It is therefore not hard to understand why eighteen-year-old Al Hopkins was seduced by promises of treasure in the nearby Black Hills of the Dakota Territory. According to the Treaty of Laramie, signed by President Andrew Johnson and the Sioux chiefs in 1868, this area was set aside for the exclusive use of the Sioux Nation. Government troops were under strict orders to turn back any expedition that encroached upon this land, using force if necessary. However, in 1874 an army expedition (partly scientific in nature) of over 1,000 men led by Lieutenant Colonel George Armstrong Custer went into the Black Hills, ostensibly to subdue nonagency Indians. There Custer was awed not only by the beauty of the area but by the gold that two of his men found at French Creek. When Custer himself confirmed the rumors that there was indeed gold in the hills, and lots of it, the newspapers picked up the message and triggered one of America's biggest gold rushes.[2]

Although the War Department warned that gold-seekers were strictly forbidden to trespass in the area, adventurer John Gordon, reputed to be an experienced guide, took two expeditions into the Black Hills. Al Hopkins joined the second. News that there was gold in the hills must have been especially tantalizing to Americans in the midst of an economic depression. By 1875 Sioux City was feeling its effects. Money was scarce and opportunity scarcer still. Al's lifelong penchant for chasing rainbows and non-existent pots of gold probably was first manifested publicly by his eagerness to embark on this adventure. He, like many others, obviously felt no compunction about trespassing onto what was by law Sioux territory in order to take what did not belong to him. But what can be seen as a regrettable lack of moral fiber might also be regarded as rugged individualism. Sioux City in 1870s, after all, was a frontier town where Wild Bill Hickok and Calamity Jane were local heroes. Inevitably, the U.S. Army caught up with the expedition. Suspicious of the mining equipment on the pack animals, the soldiers ordered the group to leave the territory. When Gordon refused, the soldiers turned a Gatling gun on the would-be prospectors and then burned the entire camp in one giant bonfire. Al Hopkins saw his dreams go up in those flames, and he returned to Sioux City as poor as when he left. But he never got over the need to take a chance and try for something better.[3]

His adventure is paradigmatic of his impulsive and somewhat irresponsible character. But it also reflects Al Hopkins' enduring optimism and a belief that anything is possible if one only tries, a valuable lesson that he passed on to his son Harry. Al never went on another expedition in search of gold, but he always seemed to have a new and better plan for the future, one that was sure to improve his life. The fact that most of his plans failed fueled his cynicism and depressed him briefly but did not seem to deter him. Characteristically, Harry Hopkins' father would dream up another opportunity which he would pursue with enthusiasm.[4]

Anna Pickett, Harry Hopkins' mother, was ten years old in the autumn of 1870 when her family moved from Ontario to the Dakota Territory. Her father, Andrew, a carpenter by trade, had filed a claim for 160 acres of land in Vermilion, near the borders of Nebraska and Iowa. The Picketts had been in Canada for several generations and boasted a strong Methodist background. Anna's father was the grandson of the Reverend Daniel Pickett, born July 4, 1771, in New Milford, Connecticut. He converted to Methodism when he was twenty-one, and in 1800 the church sent him to Ontario, Canada, as a forty-dollar-a-year circuit-riding "saddle bag" preacher. He and his first wife, Lavinia, eventually settled in the tiny hamlet of Lowville, Ontario, where he acquired some land under a crown grant. His grandson, Andrew, left Ontario and settled down to life in Vermillion, earning his living as a builder. Neighbors considered Andrew Pickett a kind man, one who took his religion very seriously. His daughter, Anna, probably inherited her religious zeal from her father.[5]

Anna Pickett was a serious and dutiful young woman who, after finishing high school, became a schoolteacher in Vermillion. She was not a great beauty but she had a gentleness and quiet steadiness that must have been very appealing. Anna's schoolmate, fellow teacher, and good friend was the daughter of Samuel Hayward, who owned the local harness shop. In 1878 Al

Hopkins and his mother, Mary, moved from Sioux City to Vermillion, one year after Lewis died. Soon after their arrival Al got a job in Sam Hayward's harness shop and met and courted Anna. They were married on May 1, 1881, and seemed an odd if not ill-matched couple. His reputation as an adventurer, however, held a fascination for Anna. She, on the other hand, represented normalcy for him and a stability that he needed after the Gordon fiasco. True to her great-grandfather, the Reverend Daniel Pickett, Anna was a devout Methodist who valued piety, discretion, hard work, and, above all, education. Although her conservative values often clashed with those of her more flamboyant husband, Anna remained a devoted wife, followed him to eleven cities, and steadfastly endured his capricious business schemes, his frenetic optimism, and his subsequent bouts of moody pessimism (as well as his very demanding mother, Mary, who lived with them until she died in 1915). And she bore him five children.[6]

The Picketts' adherence to the Methodism of John Wesley reflected a significant chapter in America's religious history because this religious movement influenced the growth of the Social Gospel in America. Historian Halford E. Luccock referred to the saddle bags carried by Anna's great-grandfather and other ministers as "magic instruments, for in the providence of God, out of them came churches, schools, colleges, courthouses, and, most powerful of all, changed and empowered lives of men and women."[7] The Methodism practiced in the Hopkins' household at the insistence of Anna had an impact on young Harry's attitude toward the world around him. He grew up in an atmosphere that was permeated by a religion that demanded service to others as a prerequisite for individual salvation.

Methodism's tradition of revivalism and enthusiastic religion made a significant contribution to the Great Awakening, the burst of evangelicalism that arose in the United States during the 1740s. The Methodist church's commitment to peaceful reform gave the evangelical movement political and social import. John Wesley taught that individual holiness was incomplete and demanded more than merely personal salvation, claiming that "[p]ersonal holiness can only speak to society through the shared behavior of a Christian community. One dimension of social holiness is that which brings Christian community into relationship with the social order."[8] This challenge posed by the Protestant churches to Christians in the face of a series of economic upheavals caused by a rapidly industrializing society was taken up by Social Gospelers during the latter part of the nineteenth century. Both Methodism and the Social Gospel served as precursors for the Progressive Movement in the United States, a movement that responded to the inequities of an industrializing nation, and both cultivated Harry Hopkins' social philosophy.

Methodism, with its rejection of pretension and materialism, spoke volumes to Harry Hopkins' mother. During the early nineteenth century American religion underwent what some historians have called a distinct "feminization."[9] Historians have debated whether the feminization of religion, which reinforced women's domestic role, was actually liberating for women. A. Gregory Schneider, in his recent work on the domestication of Methodism, stated that within the Methodist tradition, which "tended, in a limited way, to transcend distinctions of gender identity," women were able to assume a more active public role and thus expand their sphere of activity through their association with a religious institution. At the same time, Methodism encouraged women to remain safely within the domestic sphere acting as an inspiration to men.[10] For Anna Pickett this powerful but essentially domestic role would remain integral to her manner of influencing her family's decisions. She easily and willingly took on the mantle of religious piety and, with an iron will born of righteousness, directed the lives of her husband and children from a power base of hearth, home, and church. With a faith inherited from generations of her pious forebears, Anna attempted to pass on to her children the ideals of Methodism—a spirit of voluntarism, a commitment to service to others, and a sense of an interdependent Christian community. Anna was only partially successful in this endeavor.[11] But when she married Al, her strong religious background sustained an optimism for the future.

Soon after Al and Anna's marriage in 1881, a huge ice jam formed in the Missouri River. When it finally broke apart, flood waters destroyed the entire business section and much of the residential area of Vermillion. The young couple was forced to leave. Al and Anna (and mother-in-law Mary) moved to Nebraska, first to Freemont and then to North Bend, where Al got a job in a harness shop. Soon after in 1882 Adah May Hopkins was born, followed by Lewis Andrew Hopkins in 1884 and Rome Miller Hopkins in 1887. Anna began to feel that their life was finally secure. Of course, they did not have a lot of money, but her husband did have a steady job and her children were growing up in a settled household. But times were difficult in Nebraska during the 1880s, and the Hopkins family never seemed to get ahead of the bill collector. An old friend, Rome Miller, lent Al a large sum of money to open a store in Norfolk, Nebraska. In 1937 Miller wrote a letter to Harry Hopkins saying "I have no recollection of your father ever taking a drink, smoking, or swearing. Neither do I recall him ever tending strictly to business."[12] This was painfully obvious; the business failed within a year.

The Hopkins' odyssey continued. It must have been increasingly tedious for Anna, for the moves usually occurred when she was either pregnant or had a small child to care for. Years later she wrote a letter to her son Harry that gave some indication of the difficulties she had endured as well as the strength she had developed during the hard times. She told him that she survived these unpleasant experiences by learning "not to let them overcome me for we can do without so many things if we only think so." In 1889, just after their third child, infant Etta, died, the family moved from Norfolk, Nebraska, to Sioux City, Iowa, where Al again found employment in a local harness shop. On August 17, 1890, their fourth child, Harry Lloyd, was born in the city where Al had first exhibited his adventurous spirit by embarking on the Second Gordon Expedition. Soon after Harry's birth, either wanderlust or financial straits caused the family to move again, this time to Council Bluffs, Iowa, in 1891, then to Kearney, Nebraska, where in 1894 John Emery was born. From there they went to Hastings, Nebraska, in 1896 and Chicago in 1900. By this time Anna must have had enough, for she put her foot down and declared that they would settle down in one place where her children would get a good education. They—she—chose Grinnell, Iowa, because of the town's excellent schools. In 1901 the Hopkins family rented a house on the corner of Sixth and Elm streets. Al, now called "Dad" by family and friends alike, worked as a traveling salesman for a Milwaukee harness wholesaler for several years. While in Chicago on a business trip, he was run down by a horse-drawn truck and badly injured. A successful suit against the company that owned the truck brought several thousand dollars in damages. Al Hopkins used this money to buy a harness and leather store in Grinnell, which he ran with varying degrees of success and a great deal of complaining. Many of his complaints had to do with the fact that he could not devote all his time to bowling, a sport at which he excelled. Known as a "money bowler," his side bets on games often added to the family income. The family usually needed the money and what could be wrong with a little fun along the way? But more often than not, Dad Hopkins did stay home and mind the store.[13]

Harry Hopkins was eleven years old when the family moved to Grinnell. He seemed to have inherited more of his father's impiety than his mother's piety. He, along with his brothers, entered the Cooper School, located across the street from their house, and did very well academically even if his report cards indicated that his deportment was less than stellar. In the local high school, Harry developed other skills. He arranged for some friends to stuff the ballot box during a school election because he disliked how the teachers always made sure that their choices were elected to class offices. His plot, of course, was uncovered, and the election was invalidated, but his candidate (a totally inept student) won on the next election. Young Harry learned a valuable lesson about the foibles of the voting public from this experience. Yet, under the strict eye of his mother, he also attended to the spiritual and practical side of life. He regularly attended church with his family (except for Al), sometimes as often as six times a week when the revival meeting came to town. During the summers Harry helped pay for his schooling by delivering newspapers and working on farms and at the railroad yards. Once he even worked as a bricklayer.[14]

The economic well-being of the Hopkins family depended on their harness and leather business, which seemed to have more downs than ups. Dad Hopkins was well-loved by students and townspeople but he never made much money. Piqued at some farmers who neglected to pay their bills, he often complained about "poverty staring us in the face." His son Lewis, however, attributed the family's situation to his father's "champagne appetite." Anna blamed it on his obsession with bowling and his love of travel, needlessly spending money going to bowling and business conventions. Whatever the cause, by May 1915 Al Hopkins was forced to auction off most of his stock in order to pay his bills. The family had planned to liquidate the store and move out west, but because the sale did not bring them as much as they had expected they decided to stay in Grinnell, much to Anna's delight and to Al's chagrin. His dream of opening his own bowling alley would have to wait for better times.[15] For Al, good times seemed far away. His pessimistic mood continued and he became so desperate to get out of the leather business that he even looked into chicken farming as an alternative. Anna wrote to her daughter that Al was "downcast" because it looked "as though the rich were richer and the poor poorer."[16] Al Hopkins' moods continued to swing during most of his life in Grinnell, but he always managed to provide his children with a respite from Anna's rigid discipline.

Harry inherited from his irreligious and sharp-tongued father a reverence for William Jennings Bryan (which he later discarded) and an intense dislike for pretentiousness. Adopting many of the Populist ideas of his rural neighbors, Al Hopkins equated inflation with debt relief and fully supported Bryan's free-silver monetary policy—probably in the hope that it would enable the farmers to settle their debts. He tended to describe his rural neighbors as deadbeats because the farmers always seemed to owe him money for leather goods bought with their dubious credit. Yet the fact that he extended them credit speaks to a generous heart. In a letter to his son Harry in 1914 he complained "Grinnell is the same old dead country village. . . . [C]rops are good, prices high, but business is rotten. I am sick and tired of this peanut business and this town and shall get out at the earliest possible date."[17] The following winter he wrote another pessimistic letter, stating that if they were not so poor he and Anna would be able to go to New York City to visit their new grandson; but he characteristically ended the letter on an optimistic note: "But just wait until the birds sing again. There will be something doing."[18] Al's ability to sniff at his rural neighbors and to poke fun at the self-importance of local authorities may have encouraged

Harry to gravitate to city life and certainly engendered in him a dislike of formalism, but, more important, his father's attitude that things will always come out right in the end encouraged in Harry Hopkins a "can-do" attitude, an approach that served him very well as New Deal relief administrator.[19]

By the time the Hopkins family had settled in Grinnell, Anna had developed into a somewhat harsh woman who took her religion very seriously and eventually became president of the Iowa Methodist Home Missionary Society. Letters she wrote to her family reveal that she placed a great deal of importance on education as a means to a higher, more spiritual end. Anna was determined that her children would have the opportunities that a college degree provided—the chance not only to succeed materially but also to improve the world in which they lived. Simmering with moral righteousness and religious fervor, she instilled in all of her children values that stressed one's moral obligation to help the less fortunate and insisted that service to others was the most important way to manifest one's religious feelings.[20]

In a 1964 interview Harry Hopkins' first wife, Ethel Gross, described his relationship with his mother: "I think Harry admired his mother very much and I think that while he was at Grinnell that he probably attended church very regularly. I think that religion always meant a great deal to him." She stated that while his concept of religion changed over the years and eventually was reduced to "do unto others as you would have them do unto you," he never lost his deep belief that "service to others was the most important way to manifest [religious feeling]."[21]

Harry Hopkins forged the foundation of his social philosophy out of the sparks that flew between his parents. The blend and clash of opposites provided a vibrant texture to his early life. Al Hopkins' business failures did not foster in his son an excessive need for financial success, but they did encourage a healthy ambition to achieve more; neither did his cynicism smother his son's idealism. Anna Hopkins' stern morality did not turn her son into a hard-edged Christian but rather instilled in him a sense of righteousness and a commitment to service to others. Because he was never forced to choose between either of his parents, Hopkins was able to inherit the best of both. Moreover, he learned the important lesson that people with divergent beliefs could work together for a common end. In 1939 Hopkins visited Iowa and declared "whatever I do and think is profoundly influenced by the way [my parents] brought me up. That heritage from my home has always been a source of abiding strength to me."[22]

Moral Christianity turned Hopkins into an ambitious man. The example of his father's unfulfilled dreams also might have pushed him to strive for success. But his ambition was driven by the need for a platform from which to effect changes for the good of society. His education at Grinnell College provided him with the prerequisites for the realization of this ambition. In 1900 Iowa ranked tenth highest in population and second highest in the number of children attending school. Historian John W. Schacht observed that the nature of an Iowa background encouraged the "kind of life designed to inculcate the Puritan staples of hard work, thrift and self-reliance, salted with shrewdness and ambition." Significantly, men and women influenced by this milieu reached their maturity in the 1930s.[23]

The ideals of Grinnell College, especially its early commitment to the Social Gospel, had great appeal for Anna Hopkins. She very purposefully selected the town as a home for her children because the college was situated there, but she soon found that this institution reflected her own strong social and religious attitudes. The Social Gospel that permeated the college dovetailed neatly with the social imperatives of Anna's Methodism. The intertwining of theology and ethics with politics and sociology at Grinnell College, so distinct in progressive reform, suggests a religious framework for Hopkins' social conscience.[24] While he was never formally religious as an adult, Hopkins did have a strong commitment to the principles of social justice, principles that were firmly rooted in the religious elements present in his upbringing and education in Grinnell, Iowa. Because the ideals that Hopkins took with him to Washington in 1933 were first instilled in him at Grinnell College, the background of this institution is relevant to the formation of the American welfare state.

Over one hundred fifty years ago, in 1846, James Jeremiah Hill presented a silver dollar to the trustees of the Iowa College Association as the beginning of an endowment for Iowa College, an institution "founded in poverty and in prayer" in order to "leaven with Christian influence the rising commonwealth in which it was located." Eight years earlier, in 1838, Hill and nine others had formed a group they called the Iowa Band and responded to Congregational minister Asa Turner's plea for missionaries to come to Iowa "to secure a title to heaven" by founding a church and a college. Turner also warned his followers: "Don't come here expecting a paradise. Our climate will permit men to live long enough, if they do their duty. If they do not, no matter how soon they die. . . . Come prepared to expect savage things, rough things. Lay aside all dandy whims." Undaunted by this warning, the members of the Iowa Band formed the Iowa College Association in 1845 and selected Davenport, a frontier town "on the western fringes of civilization," as the site of their new institution, which was incorporated two years later. The college, modeled after the New England example of classical education, found that there was little financial support in such an "uncivilized" wilderness. It consisted of one shabby building and, according to one of its first graduates, "its most salient feature was its poverty," having only four professors, no laboratory, dingy classrooms, and few amenities for students. Also prominent at the all-male college, however, was a religious heartiness that allowed students to endure such privations. According to contemporary accounts, "this combination of poverty and religion" led to "a strong spirit of earnest work" and high academic standards. Students, whose "amusements were intellectual rather than physical," spent their free time studying, attending sermons, and lecturing in nearby communities. Despite the academic achievement and seriousness of its students, the college at Davenport was not popular in the community. Its "spirit of sectarianism" alienated other churches, and when the city attempted to build a street through the middle of the campus, the college rebelled. A means of rescue came from a nearby town.[25]

The town of Grinnell had been founded as a temperance community with strong abolitionist tendencies in the early 1850s by a dour Congregational minister from Vermont named Josiah Bushnell Grinnell. The Reverend Grinnell was forced to leave his previous post in Washington, D.C., for preaching an impassioned sermon on the evils of slavery. He bought a tract of land in Iowa with the intention of establishing a university modeled after Mt. Holyoke and in 1859 enticed the endangered Iowa College to move its "scanty library," some papers, and a safe with $9,000 to Grinnell from Davenport. From its very early years, Iowa College committed itself to social reform and progressive ideas, admitting women beginning in 1857 and banning fraternities.[26] But seminal to the development of that institution was the influence of social Christianity, a reform movement responding to the social and economic upheavals occurring in a rapidly modernizing nation.

The tensions manifested between an increasingly secular, scientific society in the throes of industrialization and the religious tradition of compassion for human suffering set the stage in the latter part of the nineteenth century for the emergence of a new social philosophy that would address the relationship of man to society. The Social Gospel Movement was, in many ways, a response to the Gospel of Wealth. Social evils, including child labor, urban slums, an undemocratic concentration of wealth, political corruption, and the dehumanizing effects of industrialization, pricked the conscience of Christians who saw the established church deserting the poor for more profitable ministrations to the rising middle class.[27] Using the church as a conduit for reform, a new breed of clergymen, including Walter Rauschenbusch, Washington Gladden, and Josiah Strong, proclaimed that the Christian spirit was capable of solving the complex social problems confronting the nation and that, moreover, it was the duty of Christians everywhere to be the instruments of social improvement.[28]

In 1893 Iowa College president George Augustus Gates, who had held the office since 1887, declared that "Iowa College has always taught, teaches today, and, so God will, will always teach the actual applicability of the principles of Jesus Christ to every department of human life."[29] Calling for the application of Christian principles to ameliorate the evils engendered by industrialism, Social Gospelers such as Gates preached from their pulpits and in classrooms that social institutions had a moral responsibility to find new ways to improve life for all ranks of men and women in America. Thus the Social Gospel, called by historian William Deminoff "the middle ground between Marxism and the Salvation Army," rallied Christians to the cause of reform.[30] This ideal molded much of the ideology that Grinnell College hoped to pass on to its students.

The Social Gospel, reflecting the religious aspect of progressivism and the influence of religion on sociology, became firmly entrenched at Grinnell College (officially named in 1909) during the late nineteenth and early twentieth century. George Davis Herron, born in Indiana in 1862, had much do with this tradition. He became a Congregational minister despite an impoverished childhood, constant illness, and a rather "spotty" education. Nevertheless, the zeal evident in his preaching and his declaration that selfish competition had no place in a moral world, that every man was his brother's keeper, attracted a Burlington, Iowa, search committee looking for a minister to assist and then succeed the rather conservative Dr. William Salter (of the Iowa Band) at his Congregational church. The committee offered the job to Herron, who quickly accepted the position.

During his time in Burlington, Herron met a wealthy widow, Mrs. E. D. Rand, and her daughter, Carrie, two women who exerted an enormous impact on his life and career. Grinnell president Gates invited the minister to speak at the college and was impressed by his enthusiastic style. He remarked that Herron "did set the souls of our young men and women on fire with a high and holy passion." When Mrs. Rand, a frequent and generous benefactor of the college, endowed a chair of Applied Christianity specifically for the charismatic Herron in 1893, his career at Grinnell seemed assured. Herron brought the Social Gospel to that institution. He gradually developed into "a romantic leftist" and a theological radical, teaching his students that businesses using wealth for their own selfish ends were guilty of committing the greatest sin against mankind. Passionately opposed to industrial capitalism and trustification, he taught that existing institutions stood in the way of Christian ideals, and he emphasized the collective nature of social Christianity.[31]

Eventually, Herron's career at Grinnell was characterized less by his spirituality than by his excesses. His radical socialism, his messianic oratory, and his questionable morals led to his resignation in 1899. According to Grinnell historian John Nollen, he was "a victim of his own extraordinary qualities and he lacked the strength of character to overcome his peculiar temptations." Not only did he neglect his academic duties and his students, but he developed what church members regarded as an unseemly love of luxury. He also developed an equally unseemly attachment to Mrs. Rand's nineteen-year-old daughter, Grinnell's dean of women, Carrie Rand. In 1901 he divorced his wife and married Rand. The Grinnell community reacted to the scandal by rejecting him; the First Congregational Church found Herron guilty of immoral and unchristian conduct and deposed him from the ministry.[32]

Herron alienated his fellow Social Gospelers as well. Although many advocates of Social Christianity, especially Richard T. Ely, founder of the prestigious American Economics Association, were concerned with the struggle between labor and capital, most did not believe in the inevitability of class conflict. Pursuing social reform within the framework of democracy, they looked forward to a classless, utopian society where people would be ruled by a just law. Unlike the radical Herron, these Social Gospelers did not look to socialism as an answer to society's dislocations but rather to a re-emergence of Christ's law to capture the spirit of social justice within the democratic system.[33]

Despite the scandalous nature of Herron's divorce and his radicalism, Grinnell College emerged unshaken.[34] The Herron episode, erupting just as the Hopkins family moved to the little town, "made Grinnell the center of nationwide interest in the bold experiment of applying the teaching of Jesus to the solution of social and economic problems." The Social Gospel had acquired a secure foothold on campus and continued to exert a strong influence on students and faculty as well as in the community.[35]

Historians have noted a strong connection between the Social Gospel and Progressivism because both reacted to the inequities arising out of industrial capitalism and the growing concentration of wealth. The application of Christian principles to social problems as taught at Grinnell College had a great influence on the students who went there to study, among them Harry Hopkins, two of his brothers, and his older sister, Adah. These lessons led them both to pursue careers in social service. The critique of laissez-faire economics heard in the classrooms echoed much later in a 1934 speech Harry Hopkins made at Grinnell. He declared "the old order of things is definitely past and finished. Rugged individualism and 'laissez faire' are of the past and have no place whatsoever in the New Deal." He went on to say that he believed in four main principles: "(1) complete government supervision; (2) the government is in the people themselves and exists primarily to bestow benefits on the people; (3) the days of great wealth for a few and a bare living for the many are over; and (4) colleges on the order of Grinnell are best qualified to teach and instill in their students this new order."[36]

Harry Hopkins' commitment to public service certainly was grounded in his experience at Grinnell College, and the social ideals he absorbed there made up a good part of the social philosophy he carried with him to New York and later to Washington. As a resident of the town and a student at the college, he could not escape the Grinnell influence. From its very beginning, Grinnell College defined the community surrounding it. In the college bulletins, prospective students and their parents were informed that the town, besides being conveniently located on the rail line and blessed with good water, was also a "center of religious and educational influence" and as a result has attracted "cultivated and intelligent people, many of whom have made this their home for the sake of the privilege of the College for their children." The early bulletins proudly added, "[t]here has never been a saloon in town."[37] These were precisely the reasons that brought the Hopkins family there in 1901.[38]

That year Adah May Hopkins, the eldest of the Hopkins children, entered the freshman class at the college.[39] She was eight years older than Harry and his only sister; three of her four brothers also attended Grinnell College. Adah graduated with the class of 1905 and her transcript shows a strong academic record, with slightly over a B average. During her four years there, Adah Hopkins became a campus leader. She held student offices and edited *The Unit,* the college literary magazine to which she was a frequent contributor. In her junior year she delivered a prize-winning oration against child labor entitled "The Curse of Childhood." She spoke of the

> cruel employment of children in exhausting occupations before maturity. Noble manhood is founded on happy childhood and it is impossible to think that good citizens can come from the little ones that toil in cellars, sweat shops, department stores, factories, fields and mines. The dormant civic spirit must be roused to a realization of the danger of this pernicious system. Children should first of all be educated instead of stunted and maimed in the race of life. The prosperity of to-day robs the community of its resources of to-morrow.

"The curse of Child Labor," she concluded, "calls for instant action."[40] No doubt these sentiments had been instilled in her by her professors. By her junior year, Adah already had taken four semesters of Applied Christianity from the famous Social Gospeler Edward Steiner. In 1905 she was chosen outstanding senior. At her commencement ceremony, she spoke on "Modern Philanthropy" in an extemporaneous speech that emphasized efforts to stem tuberculosis, a disease regarded as a primary cause of poverty. She won second prize.[41]

When Adah entered the freshman class, the college was still somewhat shaken from the Herron episode. The president of the college, George Gates, had resigned in 1900 over the scandal, and Dr. J. H. T. Main took over as acting president, fully expecting the permanent appointment. However, Main's initial sympathy for Herron lost him the support of the trustees who named Dan Freeman Bradley as president. Although the school yearbook described him as having a "hearty optimism," his was a rather lackluster career, and in 1903 Main again took over the presidency of the college, a position that he held for the next twenty-five years.[42]

President Main continued the religious traditions of the college. During the early years of his administration he ensured that there would be "no dancing or card parties . . . no strolling or driving of men or women on Sundays." But he also added to the progressive traditions of his institution. He strengthened the college's commitment to a high standard of scholarship by establishing a chapter of Phi Beta Kappa, improved the curriculum, and enthusiastically supported intercollegiate athletics.[43] Main lured prominent and controversial speakers to the campus, men and women who brought a wide range of issues to the students and broadened their perception of the world outside of Grinnell. For example, Jacob Riis visited the campus in 1901 to speak on social settlements. The school paper described how 800 people listened with rapt attention to his speech full of "[p]atriotism and sympathy for humanity." In 1905 William Jennings Bryan lectured on the topic "Honesty Will Never Perish." Former reform mayor of New York City and president of Columbia University Seth Low visited the campus in 1908 (when Harry Hopkins was a freshman there). That same year Eugene Debs came to town, arriving on the "red Special" and delivered a rousing campaign speech. The local paper reported that the audience was merely amused at his reference to George Herron as a martyr.[44]

Main headed an impressive faculty at Grinnell, some of whom he himself recruited. Probably his most significant recruitment effort occurred before his appointment as president. Aboard a steamship on the way to Europe (during Bradley's tenure), Main met and was impressed by Dr. Edward Steiner, who was on his way to Russia to write a biography of Leo Tolstoy for the journal *Outlook*.[45] Upon his appointment as president of the college, Main offered this remarkable man the recently vacated chair of Applied Christianity. Steiner reluctantly agreed—and held the chair from 1903 to 1941. In his autobiography Steiner related that Main offered him the position when he was "unknown, untrained and untried" but that he willingly took up the task of "awakening the churches to the great economic problems" that plagued the nation.[46]

Dr. Steiner left an indelible impression on both the college and his students, among them Harry Hopkins. He carried on the tradition of the Social Gospel at Grinnell, although in a less radical manner than Herron.[47] He was born a Czechoslovakian Jew in 1866 and probably was educated in Germany, although there is no record of his receiving any degrees from institutions there.[48] When he immigrated to America he converted to Christianity, graduated from

Oberlin Theological Seminary in 1891, and became a Congregational minister. The 1906 Grinnell yearbook, *Cyclone*, dedicated to Steiner (Adah Hopkins was a senior when it was published), noted his European birth and his education at the University of Heidelburg but curiously avoided the fact that he was born a Jew. Steiner, in fact, took great pride in his cultural heritage. While his courses in Applied Christianity emphasized Christian principles, he also taught a course on the Old Testament in which his students looked at "the ethical and religious development of the Jewish people," reading "the poets and prophets of Israel." W. D. Mackenzie of the Hartford Theological Seminary and author of the yearbook dedication stated that Steiner "came to taste the two supreme values of life. These are the grace of God in Jesus Christ and life in a free and self-government democracy," and that only those who have "lived outside of these blessings" can fully understand them. This statement made oblique reference to the fact that Steiner was born outside of the church and in a foreign land; it also isolated the two basic values held in such high esteem at Grinnell College: Christianity and democracy.[49]

Mackenzie also wrote: "If all immigrants from central and southern Europe were of his type, happy would be the land which received them," lamenting that too few "come with his experience and training." Steiner knew well the immigrant experience. In 1885 he endured the rigors of traveling steerage across the Atlantic to New York. Yet he did not believe in the melting pot ideal and saw great value in the cultural diversity that immigrants brought to America. After an extended trip abroad with five of his students to study immigration, he spoke of what he had discovered, claiming that the immigrants who came to America consisted of the more ambitious, "the flower of the peasant class of central and southern Europe" who often returned to their own country to become property owners.[50] While this may not be unmitigated praise for these "birds of passage," it does speak to their contributions on both sides of the ocean.

Steiner's ideas certainly influenced Hopkins in his work among immigrants in New York City, enabling him to better appreciate the rich culture of the Lower East Side ghetto. In 1904 Steiner addressed the school YM-YWCA, and his sermon exemplified much of the Social Gospel at Grinnell as he taught it to Hopkins and his classmates. Conditions confronted the church, he declared, to which it must "turn an open eye. . . . The church has done more to solve social problems, to wipe out evil, to regenerate the world and lead it to righteousness than all other institutions of the world combined. Take away the influence of the church . . . and you reduce the human race to savagery."[51]

Jesse Macy was undoubtedly Grinnell College's most famous professor. A Quaker by birth and member of Grinnell's Congregational Church, he was vitally concerned with problems of democracy and social reform. According to

Hopkins' biographer Robert Sherwood, Macy was "the originator of the first college course in political science." Seeking an understanding of politics, Macy looked to the scientific revolution for answers. He believed that "[w]hat men say and think about the operations of oxygen and hydrogen makes no difference to the phenomena; but what men say and think about the relations of capitalists and employees does make a difference." For Macy, political scientists had to inquire into actual human behavior. He eschewed learning by rote and used events in the real world to teach his students. Macy, a Darwinist, an internationalist, and an unsentimental humanitarian, transmitted to his students a clear understanding of government in operation through the science of politics.[52] Hopkins' dedication to the scientific method as applied to social work can be traced in part back to Macy's classroom.

While President Main reinforced Grinnell's commitment to Christianity and democracy, he did change one direction of the college. Whereas the Iowa Band founders had used the eastern university as a model for their college, Main worked tirelessly toward his goal of building a financially independent and distinctly Midwestern institution. In her study of Grinnell College, Joan G. Zimmerman (class of 1971) notes that in the early twentieth century, there were more women than men at Grinnell, and that from 1892 to 1907, the percentage of women enrolled in the college rose dramatically. Main, well aware that women alums usually did not have a great deal of money to contribute to their alma mater, worked to move the curriculum in the direction of more practical vocational courses in an attempt to correct the gender imbalance. Hoping to attract men away from the state universities, and recognizing that women were attracted to liberal arts courses, President Main strengthened the more practical courses such as business and engineering.[53]

Grinnell College had admitted women since 1861, yet its academic and social policies reinforced the Victorian ideal of separate spheres for men and women. While President Main did not hold with the then-popular belief that higher education diminished the reproductive capabilities of women and injured their mental and physical health, he fully ascribed to the tenet that women's influence emanated from their domestic role. However educated they may be, women properly belonged at home. Main, according to Zimmerman, "regarded the presence of women as a disruptive intrusion into a male defined college" and sought to keep them safely separate from the men. During the early twentieth century the cult of true womanhood, which emphasized that women fulfill themselves as preservers of home, children, and culture, defined the female experience at the college. Women students at Grinnell were housed together and given special considerations and extremely careful supervision. Almost all took courses leading to a Bachelor of Philosophy degree (Ph.B.), a degree that did not require the study of Greek. Women graduates were encouraged to pursue traditionally female jobs and were warned away from the perceived evils of city life. According to Zimmerman, women at Grinnell during this period did not challenge these ideas and indeed "were complicit in their own domestication."[54]

Adah Hopkins, who graduated in 1905, was in many ways representative of the ideal female college student at Grinnell.[55] She typified Zimmerman's description of the woman student of that era in that she did not really challenge the outer limits of traditionalism.[56] Nevertheless, Zimmerman found that Adah was "mildly skeptical of the ideal of womanhood held up to college women as 'a cross between Joan of Arc, a state YWCA secretary, and a favorite lady professor'" and did not wholly agree with President Main's attempts to instill his ideals of womanhood in Grinnell's female students.[57] In a sense, Adah Hopkins can best be understood as a combination of the true woman and the new woman. For her, the Social Gospel as taught at Grinnell provided her with a way to adapt Victorian principles to the social realities of a modern industrial nation. The Christian imperative to reform society gave her life direction and led her to a career in social work, one of the few professions then open to women.[58]

Harry watched Adah's career with a great deal of interest and admiration. He always had a high regard for his older sister, and he learned from her example much about the nature and value of women's work in the public sphere. Adah's reaction to the Grinnell experience reflected for him, in many ways, the proper position of women in the larger world—they should use their talents in the public sphere in order to help others, but their most valuable role would always be as wife and mother. Like her mother, Adah believed that women as well as men had a moral and religious responsibility to take an active role in the affairs of the community, and her career reflected this commitment. However, she seems not to have inherited Anna's religious zeal. In 1915 she wrote her brother Harry that she had been "distracted by the awful clamor of church chimes. . . . They always annoy me. . . . Perhaps the pricklings of conscience."[59]

Adah Hopkins' career is not as well-documented as her brother's. Immediately upon graduation, she entered the University of Pennsylvania to study sociology[60] and then worked as a visitor for the Philadelphia Society for the Prevention of Cruelty to Children. She then traveled to New York City, where she worked with Christina Isobel MacColl, head worker and founder of Christodora Settlement House. Adah later took a position as registrar of the New York School of Philanthropy. Although little is known of her experiences there, undoubtedly she came into contact with Dr. Edward Devine and the efforts of the Charity Organization Society (COS) to apply scientific methods to relief efforts.

Adah's work at Christodora in New York City would not have been her first experience with a settlement house. She had been active in Grinnell's Uncle

Sam's Club, an experiment with the college settlement house movement, which Jesse Macy called "one of the most significant movements of the generation."[61] The Uncle Sam's Club did not directly replicate urban settlements because the young workers did not actually reside there and their neighbors would not have been immigrants. Nevertheless, when Adah did finally get to New York City and Christodora House in 1908, settlement work would not have been a totally new experience for her.

By 1912 Adah Hopkins found herself back in Grinnell and involved in an experimental project called the Social Service League, which reflected a modernizing trend in social work then prevalent in many U.S. cities. It is not clear why she returned to Grinnell but her mother's illness and subsequent hospitalization with tuberculosis may have been the compelling factor. She was also recruited by the County Board of Supervisors for a job as overseer of the poor. Her work with the New York School of Philanthropy and the COS had given her the experience necessary to make her eminently suited for this position.

The town of Grinnell had formed its own Charity Organization Society in the 1890s in order to provide a more efficient and positive administration of charitable gifts and county poor funds. Similar societies had been formed in many cities in order to avoid duplication of social services and, it was hoped, to discourage pauperism. In 1912 the Grinnell COS, suffering from mismanagement and a shortage of money, conducted an investigation into how county poor funds were being spent and reported that their methods needed some improvement. Consequently, the County Board of Supervisors and the COS, both conditioned by the feeling that charity had to be both helpful and wise, joined forces to solve the problem. They made the somewhat radical proposal that, upon nomination of the COS, the County Board of Supervisors should appoint a trained social worker as overseer of the poor. This would be a salaried, full-time (rather than the usual voluntary, part-time) position with the salary paid partly by the board and partly by the COS. League reports noted that a search committee took a considerable amount of time but finally offered the job to Adah Hopkins, who was at that time registrar of the New York School of Philanthropy, a center for the COS ideals.[62]

Soon after Adah accepted the position, the Grinnell COS formed the Social Service League (SSL), called "A Bureau for Community Service," to carry out the work for distributing aid and services to the poor in the community more effectively and efficiently. Almost immediately it merged with or, more exactly, absorbed, the Grinnell COS. Adah Hopkins acted as both the town overseer of the poor and an agent of the COS, with one foot in the public sphere and the other in the private. In the words of the chairman of the Board of Supervisors of Poweshiek County, "private supervision was given the expenditure of public funds."[63] It was indeed a significant departure to have a professional social worker as overseer of the poor, especially in a small town like Grinnell with only about 5,000 people. But what was even more radical was the combination of public and private funds within one agency for the purpose of providing relief to the needy.[64] The complicated interrelationships between public and private relief became a recurring theme during Harry Hopkins' career. His sister's early years in Grinnell with the SSL reinforced for him the importance of close cooperation between both spheres. The organization's Second Annual Report stated: "We believe that there can no longer remain any doubt but that there is work to be done in our city which cannot properly be handled either by the state or any isolated religious or fraternal order. The term 'social service' implies activity of a communal character in a field all its own."[65] The dynamic between the public and private arenas continued to concern Hopkins during his entire social work career.

The Social Service League, unlike the COS, did not merely act as a clearinghouse or referral agency for the needy. Committed to modern, scientific methods of administering relief and using its close ties with the college to support its activities, the league actively sought to prevent social problems that could lead to poverty. Consequently, it refrained from giving any form of relief that might, in the eyes of its members, encourage laziness, drunkenness, or immorality among the recipients. The SSL defined its goal in its by-laws: "To secure adequate material assistance and intelligent care for needy family in their homes and for the homeless [and to] discourage indiscriminate giving." Its membership called for "stronger feelings of democracy and community interest," an end to the "old idea of charity as affording a means of self-satisfaction to the giver," and an adherence to the "new conception of social and civic responsibility."[66] In order to do this, its members worked to centralize the efforts of all organizations concerned with social service and relief for the needy, using terms in their literature such as "harmonize," "systematize," and "correlate."[67] The ideals of the SSL and the COS also reflected an effort on the part of caregivers to economize and to ensure that only the deserving would get help. They worked to avoid "reckless gifts" that "tend to degrade the manlier poor, tempt the weak to abject conduct and entice a newer degradation to the dissolute pauper." In the minds of these reformers, not only would scientific administration techniques eliminate indiscriminate charity, it also would save money.[68]

As secretary of the SSL, the general executive of the league, and the only appointed officer, Adah Hopkins gave important direction to the organization.[69] Her first report stressed that the primary task of the SSL was the "sympathetic and adequate treatment of families and individuals who are in distress." Pointing out that both personal service and financial assistance were important, she also noted in her second annual report that this was indeed an important departure from the traditional methods of providing assistance for the needy that kept public and private spending very separate.[70] Adah Hopkins' financial report reflected savings—in 1912 the county spent $8,000 in Grinnell for public relief; in 1913 this amount was reduced to $4,200, with $600 of it coming from private donations. Thus the efforts of the SSL reduced expenditures by a startling 60 percent. At the County Board of Supervisors meeting in 1913 the SSL reported that the number of persons receiving aid had decreased by 27 percent and that only twelve families in Grinnell were receiving permanent relief. Adah stressed that this in no way was done at the expense of the needy but was the result of improved investigatory methods, more frequent visits to families in need, and better record-keeping techniques. She reported that various activities of the league, including close supervision over school attendance, preventive medical work, improvement of conditions in the county jail, expanded recreational facilities, the establishment of organizations such as Boy Scouts and Camp Fire Girls, birth registrations, and movie picture censorship were all intended to eliminate the causes of poverty. As secretary of the SSL, Adah also investigated widows' pension applications and supervised the administration of these funds, a job her younger brother, Harry, would duplicate in New York City three years later.[71]

The Board of Supervisors was so pleased with the results of the Grinnell experiment that in 1914 it took over responsibility for the secretary's entire salary.[72] Although there had been some controversy when the league was formed, with critics predicting that such an "unwarranted and extravagant" expenditure of public money would soon cause it to end in failure, the SSL experiment seems to have worked because it continued to function successfully for several decades. In 1936 Adah sent a letter of congratulations to the SSL on the twenty-fifth anniversary of the SSL's Grinnell Plan, giving credit to longtime sociology professor Garrett P. Wyckoff, chair of the economics department.[73] Adah had always believed in what the league stood for. She lectured in neighboring towns on the subject because, as she reported, "a year's experiment of cooperation between public and private agencies seems to warrant our recommending the county plan for towns similarly situated."[74] Despite her success with the SSL, in June 1914 Adah again left Grinnell and went to Pittsburgh to set up a department of social service for women in the Margaret Morrison Carnagie School.[75]

During Adah's experience with social work in Grinnell, Harry Hopkins was a student at the college and living at home with his family. The four years he spent at Grinnell College certainly did much to shape the young man, although he could not measure up to his sister's academic record. Hopkins' classmate and fellow New Dealer Florence Stewart Kerr said that she "used to wonder if he'd ever graduate, because he was always turning up missing with required credits."[76] In fact, Hopkins was listed as a freshman two years in a row, 1908 and 1909, having failed to make the minimum grade point average required for sophomore standing.[77] There was one important exception in his generally poor performance during his first years at Grinnell. In his first semester Hopkins took public speaking from Professor John B. Ryan, a much-loved and renowned member of the English faculty. The purpose of his course was to "cultivate a simple, effective manner of speaking" and included "practice in the preparation and delivery of speeches." Ryan rewarded Hopkins' work with an A, one of the very few he got at Grinnell. Years later journalist Heywood Broun praised Hopkins' speaking ability, saying that "[a]mong public speakers I would rank him high because he speaks with deep feeling and utter simplicity." These were the very qualities that Ryan drummed into his students.[78]

Hopkins majored in history and political science (Grinnell required a dual major) but did not seem to hit his academic stride until late in his junior year, amassing an embarrassing number of Ds during his first two years, even failing an elective English course, Literary Masterpieces. During his junior and senior years Hopkins had the benefit of Grinnell's finest professors, including Jesse Macy and John W. Gannaway, who taught him political science. He earned a respectable B in European history from Professor John Frederick Peck, who had been the Parker Professor of History at the University of Chicago. In his first semester of his senior year, Hopkins took Professor Steiner's course in Applied Christianity, "The Development of Social Consciousness in the Old Testament." The 1911 bulletin describes the course: "A study of the social evolution of the Jewish Commonwealth must necessarily rest upon proper historical knowledge of that people [and] involves the ethical and religious development of the Jewish people [and] the inspiring personality of the poets and the prophets of Israel." Hopkins got an A.[79] It would take him a year, however, to experience Jewish culture firsthand in the New York City ghetto. In fact, Hopkins had not been exposed to many hyphenated Americans at Grinnell. When he first arrived to New York City in 1912, the Lower East Side melting pot fascinated him.[80]

If Hopkins had a favorite professor, it was Jesse Macy. From him Hopkins learned the indelible lesson that it is the duty of every individual to work unstintingly for a more just society, *whether success is assured or not.* Macy's try-anything attitude left a strong impression on Hopkins, who used it to good advantage during the New Deal years.[81] Hopkins also studied with Professor Wyckoff, who explained to students who took his course on charities how to use the social sciences to solve the practical problems of life, and with Professor Charles E. Payne, who emphasized that history happens in the present and is found in newspapers as well as in textbooks. Hopkins took political theory from Gannaway and psychology from Louis D. Hartson. Grinnell also was home to John D. Stoops, professor of philosophy, who taught that one must learn about the human condition through firsthand experience, and to President J. H. T. Main, who insisted that social improvement was man's ultimate goal. Although Hopkins did not take formal courses from these two professors, they exerted an important general influence on the college from which all students benefited.[82]

At Grinnell, Hopkins formed close friendships with many of his classmates, some of whom also were called to Washington in the 1930s. In fact, Grinnell boasted an inordinate number of students who went on to become New Dealers: Florence Stewart Kerr (class of 1912), Chester Davis (1911), Hallie Ferguson Flanagan (1911), and Paul Appleby (1913). Kerr first worked with Hopkins when he was with the American Red Cross in the South during World War I, and then he brought her to Washington to work in the Works Progress Administration (WPA) Federal Theater Project, succeeding Ellen Woodward.[83] Chester Davis and Paul Appleby both worked with the Department of Agriculture, and Hallie Flanagan headed the WPA Federal Theater Project before Woodward. These were Hopkins' close friends and they participated in many school activities together, including working on the yearbook staff and on the editorial board of the college literary magazine, participating in the debating club, and sitting on the student council, the Grinnell Institute, and the YMCA cabinet.

In addition to this impressive array of activities, Hopkins was also active in college athletics. In fact, this was where he seemed to excel. He was a "big man on campus," and earned an Honor G for playing on the championship basketball team. He also played on the tennis and baseball teams. Kerr described him as "tall and lanky, and a great basketball player, and for the four years of his college career, the Grinnell basketball team was the state champion. . . . Sometimes they called him 'Dirty Harry' because he had so many personal fouls called on him. He was very active, very athletic, very popular—*very* popular." Largely because of his high sports profile, his classmates elected him senior class president, the only elective office he would ever hold.[84] He organized the Woodrow Wilson Club at the college during his senior year, possibly a foreshadowing of his future political stance but an activity that also might be regarded as part of a flurry of school activity he engaged in with little thought to political ideology.

Hopkins, with such a shaky academic record, probably was delighted to be graduating. At his commencement exercises he listened with interest mingled with relief to William Allen White address the graduating class. The Kansas editor told the graduates that they had "two objectives in life: to promote social justice; and to develop in the masses such an enthusiasm for this social justice that they will be willing to follow the proper leaders at a personal sacrifice." White referred to Christ as "the greatest social reformer and the greatest democrat of all time." He called on each graduate to "play his part in the evolution of political and social betterment." President Main had preached a sermon to the graduates the previous Sunday dwelling on the theme that man plays an important part in solving the problems of the world, claiming that "service to man is the greatest vocation to which man can aspire."[85] Thus Hopkins graduated with the two primary themes taught at Grinnell echoing in his mind: service to others and the value of the democratic system.

Harry Hopkins always spoke with great pride of his education at Grinnell College and credited the institution for having a very positive influence on his career. When he returned to his alma mater in 1939, his speech to the student body reflected those two dominant themes he learned in the Grinnell class-room—democracy and public service. He told the young men and women of Grinnell, most of whom had experienced the hardships of the Great Depression, that "the government is going to treat people in ways we have never dreamed of before, and, therefore the government should be good." The government, as "the last stronghold of Democracy," deserved to be honored, he declared. "Don't treat it as something to sneer at; treat it as something that belongs to you. We have got to find a way of living in America in which every person in it shares in the national income, in such a way, that poverty in America is abolished. There is no reason why the people of America should dwell in poverty. A way must be found, and a way will be found."[86]

When Ethel Gross first met Harry Hopkins in the hallways of New York City's Christodora House early in 1913, she recalled that he was lighthearted and certainly very likable but what initially attracted her were his "high ideals" and "the fact that he cared so much about helping people who needed help." She credits his education at Grinnell for these traits.[87] Grinnell's popular professor of Applied Christianity, however, did not have such a high opinion of Hopkins' abilities. When Hopkins sought advice from Edward Steiner about the direction his future should take, Steiner told him that he would never have enough compassion to make a good social worker.[88] Undaunted, Hopkins sought advice from other quarters. He had better luck with his psychology professor, Louis Hartson, who had graduated only four years before Hopkins took his course in social reform. In the spring of 1912 Hopkins stopped by Hartson's office to discuss his future, telling the young professor that he was thinking about going into social work. Hartson suggested that Hopkins go along with him to work for the summer at a boys' camp run by Christodora Settlement House. The camp was located across the river in New Jersey, but Hartson assured Hopkins that there would be ample opportunity to see New York City. Hopkins knew about this particular settlement because his sister had worked there and, in fact, had gotten Hartson the job there in 1908. Hopkins eagerly agreed to join Hartson and the two traveled east together, stopping off for three days in Washington, D.C., because Hopkins had a yen to see the White House.[89]

CHAPTER THREE

HOPKINS AT CHRISTODORA HOUSE

The first tenement New York knew bore the mark of Cain from its birth, though a generation passed before the writing was deciphered.

—Jacob Riis, 1890

ON THEIR TRIP FROM IOWA TO NEW YORK in the summer of 1912, Louis Hartson and Harry Hopkins felt the excitement brewing during that election year. The duo first stopped off in Chicago, where Hopkins crashed the Republican National Convention by posing as Elihu Root's secretary and witnessed Theodore Roosevelt bolting the party. After spending three days in the nation's capital, they continued on to Baltimore, where the Democrats were holding their convention. Hartson remembered particularly "Harry's conversation with the Tammany delegates who were supporting [New York City Mayor William J.] Gaynor, and his putting in a word in favor of Woodrow Wilson."[1] Hopkins' friend and biographer Robert Sherwood wrote that "the sight and sound of the political giants excited him and for the next twenty years he nourished a desire to become combatant in that bloody arena."[2]

Historians have not portrayed Hopkins as an ambitious man.[3] It is true that he did not seek financial gain or even elective office, but he did want a place of power in the political hierarchy that would allow him to implement the policies he developed during his years as a social worker. Florence Stewart Kerr, Grinnell College classmate and fellow New Dealer, stated that in 1939 Hopkins, long a foe of those he called "predatory" industrial capitalists, made a "landmark historical watershed speech" in which he seemed to be placating big business. Kerr declared that she had helped him write this speech and that political ambition was the reason for his "great turnabout."[4] This ambition for political influence began to grow very early in Hopkins' career.

Despite his fascination with the political scene in 1912, Hopkins was eager to get to New York City; he had been there before on a trip with his mother and now looked forward to the excitement and the opportunities it had to offer him. There were other reasons. His sister Adah was there working for the New York School of Philanthropy; one of his brothers, Lewis, was also there attending medical school.[5] Hopkins, the small-town boy, was about to become an urban social worker.

Hopkins' first job at Christodora House was working as a counselor at its Northover boys' camp in Bound Brook, New Jersey, a short ferry ride across the river. He then became head of the boys' programs at the settlement house on Avenue B in New York City's Lower East Side. Social settlements such as Christodora served as training fields for many progressive reformers. Historian Judith Trolander correctly observed that settlement work gave influential people such as Frances Perkins, Eleanor Roosevelt, and Harry Hopkins a new awareness of the horrors of urban poverty and opened up for them important channels of communication with the poor.[6] The Christodora story is, of course, tied to the larger study of the place of the social settlement in the development of social reform. Much of this history has a strong connection to religion and the Social Gospel in America. Coming to Christodora House from Grinnell College, Hopkins was particularly immersed in the spirit of Protestantism, a spirit that sparked a good deal of social action during the Progressive Era.

While social Christianity permeated many settlement houses, the religious conversion of immigrants was not a primary aim for most of them. Stanton Coit, who started the first settlement in America after spending three months at Toynbee House in London, stressed the secular nature of his Neighborhood Guild.[7] Likewise, Jane Addams, in her book *Twenty Years at Hull-House,* addressed the place of formal religion in the settlement movement almost as an afterthought. She admitted that "a certain renaissance going forward in Christianity" impelled the settlement movement, that the simple gospel message to love all men had to be put into action. But if Christian charity was important to Addams as a motivating force for the settlement movement, it was not a Christianity "that tears down temples" but a tolerant humanism that accentuated likenesses among men.[8] Lillian Wald also eschewed the religious element in her Henry Street Settlement and left no room for misunderstanding when she announced: "As a settlement, nothing is said of religious teaching."[9] Yet although settlement workers did avoid organized religion, their work was essentially redemptive and thus, in a broad sense, religious. However much they desired to distance themselves from institutional Protestantism, their aim was to create what Social Gospeler Walter Rauschenbusch called "a Christian social order."[10]

Harry P. Kraus noted in his 1980 study, *The Settlement House Movement in New York City,* that although some settlements (East Side House, Union Settlement) "were originally motivated and supported by religious institutions, they soon found that their value to the community was an inverse ratio to their religious emphasis" and that "Community salvation rather than personal salvation gave the settlement its basic appeal."[11] Historians such as Allen F. Davis and Mina Carson have described the more prominent social settlements established in the Gilded Age and Progressive Era as "spearheads of reform" and the work they did as models for the reforms institutionalized by New Deal and Great Society programs.[12] Yet religion seems to be missing from this history. Davis stated that "[a]lmost without exception, the settlements that became important centers of social reform attempted to avoid anything that might give the impression of proselytizing."[13] Christodora, however, seems to be an exception to this. Arthur C. Holden's 1922 study is one of the few histories of the settlement house movement that mentions Christodora, and interestingly enough, he refers to the ways in which it treated the religious issue in its day-to-day activities. He protested that even though the spirit of Christianity dominated the house, "its policy has always been non-religious" and that despite its name there was "no effort to convert Jews but anyone coming into contact with the settlement is influenced by its Christian spirit."[14] A close reading of Christodora's records, however, reveals evidence of a strong religious spirit and an assertively Protestant atmosphere. Not only did this settlement attempt to inculcate Protestant ideals of family and work in the immigrants who came in great numbers to its doors, but it also rearticulated Protestant middle-class values for its resident workers.

An investigation into the origins and nature of Christodora House, where Hopkins began his social work career, is illuminating because it reveals how Protestantism shaped much of the social policy from which the American welfare state emerged. Christina Isobel Proudfoot MacColl, along with her friend Sarah Libby Carson, founded Christodora House in the slums of New York City's Lower East Side in the late nineteenth century. They brought with them a strain of evangelical Protestantism that permeated the settlement's atmosphere to an unusual degree. Hopkins found this familiar ideological ground, as did his sister, Adah Hopkins, and Grinnell professors Louis Hartson and Edward Steiner, all of whom formed strong connections with Christodora.

While historians have not recognized Christodora House as one of the major settlements in the United States, over 17,000 neighbors participated in its activities during the month of November 1914, making it one of the largest and most active settlements in New York City.[15] Its residents also participated, albeit marginally, in the progressive reform movement. Records of club meetings indicate an interest in issues such as child labor laws, the protective tariff, Woodrow Wilson's campaign in 1912, and woman suffrage. An investigation into the nature of Christodora House and its head worker, Christina Isobel MacColl, an influential woman who became a lifelong friend to Hopkins and his family, sheds light on Hopkins' development as social worker. This story takes on added significance because it played such an crucial role in the life of Hopkins' first wife, Ethel Gross, a remarkable woman who had much to do with his early successes.

On the first pages of a scrapbook begun by the settlement house in 1897 is an announcement that reflects the founders' frame of mind: "In the belief that the time was ripe for an organization which should combine the fine principles and methods of the 'settlement idea' with definite religious work, the Christodora House of the Young Women's Settlement was opened June 10, 1897 at 163 Avenue B, New York City. . . ."[16] Christina MacColl was not a trained social worker; neither was her co-founder, Sarah Carson. They had met while they were both working uptown in the Young Women's Christian Association's Harlem Annex. From this experience the two women took away not only a forthright piety but also a firm belief in the Victorian doctrine of separate spheres of activity for men and women.[17] According to Kraus,"[a] conversation with a frustrated Protestant pastor led MacColl and Carson to consider a settlement, for he told them 'we can't do anything with these people,' meaning the Italians, Jews and some few Germans in the neighborhood."[18] The two women decided to establish a settlement house in the Lower East Side, "a social center that should be tolerant, educationally effective and conducted without evasion on a truly religious, non-sectarian basis."[19] No matter that some observers had found many of the young people in the neighborhood to be alarmingly "fierce" and "as untamed as so many little wildcats." The two young women intended to settle in the slums of New York City and form bonds of "love and loyalty" with their immigrant neighbors. At the same time they would help them adjust to the deplorable living conditions there, conditions dangerous to both body and soul.[20]

In June of 1897, although they had no outside support and very little money, MacColl and Carson rented the cellar of a delicatessen at 163 Avenue B, just a few blocks from Tompkins Square Park, also taking rooms on the second and third floors as living quarters. They called their enterprise, which at first had a somewhat seedy quality about it, the Young Women's Settlement. The basement room that they used as their main activity area also served as the delicatessen's storeroom for limburger cheese and sauerkraut. Until they moved to larger and more genteel quarters down the street at 147 Avenue B, the settlement house's activities had a distinctly German flavor.[21]

Undaunted by their inelegant quarters, MacColl and Carson filled the basement with flowers, stuffed daisies in the holes they found in the walls, and, with less confidence than bravura, painted signs announcing the establishment of the Young Women's Settlement and inviting the girls of the neighborhood to attend the initial meeting. They were worried that no one would respond to their invitation, but ninety-eight girls, mostly Irish and German, came that first night, many straight from their jobs in the nearby pencil and tobacco factories. Although the area had a substantial population of Jews, only four Jewish girls initially responded.[22] MacColl admitted to being frightened at first by the roughness of the girls, claiming that she "had no experience with such people." Happily, this fear evaporated with experience.[23]

That evening the founders, responding to individual requests from the girls, established classes in millinery, dressmaking, and typewriting.[24] Within a few months, with the unanimous approval of its council, the settlement's name was changed to Christodora House, meaning Gift of Christ, admittedly as an anchor against the secularization of so many settlements during that time. Christodora's roots might have been in the cellar but, as MacColl repeatedly said, "it always reached upward and onward."[25]

When it opened in 1897, Christodora House was the only settlement in New York's Sixth Assembly District, an area of the Lower East Side rife with social and economic problems. Fifty-five percent of the inhabitants (54,714) were foreign born, and the neighborhood supported the greatest concentration (4,000 per block) of immigrants in the United States. The settlement hoped to instill "a sane and reasonable attitude" in order to keep these beleaguered, hardworking people from becoming embittered over what MacColl labeled "their lost dreams."[26] As a settler in the slums, she saw firsthand that the reality of life in New York City's Lower East Side had shattered many immigrants' fantasies of the good life in America. Not only would the educational and recreational activities provided by her staff temper the effect of the urban slum on its inhabitants, but the strength derived from living a Christian life would, in her mind, enable the immigrant to adjust to a largely hostile and cheerless environment. Following the dictates of Social Gospelers, she sought to ameliorate the conditions of urban life for the immigrant by treating what she believed were the environmental and spiritual causes of social disorders.

Although the Jews of the neighborhood (and some Catholics as well) would have good reason to be suspicious of the proselytizing that would likely come out of a place called Christodora, supporters asserted that no attempt was made to change the religion of immigrants who came to the settlement.[27] However, documents indicate that the settlement workers did, in fact, rejoice when a Catholic or Jew embraced Protestantism, which presupposes that evangelical Protestantism played a role in this particular settlement house. Religious services were held at Christodora each Sunday and the fact that both Jews and Catholics attended gave the workers a great deal of satisfaction. They remarked that "even the Jews and Catholics feel the influence of the Settlement" and that "through its influence many of the members have been led to Christ."[28]

Christodora's council, composed mostly of wealthy benefactors, clergy, and former residents, met monthly, sometimes more often.[29] At one of the early meetings of the council, Christina MacColl "spoke of the evidence of the Holy Spirit's work among the young women in the fact that weekly one or more letters are received by her speaking of conversions through the Settlement work."[30] MacColl always seemed much more interested in conversions than in the state of the coffers. Despite the feeling that God would always provide, the house was constantly in need of money. In 1901 she noted that the treasury was empty but that there was "much interest shown in Bible Classes and some have lately expressed a wish to follow the Savior."[31] Describing Christodora's activities, the Reverend Charles H. Parkhurst, a member of the Council, remarked that "this is distinctively religious work" and that "any work is comparatively thrown away if not distinctly and confessedly based on the gospel of Jesus Christ. There is the Divine One to stand back of this work." At the same meeting, another prominent council member, Mrs. Margaret Sangster, proudly gave an "account of one of the Jewish girls who had found the Messiah and who wished to prepare herself to be a missionary."[32] Prominent Social Gospeler Josiah Strong attended the very first public meeting of the Young Women's Settlement and chaired many of the monthly meetings. It was he who usually read the opening psalm and led the group in prayer.[33]

Showing the characteristic practicality of the settlement worker, MacColl did recognize that the young women of the neighborhood needed much more than religion.[34] She declared that the settlement was "not to be a mission. We are to have entertainments, musicals and social gatherings—good jolly ones— and while we will, of course, have the word of God, we do not intend to get unconverted girls out of heated shops and filthy tenements to preach to them. We will meet them as our sisters, our friends, and try to be a help and a blessing and God will do the rest." But she then went on to emphasize the importance of the religious element in settlement work: "It is a mistake to think that a settlement should not have the Bible. Every woman has a divine spark in her nature. . . . Of course, the foundation of the whole thing is the Bible, and our aim is to bring the girls and women to Christ, and away from the possibility of following so many of their sisters to the Bowery and Chinatown."[35] For MacColl, the spiritual state of her neighbors was always of prime importance. She did not minimize the physical effect of slum living, but for her the moral dangers inherent in the urban environment presented a much stronger challenge. Where Josiah Strong pleaded with the reformers to look to improving the environment before attempting to preach to the poor, MacColl believed that a Protestant milieu, which emphasized the traditional family structure and the work ethic, could at least ameliorate some of the deplorable physical conditions existing in the neighborhood. Although she fully realized that many of the women who came to the settlement had to work in order to support their families, she nevertheless encouraged women to stay at home and care for their children. All of the programs at Christodora House stressed women's primary role as mothers and men's role as the family breadwinners.

The nineteenth-century Victorian cult of domesticity permeated Christodora House. In 1907 the *Christodora,* the house magazine, carried an article explaining the value of the Mothers' Club, which reflected the attitudes of the staff at Christodora House. "Clubs are like a great many other things, very good when taken in moderation. When a woman belongs to so many clubs that her home duties must be neglected to attend these meetings, the result will certainly be disastrous to her home." Participation in clubs was beneficial only when it led to "views broadened and knowledge gained for the better management of self, home and family."[36] An important element in the Americanization of the immigrant, the Mothers' Club provided the overworked woman with a window on the world and was a vital part of Christodora. Yet the staff was careful to articulate concerns that the woman's first duty, no matter how desperate for company, no matter how exhausted from the rigors of slum living, was to home care. Christodora fully supported what historian Sheila Rothman called the "ideology of educated motherhood." She asserted that "some of the programs that took place within the settlement represented a self-conscious and even somewhat heavy-handed effort to make the immigrant over into the image of educated mothers." Appropriately, the settlement house clubs became the vehicles of this enterprise, "an almost direct translation of popular female associations into the special environment of the ghetto."[37]

The Christodora story illustrates the problematic relationship among the settlement worker, the immigrant, and the Protestant churches that formed much of the context for the complex power struggle going on in urban America during the late nineteenth and early twentieth centuries. Dr. Edward Steiner who taught

Hopkins his course on Applied Christianity at Grinnell was a frequent guest at Christodora. He wrote a short, unpublished history of the settlement in which he claimed that although Catholic churches and Jewish synagogues can provide the immigrants with some "insurance against loneliness, sickness, death," they also acted as "astringents, contracting rather than enlarging vision, and prolonging the period of adjustment to the new world. . . ." In addition, Protestant churches, "not infrequently greeted with brickbats rather than 'Hosannas,'" were more than a little uncomfortable with "these strange and unassorted sheep. . . ."[38] He claimed that the social settlement solved the dilemma of the inability of religious institutions to respond effectively to the problems experienced by immigrants. The settlements, Christodora House in particular, used "cultured" men and women to help individual immigrants solve their own problems. Steiner described three strands that formed the pattern of Christodora's methods: religious idealism, cultivation of the arts, and service. But there was no doubt in this Social Gospeler's mind that religious idealism was the most important. He clearly stated that "Christodora was built upon a religious foundation" and that "religion was the motivating power" behind the house.[39]

Much of Christodora's work was done through the immigrant children who were attracted not so much by Christian ideals but by the playgrounds, libraries, and clubs as well as by the "roominess, the cleanliness of the House [and by the] fresh air sweetened by the fragrance of flowers." They saw "walls made beautiful by draperies and pictures when at home they saw them mostly in grime and soot." To these children the settlement became a "larger and finer home and its residents their noble kinsmen. . . ." While this attitude certainly rings of elitism, in the minds of the Christodora residents, contact with the settlement house brought the best of American culture to immigrant children and thus to their parents. For Dr. Steiner and certainly MacColl, the best of American culture included the spirit of Christianity.[40]

The particular aim of the clubs that formed the basis of all of Christodora's activities was to instill middle-class American manners and morals in the children and, through them, in their parents. The Loyalty Club, for girls ten to fourteen, chose as its club song "Loyalty to Christ," which the members sang at every meeting. The Sangster Club included girls over fourteen, and its influence seemed to have had an immediate effect on its large membership. At the second meeting, on July 6, 1897, the minutes indicate that the girls of the Sangster Club were "already becoming more gentle and polite, and even rise to offer a chair to any one entering the room." In describing the Children's Club, for girls seven to ten years old, the minutes record that "the little ones learn to wait at the door, make beds, set the table and other useful things."[41] In an interview, MacColl remarked that "everything should be done in the very best way possible, one should put forth his best effort." For her this reflected "maintaining the standard."[42] She was remembered by those who frequented Christodora as a perfectionist. She would tell the children, "Do not be content with second best. . . . Give yourself the best that you have, because in giving yourself the best that you have, giving the world the best that you have, you can then really and truly justify yourself."[43] This emphasis on child saving, along with close attention to child development, had a significant influence on Hopkins when he was affiliated with Christodora House, and much of his work in the widows' pension movement in 1915 reflected this. For him, children ideally belonged in the home under the close supervision of a mother whose domestic activities defined her role in life.

Christina MacColl used the programs at Christodora House to find religious solutions to the destitution that Jane Addams had ascribed to social and educational disadvantages. Thus MacColl strongly endorsed an intimate connection between spiritual salvation and a literal, physical salvation from the degradation of the urban slum. Her brand of Protestantism idealized domesticity, maternalism, and hard work. For her, Protestantism became a vehicle by which she could *convert* her immigrant neighbors to an "American" way of life: a middle-class ideal that dictated that women's duty and responsibility lay within the confines of the home, dependent on a male breadwinner. Historians have largely ignored both the role evangelical Protestantism played in the American settlement house movement and, more significantly, the doctrine of separate, gendered spheres that this religious presence endorsed. MacColl's explicit use of Protestantism at her settlement house highlights the intimate relationship among gender, religion, and reform.

Social Gospeler Josiah Strong, from the very beginning a constant and influential presence at Christodora House, turned his attention to the immediate environment. He called on Protestants to attend to their brothers and sisters who were enduring inhuman conditions in slums, those "putrefying sores of the city."[44] Strong believed that industrialism had led to such wretched living conditions for the urban poor that it posed a serious threat to morality as well as to the Victorian framework of family life. A zealous advocate for the urban poor, he claimed that the city could not be saved while its people lived in squalor. For Strong, the challenge of the Social Gospel to apply Christian theology to social problems meant a synthesis of the sacred and the secular. An advocate of the Kingdom Movement (started by Grinnell College's George Gates), he declared that the Kingdom of God, the ideal society on earth, must combine the physical with the spiritual. Proclaiming that "[m]oral suasion is impotent with bad ventilation," he called particularly on social settlements to rise to the challenge of social Christianity and to look to the physical as well as the spiritual well-being of their neighbors. In 1902 he wrote: "When settlement workers make no use of religion, they neglect the longest lever for the uplifting of the people."[45] Christina MacColl was one of the few settlement leaders who did not neglect this lever. Protestant theology became the driving force behind the cultural expectations she transmitted to the immigrant neighbors. It was here, in this milieu, that young Harry Hopkins had a first-hand introduction to the urban poor and to the various methods devised to alleviate their condition. He also became acquainted with the use of relief as a lever to uplift the dependent, a strategy he later applied and then rejected in his work as New Deal relief administrator.

When Hopkins' summer job as counselor at Northover Camp ended, MacColl offered him a job as head of activities for boys. He happily accepted it. Like the other workers, he lived at the settlement house, in the midst of Lower East side ghetto. A coworker described him as "very eager and young . . . and full of the desire to help."[46] In charge of boys' work, Hopkins brought a good deal of enthusiasm to his job. Yet along with this came a realization that the immigrants he came into contact with did not benefit equally from the democracy he had learned about in the classroom. Like other young social workers, he entered into the lives of the inhabitants of the ghetto, climbing dingy staircases to tenements where he saw immigrant families living in overcrowded, unsanitary, and often dangerous conditions. This work as what was then called a "friendly visitor" opened his eyes to a type of poverty shockingly new to him. In the Lower East Side slum Hopkins saw poverty in its ugliest form. This was not the dignified lack of ready money he had seen among his neighbors in rural Iowa, a problem that even his own family had experienced from time to time. The filth and degradation of everyday life in the New York City ghetto shocked and enraged him. While Hopkins had read textbook descriptions of urban squalor, his firsthand experience served as a vivid confirmation of the existence of undeserved poverty. While Hopkins developed an immunity to the horrors of life in the ghetto, he did not become immune to human suffering. His experience with settlement work had an enormous impact on his life. According to biographer Robert Sherwood, "this was his real birth as a crusader for reform."[47]

Hopkins' total immersion into an urban environment rich in cultural diversity had far-reaching effects on the young man from Iowa. In Grinnell he had lived among a homogeneous society where his friends and neighbors were cast from the same mold as the Hopkins family. Edward Steiner's Jewish heritage had merely been an interesting cultural appendage, one more dimension of the popular professor rather than a racial distinction. There was no anti-Semitism apparent in Grinnell because there were essentially no Jews. In New York City, the ethnic mix fascinated Hopkins and provided a new and exciting element in his continuing education.

Working with the immigrant boys at Christodora House, Hopkins learned that the value system that they espoused did not always conform to his own. The distinction between right and wrong might not be as clear or as simple as his family and teachers had taught him in Grinnell. An especially telling incident occurred in 1914 when Hopkins had been working in the settlement house for almost two years. The following short essay written by Hopkins and published in the prestigious journal for social workers, *Survey Graphic,* testifies to his growing awareness of the complexity of moral codes:

CAPITAL PUNISHMENTS AND BOYS

"I move that the whole club stand for two minutes in honor of the four gunmen who died today."

The scene was the meeting of a club of small boys in a settlement on the Lower East Side of New York on the evening of the day that society had taken its revenge on four gunmen for the murder of a fellow criminal.

It was a slip of a boy, scarcely fifteen, who spoke, learned in all the vices of city streets, the recognized leader of his gang, yet highly responsible in that at this early age he is the main support of a large family. Tonight there was no sign of his usual rollicking deviltry.

"Aw, what 'yu talkin' about. Dago Frank went to the chair first."

"They had a hard time killin' Gyp."—this last from an underfed youngster whose widowed mother is trying desperately hard to keep him straight.

"They was all dressed in black, and they poured water over 'em to make the electricity work better."

"They sure died game," was one sentiment to which all agreed, for didn't every newspaper in New York announce that fact in glowing headlines? These and many other gruesome facts had fixed themselves firmly in their impressionable minds.

These boys were exceptionally keen, ambitious and clean-minded, a few of them wage earners, most of them in the public schools—a club formed by the union of two gangs from rival streets, now welded together with a fine club spirit. The basket-ball championship won the previous week, the club's annual play not only a few days off, the debate of the evening were all overshadowed tonight, for the gunmen had been electrocuted, and the details of their death must be firmly impressed on the minds of each one.

What is responsible for the fact that thirty-five boys, all under sixteen, should wish to rise to their feet to pay homage to four men whose crime their keen sense of right and wrong would naturally condemn under normal circumstances?[48]

Hopkins' tone reflected a singular respect for these "keen, ambitious and cleaned-minded" boys. He did not denigrate them; rather, he wondered why these otherwise moral and hardworking youngsters should so admire criminals. Neither did he blame the boys for what he obviously considered a "moral lapse"; instead, he blamed social institutions for the negligence that caused this misplaced hero-worship.

Hopkins' experience at the settlement house broadened his social perspective. Feeling newly sophisticated and liberal, he referred to the "conservative narrowmindedness" of those he left behind in Grinnell, thus exhibiting the normal reaction of a young man against the pedestrian minds that suddenly seemed to populate his hometown.[49] There is no doubt, however, that Hopkins' experience at Christodora House, where he rubbed elbows with a broad mix of people, blurred any class and ethnic barriers that he might have brought with him from Grinnell.

Christodora House had a further, more personal, influence on Hopkins. The settlement provided a context for what historians refer to as the dual migration to American cities during the late nineteenth century—Hopkins and his ilk coming from the American Midwest and masses of immigrants streaming to America from Europe, especially eastern Europe, meeting and mixing in urban centers such as New York City. At Christodora House Hopkins met his first wife, Ethel Gross, a young Jewish immigrant who had migrated in 1891 from Hungary. She lived with her family in one of the grimy tenements on 10th Street, a few blocks from Christodora, and may even have been one of the girls in attendance the first night the settlement opened in 1897. In her own words, her life started with her introduction to Christodora. Her particular experience at the settlement was played over many times in various cities and exemplifies the way settlement houses helped so many young immigrants adjust to life in America. Like Anna Pickett Hopkins and Adah Hopkins, Ethel joined the ranks of strong women who exerted a distinct influence on Harry Hopkins' life. Her story is especially relevant to his development as a social worker.

Ethel Gross was born in 1886 in Kaschau,[50] a small town in Hungary not very far from Budapest. Her parents, Bencion Gross and Celia Rich, were members of the town's Jewish middle class. Celia, one of ten children, had been raised by a loving and indulgent grandmother. She was reputedly a beautiful young girl with large blue eyes and chestnut hair whose lightheartedness and sense of humor attracted many suitors. Bencion was tall, bookish, and physically frail. He had been educated at the Theological Seminary at Pressburg and periodically worked as a manager in his family's glass factory in Hutta. Although Celia and Bencion enjoyed a comfortable middle-class life in Kaschau, they endured the humiliation of social, legal, and economic restrictions placed on Jews. Like so many others, Bencion dreamed of taking his family to America, where he envisioned opportunity, education, and upward social mobility. However, his dreams were shattered when he contracted tuberculosis and realized that he could never make the arduous trip across the Atlantic.[51]

Ethel was just five years old when her father died in 1891, at the age of thirty-nine. Many years later she would recount in a journal her memories of his illness. She remembered seeing him propped up in his bed, writing endless letters to relatives in America. She wrote: "My only memory of the death of my father was my mother weeping—in the doorway—her face pressed against the door jamb, her slight figure leaning against it in helplessness. It is one of the few times I ever saw my mother weep." Just after her husband's death, Celia's grief was compounded by the death of her nine-month-old son. Nevertheless, she was determined to carry out her husband's wish that his family migrate to America. She sold everything the family owned, paid the medical bills and all the debts, and had just enough money left over to purchase steerage passage to New York. The thirty-seven-year-old widow and her five children, ages three to fifteen, left for America in late 1891, joining a wave of about 34 million immigrants. The trip (which lasted about twelve days) would have been a difficult one, berthed as they were in the bottom decks where the steering mechanism was located. Even though she was very young, Ethel Gross remembered much of the voyage: "I can remember the smells of steerage . . . I can remember my mother only as the moving, guiding spirit of the whole expedition—very quiet, very adequate. I never felt anything but a sense of security—of adventure, perhaps—but never fear." Ethel wrote: "It must have a pleasant experience on the whole—because I have always since then loved the sea and boats."[52]

When the Gross family arrived in New York, however, they quickly discovered that this was a very different place from what they expected. It was worse in some ways than what they had left behind. Celia and the children settled in New York's Lower East Side. Although Ethel mentions an aunt and a cousin in her correspondence during 1913, there is no indication in any letters or journals that any of the relatives who had preceded them to America ever helped Celia when she arrived in New York. Soon after the landing, Celia had to endure yet another loss when a daughter, Henrietta, died.[53]

In 1900 the Lower East Side of New York was a densely populated urban ghetto. The Gross family lived in a typical dumbbell-shaped tenement—airless and dark and affording its occupants little in the way of comfort. Celia probably supported herself and her children by doing piecework for the garment industry in her home, one of the few jobs available to women like her who, although educated, did not speak English and had few marketable skills. However, there is no occupation listed for her on the 1900 census report. Ethel recalled that her siblings went to work as soon as they were old enough. The eldest, fifteen-year-old Francesca, probably got a job immediately.[54]

The children, with the possible exception of Francesca, worked hard to assimilate into their new country. Ethel, especially, wanted to look, act, and speak like an American.[55] Immediately upon arrival in New York, she entered the local public school on East 5th Street between Avenues B and C, just a block away from her family's first tenement apartment on East 4th Street. She hated it. A much older Ethel wrote about the frightful experience of school in a strange city. At first she could not speak English. She was self-conscious about her foreign-looking clothes, her curly hair, her earrings, and she recalled that whatever she learned, she learned out of fear. Her short, undated journal reads:

> I could probably write a wonderful essay on the value of education—never having had any. The elementary school which I attended, entering at the age of five—feeling ashamed of the difference between myself and all the other children around me, because I was the only little foreigner,[56] probably did more harm than good. Fear is the emotion that I remember most as I look back on that period. Fear of not doing what the teacher wanted. Fear of being and acting differently from my classmates. Fear of looking different because of my clothes. Fear seemed to predominate everything I did. It became the motive for doing nearly everything I did at school.[57]

This must have been an exceptionally traumatic experience for her because Ethel left school after the eighth grade. She later explained this by claiming that the family needed her wages, but doubtless her unhappy experience with school contributed to her leaving. Because educational opportunity for her children was what had driven Celia to endure the long journey to America, she must have been terribly disappointed with her daughter's decision.[58] Ethel never returned to school, and all her life she hid what to her was a shameful lack of formal education. Later, although working full time, she did attend classes at the State University of New York and New York University. In 1903 Ethel successfully passed Regents examinations in writing, elementary English, geography, reading, spelling, and arithmetic.[59]

Ethel's primary ambition was to get a good job outside of the ghetto and enter into the mainstream of American life. When she was about eleven years old, she came into contact with the local, newly established, settlement house located at 147 Avenue B, just around the corner from where she lived. Christodora House and Christina MacColl were to be the defining influences on Ethel's development for many years to come. When Ethel left school, MacColl arranged for her to spend the summer in the country, in Dalton, Massachusetts.[60] Ethel was anemic and had fainting spells, and MacColl wanted her to get out of the city in order to regain her health. It must have been effective, for when Ethel returned to the city, she went to work for Christodora House supervising recreational programs for very young children. She was just twelve years old, still a child herself, yet proud to be earning some money, even if it was just a few dollars a month. MacColl became Ethel's mentor and arranged for her to take lessons on the new typewriting machine and to learn shorthand. These skills eventually enabled her to get a job in an office as a clerk/stenographer for the Engineering News and Publishing Company when she was fourteen. The fact that Ethel got a much-coveted clerical job attests to her lively ambition as much as to MacColl's efforts. She worked there for two years and then moved to the M.P. Foster Electrical Company as a clerk/typist. At the same time, she continued to work for the settlement house as MacColl's secretary and as a counselor for the children. Ethel's ties to Christodora House were very strong and very important. This was her link to what she considered to be the real America. Here, from middle-class social workers like MacColl, Ethel learned how twentieth-century Americans spoke, dressed, and acted—and she learned quickly.[61]

In 1908 MacColl recommended Ethel for a job as a private secretary to Katherine Mackay, wife of Clarence Mackay, owner of U.S. Telegraph and Cable Company. Katherine Mackay used her wealth and social position to create a suffrage organization for women called the Equal Franchise Society (EFS). Ethel's work with the EFS and her relationship with Katherine Mackay represented her first giant step out of the Lower East Side ghetto and into the American mainstream. She organized speaking engagements for the EFS rallies, wrote press releases for the media, attended dinner parties with the elite of New York City, and met such notables as Carrie Chapman Catt, Crystal and Max Eastman, and Harriot Stanton Blatch. It was an exciting and heady experience for her.[62]

Life for the Gross family was difficult, especially for Celia, whose life in the ghetto was not what she had expected or had been used to. In Kaschau, she and Bencion had enjoyed a relatively comfortable life, complete with servants, holidays, and small luxuries. Celia missed these, of course, but even more she must have missed the support and love of her husband, for whom she never stopped grieving. She never really adjusted to life in what to her would always be a foreign country. In 1910 or 1911, knowing that her children were grown and independent and probably feeling that they no longer needed her protection, Celia killed herself. Ethel Gross was twenty-four years old when she found her mother's body in the kitchen of their tenement. She did not speak of her mother again until 1964, during a taped interview fifty-three years after the suicide.[63]

After her mother's suicide, Ethel became Katherine Mackay's resident private secretary and went to live in the splendor of the Mackays' estate in Rosalyn, Long Island. She also accompanied the Mackay family on at least two trips to Europe. In the autumn of 1912 Ethel was in Paris with Katherine Mackay, but it was a difficult time for both women. Katherine was having a rather public affair with Dr. Joseph Blake, a noted surgeon who had treated her husband, Clarence Mackay, for throat cancer and essentially saved his life. An irate Mrs. Blake was in the process of suing Katherine Mackay for alienating the doctor's affections. Because the Mackays were wealthy and in Manhattan's social vanguard, and because Katherine was a tall and dramatically beautiful woman, the newspapers were boosting sales by giving this scandal full coverage. The impending "sordid divorce," made more acrimonious by Katherine's animosity toward her husband's Catholicism, made Ethel very uncomfortable. What shocked her even more was the fact that her employer gave up custody of her three children to marry Dr. Blake. When Ethel went back home to visit her sister over the Christmas holiday, she decided that, despite the lure of first-class hotels, she could not return to Paris or to Mrs. Mackay's employ. Instead, Ethel went to her old friend Miss MacColl and asked her for a job. Even though money was tight at the settlement house, MacColl hired Ethel, who now lived with her married older sister, to run the drama program for young girls.[64]

There can be no doubt that Christodora House provided Ethel Gross with a bridge from the Lower East Side ghetto to middle-class America. When she joined Christodora's paid staff in 1912, she was a relatively sophisticated twenty-five-year-old New Yorker. She had rejected the orthodox religion of her mother and embraced all things American, including the ambiguities inherent in the nineteenth-century attitude toward gender roles. On one hand she learned typing and shorthand and took courses at New York University so that she could benefit from the new employment opportunities opening up to women in the early twentieth century. She fought for woman's suffrage by actively participating in the Equal Franchise Society and later the Women's Political Union. But she also considered her future role as wife and mother as ultimately more important than anything she had ever done, largely because of the early influence of MacColl with whom she formed a lifelong friendship.[65]

Ethel Gross from eastern Europe and Harry Hopkins from the American Midwest met in the hallways of Christodora House. They typified the mutual fascination of east and west—they fell in love almost immediately and were married within a year, on October 21, 1913. It is significant that the marriage ceremony was performed at the Ethical Culture Society, of which Ethel was a member, by John Lovejoy Elliot, head worker of the Hudson Guild Settlement House and associate of Felix Adler, who started the society in 1875. The society had close ties to the settlement houses and to progressive reform. Adler (1851-1933), son of a rabbi and a pioneer in social work, believed that religion should be based on intellectual truth rather than theology. Although an adherent of secularism, he vehemently denied charges of atheism, declaring that he believed in the "supreme excellence of righteousness" and in "the sanctification of human life . . . in the service of the unknown God."[66] Hopkins was particularly attracted by Adler's proclamation that "[w]hen we are smitten by the rod of affliction, do not let us sit still but rather get to work as fast as we can. In action lies our salvation."[67] Hopkins did follow Ethel Gross into the Ethical Culture Society, but there is no evidence that this was a long-standing membership. It did, however, reflect his drift away from formal religion, a time when he developed his "do-unto-others" beliefs that became the essence of his bare-bones theology.

Harry Hopkins and Ethel Gross exerted a tremendous influence on each other. Although they worked in the same building, they wrote each other at least one letter a day during most of 1913 (before their marriage), and this correspondence provides interesting insights into Hopkins' personality . The couple were immediately faced with the very serious issue of their religious differences. The fact that Ethel was a Jew would have held a certain attraction for Harry Hopkins, fresh from Professor Edward Steiner's course that stressed the richness of Jewish culture and tradition. Yet he was very much aware that their families would be shocked by their association with one another. Just after meeting her, Hopkins wrote: "But girl, there is going to be an awful row when your family learns how you have fallen from grace . . . Oh! but my father! Ye Gods—it is lucky that he hasn't any money for he certainly would leave me out. I love to think how it will rock the very foundations of our dining room. The poor old dears are badly in need of something to talk of and they are going to get enough to last for at least a week."[68] Ethel's family was likewise opposed to her engagement to Harry. She wrote to Harry that her sister, Francesca Gross Kohn, warned her that "she doesn't believe in inter marriage because [anti-Semitism] might be slumbering sometimes but it is never dead no matter how broad-minded they are." But, Ethel added in her letter, "I can't imagine you with that kind of prejudice 'slumbering' anywhere about your person . . . Why can't people get away from stereotyped phrases and understand how two people can be in perfect harmony and absolutely suited to each other—in spite of the fact that they were born to different faiths."[69]

Harry and Ethel were really less different than it might appear on the surface. Years before, in her overwhelming desire to be accepted into mainstream American life, Ethel had turned away from her family's Judaism.

Her involvement in the settlement house and the suffrage movement exemplified this. Harry likewise was gradually sloughing off the Methodism his mother had drummed into him at home and also was altering his concept of the Social Gospel taught to him at Grinnell. Both young social workers embraced a secularism, a rejection of formal religion, that allowed them common ground upon which to build a strong relationship.

During their courtship, in March of 1913, Ethel got a job working with Harriot Stanton Blatch, the daughter of Elizabeth Cady Stanton. Blatch had formed the Women's Political Union (originally called the Equality League of Self-Supporting Women) when she concluded that the suffrage movement "was completely in a rut in New York State." Convinced that only a constitutional amendment could ensure the success of the suffrage movement, Blatch pursued political means to that end. She engaged the help of working women and of unions, and she campaigned for those legislators who supported the amendment and against those who did not. Blatch had worked closely with Ethel's previous employer, Katherine Mackay and the EFS, but the two women never did agree on tactics. Mackay's rather genteel group abhorred the public, political strategies used by the Women's Political Union (WPU), and Blatch denigrated the white-gloved approach of the EFS. When Blatch decided that a suffrage parade would arouse the public to their cause, the EFS women expressed shock that women would march in the streets. Ethel's position was clear. Clad in the white suffragists' dress, she not only marched proudly in many of the suffrage parades, but she carried the flag at Blatch's side.[70] Although Hopkins poked good-natured fun at her activities, referring to her as "a girl who is giving the best years of her young life for the sole purpose of jogging elbows with men,—respectable and otherwise,—at the voting booth," he was very proud of her activism and thoroughly supported her.[71]

Hopkins himself began to look around for employment opportunities, and at the suggestion of MacColl, turned to the Association for Improving the Condition of the Poor (AICP), one of the largest social welfare agencies in the city. Hopkins filed a job application in April of 1913 and the following month was offered a position. With this job came his introduction to the movers and shakers of the city. He seemed to have felt little regret in leaving Christodora House to work for the AICP. He wrote to Ethel:

> You know this is the first time I ever really felt good about losing a job[72]—I have
> learned to like the boys very, very much and hate to think of giving them up
> altogether but as for the residential sections of this plant—I feel sure that their
> spiritual food would be more palatable with me far away. I have fully decided
> that if this house is on the side of the Lord, I am going to straightaway apply

below. But still they are dear, innocent people and will never hurt anybody especially themselves intentionally.[73]

This sentiment indicated that he had problems with some of the resident workers at Christodora and that he disliked the religious message that pervaded the settlement. It also revealed a youthful arrogance and a rather judgmental attitude. However, it may have been a manifestation of Hopkins' developing social philosophy. Half a century later Ethel spoke about this period in their lives and commented that religion had meant a great deal to Harry Hopkins. "His concept of religion changed as the years went by," she declared. "He felt that the 'Do unto others as you would have others do unto you' was enough to know." He had picked up the very basic tenet of the Ethical Culture Society, which taught that there should be no divisions between religions. Harry Hopkins never joined a formal church but, according to Ethel, he believed that "service to others was the most important way to manifest religion."[74]

Hopkins' work in Christodora House did much to mature him as a social worker. He reveled in life in the ethnic diversity and richness of life in New York City's Lower East Side.[75] He had no intention of leaving. In addition, his relationship with Ethel Gross broadened his outlook considerably. Through her Harry was exposed to some of what the couple considered the more radical elements of the city. He told her that he had thought "about bigger and better things since you came into my life."[76] These bigger and better things would involve Hopkins in the birth of America's system of welfare, a process that had been slowly gathering momentum while he was learning the ropes under MacColl's tutelage.

During Hopkins' tenure at Christodora House, New York City was undergoing tumultuous social and political changes. Fusion mayor John Purroy Mitchel had just been elected through the support of the reform wings of both political parties. The new reform administration, however, enraged private charities because of its attachment to modern, more scientific methods of administering help to the city's needy population. Leaders of voluntary (and largely religious) institutions, declaring that the mayor and his cronies lacked compassion in their drive to economize, saw their position as caregivers being threatened by secular philanthropy controlled by the city. Hopkins' admiration of John Kingsbury, the city's director of Public Charities, impelled him to place his sympathies on the side of Mitchel's administration. While the religious atmosphere at Christodora House would have felt congenial to Hopkins when he first arrived, his subsequent introduction to the Ethical Culture Society, the woman suffrage movement, socialism, and reform politics changed this. Adah Hopkins, who often visited her brother and sister-in-law, reinforced Hopkins' commitment to scientific charity, a movement to which she demonstrated considerable attachment during her work as Grinnell's overseer of the poor.

In addition to ideological changes that diminished his religious idealism, Hopkins' ambition was also a factor in the direction his career began to take in 1914. He looked at Kingsbury's job with a good deal of envy, believing that this was a position of considerable influence and power. Ethel Gross Hopkins remarked that her husband often expressed a wish that one day he would have such a position because of the freedom he would have to implement programs he believed in. He wanted "to get into government," she remarked, because he could be more effective and "achieve much better results than all this relief giving." Ethel was very ambitious for her husband; she thought he "could go very far in government" and could even one day be president of the United States.[77]

On their way to New York in June 1912 Hopkins and Hartson's detour had taken them to the Republican National Convention. Hopkins could not have known it then, but a group of progressive reformers—some of whom would have a lasting influence on his career—were also at the convention. John Kingsbury, Paul Kellogg, Margaret Dreier Robbins, and Owen Lovejoy had drawn up a plank for the Republican platform called "Social Standards for Industry." This program was the work of a coalition of social reformers and social workers founded in 1874 through the Committee on Standards of Living and Labor of the National Conference of Charities and Corrections. This coalition began to focus its attention on exposing conditions that made charity necessary and on encouraging preventive measures rather than just ameliorating conditions through charity. The plank called for national insurance against industrial accidents, labor regulation for women and children, a living wage, and old-age and unemployment insurance. The authors of this plank considered themselves in the midst of a revolution in social welfare, where social reform and political forces were merging and when social work was attaining status as a profession. When the Republicans turned them down, the group turned to Theodore Roosevelt's Progressive Party. The Progressives accepted the plank as presented, and Roosevelt earned the active support of newly politicized social reformers who wanted to use the candidate "as a sounding board against which to echo the national social program. . . ." After Roosevelt's defeat, the disappointed but undaunted social workers turned their attention to city politics and the newly elected Fusion administration.[78] Hopkins, through his connection with John Kingsbury and the AICP, soon was drawn into the maelstrom that transformed the city's relief policies.

New York City's philanthropic landscape during the first two decades of the twentieth century provided fertile ground for Hopkins' ideas to take root.

The social and economic turmoil caused by the huge influx of immigrants, by high unemployment due to a recession, by religious controversy, by turf battles between philanthropic organizations, and by changing attitudes toward the causes and treatment of dependency allowed Hopkins ample occasion to practice his newly acquired talents. With the enthusiastic support of his new wife, Ethel, Hopkins set out on a grand adventure in social work.

CHAPTER FOUR

POVERTY AND UNEMPLOYMENT IN NEW YORK CITY

The poor shall never cease the land.
> —AICP First Annual Report, 1845

The chief difficulty at present in the problem of unemployment is to convince the public at large that there is a problem
of unemployment at all.
> —Harry Hopkins, 1913

DURING THE FIRST TWO DECADES OF THE TWENTIETH CENTURY, New York City
presented a political arena for energetic social workers faced with a myriad of
new problems arising from industrialization and increased immigration. There
Harry Hopkins came into contact with politically active progressive reformers.
Many of these men and women vociferously blamed the eastern industrialists
and financiers for the country's economic and social ills and called for positive
government action to correct an unequal distribution of wealth and opportunity.
The echoes here of Midwestern populism must have been unmistakable to
Hopkins.[1] But unlike the populists, these urban reformers had a comprehensive
plan for social action. Reformers such as Lillian Wald, Homer Folks, John

Kingsbury, William Matthews, Mary Dewson, Frances Perkins, and now Harry Hopkins were part of a tightly knit, interactive coterie of New York City welfare administrators who were later called upon by President Franklin Roosevelt to implement his New Deal programs.[2] They brought from their diverse backgrounds common social, religious, political, and economic precepts that both shaped and reflected progressive values. Their shared experiences working in private and public social welfare agencies in New York City instilled in them a new attitude toward poverty. Blaming poverty on structural defects inherent in a capitalist society, they created preventive rather than ameliorative programs to help the needy. In addition, these reformers became increasingly convinced that the government had to take an active role in providing for the public welfare.

Once in New York City, working for and with like-minded activists, Hopkins began to develop as a social worker. The progressive ideologies, methods, and programs that he was exposed to helped to reshape his social conscience along more pragmatic lines. Not only did he become politically sophisticated, but he also sharpened his administrative skill. At the same time, the New York political environment fed his ambition.

The years from 1913 to 1918 were marked by an economic downturn and hard times for many of the residents of New York City, and social workers began to search for reform programs that would address the causes as well as the effects of involuntary unemployment. The city became a laboratory for progressive reformers who were seeking a method of welfare administration that would lead to the re-formation of democratic institutions and the adjustment of the capitalist order to promote social justice and economic equality. They rejected nineteenth-century laissez-faire liberalism and adopted a new liberalism based on active, interventionist reform methods. The new tenets of Progressivism that extended the responsibility for the welfare of citizens from the individual to a democratic government found fertile soil in the mind of Hopkins. The programs in which he immersed himself during these early years of his career served as the foundation for later experiments during the economic crisis of the 1930s. His active involvement in formulating solutions for unemployment in New York City and his administration of the city's widows' pension program were especially significant to his future career. These two projects take on added significance when examined in light of Hopkins' activities as New Deal relief administrator. The former laid the foundation for his New Deal work-relief and jobs programs while the latter informed his policies concerning Title IV of the Social Security Act, Aid to Dependent Children.

This was a seminal time for Hopkins. Because of his approaching marriage to Ethel Gross, he needed more money than he was earning at Christodora House. He therefore cast about for a better-paying social work position. It is significant that Hopkins did not seem to consider anything else but a job in social welfare. Very likely he saw this particular career path as one that would satisfy his altruism as well as his ambition. Florence Kerr, in reminiscing about Hopkins' career, remarked that during the early part of the twentieth century, women dominated the ranks of social workers. "An active, vigorous personality boy in the social work field [Hopkins] naturally went to the top very fast . . . he was an outstanding male social worker."[3]

In mid-1913 Harry Hopkins, with the help of his friend and mentor, Christina MacColl, turned to the Association for Improving the Condition of the Poor (AICP) for a job. The organization was the prototypical welfare agency and representative of the changing methods of dealing with poverty and dependence. In 1843 Robert M. Hartley, in an attempt to coordinate the many and often overlapping charitable endeavors of private philanthropic institutions in New York City, established the AICP for "the elevation of the moral and physical condition of the indigent; and so far as compatible with these objects, the relief of their necessities."[4] The order of the purposes reflected the founder's priorities. Hartley and other philanthropists were concerned with curtailing indiscriminate charity that seemed only to encourage pauperism. They had spent a year researching new and more efficient ways to help the deserving poor and at the same time to eliminate "artful mendicants" from relief rolls. Hartley held fast to the traditional mid-nineteenth-century belief that poverty very frequently had its roots in a person's moral failings; his association directed its energies only toward those who either had no agency in their poverty or whose delinquency could be redeemed. He declared that the Association's objective would be "not merely to alleviate wretchedness, but to reform character; and as far as possible, to exterminate from among us, the very germ of professional pauperism."[5]

The AICP always had combined charity with sermons for the moral improvement of the recipient. Moreover, the agency's charitable efforts were intended to safeguard the general public from degrading contact with the contaminating evils of pauperism. The association presented graphic accounts of urban slum conditions, not so much as a plea to the charitable instinct of the affluent but as a warning that unless something were done for the poor, the problems of criminality and degeneracy connected with poverty could very well spread into their well-kept and cherished neighborhoods.[6]

For the first several decades the AICP did not waver in its original objective as stated in 1843—"to relieve none . . . whom we cannot elevate."[7] This attitude reflected the popular belief that, in a bountiful land like America, there was always a way for an industrious person to earn a living and that only the intemperate, the indolent, or the vicious could be plagued by want. The AICP would make every effort to reform such people and rescue them from the debasement of pauperism, but only if they showed a willingness to assist in their salvation. Hartley believed, as did many others, that "the cold hand of want must often be permitted to press on some . . . to spur them to exertion."[8]

The self-help gospel that "the good life" was available to all who worked hard, with its religious corollary that man could cure himself of the moral frailties that led to indigence, engendered an individualistic interpretation of poverty. Many of those administering public and private charity felt that offering outdoor relief—that is, relief given to people in their own homes without requiring institutionalization—would only increase the dependency of degenerate individuals and eventually pauperize them. Gradually, however, the economic depressions in the latter part of the nineteenth century, the cyclical unemployment that resulted, along with Social Gospel and progressive rhetoric, convinced reformers that poverty also might be created by an inhospitable social and economic environment.[9] Toward the end of the nineteenth century, some of the more enlightened social reformers increasingly began to admit that there were impersonal forces at work over which man had no control, thus weakening the individualistic theory of poverty.

The beginning of the twentieth century ushered in "the golden years of social work," an era of great hope when reformers believed they could bring about significant institutional changes to further the cause of social and economic justice. Solutions seemed to be at hand, and at this moment in history social workers were especially enamored with scientific methods to achieve their ends. New interest in working conditions, unemployment, wage levels, housing, child labor, social insurance, and health issues led them to seek statistical information about the causes of poverty. They hoped that they could use this data to overcome the widespread public perception that receiving assistance from public and private agencies was somehow an admission of one's social, moral, and professional failure. Casework techniques and statistical surveys became characteristic of a new, scientific philanthropy. Adah Hopkins had experienced this movement at the New York School of Philanthropy and brought its ideals back to Grinnell in 1912. The success of her work with the Social Service League there testified to the popularity and possibly the efficacy of this cutting-edge method of relief administration.

Despite efforts to educate the public to the contrary, however, the stigma of being "on the dole" kept many of the deserving poor from seeking help. Progressive organizations such as the National Consumers' League (NCL) and the Women's Trade Union League (WTUL) attempted to overcome this prejudice and worked to educate the public to an awareness of the structural causes of unemployment and poverty.[10] By the turn of the century the AICP, an agency that took the lead in advocating preventive services rather than cash relief, was providing a vast array of services including Sea Breeze, a summer home for convalescent mothers; Hartley House, a social and industrial settlement; the Cooper Union Labor Bureau; sewing rooms for women; school lunch programs; pure milk campaigns; health and dental clinics; summer camps for children; and a wealth of educational programs. The association's traditional rigidity toward the poor had softened gradually. In 1899 its board reported that "we have learned the humanity of preferring to be occasionally imposed upon rather than to turn away any case which may perchance be one of genuine distress."[11]

During the early decades of the twentieth century, progressive reformers had been struggling with the moral and economic ramifications of unemployment as a primary cause of poverty. If periods of temporary unemployment were, as many believed, an inevitable result of industrial progress, then workers could not always be held responsible for their idleness. Natural business cycles, seasonal industries, technological improvements, and industrial consolidations caused layoffs. Workers also could lose their jobs due to industrial accidents or an oversupply of labor. Employers, at the mercy of a fluctuating market, could ill afford to keep workers on the payroll during slack times.[12]

Those who were concerned with relieving the distress caused by unemployment were, however, not of one mind. Many, like Robert Hunter, made a very clear distinction between poverty and pauperism. In his 1904 study of the problem, he reflected the still rather common opinion that there are those "litter of miserables" who are very satisfied with their dependence on charity."[13] Such paupers did not deserve charity because their poverty resulted from their own vices—their unwillingness to work. However, for progressive reformers, those victims of industrialism—workers owning nothing but their labor and living always on the brink of destitution—formed a distinct social class deserving of help. They were poor because of an industrial system that could not or would not guarantee consistent employment.

With an industrial working class becoming increasingly necessary for national prosperity, but also subject to the vagaries of an unfettered law of supply and demand, a new face of poverty appeared. During an era of business monopolization and an enlarging labor force, those stalwart workers whose involuntary idleness threw them upon the mercy of relief organizations became a special, almost elite, class of the deserving poor. What should be done with the unfortunate but industrious American worker whose family faced poverty merely because of the shortcomings of a modern industrial society? Reformers such as Hunter believed that cash relief would only pauperize the unemployed worker[14] and instead called for social reforms, including safer working conditions, worker education, wage regulation, and workers' compensation. Other more progressive reformers, such as Isaac Rubinow, who was a strong advocate of social insurance, argued that the average American worker needed the help of government-mandated and government-supported insurance programs in order to survive the economic pitfalls inherent in an industrialized society. Rubinow pointed to the fact that in 1907 only a few fortunate workers were able to set aside any money to tide the family over during the inevitable times of unemployment. This precarious economic condition, he argued, necessitated state intervention to provide unemployment insurance for the worker based on the theory of distribution of loss.[15]

A 1908 report conducted by the AICP concluded that unemployment was second only to illness as the most frequent cause of poverty and dependence. Therefore, the association should do more to eliminate it.[16] In New York City applications to the AICP and the Charity Organization Society (COS) had increased 147 percent during the recession of 1907. An alarming 34.4 percent of union workers were unemployed. When they went to the AICP's Joint Application Bureau, desperate men gratefully accepted jobs working in the COS woodyard where the only remuneration consisted of two ten-cent meals and a night's lodging.[17] Both public and private relief administrators urged that plans for public works projects be stepped up in order to meet the increased need for jobs. Consequently New York City authorized $195,000 for such projects "in order to relieve the distress of the unemployed in our city."[18]

Robert Hebberd, who was then New York City's commissioner of public charities, invited prominent social workers to come up with other solutions to the problem of unemployment. He himself called for the establishment of farm labor colonies to put men to work; progressive social worker W. Frank Persons suggested that homeless men be hired to sweep the city streets; Fulton Cutting, head of the AICP, recommended that some of the unemployed be put to "work on the country estates of wealthy land owners." Others recommended the establishment of municipal employment bureaus that would be run on a businesslike basis.[19] Despite the seemingly classist nature of Cutting's suggestion (one that was apparently rejected), the AICP joined with progressive reformers in their efforts to address the structural causes of poverty.

In 1913 when Harry Hopkins applied to the AICP for work, it was probably the most prestigious private charity in New York City. The association was then under the directorship of John Adams Kingsbury. This prominent social worker and reformer became Hopkins' enthusiastic mentor and good friend, and as such had a great deal of influence on Hopkins' social and political conscience. Kingsbury expressed his agency's mission when he addressed the annual meeting of the AICP in 1913, on the occasion of its seventieth anniversary. He reiterated Robert Hartley's original intent of improving the physical and moral condition of the poor and giving relief to the destitute. But Kingsbury added his own vision—his hope that New York would become a city "in which the well-to-do are endeavoring through organized effort in every way to help to uplift the less fortunate."[20] Significantly, he emphasized material assistance as well as moral improvement.

Kingsbury must have been impressed when the twenty-two-year-old Hopkins applied to him for work, because even though he had no position open, he put the young man on the AICP payroll in April 1913 as a trainee. He gave Hopkins an "allowance" of $40 per month, but even more important, he gave him a chance to learn about social work.[21] Factors other than a good first impression on Kingsbury may have worked in Hopkins' favor. In 1913 Elizabeth Milbank Anderson donated $650,000—an enormous sum—to the AICP to establish the Milbank Memorial Fund. Anderson outlined a program by which the association would reorganize and establish two new departments: the Department of Social Welfare under the directorship of Bailey Burritt and the Department of Family Welfare directed by William H. Matthews. The influx of this funding most likely allowed the association to hire Hopkins.[22]

Hopkins still lived at Christodora House, working with the boys at the settlement house during the day and for the AICP during the evening. He began as a regular district visitor doing fieldwork on Manhattan's Lower West Side, going to places considered too dangerous for the women social workers to visit after dark. Within a short time Kingsbury appointed Hopkins supervisor of the association's Employment Bureau. The apprentice social worker was delighted and used his position to good purpose.[23]

Progressive ideas about public responsibility for poverty and scientific philanthropy were already popular in New York City when Hopkins entered into the social work profession. Hopkins, of course, came to the profession armed with the ideals of Applied Christianity, which had a comfortable similarity to many of the ideals of the social reformers with whom he came into contact. In this progressive climate, Hopkins took up his work with an enthusiasm that remained with him throughout his career. Ethel Gross Hopkins described this attitude: "He always felt very deeply about the fact that there were masses of people who had a terrific struggle . . . for mere existence, and on the other hand there was this extravagance of great wealth and waste. I think he felt that very strongly. And he felt that something could be done about it in our own democracy."[24]

Nevertheless, discriminatory attitudes against the dependent still existed among even progressive social workers. Although city officials and social workers recognized that economic fluctuations inherent in a complex industrial nation caused men to be thrown out of work, there was still a subtle fear simmering beneath the progressive surface of many social reformers, a fear that "schemes to provide work for the unemployed" would always fail because of the "lack of stamina and will-power in the man" and because of "the inferior productive talents of the unemployed." These sentiments were expressed in the Minority Report of the Poor Law Commission in England, a document Hopkins, now head of the AICP's Employment Bureau, referred to in a report he wrote in 1913. This "Report on Unemployment Department" demonstrated that he, too, might have had reservations about providing relief of any sort for the able-bodied unemployed. Hopkins wrote: "We must always bear in mind that by the time the individual is dependent upon relief he has deteriorated in mind and body . . . and that no social or industrial reform can be successful without the regeneration, to a certain extent, of the individual." Citing "intemperance, irregular habits, laziness and want of ambition" as causes for unemployment in the same paragraph along with "industrial mal-adjustments, like casual trades, slack times, industrial accidents and disease," Hopkins reflected the ambivalence of many social workers. On one hand he recognized that there were economic forces at work over which the ordinary person had no control, forces that could throw the most upstanding wage earner out of work. On the other hand, Hopkins echoed the old moralistic attitude that the able-bodied unemployed were merely lazy and that any sort of relief would only exacerbate their delinquencies. While the family of the unemployed breadwinner should always be cared for, relief given to "men of a lower grade of intelligence and already demoralized by idleness and bad habits" usually will cause them to develop the bad habit of permanent dependency, that is, pauperism. The way to avoid what was considered to be the pauperizing effects of direct relief, Hopkins suggested, lay in the establishment of a separate department of employment. This would be the most effective way to help the unemployed avoid the stigma of charity; at the same time it would ensure that those who got help really wanted to work.[25] This position seems to be the beginning of Hopkins' commitment to jobs as the ultimate solution to poverty, a commitment that endured through the Depression years. Jobs at fair wages not only would allow workers to retain their dignity but also would reinforce the American tradition of male self-sufficiency.

Reform mayor of New York City John Purroy Mitchel seemed to walk in lock-step with the progressive reformers. Elected in 1913 on a "good government" ticket, he promoted governmental economy and efficiency. He was concerned with the increasing instances of radical agitation in response to the widespread unemployment that continued to plague the city throughout the winter of 1913-1914.[26] City Chamberlain Henry Bruere reflected this fear when he declared that "indifference to these facts [of high levels of unemployment] leaves the distress of unemployment to the exploitation of those who advocate the complete subversion of our present industrial system." John Kingsbury, former head of the AICP and newly appointed commissioner of public charities for New York City, added the familiar dictum that indiscriminate relief, "by improving the lot of the dependent [makes] them grow in number." Yet he reiterated Bruere's fear by stating that "the huge army of unemployed has gathered in our streets . . . and that army is a menace."[27] Fear of the social disorder that might be caused by extensive unemployment exerted a significant influence on the city's relief policy.

By the winter of 1913 the unemployment situation in New York City had grown increasingly grave. More and more able-bodied family men applied to the AICP for help because they were unable to find work. At the AICP's behest, Hopkins, head of its Employment Bureau, outlined a partial solution to the unemployment problem.[28] Recognizing the need for some sort of clearinghouse to assist workers seeking a job, Hopkins suggested the establishment of state-run employment agencies. He wrote: "The prime purpose of a labor exchange is to adjust the existing supply and demand of labor, so that the manless job and the jobless man may be brought together with the least possible delay."[29] Underlying this plan for coordinated labor exchanges was the belief that, despite an excessively large labor force, there were at least some jobs available for unemployed workers and it was just a matter of organizing information.

Although it was hard to get accurate statistics, Hopkins admitted that "the supply of labor, particularly of unskilled labor and in many cases that of skilled labor, is greatly in excess of the demand." The fact that 325,000 men were listed as unemployed in the city on any given day during the winter attested to that fact.[30] His realization that there were not enough jobs to go around seemed to contradict his optimism that efficiently run employment bureaus could solve the city's problem of unemployment. Yet the plan for employment bureaus fell within the realm of the possible for Hopkins, while restructuring the relationship between capital and labor so as to ensure a secure job at an adequate wage for all workers seemed an impossible dream. Hopkins was not a radical. His pragmatism always impelled him to opt for the attainable, and he believed he could change the public's attitude toward the poor; he also hoped to change the self-degrading attitude the poor traditionally had accepted as their lot.

Hopkins also recognized very early in his career the importance of allowing unemployed workers to retain some of their natural dignity when forced by adverse circumstances to request assistance. In his unemployment report for the AICP he argued that

> [e]very effort should be made to free the Bureau from any association or stigma
> of charity in order that the most skilled and efficient workmen should feel
> perfectly free to use the exchange at all times. They should feel that it is an
> industrial agency which has no interest whatever in the private affairs of the

applicant outside of determining his fitness for the position which he is applying for. No questions of a personal nature should be asked not leading up to the question of a man's efficiency.[31]

Despite some of his early ambivalence about where to place the blame for poverty, Hopkins did make an effort to overcome the old moralistic attitude. When he became aware that the men referred to the National Employment Exchange by the AICP had been treated contemptuously, he went on record and complained that personnel at the exchange were "not even courteous to men sent by the AICP to them for jobs." The annual report of his Employment Bureau further noted that many of the unemployed had been placed indiscriminately in jobs, irrespective of their previous experience or ability. He strongly recommended that efforts be made to ensure that men placed by the employment bureaus would not only be treated with respect but would be carefully screened so that they could be placed permanently in appropriate jobs.[32]

In a handwritten document that was probably a draft for his AICP report, Hopkins demonstrated what he felt to be a most insidious part of the problem— that a large segment of the population refused to believe that an unemployment problem actually existed:

> The chief difficulty at present in the problem of unemployment is to convince the public at large that there is a problem of unemployment at all. There seems to be still a large number of people who in the comfort of their own home and the security of their own job insist that any man who really wants work can find it—that the men who can't find work are drunkards and vagrants or else downright lazy. This position is held by not a few well-meaning people and until that position can be made untenable and the public awakened to the extent and nature of the problem there can be no vigorous measures looking to the ultimate solution of the problem—for it is an ultimate solution that we are interested [sic]—the absolute prevention of this social maladjustment. Temporary relief can but prolong the disease.[33]

For Hopkins, the "nature" of the problem included the unfair attribution of moral delinquency to those involuntarily unemployed. This document also noted that a lack of statistics stood in the way of an accurate reading of the unemployment problem. Hopkins' solution for this may well have come from lessons he learned in the Grinnell classrooms. He went to places where men were seeking jobs, and he used this firsthand experience to assess the scope of the problem.

Seeing hundreds of men "walking aimlessly from factory to factory looking vainly for work," Hopkins concluded that there were good, hardworking men unemployed through no fault of their own. No civilized society, he wrote, would refuse them the opportunity to earn a living for their families. He recommended institutional care or work colonies for the unemployables; for those out of work due to economic conditions, he proposed organized and well-coordinated municipal employment exchanges run on a not-for-profit basis. He also recognized that jobs were scarce. He therefore recommended reforms to remedy the imbalance between jobs and workers: the regulation of businesses to prevent factory closure in hard times, the use of public work projects during times of depression, the assignment of work to a regular crew instead of the division of work among a large number of men, the constriction of hours of labor, and the establishment of unemployment insurance and workmen's compensation. He scrawled at the bottom of this draft report: "Not necessarily a panacea but will go a long way towards ultimately curing the problem."[34]

Awakening the public to the problem of mass unemployment was only a first step. The ultimate solution for Hopkins lay in finding work for the increasing number of unemployed. This echoed the AICP's newly-acquired belief that the problem of unemployment was "purely an industrial one and that it is through the reformation of the business world rather than through the reformation of pastors or of philanthropists that its solution will be brought about."[35] Nevertheless, his conversion to the new view of poverty was not complete. Hopkins still made a clear distinction between employable (deserving) workers who were efficient, able-bodied, and willing and those unemployables who refused to work. His plan for a centralized employment bureau gave preference to skilled workers and especially men who supported families. Only "respectable" workers need apply, he wrote, because otherwise the bureau "would fall into disrepute at once and neither the better class of employers or the more efficient employees would care to avail themselves further of its privileges." He divided the bureau into four separate departments: skilled, unskilled, women and girls, and boys. Preference always would be given to married men. The department for skilled workers was deemed the most important because "it would come into contact with the more efficient men who are looking for employment . . . since casual labor requires little or no skill, and very little intelligence. . . ." Since jobs for women and girls, the report states, "would consist largely in dealing with house-wives who want maids, cooks, laundresses, etc., . . . it would be advisable to have a woman in charge."[36] Hopkins came from a family that adhered to traditional, gendered roles; the model of male breadwinner and female dependent would have felt very natural to him.[37] This division between male and female jobs remained a characteristic of Hopkins' unemployment programs throughout the 1930s.

In late January of 1914, Mayor Mitchel called a meeting of community leaders to discuss and come up with solutions for the severe unemployment problem, which, according to the census of the city's Municipal Lodging House (MLH) and State Department of Labor statistics, had almost doubled since 1910. Among the luminaries present at the meeting were Edward Divine of the COS, John Andrews of the American Association for Labor Legislation (AALL), Lillian Wald of the Henry Street Settlement, Professor Henry R. Seager of Columbia University and president of the AALL, labor activist Mary Dreier, and Henry Moskowitz, chairman of the Municipal Civil Service Commission. Commissioner of Public Charities John A. Kingsbury opened the discussion and essentially set the tone of the meeting by pointing out that "New York City is a dumping ground" for what he called the "Weary Willies who believe that the world owes them a living" and who take advantage of the city's generosity to the needy. The MLH, where it is comparatively easy to get help, he declared, acted as a magnet for this class of undesirables. It was absolutely essential that the city find employment for the unemployed worker deemed "fit," that is, those willing and able to work, and to apply the work test to those he called "unfit," those able but unwilling to work. "It is the height of folly," Kingsbury stated, "it is the height of unwisdom, to undermine self-respect by breaking down the barrier of self-dependence by giving a man relief when he asks for work." In his mind, only the "unfit" would ask for relief without work. He quoted Frederic Almy of the Buffalo COS who said that "relief is like cocaine; it relieves pain but creates an appetite," and that offering relief to those who come to New York City because of "easy pickings" is a "social crime."[38] In order to avoid this indiscriminate aid, he argued, the city must impose the work test for all applicants to the MLH.

Kingsbury, however, did admit to the existence of involuntary unemployment and stated that the most important element in addressing that problem was finding jobs for those laid off because of the economic depression (begun by the Panic of 1907 and exacerbated by high food prices caused by the war in Europe). In his statement, Kingsbury repeated Hopkins' plan to bring "the manless job and the jobless man together" and to institute unemployment insurance.[39]

Edward Devine, head of the Charity Organization Society and strong advocate of scientific philanthropy, agreed that the work test had to be applied, but he did not think that merely instituting a municipal labor exchange would solve the problem. As he pointed out, due to the huge influx of immigrant labor, there were not enough jobs available in New York City to absorb the labor force. Although he suggested public work projects to absorb excess workers, Devine doubted their overall efficacy because "according to the theory of our law from time immemorial we have said 'while we will take care of you and provide you with lodging and meals [at the MLH], if you are an able-bodied man the responsibility of finding employment is with you, and while we will take care of you, the only institution we have to take care of you is the Work-house."[40]

Sarah J. Atwood, representing private employment agencies, also took a hard line. She declared that most of the single men who come to the city looking for work usually "sponge too much of their money and rely on Lodging Houses." She referred to Coxey's Army of unemployed who marched to Washington in the 1890s as a group of people who were unwilling to apply themselves to hard work and thought "the world owes them a living." She denied, moreover, that there was any lack of jobs and insisted that giving help to the unemployed only increased pauperism.[41] It seems clear that a deplorable lack of statistics on unemployment made it very difficult for either side to make an unassailable case.

Not all speakers reflected the apparent coldheartedness of scientific philanthropy. Timothy Healy, a Catholic representing organized labor, opposed applying the work test, saying "this city should be big enough to shelter all comers. . . ." Healy supported public work projects as "good substantial relief," especially for men with families.[42] Mary Dreier called for the establishment of workrooms for the increasing number of unemployed women who also wanted work and not charity.[43] Most of the other professionals at the meeting agreed that employment exchanges would go a long way in helping some get jobs but that the main problem was always to separate the "Weary Willies" from men and women deserving of relief. Those workers in good standing, especially skilled workers, should be given a job, a loan, or some sort of relief. Others, they all agreed, should be sent to the workhouse.

In 1915, in another attempt to deal with unemployment caused by the economic downturn, Harry Hopkins teamed up with William Matthews, head of the AICP's Family Welfare Division, to put together what was the most widely discussed, if not the first, work-relief program in New York.[44] Because of the unusually high unemployment in New York City, men and women were flocking to the AICP for help. Hopkins' interviews with them only reinforced his conviction that they sincerely wanted to work rather than accept charity. They simply could not find jobs. Hopkins remarked to Matthews that the number of able-bodied unemployed men applying to the AICP for relief had recently, and alarmingly, escalated. Earlier that same day Matthews had noticed in the paper that a large tract of property belonging to the Bronx Zoological Park had remained unimproved due to lack of funds. Matthews approached the park commissioner, Hermann Merkel, with a proposition. If the commission would employ and supervise one hundred men, the AICP would pay them to work on the property. The commissioner agreed to this unconventional use of relief funds, and, according to Matthews, "before night young Mr. Hopkins was enthusiastically writing letters to a hundred men calling them to 'real work at real wages.'"[45]

The men involved in Hopkins' and Matthew's Bronx Zoo work-relief project drew wages of $2 a day but were limited to working only three days a week so that more would be given an opportunity to work. Six dollars a week was certainly not a living wage for a family, even in 1915. However, neither was it charity, and this was extremely important for all involved. In the end, 231 men were employed under this program.[46] According to Bailey Burritt, the general director of the association, this project represented the best form of relief because it had the important element of real work for real wages without competing with private industry. In addition, he added, "[t]he plan enabled us at once to discriminate justly between the man willing and anxious to work and the work-shy man who, even when jobs are plentiful, never works regularly and . . . was quite ready to settle down to a period of rest."[47] In other words, it had the ring of the work test.

The Bronx Zoo project, although funded with private money, served as a prototype for future public work programs. The AICP Yearbook for 1915 reported that "[t]here has never been more effective co-operation on the part of both public and private agencies in dealing with the problems arising from a period of industrial depression in New York City than that which was manifest last winter." Although AICP director Burritt saw the value of the Bronx Zoo project—"a demonstration on a small scale of the practicability of employing idle men in times of industrial stress to improve public property"—he was not convinced that the idea would take hold. He stated that "there is not much evidence that permanent plans for dealing with unemployment on the basis of experience acquired during the past winter are likely to be adopted on the part of the community either to prevent its recurrence or to deal comprehensively and systematically with it when it does occur."[48] The city's chief engineer, on the other hand, saw much value in the project which provided the park with work the city could not have afforded to carry out. He respectfully suggested to the AICP that "we begin some permanent improvements, as for instance the railings which are to protect both banks of the Bronx River, or the walls to be built between Boston Road and the River."[49] At the mayor's Conference on Unemployment held late in 1915, Burritt pointed out the Bronx Zoo project as "a definite contribution to the unemployment situation" and one that "it is perfectly possible for any municipality to adopt, with modification, on a larger scale."[50] The next month he wrote to the Zoological Society that the project ended only because of lack of private contributions. "We are quite convinced that no money that we spent last winter for relief purposes was spent more wisely and with better results than that which we spent for wages of the men sent to the Park for work."[51]

Harry Hopkins was familiar with this combination of public and private efforts; his sister, Adah Hopkins, was at that particular time experimenting with this methodology in her work with the Grinnell Social Service League. Hopkins would have been aware of the necessity for such cooperation in times of economic depression. In his memoirs, Matthews wrote that the Bronx Zoo project was "the beginning of work relief in the United States, a method of relief which sixteen years later was to become a major form of aid for the casualties of the Great Depression."[52] However, the historian has to question the impact of this cooperation between public and private agencies on Hopkins in light of his later rejection of local private agencies and his insistence on using federal officials as relief administrators for his New Deal relief programs. Nevertheless, this experiment in work relief left a lasting impression on Hopkins.

Matthews was not surprised that Hopkins later became chief "protagonist" for work relief during the Great Depression; he had witnessed his earlier conversion to its philosophy.[53] In several ways the Bronx Zoo project foreshadowed the Civil Works Administration (CWA) of 1933-1934. No investigatory work was done by social workers and no means test was required, although Matthews did give preference to married men. The general assumption was that every unemployed man wanted to work. (In 1915 this assumption did not apply to women.) The rate of pay was equal to the prevailing wage for unskilled labor, and workers were encouraged to take supplemental jobs to increase their income. Through their direct contact with the destitute, both Hopkins and Matthews came to share the view that unemployed workers on bread lines wanted jobs rather than charity. Matthews wrote a rather lengthy poem describing the plight of the unemployed worker. Despite its lack of literary merit, it does reflect a characteristic attitude held by these social workers. It concludes:

> Breaking in spirit, hope and courage gone,
> Weary of trudging up and down the streets,
> What shall we say, what shall our answer be
> To men who ask just for a chance to work?[54]

For Hopkins, the answer always would be jobs. His New York experience during this period of economic depression led him and many of his colleagues in other cities to conclude that the long-range planning of public works could do much to stabilize the national economy. He and other professionals realized that in an industrialized nation, the central economic problem continued to be involuntary unemployment and that this problem could be largely ameliorated through the rational planning of public construction projects to absorb idle able-bodied (male) workers in times of depression. The establishment of planned public works programs became one important way to ensure the American workers' right to a job.

By this time Hopkins had acquired an implicit belief in the dignity of labor and in the basic human right to have access to useful work to earn a living for oneself and one's family. Beginning very early in his career, Hopkins wanted to put unemployed people to work at useful jobs and pay them a living wage. In the absence of private funds, government money should initiate such programs. Much of his social philosophy had taken shape under the influence of progressives such as John Kingsbury and William Matthews and continued to evolve throughout his career as a social worker.

CHAPTER FIVE

THE NEW YORK CITY CHARITIES CONTROVERSY

In a word, then, it became clear to me that this was my duty and the Mayor instructed me to fulfill my duty to turn the light into the realm of darkness which for a century has enshrouded the private institutions caring for this great City's foster children.

—John A. Kingsbury, 1916

The Department of Charities, to gratify its hatred of the State Board, under the advice of the heads of the "Charity Trust," has used the institutions for its own purposes, and the earmarks of conspiracy stick out all over the proceedings.

—The Reverend William B. Farrell, 1916

HARRY HOPKINS' ASSOCIATION with a new breed of professional social workers dedicated to modern methods of providing help for the needy placed him in opposition to many of the ideals held by entrenched and largely religious charitable institutions. He watched from the sidelines but with active interest while a controversy raged across the political landscape of New York City from

1913 to 1916, one that would have a significant impact on both public and private relief agencies. It began with the Mitchel administration, during the height of the Progressive Era. Newly appointed charities commissioner John Kingsbury appointed an Advisory Committee in 1914 to investigate the activities of private child-caring institutions in New York City, which had been receiving public funds. When city investigators working for the committee reported shockingly substandard conditions in many of these institutions and accused the State Board of Charities of not supervising them properly, the governor ordered a state commission headed by Charles Strong to look into the charges. The ensuing Strong Commission hearings polarized the city's caregivers and led to the publication of defamatory pamphlets, to charges of libel and conspiracy, to wiretaps, and to a criminal indictment against Commissioner John Kingsbury. For Hopkins, this controversy became a living textbook in his postgraduate course in social welfare methodology. Because it clarified a significant number of important issues, this face-off between public and private caregivers did much to influence Hopkins' belief in public responsibility for relief of the needy. In addition, the controversy strengthened his dedication to the efficacy of professional social work.

Those closely involved in the charities controversy differed in their assessment of the final outcome, but there seems to be little doubt that when the dust settled in mid-1916, new methods had emerged to aid dependent children. The controversy marked one important step along the way to a modern welfare state, a movement from voluntary to coercive, from private to public, and from religious to secular. The ideals of the progressive reformers eventually subsumed those of the church. The controversy clarified the debate and polarized the philanthropic community in such a way that scientific charity appeared the wave of the future. Hopkins cut his teeth as a social worker against this background. Although many children continued to be placed in orphanages, the traditional reliance on institutionalism essentially had ended and placing children in private homes ("placing-out") became the accepted strategy of the child-savers; the cottage plan took preference among charity workers over congregate institutions; home life became recognized as most beneficial for children; and, probably most important, many of the child-caring activities passed from private philanthropy to municipal bureaus that attempted to apply rigid and less personal methods of caregiving.[1]

Hopkins, a young, ambitious, and energetic social worker looking for innovative methods to solve the problems of poverty, unemployment, and dependency, watched closely and learned. In 1917 his colleague William Matthews described Hopkins as "a strong advocate of state assistance as against the private relief system."[2] This was an important milestone in Hopkins' emerging welfare ideology. The issues debated during the New York City charities controversy—professionalism, public responsibility, and modern scientific charity—continued to define Hopkins' emerging social and political ideology. It is important, therefore, to understand fully this crucial debate that formed the background for Hopkins' practical education in social work.

New York's charity landscape in the late nineteenth and early twentieth centuries was dominated by what was known as the New York System, a system whereby city funds were used to subsidize private charitable institutions on a per-capita basis for the care of dependent children. The New York System developed as a result of both law and tradition. During the nineteenth century, the inadequacy of public institutions caring for the city's dependent population led to the proliferation of private orphanages that had to rely on irregular and often insufficient donations. Although the city of New York voluntarily donated funds, by mid-nineteenth century these institutions had secured laws requiring the city (and until 1874, the state) to help finance their work. Many of these laws were brought about through the energies of Catholic Charities. During the latter part of the century, fueled by an increase in the needy population brought about by a sharp rise in the number of immigrants (many of them Catholic), by the relative ease in obtaining city money, and by restrictions on placing children in public almshouses, the number of private child-caring institutions in New York City grew from 130 to 204.[3] Public support for these private and largely religious institutions developed out of necessity; the city could not afford to care for the rising number of dependent children. When city funds were made available to care for these children, private institutions jealously guarded their right to this support.

Key to New York's subsidy system was the Children's Law of 1875, a milestone in the history of child welfare. The law mandated that all children between the ages of three and sixteen be removed from public almshouses, away from the dangerous influences of adult paupers and criminals, and placed either with families or in institutions exclusively for children. This law also required that "as far as practicable, a child shall be committed to an institution controlled by officers of the same religion as that of the parents of that child."[4] By the end of the century, public funding to private/religious child-caring institutions had become an entrenched and indispensable part of the city's charitable system.

The 1894 New York State Constitutional Convention gave new powers to the State Board of Charities (which had been established as a constitutional entity at the State Constitutional Convention of 1867) and authorized it to issue regulations for the reception and retention of children in orphanages. Joseph H. Choate, chairman of the convention, declared that the State Board should ensure that all of these children received "proper and intelligent care and protection."

Those institutions that were not up to the Board's standards would not receive any money. However, because there was a lack of inspectors, the State Board allowed each institution to file a document in the form of a letter attesting that it was in compliance with the regulations. In New York City the comptroller relied on that document, called "the green certificate," for authority to fund private orphanages caring for young public wards.[5]

By 1900, there were about 110,000 children in 1,200 private institutions in the United States; of these, 37,000 were in New York State receiving public funds. Close to two-thirds of these dependent children (23,397) were cared for in New York City. Thirty-nine institutions there received city money.[6] Catholic institutions, usually staffed by unpaid nuns, housed almost 16,000 of these children. Because New York City had both the legal *right* to support private institutions with public money (which the state did not have) and the legal *obligation* to remove children from public almshouses, city officials willingly paid a per-capita fee for every public ward committed to these private, mostly religious institutions. It was simply cost effective. James J. Higgins, secretary of Catholic Charities in Brooklyn, affirmed that his institutions were giving the city much more than their money's worth. He pointed out that each child committed by the Department of Public Charities to private institutions received from the city about $2.57 per day while the institution spent from $3.15 to $4.85 per child per day. This amounted to a substantial saving for the city, which could not otherwise adequately care for these dependent children.[7] But, as the Catholics caring for these children claimed, economics should not be the only reason for supporting this subsidy system. They also were providing important religious and moral training to the children—training, they argued, that would prepare them to be better citizens.

From the very beginning, the State Board of Charities had taken the lead in the movement to separate children from what reformers considered the degrading and dangerous conditions of the public almshouses. The State Charities Aid Association (SCAA) supported the board's efforts and led the way in the next step—placing children in private homes. Leaders of this Protestant-led placing-out movement, founded by Charles Loring Brace and his Children's Aid Society (CAS) in the 1850s, believed that it would be infinitely better for the child's welfare to place him or her in a private home. Because these child-savers also believed that it was easier to place children from private orphanages rather than from public almshouses, they supported these institutions, but only as a necessary step to foster care. Many Catholics agreed that "friendless children"—that is those who had no relatives who could (or would) reclaim them sometime in the future—would be better off placed in Catholic homes rather than in Catholic institutions.[8] In 1905 the church established the Catholic Home

Bureau for this purpose. However, the Catholics were adamant that Catholic children *temporarily* committed to their custody remain in the orphanages. Many other Catholics were generally suspicious of this placing-out movement because it seemed to remove Catholic children from the beneficial influence of the church and threaten their spiritual well-being. The controversy between those committed to placing-out and those committed to institutionalism thus became a religious issue.[9]

During the early years of the twentieth century, an awkward system evolved in New York to administer funds and supervise charitable institutions. This led to increasingly strained relations between the city and state agencies. In New York City, the commissioner of public charities was responsible for committing dependent children to private institutions as public charges. An 1894 amendment to the city constitution provided that "no such payments shall be made for any inmate who is not received and retained therein pursuant to the rules established by the State Board of Charities." Furthermore, no payment could be made to any private institution caring for dependent children unless the commissioner (a city official) certified that the child was a legitimate public ward. Because it was left up to the State Board of Charities to enforce its regulations and to certify institutions, the city's only responsibility was to ensure that every child placed in an institution and getting city money was a proper public ward. However, the ability of the institutions to issue their own "green certificates" created a situation reminiscent of the fox watching the henhouse. This state of affairs eventually gave rise to enormous dissension.[10]

The Catholic attitude toward the perfunctory authority and investigatory power of the State Board of Charities was, understandably, perfectly amiable. Most of those connected with the institutions did not resent the board's (largely unused) power to impose standards and regulations. Thomas Mulry, member of the COS, president of the St. Vincent de Paul Society, and a prominent Catholic, declared that "where the public contributes to the support of the inmates of an institution under private control, the State has every right to adopt measures of a supervisory nature."[11] For Catholics, however, while efficient standards of operation and economy were desirable goals, religion always constituted the most essential element in the care of the dependent child. They resisted the new, more secular ideas about philanthropy that had begun to emerge among a new breed of professional charitable workers, including John Kingsbury, in the early years of the twentieth century. These ideas clashed head on with the older attitude toward charity because they seemed to threaten the religious impulse behind the sectarian child-caring institutions. Although the AICP always had been concerned with the moral character of its recipients and used relief to impose what it considered proper behavior, the religious element was largely absent.

The well-being of the children became the stated objective for both sides during a three-year controversy (1913-1916) that brought widespread dissension to the city's administration. This was precisely the period when Harry Hopkins began to formulate a standard for his methods of providing help for the needy. New York City became the battlefield where professional social workers fought for the modern standards of philanthropy and where, in the end, scientific methods seemed to triumph over the human charitable impulse. Each side vehemently professed the most altruistic reasons for the unceasing spate of verbal assaults raised against the other. Hopkins, an advocate for secular and scientific charity, sided with the city and with his mentors in the AICP. The social Christianity that he had absorbed at Grinnell had by this time become tempered and secularized.

The rhetoric used by both sides reveals the depth of the fear and animosity felt by those embroiled in the conflict. In early 1915 Bird Coler, a strong Tammany supporter who had held the post of New York city comptroller since 1898 and was an advocate of the New York System, lambasted city officials as "experts, sociologists, Socialists" and called the government "humbug." He depicted professional social workers as a "parasitic class who formerly practiced necromancy or astrology [and] have abandoned that profession for the more profitable field of sociology." He declared that these social workers "have flocked to the City of New York from all parts of the world because it is known that New York is rich and foolish. Their theories and fads take the place of useful work." According to Coler, only charitable institutions with a religious base were effective because "they manage to get along without elaborate demographic charts and huge salary rolls and it doesn't cost them eighty cents to do twenty cents of good work."[12]

In mid-1916 an article in the Catholic journal *America,* written by Paul L. Blakeley, S.J., further exemplified this conflict between the old and the new. It made reference to "modern pagan philanthropy" that, along with its allied product, modern sociology, posed a great danger to religion. It noted the antagonism between the principles of modern sociology and the principles of Catholicism and called modern sociology "craven, dishonorable and despicable." The article described the modern social worker as "trained in principles ultimately destructive of faith and morality" and called on Catholics everywhere to fight against the "crass materialism that would turn the State into a god, and would recognize no creed save one, the omnipotence of the Commonwealth." The author declared that "[f]or modern sociologists, revealed religion is nothing more than a social value like clean streets or education." For Catholics, he claimed, "religion is not merely a sentiment but a rule of life."[13] The *Nativity Mentor,* another Catholic publication, echoed these sentiments several months later when it distinguished between the "professionals and the amateurs of charity in New York," calling trained workers "hirelings" motivated by profit and power.[14]

The other side was no less hyperbolic. Francis Hackett's article in the *New Republic,* "The Sacred Cow," supported the mayor's position by declaring that the city's financial crisis was the result of "the vicious immunity" of the private institutions that took public funds and yet refused to submit to supervision. Arguing that these Catholic institutions did not accept the modern conception of charity, which was properly a matter of the head and not the heart and which should be "a cooperation in social uplift rather than a mere avenue to saintliness for the giving of alms," the article insisted that "in so far as they are stupid, dirty, ignorant, and lax," the Catholic orphanages must be carefully supervised by the state "not only as economy requires, but as modern conceptions of charity plainly demand."[15]

Into this contentious landscape burst the reform administration of Fusion mayor John Purroy Mitchel, a thirty-four-year-old Irish Catholic, anti-Tammany attorney who was elected in 1913. Mayor Mitchel's reform administration was plagued with economic woes from the very beginning. Faced with unprecedented levels of unemployment, private agencies were unable to handle the emergency. Over 400,000 workers in New York City were unemployed. When Mitchel turned to business interests to help solve the city's financial problems, businessmen were given the power to set many of the conditions for care giving.[16] Thus the attitude that only the deserving should receive assistance took on new meaning. No longer did it have religious import; now it had the ring of fiscal responsibility. Elbert Gary, chairman of the board of U. S. Steel and chairman of the Mayor's Committee on Unemployment and Relief created in 1914, declared that "[p]ublic support of the non-productive human individual is plain waste."[17] Good business methods dovetailed with modern philanthropy in rooting out the undeserving.

As president of the Board of Aldermen in 1910, Mitchel had conducted an investigation into private charities receiving public funds and found that there was very little information available on these institutions and very little city supervision. In his 1911 report to Mayor William J. Gaynor, Mitchel wrote: "This condition of aloofness with respect to the management of private institutions has been characteristic even of the Department of Public Charities, which is the medium through which the great majority of the 22,000 dependent children now maintained in private institutions at the City's expense have been committed." Nothing was resolved as a result of the investigation, arguably because of noncooperation of the Department of Public Charities.[18]

When Mitchel was inaugurated mayor in 1914, he again took up the issue of public funding to private institutions. Almost immediately he sought to ameliorate what he considered substandard conditions in orphanages receiving city money. His stated purpose was to establish new standards for these institutions and to compel them to measure up to these standards. However, an anti-Tammany animus along with a need to attack the Catholics who were siding with Tammany may have served as an additional motive for the mayor to direct Commissioner of Public Charities John Kingsbury to inquire into "this realm of darkness which for a century had enshrouded private institutions caring [for] the City's foster children."[19] Kingsbury was to do this by closely supervising the allocation of the approximately $5 million given to private institutions each year by the city and by determining the conditions under which those institutions received children as public wards and were allotted money for their support. Mitchel reported that almost immediately there began:

> a subterranean opposition . . . which led to threats, menacing the lives of the Commissioner and his Deputy, . . . to an actual attempt at suicide by one of the officers bitterly persecuted for performing his duty; opposition which laid at the door of the Commissioner and his Deputy, and of the Mayor, the death of prominent citizens who happened to pass away in the course of the controversy which raged; opposition which led the Secretary of the State Board of Charities to perjure himself and then to resign under fire in the course of the inquiry; opposition which led to conspiracy entered into by certain Catholic priests co-operating with certain of the laity, both Catholic and Protestant, an ex-Baptist minister, and the then Secretary of the State Board of Charities to obtain undue control over the Department of Public Charities, and failing that, to wreck its administration and the administration of the Mayor."[20]

There can be no doubt that the investigation was done at the behest of Mitchel in order to finish what he had started as alderman in 1910.

Kingsbury was exactly the type of progressive reformer the Catholics resented. After a stint as a teacher in the public school system in Washington state, Kingsbury traveled east to study at Columbia University's Teacher's College. There he met Homer Folks who, as secretary of the State Charities Aid Association (SCAA), had long opposed institutionalism. Folks was quite impressed with Kingsbury's energy and idealism and said of him, "[h]ere is the man whom Diogenes was looking for with his lantern." In 1908 Kingsbury met prominent photo-journalist and reformer Jacob Riis in Folks' office at the United Charities Building. It was Riis who convinced Kingsbury to become a social worker instead of a teacher. When Mitchel was elected mayor in 1913, Kingsbury had already served as assistant secretary of the SCAA and as general director of the AICP.[21] His status as a well-known social worker afforded Kingsbury the prestige necessary to carry out the mayor's agenda.

Influenced by progressive reformers who believed that poverty could be prevented through the modern methods of scientific philanthropy that eschewed indiscriminate almsgiving, Kingsbury believed that the causes of poverty, whether illness, irresponsibility, unemployment, or widowhood, had to be discovered and eliminated. He believed that

> [i]mpulsive benevolence is selfish, indolent, indiscriminating and generally produces evil [while true charity] ascertains the character and condition of the needy . . . and must look beyond present temporary relief to progress and permanent advancement. The sufferer is not only contemplated individually, but as a prototype of other sufferers in a long succession for whom our labors must aim to provide in some degree by well adapted far-reaching agencies which strike at the fundamental causes of poverty.[22]

As far as Kingsbury was concerned, there was no religious issue involved in the current controversy. He insisted that the city's investigation into the subsidy system did not represent an attack on Catholic institutions, which were doing valuable work in the community. Rather he declared that he had a duty and responsibility to the taxpayer to ensure that "all cases admitted to private institutions as public wards are properly admissible." He further insisted that he wanted "to nip in the bud any attempt to inject any religious prejudice into this controversy."[23] Yet beginning with his appointing an Advisory Committee to investigate private charitable agencies, a series of events made it impossible to avoid the religious issue.

The Advisory Committee, which was to inspect the institutions and report back to Commissioner Kingsbury, consisted of Dr. R. R. Reeder, a Protestant and superintendent of the New York Orphan Asylum at Hastings-on-Hudson, Dr. Ludwig V. Bernstein of the Hebrew Sheltering Guardian Society, the Reverend Brother Barnabas MacDonald of the New York Catholic Protectory, and, at the helm, William J. Doherty, second deputy commissioner of the (city) Department of Public Charities and former secretary of the Catholic Home Bureau. Reeder, who asserted that New York was the "worst institution ridden state in the US," had been accused of bigotry by the Catholics. Doherty, who had been raised in a Catholic orphanage, was resolutely in favor of placing children in foster homes and outspoken in his opposition to orphanages.[24]

In a 1915 speech before the National Conference of Charities and Corrections, entitled "A Study of the Results of Institutional Care," Doherty gave some indication of the reason for the charities investigation. He declared that he was opposed to institutionalism in general. Nevertheless, he reiterated that his investigation was driven only by a desire to see that children in orphanages were given a "square deal." Doherty announced he had discovered that in a number of institutions children were not getting proper medical treatment or nourishment, that they had few educational opportunities and little recreation; and moreover, many were kept there too long. The frightening consequences of these "woeful inadequacies," he continued, would be physically and mentally defective children utterly unprepared to take their place in society as productive citizens. Doherty denied that the inadequacies in these private institutions could be blamed on lack of money; he attributed many shortcomings to "the attitude, spirit and underlying purpose of the institution." The investigations, of course, also implied that the State Board of Charities, officially responsible for the regulation and certification of orphanages receiving public funds, had not been doing its job.[25]

Mayor Mitchel and Commissioner Kingsbury claimed that they were not "out to get the State Board of Charities" and were primarily interested in "lifting the standards of child-caring in our children's institutions."[26] Furthermore, they only wanted to compel those institutions to conform to state standards. However, political reasons also drove the mayor's campaign against these institutions. For political reformers, this campaign would mean a blow against Tammany Hall. Progressive reformers supported the mayor because they wanted to end Catholic domination of the charitable arena and ensure the ascendancy of modern social welfare practices. If, as the reformers protested, no religious bias lay behind their efforts, criticism nevertheless was aimed in the direction of the Catholic church and its supporters. If their bias indeed had no theological or doctrinal basis, it still infuriated some of the more powerful and active church members.

The Advisory Committee's investigation began in April 1914 and continued for about a year. But each step along the way seemed to lead to another crisis, to more friction and dissension, and finally to public scandal. The Department of Public Charities became the storm center for what was to be an extremely mean-spirited and protracted conflict between Catholics and non-Catholics, between city and state officials, and between professional and volunteer caregivers. And Hopkins watched the events unfold with the fascination of an ambitious neophyte.

An array of prominent Catholic priests and laymen who had long been involved in Catholic Charities and the State Board of Charities aligned themselves against the city officials, targeting especially John Kingsbury. Thomas Maurice Mulry, a prominent Catholic layman and president of the Emigrant and Industrial Savings Bank, had a leading role in strengthening the relationship between Catholic and non-Catholic charity workers. A longtime member of the St. Vincent de Paul Society, he had been one of the founders of the National Conference of Catholic Charities in 1910. While his father's firm had ties to Tammany Hall and had constructed the foundation for Tweed's Wigwam (Tammany headquarters) on 14th Street, Mulry maintained a commendable distance from New York City's political bosses. Despite his close association with Catholic charity workers, Mulry was a longtime friend and associate of progressive reformer Homer Folks and served on the Central Commission of the State Charities Aid Association from 1900 to 1907. While Mulry was always a strong supporter of the New York System and defended Catholic charitable institutions, he nevertheless could see the value of placing children in private homes. It was he who had organized the Catholic Home Bureau for the placement of Catholic children. He also sponsored William Doherty, later John Kingsbury's lieutenant, as field secretary for the bureau. Mulry was a member of Charity Organization Society's Central Council from 1891 to 1916 (despite COS efforts to remove public funding from Catholic institutions). Along with Folks, Mulry helped organize the 1909 White House Conference on Children, which declared that no child should be removed from the home for reasons of poverty alone. Mulry sat on the State Board of Charities until his untimely death in 1916, at the height of the charities controversy.[27]

Robert W. Hebberd, a Catholic and the secretary and admitted leader of the State Board of Charities, had had serious disagreements with Kingsbury prior to 1913, and the two men would continue to lock horns for years to come. As New York City Commissioner of Public Charities in 1907 (the position Kingsbury held from 1913 to 1916), Hebberd had adopted the policy that this office had no responsibility to inspect charitable institutions receiving city subsidies and could properly rely on certificates of compliance issued by the State Board of Charities based on the assertion of individual institutions. According to Kingsbury, Hebberd and Mulry did all they could to thwart the investigations into private charitable institutions receiving public funds.[28]

Kingsbury's Advisory Committee inspected thirty-eight child-caring institutions and found that twenty-six of them did not measure up to modern methods of caring for dependent children. These institutions were placed on what was called the controverted list; fourteen of them were Protestant and twelve were Catholic. To refute charges that the investigations were sparked by anti-Catholic sentiment, Kingsbury and his supporters pointed out that only twelve Catholic institutions appeared on the controverted list and that the Catholic institutions on both the controverted and non-controverted list generally received higher ratings from the inspectors. Kingsbury's Final Report to the Mayor on the investigations carried out by the Advisory Committee (which comprised part of his Annual Report on 1914 departmental activities) was sent to Governor Whitman. The following day, November 18, on the recommendation of Homer Folks, the governor appointed his old friend, Charles H. Strong, to head up a commission to look into the activities of state agencies having authority over charitable institutions and make recommendations for changes.[29]

The Strong Commission held hearings in New York City from January 31 to April 24, 1916. As the hearings progressed, emotions boiled over and the press gave the combatants ample coverage, with the New York City papers supporting the administration and the Brooklyn papers supporting the Catholics. Headlines likened conditions in private orphanages certified by the state to those endured by Oliver Twist. Every day newspaper articles printed often-graphic testimony describing the orphanages.[30] The extensive press coverage of the testimony of the various witnesses (including priests, nuns, Catholic laymen, and prominent state and city officials) led to an unfortunate public outburst, with charges of unfit conditions leveled against Catholic orphanages and counter-charges of religious bias on the part of the city officials.

Father William B. Farrell, a Brooklyn priest who was one of the directors of the Associates of Private Charities and a vigorous defender of the independence of Catholic charitable institutions, purportedly wrote an open letter to the governor charging that prejudice against Catholics motivated the inquiry. This letter, published on February 16 as a pamphlet entitled "A Public Scandal: Being an Analysis of Men and Motives Underlying the Investigation of the Charitable Institutions," initiated an incredibly mean-spirited pamphlet war that lasted from about mid-February to mid-March of 1916.[31] This first pamphlet was followed quickly by several more including "How the Strong Commission Discredited Itself," "Charity for Revenue," and "Priest Baiting in 1916." One in particular castigated Kingsbury unmercifully. A section entitled "The Mayor's 'Best Man in the City'" asserted that "no public figure in the history of the city has offered the Catholic element in this community an insult so gratuitous, so outrageous, so contemptible" as to appoint William Doherty to head up the Advisory Committee.[32] These pamphlets, all excoriating the city investigation and the testimony of the Advisory Committee, were printed by the hundreds and distributed in Catholic churches all over the greater metropolitan area.

There was the expected response from the city. Kingsbury contended that the pamphlets were not written by Father Farrell "but by a brilliant mind though one of the most despicable individuals in the community," referring to Dr. Daniel Potter, an ex-Baptist minister who vigorously supported religiously sponsored child-caring institutions.[33] An *S.C.A.A. News* article said that the pamphlets represented "a concerted effort to discredit the investigation being made by Commissioner Strong" and "consisted merely of innuendo and vague suggestions" and were "largely without basis."[34] Edward Moree, who did publicity work for the SCAA, produced an anonymous, twenty-four-page pamphlet consisting of a montage of newspaper headlines and copies of articles, editorials, and testimony, ostensibly in response to the first Farrell pamphlet (although it later came out that it had been put together on February 16, two days before Farrell's letter was published).[35] Especially prominent on the cover of the pamphlet was the headline from the *New York Herald* asserting that at the Mission of the Immaculate Virgin at Mount Loretto, a Catholic institution on Staten Island, pigs and orphans were fed from the same receptacles. Moree later admitted that this newspaper report was indeed a "misrepresentation of the evidence" but justified his actions by declaring that the pamphlet had already been printed when he found this out and that he did not think it was important enough to delete. Catholic Charities responded by calling the Moree pamphlet "craven, dishonorable and despicable." John Bowers, counsel for the State Board of Charities who examined Moree at the Strong hearings, contended that the Moree pamphlet was "completely one-sided" and intended to "impress the public in an unfair way and raise a prejudice in the public mind."[36]

John Kingsbury was convinced that Father Farrell and Daniel C. Potter had committed crimes. Citing the Catholics' pamphlets and the testimony during the Strong hearings, he charged them with "perjury, criminal libel, conspiracy to utter a criminal libel, and conspiracy to obstruct the administration of the law."[37] It had been the practice of the New York city police to use wiretaps to establish facts in criminal cases. Therefore, Kingsbury asked Mayor Mitchel to request wiretaps on the telephones of Farrell and Potter. From March 18 to March 30, 1916, police officers on the wiretapping squad listened in on their telephone lines, writing down pertinent conversations on slate boards. Stenographers later typed out their notes. William Hotchkiss, attorney for the city, then received the transcriptions of the tapped conversations and used them in his questioning of witnesses during the ongoing Strong hearings.[38]

Kingsbury's plan backfired. The city brought charges against him and attorney Hotchkiss, and on May 23 a Brooklyn grand jury indicted them both for unlawfully tapping the telephone of Father Farrell, stating that they violated the statute that prohibits wiretaps except for the purpose of detecting crime. The defense attempted to justify the wiretap on the grounds that both Kingsbury and Hotchkiss had sufficient reason to believe that crimes were being committed and that "they were immune from prosecution."[39]

In mid-July William Doherty appeared before Justice Samuel Green-baum of the Manhattan Supreme Court and signed a complaint against Farrell, Monsignor John J. Dunn, chancellor of the Archdiocese of New York, Potter, and Hebberd, charging them with crimes against the city, including libel, obstruction of justice, and perjury based on information obtained through the wiretaps. Justice Greenbaum took testimony from the principals to determine if there was sufficient evidence to present to a grand jury. When he recommended that the charges against Kingsbury and Hotchkiss be dropped by the Brooklyn Kings County grand jury, a press release issued by the SCAA read: "Collapse of Kingsbury Charges Gratifies City" and congratulated the commissioner on being vindicated. All charges against Farrell and Hebberd pending in the Manhattan Supreme Court were likewise dropped.[40]

Hopkins and other colleagues lent support to Kingsbury by attending the court proceedings. On May 24, 1916, Kingsbury wrote Hopkins a letter expressing his appreciation for his welcome presence in court. "If the power were given to me to express thoughts that lie almost beyond the reaches of my soul, then you would know what it did mean to me yesterday morning to see the encouraging smiles, the glances of sympathy, and the friendly wave of hand which greeted me as I looked about the court-room." He claimed that he was "fighting a good fight for a righteous cause" and deplored the injection of the religious issue into what he believed was only a political battle. "I was fighting your fight and the fight of all good citizens who believe in giving the child a chance and of those who deplore the attempt to inject religious prejudice into political life for the purpose of throttling public officials who are endeavoring conscientiously to do their duty."[41]

In late October of 1916 Commissioner Strong issued his long-awaited report. He criticized the effectiveness of the State Board in carrying out its duties and obligations and declared that the "failure on the part of the State Board to demand proper compliance with its advice can only serve to breed disrespect for the State Board." Remarking that one result of his inquiry and the controversy attendant upon the hearings was "to arouse public interest as never before in the welfare of dependent children," he recommended that a new Bureau for Dependent Children be created within the State Board of Charities in order to take selected children out of institutions and place them in homes, with the municipality paying for their cost and maintenance.[42] Strong stated that there was no basis for the accusations that New York City officials intended to destroy or to secularize private institutions, or to place-out *all* children, or specifically to target Catholics for attack.[43] Taking up the issue of the pamphlets, Strong stated that they never should have been issued and "were deplorable from every point of view and lengthened and obfuscated the inquiry."[44] Most significantly, Strong found that none of the institutions on the Advisory Committee's controverted list were "unfit" as he understood the term.[45] Finally, he censured the State Board "for failure to issue certificates of non-compliance with its rules or for failure to withhold certificates of compliance. . . ." Strong held that "the City has proved its case against the State Board."[46]

In its response to the Strong Report, the State Board protested the criticisms and claimed that the State Constitution did not intend that it should exercise control but rather "counsel, guide, and assist." If they did manage, board members contended, they could not make the "dispassionate and judicial criticisms of their own work." The job of managing and inspecting should fall to the city, they maintained, and they had every "right to assume that the City of New York was also making such inquiries as it deemed advisable as to the conditions in these institutions." The board adamantly denied that it had been "negligent of duty or inefficient in the discharge of responsibilities devolved upon it by the Constitution and the Statutes," and it appealed to Governor Whitman for recourse "from the unwarranted and often erroneous findings of Commissioner Charles H. Strong."[47]

Commissioner Kingsbury and Mayor Mitchel felt vindicated when Strong found no grounds for the accusation against the city that its officials were out to destroy or secularize private institutions, "to take God out of the hearts of the children; to found charity upon morals and not upon religion."[48] The Catholic charity community had a differing opinion. *America* ran an article that asserted that the Strong hearings "found Catholic Charities refusing to pay tribute to the modern pagan philanthropy."[49]

Although the Catholics felt strongly that the charities investigation was fueled by religious bias, *Survey,* a journal dedicated to modern philanthropic methods and therefore reflecting the feelings of the city and professional social workers, claimed that the investigation was not based on religious bias but rather on the debate of whether children were better off in institutions or in homes. The journal declared that there was no religious issue but only the question of the well-being of the children and, true to its title, asserted that an answer could be found only in "analysis and massed facts as to . . . the educational and physical results for the children; as to the effect of such an entangling alliance upon the healthy operation of both public and private activities." The journal accused the Catholics of bringing in the religious issue: "The weight of the organized forces of one great religious body has apparently been thrown into an effort to discredit the impartiality of the investigation, to inject the religious issue into state and city politics, and to make a blanket defense of the charitable institutions of this church."[50]

Whatever the true intentions of the progressive reformers, the investigations they instigated, the ensuing trials, the wiretaps, and the pamphlets all combined to help in the efforts to foster changes in New York City's welfare system. The creation of the Children's Home Bureau and the Children's Clearing House in late 1916 marked an increased commitment on the part of those concerned with the welfare of dependent children, Protestant, Catholic, and Jew, to place them in carefully selected homes. Doherty reported that this signaled "a new chapter, brimful of progressiveness," in "the history of the development of publicly administered charities in the City of New York." By mid-1917 city authorities were convinced that it was clearly possible to adopt this more progressive method of child care and that the Children's Home Bureau was no longer an experiment but a demonstrated success. The city, therefore, took over the work of finding homes for dependent children as part of the recognized activities of the Department of Public Charities and applied scientific methods to ensure that the children received proper care.[51]

By the time the charities controversy died down in late 1916, Hopkins had established his reputation as a social worker of the first order, ready to join the ranks of prominent professional social workers in New York City. William Matthews recognized the advances Hopkins had made in his profession and possibly the effect of the charities controversy on his outlook. In a 1916 letter to a colleague, he referred to Hopkins as "a splendid fellow in every way, capable, aggressive, not satisfied with doing things in the old accepted way if some other way promises better."[52]

As a result of watching the charities controversy, Hopkins decided that he wanted to pursue governmental avenues to power. He felt that this was the area where social workers could get "much better results than all this relief giving." He greatly admired John Kingsbury and coveted his job as commissioner of public charities. Ethel Gross Hopkins remembered that her husband "wanted more than anything else at that time . . . the job that Kingsbury had." She stated that "Harry felt that if he could sometime in the future be in a position so that he could qualify for that kind of job that would be what he would like to do."[53] Hopkins did not like the often-suspicious attitude of many of the charity workers with whom he came into contact; his commitment to close oversight of those receiving relief rose from a need to ensure efficient and economically sound programs rather than from any inherent suspicion he felt toward the needy.

The religious element that was so much a part of the charities' scandal had particular import for Hopkins. A clue as to how he felt about this religious theme can be found in an interesting exchange of letters between him and a Grinnell classmate, Harvey Young. In 1916 a New York State Methodist

Conference had failed to recommend Young for ordination after he had graduated from Union Theological Seminary, ostensibly because his views were too liberal for the committee. Although the bishop overruled the committee and later ordained Young, he was understandably upset at the time.[54] Hopkins wrote him a letter that revealed a great deal more about his own ideals than about his friend Young's dilemma:

My Dear Harvey,

Have just learned that the M. E. Conference has decided that your theology is not in sympathy with the administration, as it were. Congratulations. Ever since I left it, the church has deteriorated rapidly—until today they don't know a good man when they see one. My Methodist blood however rises in revolt when I think of the sissified and decidedly spineless men that grace its pulpit and the brazen effrontery of some old fogies who would turn a man down when he displays some signs of raising the church out of a more or less permanent lethargy. There is some consolation in knowing that Jesus isn't interested where a man is preaching just as long as he is preaching the truth. Although I know you are disappointed, still I can't help from being pleased and personally hope that you never get into the Methodist Church! The chief thing in this life to my mind is to work toward the founding of an ideal state, in this earth, based on social justice which will make for happiness for us all. I firmly believe that an approach to this condition is no idle dream and hope to lend my meager efforts to the culmination of this ideal.

This letter was really begun to thank you for the ticket for "Billy" Sunday [a contemporary evangelist]. Altho [sic] he consigned me and all my family to the everlasting torments of hell—still I think he is a wonder for while he speaks despairingly of "ethics"—"good conduct" etc. he seems to me to be the finest exponent of these very things that I have ever heard. I think the rest of his theology is uncivilized!

Do you ever get off to play tennis—I should like to take you on—

Very cordially,

Harry Hopkins[55]

Later that year, in July, Harvey Young sent a letter to his wife describing a visit he made to Harry and Ethel's home in Staten Island. He wrote that after dinner the three of them sat on the porch and, with a thunderstorm as a backdrop, talked for several hours about religion. The men put their feet up on the porch rail, Ethel lay in a hammock:

They seemed to be interested in the reasons that I had to give for working as a religious man, for they have come to the place where they do not stop to think of the religious significance of life. They say they try to do the things they ought to do, to help what they can to make life more tolerable and enjoyable for people who have a hard time of it. And they do not feel the need of answering questions with regard to God and His interest in the work that we are doing, and they think that they would do their work just the same whether there were an afterlife or not. They feel that men get about all that is coming to them in the way of punishment for their misdoings here, and in the way of reward for doing what they conceive to be right. They asked for themselves no other reward than the pleasure that comes to them from their effort to be true to their ideals and to be of some service to those in the world who have not had as easy a time as they. That in general was the line of their argument. They could not imagine that a future life was possible, for they had no evidence for it. And they were going right on with their work as tho [sic] it were not, for they were frank to say they did not think there would be any other life. Then they could not conceive how God could be interested in all of the things that all of men do, for they could not imagine a mind great enough to take them in, nor an affection broad enough to surround all of the interests of all men. They could not conceive either how God could have anything to do with such things as the war with all its horrors, and with sickness and with poverty with all the burden that they bring. They thot [sic] that we knew enough without him to try to remove the evils that we saw in the world and they did not get any of their incentive to work from the fact that they thought He was interested in them. They worked because what they were doing needed to be done, and the joy of doing it was all that they asked in return.

This letter indicated that Ethel and Harry believed in the redemptive qualities of charity. It is also interesting to note that they were speaking in the plural and spoke about both of them, Harry and Ethel, as equal partners, working toward a common goal. This would have been Ethel's ideal. Young tried to explain his friends' attitude to his wife by suggesting that self-reliant people, like Ethel and Harry Hopkins, may not feel they need the help of God. While he told them that he himself felt more comfortable in the belief that God was controlling "the whole process," he wrote that "[i]t is hard to say whether they will think more favorably of the part that association with God takes in the life of a man or a woman than they thot before."[56] Clearly Hopkins had been constructing his personal theology along with his social philosophy during this period of his life. New York City from 1914 to 1916 had been his social work laboratory. There he began to form and re-form the policies and methods that became his trademark as Roosevelt's relief administrator during the Great Depression. Foremost of these was a commitment to government responsibility for the welfare of Americans.

CHAPTER SIX

WIDOWS' PENSIONS

There is always the danger that in our dread of making people dependent we shall cease to do good for fear of doing harm.

—Harry Hopkins, 1914

HARRY HOPKINS DEFINED A GOOD PART OF HIS SOCIAL PHILOSOPHY during his practical education in social work during the second decade of the twentieth century. Indeed, the design of much of the American welfare system that he helped to formulate after 1933 was cast in New York City from 1913 to 1917. During these years the movement to legislate public pensions for poor, single mothers captured Hopkins' attention. In New York City widows' pensions became one of the most important issues for the child-savers and progressive social workers because the movement both reinforced the value placed on home life and reiterated the need for public funding.

Hopkins was in the thick of the debates over widows' pension, and the experience had a direct impact on his career. He actively participated in this contest for control of outdoor relief (that is, assistance given without requiring institutionalization) to a much larger degree than he did in the concurrent charities controversy. Many of the issues were the same: public vs. private relief and the importance of home life for the child as well as the state. Because the widows' pension program served as the model for Title IV of the Social Security Act, Aid to Dependent Children (ADC), Hopkins' involvement with this movement takes on added significance. A clear understanding of the issues involved, the cultural climate of the era, the choices made among alternatives offered, and the administration of the resultant program in New York City does much to explain the origins of the American welfare system and Hopkins' role in it.

During his tenure at the AICP, from 1912 to 1915, Hopkins began to develop his belief that the government had not only the right but the responsibility to intervene in the lives of citizens by providing relief for the deserving needy. Although he worked for a large charity organization supported by private donations, Hopkins learned through his experience there that only public action could adequately meet the real needs of poor families. Close investigation of prospective relief recipients and moral uplift through careful supervision—the basic tenets of scientific charity—continued to be an important part of his social work training at the AICP. However, this did not mean that Hopkins blamed the poor for their situation. He accepted the very simple fact that people were poor because, for one reason or another, they did not earn enough money. Historian Walter Trattner pointed out that the comprehensive data gathered by social workers in the early twentieth century revealed that, for a good number of those who applied for relief, poverty was caused not by moral degeneracy but by social and economic conditions that they could not control.[1] Statistical analyses of casework records amassed by friendly visitors indicated that families became destitute for a variety of reasons: illness, death, desertion, industrial accident, unemployment, or insufficient wages. In instances such as these, lack of income rather than lack of moral fiber led to poverty. Replacing the family's income could remedy the situation. While charity workers still frowned on indiscriminate giving, Hopkins realized that the rigorous investigation and strict oversight of the local charities often was driven by financial constraints rather than by the impulse to discipline the poor.

Hopkins saw very clearly that private charitable agencies could not attract sufficient donations to meet the growing needs of the poor in New York City. Public funds would have to be used to help these families. New York City, however, had been legally prohibited from providing outdoor relief since 1874. While it could and did subsidize private orphan asylums and foster care for destitute children, the city was legally barred from giving the same amount to a child's own mother, even though this was a cheaper and more humane system. Many reformers found this situation intolerable.

The widows' pension movement, like the charities controversy, took place against the background of an austerity budget for New York City. The need for economy impelled John Kingsbury, as the Commissioner of Public Charities, to make sure that every dollar the city spent was spent wisely. Thus the move to remove children kept in private institutions at city expense (totaling about five million dollars each year) served the economic as well as the political ends of Mitchel's Fusion administration. The financial benefits that would accrue to the city encouraged this movement as much as did humanitarian reasons. Yet, undoubtedly, new attention to the importance of home life gave added impetus to deinstitutionalizing children by means of public outdoor assistance.

In 1909 representatives from all states unanimously adopted a series of declarations that constituted a comprehensive program for child-caring work. Social workers came together at the 1909 White House Conference on the Care of Dependent Children and wholeheartedly endorsed President Theodore Roosevelt's pronouncement: "Home life is the highest and finest product of civilization. . . . Children should not be deprived of it except for urgent and compelling reasons." The conference declared that dependent children[2] "represent either a potential addition to the productive capacity and the enlightened citizenship of the nation or . . . a potential addition to the destructive forces of the community" and that "deserving mothers" should be enabled to raise their children in their own home.[3] This important conference, supported by those who ended up on both sides of the debate over public pensions for widows (Homer Folks of the SCAA, Thomas Mulry of the St. Vincent de Paul Society, Edward Devine, and Theodore Dreiser of the *Delineator*), emphasized the needs of the child rather than those of the mother. They depicted children as the "anchor which holds the woman to a good life," as old-age insurance for their mothers, and as a natural resource that needed to be conserved. For the mother, economic dependency seemed to have stripped her of the ability to care for her children without guardians to make sure that she did her job properly. The general assumption was that any mother who asked for financial assistance to care for her children, although seen as especially deserving, would also need close supervision.[4]

Agreeing that children should never be removed from their homes merely because the family was poor, progressive reformers began to look for new ways to conserve home life for destitute families. This fit in neatly with Mayor Mitchel's fiscal policies and with Commissioner Kingsbury's efforts to deinstitutionalize dependent children. Yet this movement to keep children in their own homes further complicated the relationship between private relief organizations and public officials. Although President Theodore Roosevelt made clear his preference that private charities rather than public agencies should provide assistance to fatherless families, many states began to enact legislation enabling governmental authorities to issue funds to needy mothers (variously called mothers' aid, mothers' pensions, or widows' pensions). In 1911 Illinois became the first state to pass a mothers' pension law, with other states rapidly following suit.

Charity workers had long characterized public outdoor relief as pauperizing, dangerously open to political corruption, placing an unfair burden on the taxpayer, lacking in proper supervisory methods, and discouraging help from relatives, friends, and private contributors. They agreed that relief should be given to families that might be destitute temporarily (that is, those not candidates for the poorhouse), but they vigorously opposed any legislation that would allow government authorities to give such aid. They believed that public relief always encouraged "the pernicious notion that the State is bound to support all who demand assistance; a notion which leads to the recipient of relief administered in this way to accept it without gratitude and to use it without discretion. . . . Relief acknowledged first as a gift, and gratefully received, is at length demanded defiantly as a right."[5] Not only would public outdoor relief lead to loss of independence and self-respect, and ultimately to deceit and crime, it also tended "directly to political favoritism, by putting into the hands of the distributing officers a most powerful engine of corruption." The widespread perception that public officials were not able or qualified to spend taxpayers' money in an efficient and wise manner also worked against public outdoor relief. Josephine Shaw Lowell of the New York Charity Organization Society (COS) expressed another objection to public relief: It was paid out of taxpayers' money. "It is not right to take money by law from one man and give it to another," she declared, "unless for the benefit of both." She repeated the most common objection to relief in general. "Human nature is so constituted that no man can receive as a gift what he should earn by his own labor without a moral deterioration."[6]

Poor mothers had a somewhat legitimate claim on outdoor relief, and the case of a destitute, fatherless family usually roused sympathy. However, this was only if the mother exhibited good moral character. There was always the danger that she would misspend her money without the guidance of social workers acting in lieu of her husband.[7] The methodology used by most charitable associations thus infantilized poor women by insisting on close scrutiny of their domestic activities. They assumed that these women had or could develop no marketable skills. Nevertheless, case studies compiled by social workers demonstrated that mothers who stayed at home and supervised their children rendered an important benefit to society in general. Children from these families were less liable to turn to a life of crime and more likely to become productive citizens. Private agencies such as the AICP, recognizing all of the beneficial effects of mothers' aid, established their own programs for these families. They stressed especially the importance of home life for the child as a way to prevent juvenile delinquency.[8] Therefore, when the movement for public pensions for needy widows began to spread across the nation, New York City's private relief agencies, led by the COS, regarded this movement not only as an outright criticism of their service methods but also as a threat to their power and funding. Consequently, they used the traditional arguments against public outdoor relief to oppose vehemently the movement.[9]

In 1912 Frederic Almy of the Buffalo COS, an avowed advocate of *private* aid for widowed mothers, clearly expressed one very important facet of the debate: the pauperizing effect of public relief. Using the rationale that "[w]idowhood is the most innocent cause of poverty" and "[n]eglected childhood is, in all the world, the very most innocent, appealing and frequent cause of poverty and crime," Almy called on organized charity to give generously to these destitute families. He declared that it would be both unfair to widows and dangerous to society to withhold help. "When organized charity learns to be generous, without blushing, it will come into its own, and the widowhood of poverty will get as liberal indemnity as the widowhood of industrial disaster." Balancing the deleterious effects of neglected childhood against the evils of public outdoor relief—that is, pauperizing by alms vs. pauperizing by neglect—he stated his opposition to public outdoor relief, even for innocent widows. In his opinion, using untrained public officials to administer relief was tantamount to administering "medicine without doctors." Furthermore, he warned that "untrained relief is poisonous to the poor" because it encouraged the public to believe that "the public treasury is inexhaustible and their right, and that they drop upon it without thrift, as they dare not do on private charity." These two main objections—that relief for these widows must not be seen as a right and that public officials did not have the expertise to administer aid efficiently—became the basis for every other argument against widows' pensions. Almy also argued that widows' pension legislation could lead to political corruption. "[S]uch subsidies lead to sectarian appeals, to lobbying and to a scrambling at the public trough for patronage." The inadequacies of public administration, the pauperizing effects of public relief, and the political corruption that would result all weighed against public outdoor relief.[10] These biases, articulated so clearly in 1915, remain central to America's attitude toward welfare to this day.

Support for widows' pensions, whether public or private, dovetailed into the controversy over public subsidies to sectarian child-caring institutions. If half orphans could be either removed from these (Catholic) institutions or prevented from entering them by enabling their mothers to care for them at home, the institutions would lose funding and therefore power and influence.

COS leader Edward Devine, probably one of the most outspoken foes of outdoor relief in general, admitted that assisting the families of poor widows might improve conditions for the family but also proposed that these needy women might be "the least efficient, the least capable, the degenerate, the unfit" and beyond the help of any relief agency, public or private. His argument against widows' pensions echoed the conservative view of poverty as being inevitable and usually the fault of the individual. He declared that in many cases "the physical, mental, and moral constitution of the individuals in the families in question is inferior" and that the answers in this instance would be "to promote conservative eugenic policies" or commit the children to institutions. He especially opposed public assistance for poor mothers. Devine claimed that such women would be capable of supporting themselves and their children if obstacles to women's work were removed—low wages, insufficient training, and irregularity of employment. In addition he advocated a "liberal, inexpensive, and safe system of social insurance" as a partial remedy against destitute, fatherless families.[11]

Defining social insurance as "the distribution of risks among all those who are naturally subjected to them," Devine declared that employers, industry, and consumers should bear the burden "of its deaths, diseases, and injuries." He challenged pensions to needy mothers as "not in harmony with the principles of social insurance" and having no claim to the name "pension." He called widows' pensions irrational, an "insidious attack upon the family, inimical to the welfare of children and injurious to the character of parents." Based on need and sympathy rather than on any right or fair exchange, widows' pensions were nothing more than public charity with all its attendant evils. Organized charity and all of its scientific principles—investigation, casework, the encouragement of self-help—combined with social insurance, institutional relief, and especially personal responsibility for one's own welfare, claimed Devine, could solve the problem of family destitution caused by the death of the breadwinner. "The ordinary expectation should be that one will provide for himself in sickness and in old age, and upon his death for his widow and orphan children."[12]

Devine warned that social programs such as widows' pensions would allow "the anti-social type of employer, who now throws his maimed and mangled workers, his exhausted, worn out workers, and the widows and orphans of those whom he has slain, indiscriminately upon the scrap heap of public relief" to further exploit workers. On the other hand, "[a]n income for widows, from a state administered fund, raised by the joint contributions of the insured and their employers, the burden lightly felt because widely distributed and borne in part by all of us . . . that is the honorable income which I covet for every mother who is widowed by the death of an industrial worker." In exceptional cases, the widow would have "recourse to public relief, to organized charity and to voluntary individual neighborly help." Calling advocates of experimental state subsidies to poor mothers "sudden heroes" and "brash reformers" Devine accused them of "building on the sand" and "following a will-o'-the-wisp."[13]

Mary Richmond of the Russell Sage Foundation's COS argued to set aside "all this claptrap" about public pensions for widows. She recommended that everyone interested in helping destitute families should soberly investigate the evidence before "stampeding our state legislatures." Richmond, like Devine, insisted that widows' pensions would disadvantage women and warned that in helping the widow or wife of a disabled husband, "we must be careful to put no further barriers in the way of the social workers who are striving to give all women a more dignified, better organized, and better safeguarded industrial status." Because they often prohibited women from working outside of home and at same time failed to provide adequate support, public pensions, according to Richmond, would lead to women's exploitation in the labor market. In addition, such pensions worked against women who preferred jobs outside of the home over state-subsidized payments for domestic duties. Richmond also made a very timely and effective argument against widows' pensions by equating them with the costly and proliferating Civil War pensions, which she branded as excessive, indiscriminate, encouraging fraud, and an "unprecedented raid on the people's treasury."[14]

According to historian Theda Skocpol, Richmond's opposition to widows' pensions, although ostensibly based on the fear of political corruption attendant upon social spending by a public agency and on the resultant retardation of social insurance and social reform measures, may have had more to do with the pauperizing effect believed to be at the heart of all public outdoor relief.[15] Richmond stated that Civil War veterans "able and anxious to seek their own way had no thought of seeking a government pension until it came to them fourteen years after the war in the overwhelmingly tempting guise of a large check for arrears." Because no inquiry was made into a veteran's need, these pensions fostered degeneracy and fraud. Drawing a parallel between this program and the pending legislation for widows' pensions, Richmond supported alternative solutions including social insurance and improved health care.[16]

Despite strong opposition from private charities, legislation for mothers' aid spread like "wildfire."[17] A unique coalition of middle-class activists, labor leaders,[18] journalists, juvenile-courts judges, settlement workers, women's associations, and progressive reformers generated the necessary momentum for mothers' pensions.[19] This powerful coalition marked what Skocpol called a significant "exception to the usual reluctance of middle class public opinion during the Progressive Era to countenance public social spending."[20] Those who spoke out strongly for legislation that would allow the state to assist destitute, fatherless families in their homes used an appeal based on women's helplessness and their unique status as mothers to legitimate public outdoor relief. The focus subtly shifted from child-saving to protecting women as mothers.

In 1915 most social workers agreed that children should not be removed from their homes and institutionalized merely because of poverty, and most agreed that women's primary role was as a wife and mother.[21] Poor widows trying desperately and unsuccessfully to support their children by working outside of the home presented a particularly appealing needy population. No one could accuse them of being responsible for their poverty unless, of course, they were blatantly immoral. Their poverty did not arise from unemployment but from the nature of their "employment." These women did not lack a job; what they lacked was an income from that job. Their alternatives were limited. They could let someone else care for their children and work; they could find a job at a high enough wage to pay for child care in the home; or they could accept a pension from the state. If, absent a male breadwinner, they accepted money from the paternalistic state to perform a publicly beneficial service, they were not recognized as employees of the state, a position that might have had some stature. Instead, social workers categorized them as recipients of public assistance: weak, unable to make decisions for themselves, prone to deception, and in need of direction.

In analyzing how politicians and social reformers used gender politics, it is useful to look at what historians Miriam Cohen and Michael Hanagan called "the context of political constraints and opportunities" that confronted those trying to build a strong coalition to make claims on the state.[22] The issues involved had to do with politics and power and responsibility for the poor. What really defined the argument over mothers' pensions was not the gender issue put forth by maternalist reformers in favor of such pensions, but rather the issue of who was responsible for the relief of a dependent population in a complex industrial society and how this relief should be administered. In 1915 the normative family consisted of a male breadwinner earning a family wage and a female caregiver concerned with domestic duties. The image of the mother as a powerful nurturing and disciplinary element within the family held sway on both sides of the debate. Supporters of widows' pensions used the image of idealized motherhood to advance their agenda for publicly controlled and funded pensions. Opponents claimed they were attempting to preserve the dignity and independence of women. As historian Roy Lubove pointed out, the issue of whether a public or private agency would administer the pensions became a much more divisive aspect of the discussion than gender politics. The cultural implications of mothers' pensions thus legitimized public outdoor relief. Its association with deserving motherhood allowed this form of relief to transcend any negative image as a mechanical dole encouraging indolence and vice.[23]

COS opponents to mothers' pensions did not deny the need to support dependent motherhood. However, they pointed out the widely accepted negative image of public outdoor relief and argued that only private charity organizations with their troops of trained investigators using methods of scientific charity could effectively screen out the undeserving and discourage "crafty pauperism."[24] Their objections to widows' pensions reflected the persistent belief that any form of assistance to the poor without the close moral supervision of friendly visitors would encourage recipients to regard relief as their right, a dangerous principle when the withholding of private charity was so useful as a lever for inducing proper behavior.

Opponents to public pensions for widows formed a committee of twenty-two representatives of private relief agencies in New York City and published their findings in a document, entitled "A Report of an Investigation of Matters Relating to the Care, Treatment and Relief of Dependent Widows with Dependent Children in the City of New York," most of which was written by Edward Devine. The report stated clearly that children should not be removed from the care of mothers for reasons of poverty alone and that adequate relief should be given to needy widows to enable them to care for children in the home. However, it emphasized the need for preventive measures. Dependent widowhood and the consequent institutionalization of poor children could be prevented through safer working conditions, social insurance, and vocational training of working-age children. Although the committee recognized the need for an adequate home-relief policy until such recommendations could be instituted, they insisted that the problem had been overstated; they found that in 1912, only 190 children from 100 different families were placed in institutions for reasons of poverty alone. Therefore, they insisted that the need could be addressed through increased cooperation between relief societies and the bureaus of dependent children. The report further claimed that "the relief of widows and their children in this city is more nearly adequately performed by the societies now engaged in this task than is any one of the important duties assumed by the municipality or the State in the care of the dependent classes. . . ." The report was signed by Frank Tucker, vice-president of the Provident Loan Society; Cornelius N. Bliss, Jr., president the AICP; Edward T. Devine, director of the New York School of Philanthropy; Lee K. Frankel, sixth vice-president of the Metropolitan Life Insurance Company and former manager of United Hebrew Charities; Homer Folks, secretary of the State Charities Aid Association; Arthur M. Howe, on the editorial staff of the Brooklyn *Daily Eagle;* Michael J. Scanlan, treasurer of the Superior Council of the Society of St. Vincent de Paul; Henry

R. Seager, professor of political economy at Columbia University and president of the American Association for Labor Legislations (AALL); Gaylord S. White, headworker at the Union Settlement; and John Kingsbury.[25]

Cornelius Bliss sent a letter to AICP Director Bailey Burritt just after this report had been produced reiterating his support of its conclusions. If private charities could not meet the need to keep these destitute families together, the solution was not to relinquish the task to public officials but rather for the private agencies to raise more money. "The Report shows very clearly, I think, that some radical step should be taken by the Relief Societies to enable them to handle more efficiently cases of this kind, and it seems to me an opportune time to place before the Associations interested in this matter the advisability of making a concentrated effort to secure much larger contributions than they have been able to secure in the past." He suggested that one way to do this would be to consolidate the AICP and the COS, with possibly the SCAA and the CAS joining in because only through close cooperation between the large charitable societies could the requisite money be raised.[26] The fact that he suggested this radical merger indicated how strongly private charities opposed public administration of these pensions.

Supporters of widows' pensions, discouraged by the repeated failure of various bills to pass the legislature, also produced a report. The New York State Legislature established a fifteen-member fact-finding commission[27] in order to inquire "into the practicability and appropriate method of providing by statute for pensions or other relief for widowed mothers." Nine months later the commission submitted a report that began with the surprising statement, "The normal development of childhood is one of the main functions of government." The State of New York, according to this report, had the responsibility to conserve the home "whenever factors, other than the improper guardianship of the parents, threaten its destruction."[28]

The commission found that private charities in New York City had been unable to do an adequate job of assisting destitute families "on account of both insufficient funds and an absence of a sympathetic attitude." The insufficiency of funds could be quantitatively proven. They estimated that more than 2,000 children had been taken away from their mothers and institutionalized for no reason other than poverty—over 1,800 more children than in Devine's report. An unsympathetic attitude was more difficult to establish although the accusation was based on the assumption that private charity workers tended to over-investigate.[29]

Recognizing that a comprehensive system of social insurance was not likely to be adopted in the near future, the commission therefore recommended "a system of direct governmental aid to the widowed mother with children." Mothers' aid, it declared, should not be considered as an alternative to but as a necessary and integral part of social insurance. This assistance, given to a unique and wholly deserving class of dependents, was not to be charity but "an indemnity for the earning capacity of the husband, so that the mother may be enabled to bring up her children as they would have been brought up had their father lived and worked for them." Thus the commission considered the pension to be payment for future service to be rendered by the mother so that children will "become intelligent, industrious, and responsible citizens, that add to the industrial prosperity of the community."[30]

The commission stated that private philanthropy had been a great stimulus in the area of assistance to widowed mothers, bringing important research and data to the public's attention and demonstrating methods to treat and eradicate "the fundamental defects in our society which contribute so largely to this dependency." But, it added, "[i]t has never been the function of private charity to supplant that of the government; rather, its field is to develop, through private effort, newer and better standards and methods for the government to undertake."[31] This interpretation of the natural transfer of responsibility from the private to the public sphere reflected the progressive nature of the commission, which did not ascribe to the traditional division of philanthropic labor: public indoor and private outdoor relief.

Charity leaders had long cited the Elberfeld system of outdoor relief as a European model worthy of emulation.[32] In operation since 1853, this system provided cash assistance to the poor in their own homes. The funds were raised by taxation and distributed by municipal boards. The system had reduced not only the number of paupers but also the cost of relief. Its characteristic features included the continuous and intense oversight by "unpaid visitors selected from representatives of the best class," a very small caseload, careful investigation, adequate aid but not enough to make charity attractive, and strict punishment for refusing to work, for wasting relief money, or "for misspending time in amusement, idleness, or drink, in such a way as to render public aid necessary." The essence of the system was constant supervision of relief applicants.[33]

At the 1904 National Conference of Charities and Corrections, Frederick Almy, opponent of public outdoor relief, cited Elberfeld as an example of a successful program where public relief followed private initiative: "If public charity in America ever makes general use of unpaid boards and volunteer visitors, it will be another illustration of an experiment tested and found successful by private charity and later incorporated into the public service on a larger scale than was otherwise thought possible." His main opposition to legislation for widows' pensions had to do with its proposed use of public officials as administrators. If this could be avoided, if workers trained by private agencies would administer these programs, Almy ventured, they might work.[34]

Sophie Irene Loeb, a reporter for the *Evening World,* was one of the leading advocates of public pensions for widows and a member of the New York State Commission. She traveled to Europe[35] (just five months before war broke out), where she conducted an investigation into methods other countries had used to solve the problem of fatherless and destitute families. She pointed to the German (Elberfeld) and English examples that clearly demonstrated that neither private charitable organizations nor social insurance would adequately provide for poor, fatherless families. She argued that in Germany, which had had social insurance since 1883, widows and their children were *not* protected. Moreover, in England, the insurance act did not take care of family members who were not part of the workforce.[36] Despite the efficacy of this argument, the impact of the war in Europe lessened considerably any weight the German example would have had for Americans.

Based largely on its observation that private charities had failed in their endeavor to support dependent motherhood, the commission recommended that the state legislature mandate the establishment of local boards of child welfare that would be permitted to grant an allowance to widowed mothers with dependent children under sixteen years of age. This assistance would be given, however, "only when the mothers are suitable persons to bring up their children properly and require aid to do so." The family would be given $20 per month for the first child and $15 per month for every additional child, with a maximum of $60 per month for any family. This law, the commission stated, would be "democratic, fundamental, conserving, and constructive . . . and an essential part of the social code necessary to advance the welfare of the citizenry of New York."[37]

The commission regarded women's domestic duties to be of utmost importance to the social order. The value of a mother's attention to her home and children far outweighed any value she would have in the labor market.[38] Historians recently have noted the strategies idealizing motherhood that lay at the heart of the movement both for and against widows' pensions and have pointed out that maternalist reformers used this emphasis on women's value in the domestic arena to reinforce gender inequality.[39] According to historian Linda Gordon, women reformers during the Progressive Era regarded domestic duties as primary for women and, at the same time, saw themselves as having "a motherly role toward the poor." The use of maternalist rhetoric, Gordon claims, allowed reforming women to "build a strategy for using the space inside a male-dominated society for an activism that partially subverted male power."[40] There is no doubt that support for widows' pensions in 1915 reinforced the family wage system (for males) and separate, gendered spheres.[41] Yet although both sides did emphasize the inadequacy of women, proponents of widows' pensions hoped to build a paternal state to take the place of the missing male breadwinner; they were not attempting to create a maternal welfare state.

Most of the commission's members were men who did not assume a "motherly" role toward the women they intended to help. Moreover, it is questionable whether the two women sitting on the commission, Sophie Loeb or Hannah Einstein, felt maternalistic toward poor widows and their children. They were more concerned with this issue of public vs. private relief. Einstein emphasized the "spirit of distrust and suspicion [that] permeates all that organized charity attempts to do for the poor. It is this spirit which leads many to hide and bear their physical misery rather than apply to our so-called charitable agencies." She deplored the attitude that widowed mother were "in a hopelessly chaotic state" and needed "a charity third degree" carried out by "grillers" before relief is realized. Her argument against forcing the widowed mother to seek work outside the home was based on the fact that institutionalism and foster care were "ineffective and costly, and in most instances serve but to add to the misery and degeneracy of those from whom death took their natural protector." The emphasis was not on their helplessness as women but on the effectiveness of the remedy and the right of these women to claim assistance from the state. Charitable societies, with their disciplinary, scientific, and rather arbitrary methods, had no place here. "This [assistance for poor mothers] can only be done by taxation; society is responsible and it must not shirk."[42] Loeb also stressed the relationship between the dependent child and the state rather than the inability of the mother to support a family. Reporting that in Europe as in America private charities did not provide adequate aid, she recommended that instead of relying on social insurance, relief legislation should be encouraged.[43]

At this point, one of the most prestigious private agencies, the AICP, broke ranks and issued its own report on the problem. This disavowal of COS standards by one of its own members revealed the complexity of the issues surrounding the debate over widows' pensions. By 1914 the AICP had expressed a belief in "a complete welding in the power and prestige of the public agencies with the initiative and elasticity of private agencies." The result of this "welding process" would be the "increased efficiency of both."[44] Most likely the agency saw hope for its survival in this position.

The New York AICP had long recognized the unique problems facing poor single mothers and had been providing them with assistance so that they would not have to institutionalize their children. One of Harry Hopkins' first assignments for the association had been administering aid to poor widows and their families. Bailey Burritt, director of the AICP, and William Matthews, head of the family welfare division, were both convinced that assistance for widows and their children lay legitimately within the purview of private charitable agencies. They at first opposed public aid for widowed mothers. However, a close, hard look at the actualities of the relief situation in New York City soon changed their minds.[45] Because of the economic downturn, private agencies were finding it more and more difficult to provide for poor, single-parent families that had lost their breadwinners. Kingsbury wrote to Burritt that "private relief organizations must raise more funds in order to deal adequately with the widows' cases. The only alternative to this would be the adoption of a program for the relief of widows by the state...."[46] He did not think that this would be best. William Matthews strongly supported his agency's widows' pension program as a means to prevent dependency. Just keeping families from starving was not enough; agencies like the AICP had to rehabilitate families. Adequate pensions to deserving widows with young children seemed to be one essential way of preventing families from falling into the spiral of destitution, dependency, and crime.[47]

During 1913 and 1914 Hopkins worked with Matthews on a project commissioned by the AICP in order to investigate how best to provide for deserving families that had lost their breadwinner.[48] The study had been prompted by "a report made by a group, sympathetic with the work now being done by private agencies to care for widows with dependent children, which pointed out that 'in a large number of cases, in spite of whatever aid is given, the health of the mother or of the children is impaired and progress toward genuine family rehabilitation does not take place.'"[49] The resultant report seemed to straddle the fence between the two sides of the issue. Firm in the belief that a woman's "first duty lay in the proper rearing of her children," the AICP had, since 1912, made regular payments to poor mothers. It undertook "to ascertain whether the Association has dealt with these families with sufficient wisdom and liberality" so as to ensure that the children would become responsible and productive citizens. For this project, it took forty-three of these families[50] and either supplemented or provided the full income necessary to maintain for the family a fair standard of living. Of course, this experiment was based firmly on the association's belief that the domestic duties of the mother required her full time and energies.[51]

The 1914 AICP report is important not only because Hopkins, one of the architects of the American welfare state, helped Matthews write it, but because it marked an important change in attitude of one of the nation's foremost private charitable institutions towards public outdoor relief. A contemporary expert on the causes of poverty, Lillian Brandt, in her study of the AICP, stated that this experiment and report "affected the attitude of the AICP towards pending legislation for 'widows' pensions' from public funds."[52] It is significant that the AICP did not express clear opposition to widows' pension legislation, as did other private relief agencies. The report insisted that those who received outdoor relief, especially poor women with children, needed direction and supervision. It also recognized the traditional imperative to "morally uplift" relief recipients. Of course, private charities, dedicated to modern methods of scientific philanthropy, were uniquely able to do exactly this. The AICP, however, had learned that moral uplift without financial support was ineffective. Its report emphatically stated that unless these families were given adequate financial assistance, the "indispensable minimum, [they would lead] dwarfed, stunted, inefficient lives." Widows with children should never be "required to work under conditions that mean the breaking of health and strength or the neglect of her children." These women should be given regular financial assistance "to remove from their lives that constant crushing anxiety that surely deadens hope and aspiration, not only in the mother's life but that also gradually lays its withering, paralyzing hand on the lives of the children, creating a downward pressure on life. . . ."[53] This assistance necessarily had to precede any uplifting work the agency might undertake.

The 1914 AICP report recommended uniformity and adequacy as necessary elements of any pension program. "The very first essential in the administration of any fund created or contributed for the aid of widows and their children should be that of universality of treatment. Without such a controlling principle there is bound to come unfair discrimination [and] feelings of bitter resentment. . . ."[54] Further, the report stated that "a fairly high standard of character and home care should be expected from the mother; that the continuous and adequate relief should be used as a lever, if necessary, to lift and keep families to a reasonable standard in such matters as care of health, regular attendance upon school, and general conduct. But it is utterly unfair to demand these things until we have supplied the means that make them possible."[55] Thus the regularity and uniformity of public pensions combined very effectively with the close supervision that always distinguished the methodology of private charities.

The AICP report, however, warned against degrading the recipient. Matthews and Hopkins stressed that widows and children, a population especially deserving of help, should not have to undergo the humiliation of excessive investigation. Widows applying for relief should not be subject to

> the same sort of investigation and inquiry as other people. . . . they are special. The most precious asset to be preserved during a period of stress and strain is the independence, the self-respect, the finer fibre. . . . Necessary as vigorous and searching investigation is in general relief work—by reason of the presence in a community of a few people who prefer begging to working—to compel women and children who have been left to battle with poverty by reason of the death of

the father to submit to that same sort of inquiry is neither necessary nor just. . . .
Self fault, improvidence and imposition on their part should not be assumed.[56]

They recommended that "women of high grade and of rare tact and sympathy" be hired as investigators to look into "the delicate needs of these families," families that always should be given the benefit of the doubt during the assessment process. These policies reflected those advocated by Sophie Loeb and the coalition supporting public pensions for widows and seem to be an effort on the part of the AICP to indicate that it was exceptionally able to carry out this program. On the other hand, the "vigorous and searching investigation" seems to be trying to engage the opponents of widows' pensions by emphasizing their commitment to scientific charity. This evidence indicates that the AICP was campaigning energetically for administrative control of the program.

The AICP's attitude toward widows' pensions did indeed reflect a commitment to preserving the dignity of women as mothers and an understanding of their unique role in shaping the lives of future citizens. Widows' access to state funds rested on the social duty they performed—the creation and nurturance of law-abiding, industrious workers—and thus could be claimed as a right. But also there remained the element of need. Widows' pensions only went to poor mothers, and, as always, this admission of dependency brought with it an assumption of inequality as a result of both class and gender.

Hopkins and Matthews knew that pension was the wrong word to use. Mothers' aid was not money earned through past service but merely replacement of a male breadwinner's wage through public charity. Hopkins wrote that he "doubted whether widow's pensions could be dissociated from the idea of relief" and thus from the stigma attached to it. He believed, however, that if these pensions could be given in the proper spirit, in the same spirit in which social insurance is given, the recipients would avoid this censure to a great degree. "It will always be a fair question as to whether it is relief itself or the methods by which it is administered that encourages dependency and creates pauperism. There is always the danger that in our dread of making people dependent we shall cease to do good for fear of doing harm."[57] Matthews later underscored this in 1917 when he declared that "in public relief, carefully administered, there is less danger of breaking the spirit and morale of those who must temporarily receive such assistance than when given from private sources. And this is all important."[58] Hopkins felt that proper administrative procedures could overcome any stigma attached to public assistance.

The AICP report, however, did attempt to legitimize widows' pensions as a right by equating them to a benefit many middle-class citizens received and giving both the same justification. Hopkins pointedly observed:

There are in this city, as is others, thousands of men and women who have and who are now receiving years of education in preparatory schools, colleges and post graduate schools by aid of scholarships and money grants. They are *given* these funds in the hope and belief that they will some day make return to the community in the way of useful, helpful lives. The assumption is that they will. In precisely the same spirit should we supply in adequate measure an income to the families under discussion . . . believing that such investment will be returned in the way of healthy, vigorous, red-blooded workers, an insurance against under-vitalized, stunted, inefficient bodies, against breakage and wastage of future citizenship, against an increase in that part of our juvenile population that keeps busy the machinery of juvenile courts, truancy schools, reformatories and like institutions. Administered in this spirit it will make little difference if we call them "pensions," "mothers' allowances," "compensations to mothers," or some other more pleasing name.[59]

Twenty years later, in 1934, Hopkins echoed these same sentiments at the November 14 meeting of the Committee for Economic Security discussing Aid to Dependent Children when he told his audience that if any of them had ever received an academic scholarship, they had received a form of public relief.[60]

Hopkins and Matthews had "[v]isions and prophecies of a day when, by large preventive social measures, the causes of want and destitution shall be cut away" through workmen's compensation and social insurance measures, but they recognized that there were families in need that required immediate assistance. These families were in trouble "by reason of the fact that we have failed in the past to check and to prevent the growth of adverse social and industrial conditions which are in large part responsible for the stress, the strain, and the want that now cruelly grip their lives." They added that the public "had to give up the wretched delusion that a mother can earn the bread for and at the same time properly nurture and rear her children."[61] While this attitude surely underlined gender inequality, it was then (and still is) a hard fact. The social work community agreed that it was virtually impossible for a widowed or deserted mother to work in order to support her children and at the same time to provide a healthful environment for them. If she did attempt this, her health would break down. She would neglect her children, and eventually they would become delinquent, a burden on the state instead of upstanding citizens. This attitude formed the basis for most of the arguments in favor of widows' pensions. As such, it reinforced the assumption that a mother's proper duty was to stay at home and raise productive citizens. According to Grace Abbott, mothers' pensions "constituted public recognition by the states that the contribution of the unskilled or semiskilled mothers in their own homes exceeded their earnings outside of the home and that it was in the public interest to conserve their child-caring function."[62]

The AICP report concluded that because preventive efforts such as workmen's compensation and proposed social insurance could go only so far in reducing the number of destitute, fatherless families, many widows with dependent children needed the immediate benefit of public pension. Stronger advocates of widows' pensions, such as Sophie Loeb and William Hard, believed that these pensions would have to remain part of the entire system of social insurance, while the AICP felt that any comprehensive plan for social insurance eventually would obviate the need for them. But no matter what position was taken on the issue of private insurance, there was an immediate need that private charities could not meet. The AICP estimated that it would have to raise an additional $120,000 annually to provide material relief for all needy fatherless families under its care, money it did not expect to get. "Theories and opinions" as to public relief or private charity should not "prevent the adoption of a program whose purpose it is to put a stop to the incalculable social loss. . . ."[63] Therefore, the AICP passed a resolution to support the pending legislation for public funds for widows' pensions. Although most other private relief agencies opposed such legislation on the grounds that this was outdoor relief and therefore properly fell within the purview of private agencies, the AICP adopted a resolution that "it was not opposed to such relief being given by the City of New York, provided the relief be adequate and that it be administered effectively and impartially."[64] This conclusion is especially interesting in light of the fact that Cornelius Bliss, president of the AICP, recently had endorsed the report issued by the group of private agencies opposing widows' pensions, a report also signed by John Kingsbury, late of the AICP. In addition, the AICP, along with the COS, had opposed the Ahern bill calling for public pensions for widows in 1897.[65] Why, then, would this agency come out in favor of public pension legislation in 1914? One reason might be that it fully expected to have administrative control over the public program.

AICP support for the legislation does not seem to have been entirely opportunistic, however. In 1914 Bailey Burritt had written a letter to Robert Hebberd, state commissioner of public charities: "Like Commissioner Kingsbury, I am myself uncertain whether governmental aid ought to be attempted in this state until private agencies shall have been more fully proved incapable or unwilling to cover the ground satisfactorily." He added that the AICP would neither oppose nor advocate any such policy.[66] Less than a year later, Burritt wrote the editor of the *New York Times* that he favored public pensions for widows "because I believe that the whole community rather than a small part of it should accept financial responsibility for the relief of widows. . . ." But he added that, contrary to what Sophie Loeb claimed, private agencies were not wholly inadequate to the task. The AICP, he declared, was spending more money for destitute families of widows than Cook County, Illinois, which was known as the home of public aid to widows. Furthermore, public aid would cost more money than institutional subsidies. Yet he declared himself in favor of public relief for these families. "We believe that adequate relief for widows and good standards of giving this relief are more important than the question of whether it should be given by public or voluntary agencies," he wrote, and added that the AICP would continue to provide this relief until the city was enabled to do so. Admitting that the AICP did not have sufficient funds to provide for all deserving and needy families, Burritt said the city should assume the financial burden "but in assuming it, it should equip itself to do the work adequately, impartially, and it should be clearly conscious of the size of the burden which it is about to assume."[67]

By early 1915 the leaders of the AICP stated openly their support of widows' pension legislation. William Matthews testified in Albany on behalf of the bill, and the AICP report he and Hopkins had written was used by the legislative investigating committee at its public hearings.[68] The report reflected an important difference of opinion between the two groups supporting public pensions for widows—the AICP and the coalition of social reformers—as to the place of private charities in the administration of the pensions. As head of the AICP, Burritt believed that the private charity model was appropriate for the administration of public pensions. He and his agency supported the legislation for the very practical reason that the AICP did not have sufficient funds to aid all the needy and deserving families. Their support had nothing to do with methodology. The coalition behind widows' pensions agreed that private charities did not have sufficient funds, but they were very concerned about the methods that would be used to administer the pensions, deploring the cold, mechanical, and demeaning procedures private charities employed using the COS model. A rather complex debate evolved out of this three-tiered controversy: (1) private charities (represented by the COS) almost unanimously opposed the legislation on the premise that public relief would encourage pauperism; only private charities had the expertise to flush out the undeserving; (2) the reform coalition argued that only public funds could meet the need and that these families had a right to assistance without intrusive and demeaning investigation; and (3) the AICP asserted that it could not meet the financial needs on its own but could administer a widows' pension program in such a way that, while care would be taken to recognize fraudulent applications, any needy widow who applied for help would be allowed to retain her dignity and would not have to undergo undue or intrusive investigation.

The legislative battle for widows' pensions was long and hard fought. Almost every year since 1897 widows' pension bills had been introduced to the New York State Legislature. Six bills had failed since 1913. Hannah Einstein, along with journalist Sophie Loeb (both on the New York State Commission), led the fight for this legislation. Einstein referred to it as "a six year's war—which knew not a day of rest until the struggle closed with victory in our hands."[69] Many social workers from the private sector took an active role and vigorously opposed the program because it would take away a good deal of their own power and control. Despite the strength of the opposition, the bill finally passed the State Assembly by an astounding vote of 129 to 8, and the State Senate concurred unanimously. On April 7, 1915, Governor Whitman signed the Child Welfare Act; it became effective in July. He stated that "[e]xperience has shown that where because of misfortune the widowed mother is compelled to give up her home and her children are provided for by persons who have no natural interest in them, such children are injuriously affected thereby and they do not become as capable as would have been the case if they had remained under the care and control of their real mother." And the governor, with unanimous support of the assembly, made special mention of the women who worked so hard for the passage of the bill: Mrs. William R. Hearst, Mrs. William Grant Brown, Mrs. William (Hannah) Einstein, Mrs. Samuel Koenig, and Sophie Irene Loeb. Supporters of the bill proclaimed that the "overwhelming vote, in view of political opposition, showed conclusively that public sentiment was strongly behind the policy of widows' pensions, and that the Legislators refused to bring party politics into its considerations."[70]

The law, although it was permissive rather than mandatory, did require each city or country to establish a Board of Child Welfare. It included requirements that the sum paid for the child should not exceed the allowance that would have been paid to an institution to support that child; that the widow be "a proper person mentally, morally, and physically"; that the husband had been a citizen at the time of his death; and that the family had been in residency for two years. In New York City Mayor Mitchel appointed Hopkins' boss and AICP colleague, William Matthews, as chairman of the newly established Board of Child Welfare (BCW), which consisted of the Reverend William A. Courtney (a Catholic), Mrs. Rogers H. Bacon, Hannah Einstein, Michael Furst, Mrs. J. Borden Harriman, John A. Kingsbury, Sophie Irene Loeb, and Edward P. Maynard.[71] When Matthews subsequently was elected president of the BCW, he accepted the position on the condition that his assistant, Harry Hopkins, be appointed as executive secretary. Hopkins was certainly up to the task—he had much to do with administering widows' pensions for the AICP from 1913 to 1915 and had collaborated with Matthews in writing the association's report.[72]

Hopkins wanted this job badly. He had solicited letters of recommendation from Grinnell professor Garrett P. Wyckoff, from Christodora House headworker Christina Isabel MacColl, and from his social work colleagues. MacColl wrote that Hopkins had a grasp of "investigation and follow-up work" as well as a "sympathetic understanding of social and economic conditions."[73] Bailey Burritt wrote an especially strong recommendation for Hopkins citing his work with widows, his collaboration on the 1914 AICP report, his tact, and his supervisory talents.[74] Helen Ingram, superintendent of the AICP Bureau of Family Rehabilitation and Relief and a member of the BCW, recommended Hopkins as having developed for the AICP "probably the best plan yet formulated for the care of widows' families." She also added that his mind was "open to suggestions and instruction from those to whom he is officially responsible."[75]

When Hopkins got the appointment in November of 1915 as executive secretary of the BCW, he resigned from the AICP.[76] Burritt wrote him a congratulatory note that said, "I believe it gives you a well-deserved opportunity for greatly increased usefulness and I know that you will make the most of the opportunity."[77]

Hopkins did. As BCW executive secretary, his first and last job with a public agency until 1931, Hopkins had the perfect opportunity to participate in the creation of a model welfare organization. He wanted to demonstrate what he had learned from his past experience. Hopkins fully recognized the importance of his work. He was also aware of the objections voiced by the private charities that had opposed the legislation and by those like Sophie Loeb who did not want program administration to fall into what she considered to be the bad habits of private charities. She probably should not have worried. Hopkins aspired to establish a widows' pension system that would be the national standard of excellence. The BCW and Secretary Hopkins made every effort to ensure that the women who applied for help be treated fairly and courteously and that a "kindly and sympathetic hearing" be given "to all who come to the offices of the Board."[78] By the end of the second year of the board's operation, New York City was spending more money than any other city in the United States for widows' pensions.[79] Hopkins worked extraordinarily hard, pushing himself to the point of collapse and, as a result, contracted pneumonia in 1917.[80]

Hopkins' work with the BCW was seminal to his career. When Matthews resigned as president of the organization in October of 1916, he wrote Hopkins that he would not have remained as long as he did "had it not been possible to have you in the position which you occupy. I do not think you fully realize yourself what a very important piece of work you have and are doing. What is more, I am quite sincere in saying that I do not know the person who could have done it with more effectiveness, more sympathy, more fairness, than you have." Despite the divisiveness of the board, Matthews wrote, "the big thing to keep in mind is the mothers and children to whom a better chance in life is being given through the Child Welfare Board."[81]

Hopkins took an active role in ensuring that his staff would do their very best for their clients, that no money would be wasted, and that his agency would build solid and lasting relationships with existing charities.[82] His staff responded well to his administrative techniques. One staff member wrote: "The weekly conferences and the personal interviews with you have been most beneficial and encouraging. It has been a privilege to us to work for you."[83]

Letters sent out from the mayor's office to prospective members of the BCW emphasized the important responsibilities that would fall to them and reflected the high hopes the administration had for these pensions. "Heretofore, the city has cared for children dependent upon public charity in institutions or by placing them out in families," the mayor wrote. This new law allowed them to remain in the custody of their widowed mothers, a situation that was both "humane and desirable." Each member had to use "judgment and considerate discretion" as well as "careful inquiry" in each case without falling into the trap of "over-investigation." Counseling them not to set up new investigatory machinery, the letter recommended that the "excellent division of child welfare of the department of public charities recently organized and equipped with intelligent and sympathetic workers is available to you."[84] Clearly, this last directive attempted to assuage the critics of public pensions as well as some of the advocates who feared that private charities would co-opt the program.

Despite the high hopes held by board members, the exigencies of financial, political, and cultural constraints prevented the widows' pension program from providing substantial and long-lasting help for most of the BCW's clients. Problems surfaced very soon after the BCW began its work, much of it due to the fact that John Kingsbury, William Matthews, and Harry Hopkins, all from the AICP, and William Doherty, Kingsbury's deputy, sat on the board. This angered advocates of widows' pensions (led by Loeb) who, suspicious of the mechanical, scientific methods of private charities, had envisioned city admin- istration of the new program. Henry Pollack, former member of the New York State Commission on the Relief of Widowed Mothers, expressed concern that the BCW, with former AICP worker Hopkins as executive secretary, was using investigators from the Department of Public Charities who previously had been employed by private charities. He wrote that he feared that the board would perform its duties "in the same way that relief was formerly given by the private charitable associations in which you and I as members of the 1913 Commission found very unsatisfactory."[85]

Hopkins used investigators working for the Bureau of Social Investigations in Kingsbury's Department of Public Charities only because the BCW did not have the money to hire sufficient staff. These investigators were recruited to inquire into the situations of widows who made applications for help. Mayor Mitchel, hoping to avoid the creation of "new and expensive machinery," sent out a letter endorsing Hopkins' decision, stating that it was in the interest of economy and would greatly simplify the BCW's work.[86] Robert W. Hebberd, secretary of the State Board of Charities, whose animosity toward Kingsbury stemmed from the charities controversy (still raging), could not support anything Kingsbury did and aligned himself with Loeb. He called Hopkins' decision "absurd" and informed Loeb that the investigators of the Charities Department were "months behind in their regular work and are in no position to undertake the work of investigation for the Board of Child Welfare." He stated that they had failed to reinvestigate children in private institutions at public expense and this failure was costing the city thousands of dollars each week.[87] In a letter to the mayor, Kingsbury related Loeb's allegation that he, as commissioner of public charities, was usurping the power at the BCW.[88]

Loeb subsequently undertook a campaign to remove Kingsbury from the board by recommending that an amendment be added to the law removing the commissioner of public charities for the City of New York as an ex-officio member. In response, Kingsbury wrote to Mayor Mitchel telling him it would be a serious mistake to reappoint Loeb to the board.[89] William Matthews, president of the BCW, naturally supported Kingsbury in his battle with Loeb.[90] Loeb, again supported by Hebberd, used her position as reporter for the New York *Evening World* to criticize Kingsbury as commissioner of public charities for failing to remove children eligible for pensions from institutions and transferring the funds for their support to the BCW.[91] The debate extended over whether to give priority to children already in institutions or to those at risk of being institutionalized.[92]

Hopkins also squared off against Sophie Loeb. In late 1917 he attempted to modernize and professionalize the BCW by adding more investigatory staff, called "district secretaries," whose job would only be to read caseworkers' reports. Loeb argued that these investigators, who would not go out into the field and have direct contact with the families, would simply add an unnecessary bureaucratic level between social worker and client. She feared that these district secretaries would rely too much on statistics and "assume an impersonal attitude toward the cases."[93] Supported by board member Father Courtney and by field investigators who resented the proposed higher salaries for the new staff, Loeb vigorously opposed Hopkins' recommendation. Eventually, however, the investigators were transferred to the BCW.

The city, nevertheless, gave its wholehearted support to the work of the BCW.[94] The president of the Board of Aldermen, Frank Dowling, underlined the political commitment to this policy on April 18, 1916: "This Child Welfare work is but in its infancy and there isn't the slightest doubt that it will cost us from $1,000,000 to $1,500,000 a year. But, if it actually keeps thousands of children out of institutions, I am in favor of granting such a sum."[95]

The BCW's first annual report reveals the divisiveness that marked the first year's activities. It noted that the bill had been amended on February 15, 1916, to allow the board "to appoint its own staff and make its own investigations" and to discontinue the "membership of the Commissioner of Charities as an ex-officio member of the Board. This was done in the belief that it was desirable to have complete separation between the work of the Board and the Department of Public Charities. Furthermore it was felt that the presence of the Commissioner of Charities on the Board made possible a subsequent return to earlier [investigatory] methods. . . ." Speaker Thaddeus Sweet, who had actively supported the legislation, stated that he was very pleased with this decision, which "affirmed the primary spirit and intent of the measure."[96] Clearly, this was a slap in the face for John Kingsbury and possibly an attempt to limit the influence of the AICP crew on the board.

Hoping to avoid the stigmatizing effect of public relief, advocates of the widows' pension legislation, including the AICP, had argued against overinvestigating families. They also had argued for an adequate level of assistance. However, the reality of the program would not bear out their hopes. Hopkins and his team conducted extensive investigations into the background of each widow in order to determine not only her need but her "worthiness."[97] The women had to fill out lengthy and complicated forms; they were required to give a sworn statement as to their financial status, to provide lists of family references, and to present a certificate of health. A BCW field investigator visited the home to appraise the family's behavior. After this, and upon recommendation of the investigator, the board would grant an allowance. However, the amount of the allowance was based on a budget that would provide for little more than the bare necessities.[98] Although Hopkins acceded to this stricture, he came to deplore the general policy of providing the lowest possible level of subsistence. As New Deal administrator in Washington, he insisted that those receiving either direct relief or wages should be given a sufficient amount of money so that their standard of living would rise above the mere subsistence level.

Funding always presented a problem. No appropriations had been made in the city budget for widows' allowances. Two months after the BCW started work, it had 3,700 applications, which it started investigating in November of

1915. By early January $100,000 had been released from the budget for subsidies to private institutions and transferred to the BCW, but only 161 allowances were awarded at that time. By April another $300,000 had been appropriated, but this still was an inadequate sum.[99] Many more women needed assistance to keep their families together. By the second year Hopkins had a staff of thirty-six visitors and six clerks and a "more than adequate" appropriation of $1,250,000 for the year. The assistance given to widows and their children had, however, strings attached. Only about 40 percent of those who applied actually got allowances. Hopkins reported that while the BCW made every attempt to see that the family received adequate relief, its staff, through investigation and reinvestigation, also carefully supervised and directed the mother in almost every aspect of her family's life: school, health, jobs, church.

Hopkins understood the necessity for detailed casework in order to assess the needs of these widows. Yet he also felt very strongly that the recipient of widows' pensions should not have to submit to humiliating and intrusive investigations in order to qualify for help. He disliked the suspicious attitude that many of his fellow social workers had toward the poor, and he tried very hard to ensure that BCW caseworkers acted with the utmost consideration toward their clients. His first wife, Ethel Gross, recalled that Hopkins, when reviewing case studies, "would rather make a mistake than to suspect someone of misrepresenting himself."[100] Nevertheless, Hopkins was alert to any attempt at fraud and was careful not to waste agency money on those whose needs were exaggerated.

Hopkins believed in the work that the BCW was doing, despite the concessions he had to make. "There is possibly no other City activity that means so much to such a large class in the community as the Widows' Pension Law. It is keeping homes together that were formerly broken up because of poverty. It will result, if properly administered, in children becoming better citizens than they otherwise would have. It is the best practical interpretation of the City's responsibility for a particular class of its dependents."[101] In fact, Hopkins was so enthusiastic about the BCW that he recommended that it combine with the Department of Public Charities, headed by John Kingsbury, in order to administer widows' pensions even more efficiently.

Hopkins' effectiveness in administering widows' pensions for the City of New York made the newspapers. In March of 1917 the *New York Herald* described him as "the presiding deity of the pension fund." Although at age 26 he was still very young, the article declared "the mere mention of his name appears to exert a magic influence on the widowed mothers who are in receipt of pensions." Investigators often would invoke Hopkins' name to convince clients, who were in awe of him, to behave in what they considered acceptable ways.[102] Certainly, for these women, Hopkins was "the man." There was no doubt that a paternalistic welfare system was at work here.

Despite wranglings with board members, budgetary problems, and a bout with pneumonia, Hopkins managed to help turn the Board of Child Welfare into a professional and efficient organization. He met often with his staff, pushed for salary increases when they were warranted, attended conventions, spread the word about the work of his agency, and encouraged his staff to use creative and innovative techniques when dealing with clients. Hopkins recommended the complete professionalization of the board of directors—exactly what Sophie Loeb had feared all along. Although this recommendation was not carried out, it was a foreshadowing of Hopkins' later determination to staff his New Deal agencies with professional social workers.[103]

For Hopkins, the time spent working for the Board of Child Welfare was a period of increasing political awareness as well as social work training. He believed implicitly in the program he had done much to create. In a letter to John Kingsbury in April of 1917, Hopkins thanked his mentor for recommending him for another, much higher-paying job but said he had to turn it down. He wrote that "[t]here are many things to be done here to get this properly started and I feel that I am more or less indebted to the City to finish the job." Over the past several years Kingsbury had become increasingly close to Hopkins and Hopkins recognized the value of this relationship. "I appreciate immensely the confidence which from time to time you have shown in my work. It has been a very real help to know that you were supporting my work here through the past year. The job, to say the least, has been trying, but we have progressed steadily and I think before the end of the year will have established an administration of widows' pensions second to none in the United States."[104]

But in Hopkins' mind, rehabilitation always should accompany relief, and this was especially true for destitute families. A family living just at the subsistence level had little hope for any real improvement. Hopkins felt that it was the responsibility of the government, through public agencies such as the BCW, to provide adequate funds to help them. And he did believe in spending the government's money.[105] However, private charities and even some progressive reformers objected that the program did not go to the root of the problem and address the reasons these women became widows in the first place. The BCW did, in fact, endorse preventive measures, but it also recognized the necessity for emergency cash relief to keep children in their homes.[106]

In the 1917 administrative report of the BCW, Hopkins expressed his belief that "the policy of widows' pensions is not the 'last step' in our social efforts to meet the needs of this group in the community." He declared that social insurance would be the wave of the future. With an effective system of insurance against sickness and unemployment established in the country, "not only will old evils of public outdoor relief be avoided" but the system will prove to be better than either private or public relief.[107] Hopkins had come almost full circle. He now agreed with the most adamant opponent of widows' pensions and the enthusiastic proponent of social insurance, Edward Devine.

In assessing the nature of the widows' pension program, it is helpful to look at what Linda Gordon refers to as "defeated alternatives" and the choices that the historical actors made within the social, political, and economic constraints of times.[108] Historian Ann Vandenpol underlined the progressive nature of widows' pension legislation by emphasizing that public aid to poor mothers in their homes ended the dominant practice of the state interfering to break up families. During much of the nineteenth century, private charities had led the fight to remove children from poor families and place them either in institutions or foster care.[109] Roy Lubove declared that the mothers' pension programs were liberating for women because they made the important distinction that poverty was caused by lack of income rather than improvident or immoral behavior. Yet, he claimed, the "failure to defend economic assistance as an end in itself . . . compromised any claim that the pension was a right, and substituted behavioral criteria for economic criteria in determining eligibility."[110] This became the fatal flaw in Hopkins' BCW's program. Using aid as a lever to encourage proper behavior eliminated any pretense that such financial assistance was a pension in the real sense of the word. If the mother knew that the aid could be withdrawn at any time, the security of the family stood on shaky ground.

Initially, the BCW made every attempt to preserve the self-respect of the women in receipt of allowances. It sent a letter to each woman upon approval for such aid that "this allowance is not granted to you as a matter of charity, but in accordance with the laws of the state." But it also made clear that she was expected to spend the money "in ways that will contribute to the health and education of your children."[111] And the inference always was that the BCW would be the judge of how well the mother was doing. Therefore, behavioral norms became the key for determining if the allowance would continue. Seen in this way, mothers' pensions were indeed the precursor of Title IV of the Social Security Act, Aid to Dependent Children, and thus contributed to the creation of what historian Barbara Nelson has described as a two-channeled welfare system with social insurance for men and public assistance for women.[112] Yet as historians Muriel and Ralph Pumphrey show, any evaluation of the widows' pension program should separate the intent of the advocates from the outcome. Those who administered these programs saw the acceptance of public assistance for needy mothers as a "process by which the new idea was incorporated into, and reached accommodation with, the older cultural and legal system."[113] The Pumphreys point out that because the BCW was underfunded, it had to turn to private agencies for staff "and thus became captives of the very organizations that had fought most vigorously against publicly administered pensions."[114] The administration by private agencies made it relief once again. However, in the New York City case, the AICP had come out in favor of the legislation by 1914. Its co-option of the BCW may have been premeditated, yet it did make every effort to administer the funds according to the ideals expressed in the 1914 report.

The administration of mothers' pensions gave the BCW an opening to investigate, supervise, and oversee the women it aided. Thus on one hand, the legislation disempowered women as workers and reinforced women's economic inequality.[115] On the other hand, the BCW did provide help for a great many families. It never had sufficient funding, however, and this led to a narrowing of the eligibility requirements and increased oversight. Yet, as Linda Gordon claimed, the "inadequacy of mothers' aid should not mask its historical significance as a welfare accomplishment."[116] The Pumphreys also point to the positive effects of widows' pensions in reversing the ban against public outdoor relief and the significant help it gave to many families.[117] Historian Molly Ladd-Taylor agreed with Gordon that the administration of widows' pensions did not meet the expectations of its advocates, and both of these historians attribute this to the weaknesses of the women's movement. However, the strong cadre of reformers who were more concerned with the transfer of the responsibility for relief from the private to the public sector, from the traditional to the modern methods of providing relief for the dependent population, had much to do with the formulation and administration of widows' pensions. Central to this program was the diminution of scientific charity methods so as to present a sympathetic attitude while at the same time ensuring that immoral, undeserving women were eliminated from any assistance. It did not seem to matter that children would suffer if funds were withdrawn from women found to be unworthy mothers. For the administrators, a wayward child was redeemable—if he or she had proper maternal love and supervision. If a mother strayed, the family was doomed.

The hard fact of widows' pensions in 1915 was that because of underfunding, families rarely received enough financial aid to allow the mother to stay home. There was also a real fear on the part of the public and social workers that if these mothers did not show that they indeed were willing to work (either inside or outside the home to help support their children), they might be "welfare chiselers."[118] Critics of widows' pensions, who accused the program of perpetuating women's marginal place in the workforce, welcomed any move to expand women's work opportunities. These opportunities were, however, extremely limited.

One of the important differences between the advocates of widows' pensions and their opponents lay in their attitude toward social insurance. The COS placed responsibility for family security upon the wage-earner, claiming that "the main responsibility for the relief of widowed families does not rest upon the charitable societies but upon the individuals themselves."[119] It recommended a living wage for workers along with a comprehensive system of social insurance against sickness and death, state control over working conditions, and workmen's compensation. The New York State Commission, on the other hand, pointed to the immediate needs of these families and declared that any form of social insurance would be insufficient and ineffective.

The establishment of a system of social insurance to protect Americans against illness, unemployment, or widowhood meant a significant diminishment of the supervision and oversight—administrative methods that had become an integral part of both public and private relief. The recipient of insurance received payments earned as a right, and , while he or she had to meet certain requirements, these payments were not needs-based. There were no restrictions as to how that money could be spent nor were there behavioral codes imposed. Devine and Richmond argued for social insurance to protect mothers from poverty caused by widowhood, declaring that individuals were responsible for their own economic fate. By extension, therefore, they sought to exempt needy mothers from excessive intrusion into their lives. This, of course, would afford them some degree of independence and agency in their own lives and the lives of their children. While widowed mothers were still regarded as "dependent"— unemployable—their claim to workmen's compensation or to some form of social insurance would be based on a right as well as need. Although advocates of widows' pensions attempted to describe their programs as payment for socially beneficial maternal services, there was never any doubt that this form of assistance was needs-based public charity. Thus, in effect, opponents of widows' pensions tended to mitigate the subordination of women while those campaigning for this aid reinforced the normative family roles. Despite attempts by the coalition supporting and administering public allowances to eliminate excessive intrusion into the lives of needy mothers, and despite their attempts to liken this form of assistance to an honorable pension, mother's aid nevertheless evolved into the antithesis of rights-based, earned social insurance. This was not the intent of those who supported the program, Hopkins included.

In 1917, while he was still executive secretary of the BCW and two years after he had organized the Bronx Zoo work-relief project, Hopkins wrote a report entitled "To What Extent Are Public and Private Agencies Supplementing Low Wages?" This report reveals a great deal about his attitude toward relief. Within a few pages he responded to the argument propounded by critics of social welfare agencies that organized relief to the needy "is to all intents and purposes a subsidy in the form of charity granted to parasitic industries" that refuse to pay adequate wages to their workers and that charity, functioning as a subsidy to business, had become an "obstacle in the fight for fair wages." Critics claimed that relief had been "used by the employing class as one of the agents in maintaining an unfair standard of wages." Hopkins quoted Devine to explain the official position of professional social workers and their relief organizations: "We are not to supply relief in order that employers may get the benefit of under-paid labor. . . . Relief is not a substitute for wages in whole or in part." Hopkins vigorously denied that any relief organization granted outdoor relief to an able-bodied man with a normal, healthy family. He did note an important exception—the Bronx Zoo work-relief project that was instituted during depression years.[120]

Hopkins was fully aware that because most workers earned barely a subsistence wage, it was impossible to save for medical emergencies or periods of unemployment or to buy life insurance for the breadwinner. In the early part of the twentieth century, the average American worker simply did not earn enough. Moreover, if he attempted to put aside money for the proverbial rainy day, not only would his family's standard of living drop to a dangerously low level, but the aggregate lowered consumption could precipitate an economic slump. In 1907 statistics revealed the shocking fact that 75 percent of male workers and 95 percent of female workers in the United States earned less than two-thirds of the amount necessary to ensure physical health and a decent standard of living. Therefore, liberal reformers began to propose a system of social insurance, with its theory of distribution of losses and elimination of risk, as the most efficient way to provide the American wage earner with economic security.[121] In 1913 Isaac Rubinow, a pioneer in the social insurance movement (and in 1935 a consultant to the Committee on Economic Security) wrote that indolence was not the essential cause of want. Rather, in an industrialized nation, lack of work opportunities and low pay caused poverty. Rubinow described the status of most American workers: "Their economic condition is precarious; the economic dangers threatening them many; and the degree of risk in each case is very high. Individual provision is insufficient, social provision through distribution of loss is necessary but costly, often much too costly."[122]

While Hopkins supported efforts to implement social insurance, he also proposed that social workers themselves had the ability as well as the responsibility to make every effort to secure fair wages for American workers by intervening with private industry, by supporting trade unions in their drive for fair pay, and by endorsing minimum-wage legislation for unorganized workers. It was simply a matter of social justice in a city where "we find on the one hand a large number of people with every luxury at their command, and on the other a large share of the working class in abject poverty."[123] He clearly stated his position:

> Personally, I cannot understand how [friendly] visitors can go amongst the miserable tenements of New York City and see, in family after family, how their need is entirely due to the inadequate wage which is paid to working members without vigorously protesting against such a condition. Employers should first be given an opportunity to increase the wage, but if they refuse to do so the relief agency should in some way acquaint the public that such a store, business or corporation pays unfair and inadequate wages to its employees.[124]

Hopkins called upon charitable agencies, both public and private, to intervene actively to force industries to provide a living wage for their workers. The COS refused to give relief to able-bodied men with normal, healthy families because they believed that this would encourage employers to pay less than subsistence wages. Of course, the assumption here was that if relief were withheld, industry would raise wages. Hopkins agreed that relief societies should not and did not subsidize industry by giving alms. Claiming expertise and experience with both private and public agencies, he denied accusations that these agencies ever gave relief to able-bodied men, even if they did not earn enough to support their families. He wholeheartedly agreed with this position, even in the extreme cases where sickness in the family caused destitution.[125] For Hopkins the solution lay in social and governmental action in order to get to the root of the problem and eliminate the need for relief.

Hopkins, however, convinced as he was that this was the correct policy to follow, lost the courage of his convictions when he saw firsthand the misery an impoverished family experienced. "Anyone entering an tenement in any part of the City and finding a little child ill from lack of proper food would seem to be heartless indeed if he did not see that it secured instant and sufficient relief." But, he added, "I still believe the theoretic policy of refusing relief to every able-bodied man, under any circumstance, is a sound one, and one, if it were put into practise [sic], would soon stir the fine sensibilities of our population to action."[126]

Hopkins was especially concerned with the low wages paid to women and children and the concentration of extreme poverty in families without a male breadwinner. He recognized that "nearly every family [getting relief] has wage earning women and children" and that relief, in these cases, does tend to supplement low wages because "[t]he general policy of relief organizations is to give assistance on the basis of need." Therefore, Hopkins stated, the widows' pension program deserved some of the criticism leveled against it by its opponents. "Girls, hundreds of them, receiving $4. to $6. a week, a disgracefully low wage, are found in families of widows receiving pensions from the City."[127]

While active intervention by BCW workers to ask employers to raise wages for women and children had not been generally successful, Hopkins urged the BCW visitors to continue to protest publicly against inadequate wages. "I believe there is enough information in the records of relief societies about the low wages paid to women and children to move public opinion forcibly in the direction of . . . the minimum wage. . . ."[128] Hopkins knew that especially in the case of needy mothers, "[c]harity is given when all that is needed is a fair wage. . . ."[129] It was his stated policy that relief should never act as a substitute for insufficient wages. The preferred remedy always would be government action in the form of social insurance and minimum wage laws. Programs that provided public pensions to widows merely provided necessary but temporary assistance to families suffering from the gross injustices of the employing class.

President Woodrow Wilson's Commission on Industrial Relations had conducted an investigation into this particular problem, calling witnesses from the AALL, the National Child Welfare League, the Women's Trade Union League (WTUL), the Consumers League, the American Federation of Labor (AFL), and political organizations and social welfare agencies. The commission issued a final report in 1916, part of which concluded that women and children were exploited in industry to an extent that threatened their health and welfare and that their competition presented a direct menace to the wage standards of working men. In addition, the report reinforced the family wage system by declaring that the employment of women threatened "the ideals of family life upon which American civilization has been established." The solution, the elimination of this unfair competition in the labor market, lay in federal legislation establishing protective legislation for all working women and children regulating wages, hours, and work conditions.[130] The widespread agreement among diverse groups as to women's secondary position in the workforce, the social importance of their domestic role, and the need for protective legislation gave added impetus to such measures as New York City's widows' pension program.

The proto-welfare system that was modeled in 1915 and aimed at single women and their children did not challenge the gendered social roles that were so deeply embedded in American culture. The system was instituted to meet a desperate and immediate need. The reformers who supported this public assistance to needy mothers did not place them in the same category as unemployed male workers whose dependency could be addressed with jobs or work-relief programs. These women were not unemployed members of the industrial workforce. For them the solution came not from jobs but from the replacement of their husband's wages. Women's domestic role and their concomitant economic subordination within the family had become a cultural norm, and progressive reformers worked within this assumption. They hoped that a comprehensive system of social insurance, including unemployment insurance, countercyclical work-relief programs, workmen's compensation, minimum-wage requirements, and health insurance, would afford enough security to the family that widows' pensions would no longer be necessary. Social insurance, however, implied a right based on participation in the workforce. The Bureau of Labor defined social insurance as a method by which wage earners secure a right to financial benefits by dint of their contributions to a fund or "by the fact of his employment. . . ."[131] Clearly poor mothers and their children could not claim their right to a public pension based on their contribution.

According to his first wife, Hopkins' work with the BCW was a determining point in his career. Ethel Gross Hopkins remarked that "[i]t all started with the Board of Child Welfare; he very soon felt that the avenue he wished to pursue was to get into government through the Department of Welfare because he felt that [he could] get much more, much better results than all this relief." Hopkins, while recognizing the need for it, condemned the whole idea of relief, especially the suspicion it bred that the poor were "chiselers."[132] But Hopkins was a realist; he knew that the BCW had to spend the people's money responsibly. Therefore, close supervision and oversight was a necessary part of his administrative method. When he entered into a public discussion at the 1917 National Conference of Social Work and outlined the administration of the BCW, he emphasized two points: the lack of political influence and the rehabilitative work that was being done by his staff of trained supervisors.[133] Thus he refuted two of the main objections voiced by the opponents of the legislation; he also justified his work providing public assistance for this uniquely deserving population.

Anna Pickett and David Aldona Hopkins, Nebraska 1884

Picture probably taken 1896
Hopkins brothers: L. to R. Harry (b. 1890), Rome (b. 1887, on top),
John (b. 1894), Lewis (b. 1884)

Harry Hopkins, New York social worker, 1912

Ethel Gross wearing "short stop" hat in suffrage parade. 1913, NYC, Fifth Ave.

Meeting with state WPA administrator Florence Kerr, Mayflower Hotel, June 1935
L. to R. Kerr (with glass) Harry Hopkins, Eleanor Roosevelt, Ellen Woodward

Facing page: Harry Hopkins pondering economic security, 1934, courtesy of Stock Montage

FDR attempting to ease tensions between Harry Hopkins and Harold Ickes by taking them on a fishing cruise, after the Emergency Relief Appropriation Act was signed. Ickes had just lost his wife. USS *Houston,* November 2-22, 1935.
Ickes (second from left in front), FDR, Harry Hopkins

CHAPTER SEVEN

WAR WELFARE AND PUBLIC HEALTH

Home Service Sections feel . . . that soldiers' families are not in any way objects of charity, but are the rightful recipients of the grateful and neighborly service which fellow-townspeople wish to give them through the Red Cross.

—Report of Bureau of Civilian Relief, 1918

You could mark [Hopkins] down as an ulcerous type. He was intense, seeming to be in a perpetual nervous ferment—a chain smoker and black coffee drinker.

—Dr. Jacob A. Goldberg,
Secretary of the Tuberculosis Association

HOPKINS' WORK WITH THE BOARD OF CHILD WELFARE (BCW) proved to be short-lived. He resigned from his position in late December 1917, publicly citing budget cuts as his reason for leaving.[1] Political pressure and administrative problems, however, led to his disillusionment with the program, which also contributed to his resignation. In addition, America's entry into the world war shifted Hopkins' focus to broader issues.

The BCW had been plagued from the very beginning with insufficient funds, which hampered Hopkins' attempts to provide adequate assistance to women who applied to the board for help. This tight financial situation increased the need for very close investigation of these families applying for assistance in order to determine need and moral eligibility, something Hopkins had hoped to avoid. However, by this time he was politically astute enough to realize that his bureau had to give the public an unambiguous impression of fiscal responsibility and economic prudence especially in the administration of public outdoor relief.

During the first nine months of the program Hopkins had received applications from 5,280 widows who qualified for pensions but the Board was only able to give assistance to 157. He and William Matthews complained to each other about how the private charities had "dumped their load over onto us before we ever had any money to work with and requested that we give their widows at least twice as much as they had ever given them."[2] The argument over which entity should be responsible for which needy population was repeated during the 1930s when Hopkins argued that women who were getting relief from the Federal Emergency Relief Administration (FERA) should have been getting money from the states' widows' pensions. Then the issue concerned a choice between two public sources of the money, his FERA (federal) budget or the local tax funds. In 1916 the choice was between public and private money. In this earlier situation, however, local politics had as much to do with funding problems as did financial constraints. As soon as Kingsbury had been ousted from the New York City Board of Child Welfare, the Board of Aldermen appropriated some $300,000 to the BCW.[3]

Although the BCW tried, with some success, to keep out of contentious city politics, Hopkins continuously confronted intra-agency politics. While he had the admiring loyalty of his staff, he often ran into conflicts with the members of the board. Matthews alluded to the divisiveness that Hopkins had to contend with in a letter recommending him for a job with the National Social Work Organization in 1916: "As Secretary of the Board of Child Welfare [Hopkins] has had a most difficult position, having to deal with a Board, some of whose members have been utterly at variance with one another most of the time. . . ."[4] These tensions, while they certainly complicated Hopkins' job, also forced him to develop administrative and organizational skills quickly. He also made every attempt to transcend the public/private rivalry. If he failed to initiate whole-hearted cooperation among members of the BCW, he managed to build harmonious relationships with local private charities by referring cases to them that did not qualify for public pensions. Most significantly, Hopkins saw his work with the BCW as groundbreaking. He had hoped to establish the efficacy of public outdoor relief for a particularly deserving group—poor women with young children—and believed that his work at the BCW would set standards for private charities and for relief administration in general.[5]

New York did have the opportunity to make its laws a standard for the nation. Illinois had passed the first mother's aid law in 1911; it took New York four years to follow suit. Many of the early experimental laws were passed very quickly, and the supporters of the New York legislation hoped that they could learn from the mistakes of others. The original acts in Illinois and Colorado targeted parents unable to care for their children, not limiting assistance to widows or deserving single mothers. However, later these laws were amended, limiting the aid to children in families with an absent male breadwinner. The New York legislation limited pensions to widows with dependent children and set as its goal the removal of children from institutions. Unlike most states, New York did not set a specified maximum amount of aid. Rather, demonstrating that the program would be cost effective and would not necessitate any increase in taxes, it linked the amount of money given the family to the cost of institutionalization. Furthermore, wanting complete control of these programs, New York was one of the few states to create a new, specialized agency to administer the pensions instead of relegating the duties to the juvenile court system or to existing local public agencies.[6] Clearly, the advocates of widows' pensions wanted to create an ideal program that could be replicated successfully in other municipalities. Social, economic, and political currents, however, made this impossible.

By 1917 Hopkins had become disillusioned by the inability of the Fusion government to initiate real reforms; he expressed this by voting for the Socialist candidate for mayor, Morris Hilquit. In 1939, during the Senate hearings for his confirmation as secretary of commerce, Hopkins claimed that he did not remember registering as a Socialist but that he did vote for Hilquit because he was "profoundly moved by a desire to keep us out of the war" and had "a great desire to see a decent administration of government in New York City. . . . I was a young man in those days, and I was expressing my idealism in that way." For Hopkins, Hilquit represented this ideal.[7]

The subsequent election of John Hylan, the Independent candidate supported by William Randolph Hearst (Sophie Loeb worked for a Hearst paper), brought to a temporary halt much of the social reform in New York City. Hopkins' disappointment with city politics, combined with the conflicts and changes within the BCW, led to his resignation. He left rather quickly, when, as Matthews wrote, "his ambitions fatally collided with politics." Despite his growing reputation as an up-and-coming social welfare administrator, he had no job offers. Having a wife and baby to support, he needed employment. When he learned that the American Red Cross (ARC) was looking for people to provide humanitarian services for the families of servicemen, he applied.[8]

The ARC provided a means for many social workers to get into war work. A memo sent out by the acting manager stated that it was the policy of the Red

Cross to employ men of draft age who were placed in Class 4 (having dependents) or Class 5 (having a physical disability) in important positions.[9] ARC Director-General W. Frank Persons (formerly of the COS and vocal opponent of public pensions for widows) was eager to hire Hopkins. He sent a telegram to Emmet White, head of the Gulf Division (consisting of Louisiana, Alabama, and Mississippi), that Hopkins "would make an excellent Assistant Director of a Bureau of Civilian Relief." He added that Hopkins was willing to serve anywhere, provided he get an annual salary of $3,000. On December 20, 1917, Hopkins accepted this offer to work as assistant director of the ARC Civilian Relief, Gulf Division.[10]

At first Hopkins had opposed American involvement in the European war, but once war was declared, he supported President Woodrow Wilson's decision, if not ideologically, at least with a modicum of patriotism. He wrote to his Grinnell classmates (who were about to celebrate their fifth reunion in 1917): "Much as I was opposed to the war in the beginning, it is my firm belief now that everyone should aid in prosecuting it as successfully and vigorously as possible." He admitted that he was merely acquiescing to the majority view and suggested that those "earnest patriots" with annual incomes in excess of $50,000 should be drafted first. "Aside from unhorsing the capitalist class, I know of no pleasanter duty than driving Kaiser Bill into Dante's retreat for autocrats."[11]

In June of 1917 Hopkins, along with 10 million others (his wife Ethel Hopkins included), registered for the draft. Because he had dependents, he was not called for his physical exam until July of the next year; by that time he was working with the ARC in New Orleans. After his physical examination uncovered defective vision in one eye, he was refused induction.[12] His position as general director of civilian relief for the ARC, however, probably would have exempted him from the draft; his work with the families of servicemen was considered vital to the war effort. Persons wrote to Hopkins' draft board informing them that "it would seriously embarrass our work if his classification were changed on the ground that he is not usefully employed."[13]

In 1918, just after Hopkins had moved his family to New Orleans, he wrote to Harvey Young, his old college chum, on the topic of the war and religion. Young seemed able to elicit religious pronouncements from Hopkins more easily than others. Hopkins asked Young, an ordained Methodist minister, if the war affected his preaching at all, adding that he himself found it very hard "to reconcile the ethics of Jesus with this war. . . . God of course is on our side." Claiming that he was no longer neutral, Hopkins wrote that he believed that it was absolutely necessary to beat the Germans. "Germany symbolizes militarism and while it exists elsewhere, it is not with the same arrogance and domination."[14] Working for the Red Cross on the home front, he wanted to do everything possible to support the war effort by helping the families of servicemen who were fighting the good fight. During this phase in his career, Hopkins, in the spirit of Grinnell College, was uniquely able to combine service to others with preservation of democracy.

President Wilson appointed Henry P. Davison, chairman of the ARC War Council, to head its Civilian Relief (also called Home Service). This division provided crucial assistance for the families of servicemen suffering from the loss of a breadwinner. These families, in one sense, had some significant similarities to the families of widows who had applied to BCW for help, and social workers had much the same attitude toward both groups—believing that not only did the families often need financial support but that they also needed paternalistic advice and guidance. A *Survey* article expressed this attitude: "The nation has taken from them more than a source of income. . . . If the ultimate victory rests with the country whose people are happiest, most healthy and of the sturdiest character, then the home of the soldier must not be allowed to suffer because he cannot be there to contribute his judgment, advice and experience. It is the task of the civilian relief worker to do this work in his place."[15] Thus the idea of the *parens patriae* continued, with a quasi-public agency acting as proxy for the husband/father. Also similar was the save-the-family impulse. The Red Cross described servicemen's families as consisting of "not merely the shiftless, the vicious, the ne'er do wells, charity's chronic objects . . . but upright self-respecting folk who ordinarily make their own way in the world."[16] Red Cross leaders declared that there was little criticism of their services because the term "Home Service" did not have the same connotation that "charity" or "relief" had. In essence, it "symbolized a democratic, considerate, neighborly relationship."[17] Although Hopkins again used this type of rhetoric during the 1930s when he portrayed unemployed workers as ordinary folks, neighbors who merely had fallen on hard times because of a national crisis, he had not used it to describe poor mothers receiving widows' pensions from the New York City BCW. Society did not expect them to make it on their own.

There was a significant difference between these groups of dependents. In 1918 America's participation in the war to end all wars endowed servicemen and their families with particular worthiness. Before the war dependent widows with children had become poor not because of an international crisis but because of tragedy on a personal level. The character of some mothers seeking public pensions from the BCW might be suspect, but the families of soldiers and sailors, as an integral part of the war effort, always would make up an unreservedly deserving population of dependents. Social service agencies, including the American Red Cross, went to great lengths to treat them with the utmost care. John Kingsbury, as New York City's commissioner of public charities, sent out a memo in June 1916 stating that the Red Cross, rather than organized charity should be responsible for helping these families "in order to apply the principles of organized charity without having the appearance of too much of the unpopular aspects of such organizations."[18] Red Cross workers did not assume that the families of servicemen needed the moral uplift that poor widows seeking pensions from the BCW might require. While financial supervision and advice was freely given, servicemen's families received considerably less oversight than did the families given mothers' pensions. Hopkins had made every attempt to preserve the dignity of widows receiving public assistance, but the general suspicion toward the poor, the fear of the pauperizing effects of public outdoor relief, and a shortage of funds had made this impossible. The emergency atmosphere of war changed this and allowed relief to be given to families with fewer restrictions.

The Red Cross Civilian Relief, as a peacetime agency, had been concerned mostly with disaster relief; with America's entrance into the war, the division focused its efforts on ensuring the soldiers' peace of mind, by making sure that their families were secure. Its stated mission was "to keep the morale of the army at its present effective state by assuring every man in our fighting forces that his folks at home are not only physically cared for, but are behind him to the limit. . . . Everyone will agree that this is one of the biggest responsibilities, if not the biggest that the Red Cross has assumed." The nation's first line of defense was a contented army, and soldiers had to know that their families were all right. Letters from home that were less than cheerful were considered "more deadly than the German bullets."[19]

The Red Cross Home Service in the Gulf Division ultimately provided support and services for 200,000 families of soldiers and sailors. Hopkins declared that "it was the business of Home Service to see to it that under all circumstances the standards of living of the families of men in service be not lowered and that Home Service Sections should, as far as possible, take the place of the men in the service while they were in the camps or at the front."[20] Hopkins perceived these families not as objects of charity but as deserving recipients of temporary assistance through the Red Cross.[21]

Hopkins spent four and a half years with the ARC, first as Director of the Gulf Division Home Service in New Orleans and then, after the war, as head of the Southern Division in Atlanta.[22] During this time he honed his administrative skills and gained national prominence as a social worker. He was personally involved in disaster relief: the Lake Charles tornado and flood of August 6, 1918, which destroyed 2,600 homes and caused a property loss of $10 million; the devastating influenza epidemic of 1918; and the Vera Cruz, Mexico, earthquake in January 1920 that caused enormous loss of life and property. Hopkins responded on-site whenever he could, often risking his life. His efforts at Lake Charles even made the newsreels. However, most of his time and energy was spent building up a strong network of Red Cross offices across the South in order to assist the families of servicemen. Hopkins brought extraordinary activity and enthusiasm to the Red Cross. He immediately set about reorganizing his division, hiring a professional staff, raising additional funds, and making sure that his division received adequate and positive publicity. If his ambition and energy unnerved some of his colleagues, these qualities attracted the attention of his superiors.[23]

Hopkins threw himself enthusiastically into his work as soon as he arrived in New Orleans. He saw this position as a great opportunity, and during the time he spent in the South, the opportunities grew.[24] Neither the Red Cross nor any other social welfare agency had been well established in the area. Consequently, there were few trained social workers. Hopkins' first order of business was to establish training institutes for Civilian Relief staff. To implement this, he hired his former Grinnell sociology professor, Garrett Wyckoff, and his fellow Grinnell alum, Florence Stewart Kerr. Hopkins' predecessor, Emmet White, had recognized the importance of a training program and had done some of the groundwork. Hopkins realized that the general attitude toward social work in the South needed "fixing" and that the ARC Civilian Relief had an opportunity to demonstrate "that honest case work with families is not only possible, but necessary." The only way this was possible, in Hopkins' mind, was to employ a staff of trained, professional social workers. Hoping to educate the public as well as the staff, he held conferences and roundtable discussions to present the mission of Civilian Relief to the community. Not only did the people attending learn about Home Relief work, but Hopkins and his staff gained important information from them on local conditions.[25]

Hopkins next attacked the general disorganization of Home Relief services. He streamlined office procedures while instituting professional standards for all of his staff.[26] Jane Hoey, who had been Hopkins' assistant at the BCW, remembered "[w]e resigned at the same time from the Board of Child Welfare because the Board would not allow us to have any supervisors in a large organization here, so I had to be the only supervisor in the agency. We couldn't go on with that, and we both resigned." Like Hopkins, Hoey worked for the ARC, the Atlantic Division, during the war years, and like many who worked with and for him, she considered Hopkins an exceedingly able and imaginative social worker.[27] In July 1918 Hopkins became acting division director of the Gulf Division when his boss, Emmet White, was drafted into the army. By this time the ARC had over 500 branches in the Gulf Division; many still did not have Home Service. Hopkins' goal was to have services in every chapter by August 1, 1918, and he urged that the ARC staff get in touch with every serviceman's family by letter. Another of his Grinnell professors joined him in this work; Paul Peck was appointed field director at Camp Shelby, Mississippi. Both Wyckoff and Peck took considerable salary cuts to work for Hopkins at the ARC.[28] Hopkins' strong support of the training institutes points to his continued dedication to the professionalization of social work. Not only did the institutes successfully turn out a group of trained social workers, but they also added to the status of the ARC worker. Hopkins, proud of his efforts in this area, reported that many of those who taught in the institutes looked upon their work as a possible profession "largely due to a genuine interest in a new method of dealing with the child and his problems."[29]

Hopkins campaigned for more ARC involvement in providing a broad menu of social services and an increasing number of families received help from Civilian Relief sections. By November 1918 17,000 families were served, 8,000 more than in any previous month.[30] This expansion, along with increased Red Cross activities in Europe, necessitated a carefully planned campaign for more contributions. With the enthusiastic support of former president Theodore Roosevelt and President Wilson, the Red Cross drew on the services of local leaders, service organizations, entertainers, and the media to solicit funds. Slackers were castigated in a somewhat hysterical press. The result was "a spontaneous and generous outpouring of contributions." Thus, due in part to the "psychosis of the war," the Red Cross did not suffer from underfunding.[31]

Home Service in the ARC's Gulf Division flourished and expanded under Hopkins' direction. In late January of 1919 one of Hopkins' assistants, W. J. Leppert, wrote that two years previously the division had presented "an absolutely virgin field for concerted humanitarian action." By 1919 more than 500,000 adults and 250,000 youngsters were members of the ARC in the three states of the Gulf Division, with 239 Home Service sections. This represented a growth from three sections with 3,000 members. Leppert indicated his strong feeling that the division's work should continue in order to ensure that the patriotism fostered during wartime would continue during peacetime. Hopkins could not have agreed with him more.[32]

By the end of the war, ARC Home Service/Civilian Relief was providing services to about 15,000 families each month, with a staff of 200 volunteers and professionals. In New Orleans the ARC handled more families each month than private charities handled in a year. Hopkins proved equal to this huge administrative task. According to biographer George McJimsey, "[a]lmost overnight, he had brought professional social work to the South." Hopkins accomplished this, in part, by establishing good relations with local organizations. He assured them that the Red Cross had no ambition to supplant them, and he held frequent conferences where he discussed ways they could work together.[33] While Hopkins demanded a great deal from his staff and would not tolerate inefficiency, he also developed very positive relationships with those who worked for him. His then wife, Ethel Gross, remembered that he had a "wonderful and personal way with them," that he liked people and listened carefully to what they had to say. This was a tremendous asset for Hopkins, especially in his later work during the Great Depression.[34]

With demobilization after November 1918, the ARC set itself to the task of preparing for peacetime programs. Hopkins sent out a letter to the governors of the states within his division suggesting a conference so that they could discuss the future of the ARC Civilian Relief. Most of the controversy was over centralization vs. decentralization. This issue boiled down to whether ARC Home Service, a national program, should absorb all peacetime activities or let local charities take over. During the war, the ARC programs essentially had taken over the delivery of social service. Historian John F. McClymer noted that the Red Cross drained staff, money, and resources from private agencies. When the war ended and military morale no longer was a concern, local social workers and their agencies hoped to regain some of their previous funding and power.[35]

Many social workers recognized that the programs established by the ARC Home Service were "the best opportunity that the country has ever presented for the widespread, practical teaching of the aims and ideals of social service." But few had any hope that Home Service could be adapted to peacetime conditions. Hopkins was at first in favor of local initiative ("on general principles"), but at a conference in Jackson, Mississippi, he saw that "local feeling runs very strongly in the direction of turning the entire work over to the Home Service Section." Therefore, he threw his support behind the continuation of Home Service sections. He consequently wrote a report in which he presented three alternatives: completely liquidate the division, expand it to absorb all civilian families in need, or leave it up to each community to decide. He and others considered liquidation of the division to be ill-advised because Home Service was "a social asset of great value and in a large part of the country the only social asset of its kind now in existence." The second alternative seemed to be merely "federalizing the direction of an unprecedented large social service enterprise. . . . It is not in tune with the traditions and mental habits of the American people who have always hesitated to federalize movements which touch intimately the lives and purposes of our people." Only with the coming of a great national emergency did Hopkins change his attitude about this. The third alternative, leaving it up to the community to decide, seemed to Hopkins the most logical solution.[36]

Hopkins agreed with ARC leaders that Home Service could do for civilians what it did for servicemen and their families in one respect. It would provide not charity but "a means of giving practical, organized expression to the spirit of neighborly helpfulness." From a practical standpoint, however, few local social service agencies in the Gulf Division, public or private, were able to take up the work. Although the end of the war brought about a new spirit within the ARC, Hopkins felt strongly that the "organized neighborliness" of Red Cross Home Relief should continue, with each community making the decision for itself whether to let the Red Cross division absorb the work of local agencies.[37] In March 1919 Hopkins declared "[a]ll of us are going after the work now with a renewed enthusiasm and with the pleasant thought that we have a big job to do, whose success and development can only be measured by our ability to transfer our present Home Service into a broader community service."[38]

The Armistice, consequently, brought internal strife to the ARC Civilian Relief. W. Frank Persons, like Hopkins, had worked diligently to build the division into an efficient organization. However, Persons had resigned from the ARC in December 1918 largely because he resented the fact that his Division of Civilian Relief had been put under the authority of the Division of Military Relief.[39] Writing Hopkins about his resignation, Persons told him this was the "wreck" of his ambition but that he "should rather be a day laborer with my conscience as it is, than to carry with me always the burden of shame and hypocrisy that would have followed the conscious betrayal of our rights and our ideals. No one has shown a truer spirit or done a better job than you."[40] Possibly as a reaction to this and to internal problems, Hopkins began to put out some tentative feelers for another job.

About this time (late in the year 1918), Hopkins had just recovered from another serious bout with pneumonia, probably brought about by overwork and influenza (contracted during the epidemic). In a weakened physical condition, he might have been especially susceptible to thoughts of moving back to New York City, the place he now considered home. William Matthews, still head of the AICP's Department of Family Welfare, sorely missed working with Hopkins. His agency had been stretched to the limits during the war years, having been forced to fill in for other organizations due to the lack of manpower. He campaigned for Hopkins' return: "I have not forgotten the old days and I have yet to meet the person other than yourself whom I would sooner have here with me."[41] But it was not to be.

Hopkins did not want to re-create the old days. Instead he looked for advancement within a national organization like the ARC. In the spring of 1920, anticipating a merger between the Gulf Division and the Southeastern Division as part of postwar reorganization, he successfully campaigned to be named division manager. When Leigh Carroll finally did resign in the summer of 1920, Hopkins succeeded him. When the merger occurred later in the year, Hopkins was appointed manager of the newly created Southern Division, headquartered in Atlanta.[42] George McJimsey correctly observed that, as a result of this astute move, Hopkins "entered the upper ranks of social work administration."[43] It was the poorest region in the nation, with a population suffering acutely from health problems, especially tuberculosis, and Hopkins directed a good deal of his efforts to health issues.

In Atlanta, Hopkins felt isolated from the larger urban social work community, and he especially missed New York City. His discontent was further fueled by his inability to initiate all of the reforms he felt necessary. Home Service was no longer expanding and Hopkins missed being at the hub of activity. Typically, he looked around for new work. The National Child Labor Committee (NCLC), under the directorship of Owen Lovejoy, offered him a position as executive assistant at an annual salary of $6,000. This might have appealed to Hopkins because the NCLC was an important national organization and the future of the ARC Home Relief seemed questionable.[44] Hopkins also looked farther afield. He wrote Frank Persons, who was then the director of administration for the International League of Red Cross Societies, that he would be interested in a job in Geneva. Persons replied in September 1919 offering him the job, waxing nostalgic about "the time when we were doing pioneer work and laboring desperately to get our log house completed before the cold weather struck us."[45] He recognized Hopkins' administrative talents and knew he could make good use of him in Geneva. However, the new chairman of the ARC, Dr. Livingston Farrand, despite pressure from Europe, refused to let Hopkins go. Hopkins regretted that he did not get the appointment. Although he was complimented by ARC's fight to keep him, he nevertheless wanted to make up his own mind about whether to accept a job offer.[46]

By 1920 another avenue opened up for him outside of the ARC. At the end of the Mitchel administration in New York City, John Kingsbury went to work for the Serbian Child Welfare Association of America as chairman of the executive committee. William Doherty followed his boss to the association as overseas commissioner and wrote to Hopkins offering him a job in Serbia. However, he advised Hopkins against taking his family with him.[47] For this reason, Hopkins never did give the offer serious consideration and continued with his work in Atlanta.

Probably in 1919 or 1920, Hopkins scribbled an interesting self-critical note on the back of some ARC stationery:

> Hopkins impresses us all here as being one of the most capable young men we
> have in the service. On the other hand he seems to me to be a little overambitious
> and this to an extent indicates a greater measure of self-seeking than I fully like.

I would not of course have him other than ambitious but for a young man he has already gone pretty far and he can afford not to aim too high at once. While I believe he has made a singularly fine record at the Gulf Dist., I am quite sure that he would not have, had not your steady hand and your knowledge of southern conditions been there to help him.

I believe it is absolutely essential to complete success in the Gulf Division . . . to have your help and influence at all times. If Hopkins keeps both feet on the ground and exercises a little patience he should become a very valuable man to the R. C.[48]

This note was ostensibly a draft for a letter that the ARC general manager, Frederic Munroe, would send to Leigh Carroll. Hopkins wanted to help Monroe convince Carroll not to resign and to remain with the Red Cross, because he wanted Carroll's help in running the Gulf Division.[49] The note demonstrates not only Hopkin's remarkable self-awareness at this time but also his willingness to engage in office intrigue for the perceived good of the agency.

Hopkins' hard work, his ability to elicit a cooperative attitude and open communication among his staff, as well as his untiring dedication to providing effective services to clients inspired those who worked for him.[50] During his years with the Red Cross, Hopkins developed a style that would become emblematic of his New Deal agencies: free and open exchange of ideas during frequent, informal staff conferences. William Matthews described Hopkins' meetings: "Well, they are just like old time prayer meetings."[51] All of these efforts were part of Hopkins' long-term plan to involve the ARC in broader social problems and at the same time to expand the scope of his work.[52]

Particularly in the South, race relations underlay many of these broader social problems. Hopkins did not seem to have involved himself or his agency in issues dealing with racial inequality, and evidence suggests that Ethel and Harry Hopkins had very little contact with blacks in the South during this period except for domestic help. Both seemed to have the impression that African Americans were happy and well cared for by their employers. In 1964 Ethel Hopkins recalled that she had "heard about the south and how they treated their Negroes" and that she expected to find "a sad, downtrodden group of people." She claimed to be very surprised when she found that they "were very happy . . . were singing and gay and they were dressed in gay clothes, wonderful colors." She and Harry found them "picturesque" rather than "the sad, [deprived], abused people" they expected to find. The Hopkins family befriended a young social worker named Belle Pike whose family owned a sugar plantation on the Mississippi near New Orleans. Harry and Ethel spent several weekends visiting there, during which time they learned something about local attitudes toward race. Ethel noted that on the Pike plantation the black workers were housed, fed, clothed, cared for when sick, and "all their needs were supplied just as though they were children."[53] Her lack of insight into the conditions that she observed here might have been tainted by the hardships she herself experienced as a young child in the urban ghetto. Her inability to see below the surface reflects a concern with basic material needs rather than a concern with the universal human need for independence and self-determination.

Ethel and Harry also learned from the few African Americans they themselves knew. Ethel remembered that when she employed a maid to help in the house, she discovered that there were "different stratas of society among the Negroes. Those who worked in the home, lived in the house and were nursemaids, house niggers they called them [and] they were just part of the family." Others who came in to do the washing in large outdoors tubs heated by charcoal burners, according to Ethel, were "expected to steal," and thought it was their right to take anything that was left out. And, she added, when blacks migrated north, "they did the same thing and would always expect that anything left out was theirs. . . . And those were all new ideas to me." Ethel and Harry Hopkins gathered these impressions from their mutual experiences, and, according to Ethel, they felt much the same way about the Blacks with whom they came into contact. Harry, however, seemed more interested in Black culture than Ethel. He attended at least one baptism held in Mississippi and visited the churches several times, standing in the back, enjoying the theatricality of the preaching and singing.[54]

The Hopkins' understanding of race relations in the South was certainly not enlightened. Their limited experience with African Americans almost ensured that they would absorb some of the local attitudes, and, although they never demonstrated overt racial bigotry, they did seem to accept the idea of a segregated society. It seems that they also temporarily adopted the paternalistic attitude so prevalent in the Deep South. Yet Hopkins' New Deal work programs always mandated equal pay for blacks, especially in the South, and he insisted that his programs be free of any racial bias. His extensive traveling during this period may have moderated the negative effects of southern racial attitudes. In addition, his early religious training surely mitigated against racial prejudice.

Hopkins' four-and-a-half-year stint with the American Red Cross, a national organization with centralized administration, marked an important step in his social work career. In 1919 he wrote: "Direction from 'above' is purely for the purpose of liberating the energies of the local communities, of helping them to express themselves better, of putting tools in their hands."[55] This configuration served as a training ground for Hopkins' growing ability to define relations between the states and the national government—an ability he tapped into a decade later. His national relief agencies were subject to central administration but still had a certain amount of autonomy at the state level.

Work with the Red Cross broadened Hopkins' view of relief work and the interdependence of communities across the nation as well as across the world.[56] Nevertheless, he saw the limitations this work had for his career, and he was an ambitious man. He wanted to leave the South, and so did his wife.[57] Hopkins resigned from the ARC in September 1922, writing to Leigh Carroll that he had been giving a lot of thought to his future career and that it seemed clear to him "that the possibilities for growth and advancement in my present job are rather meagre."[58] Most of his colleagues were truly sorry to see him go. One of his field representatives, Mrs. Butler, expressed the general sentiment of Hopkins' staff when she wrote that she did not see how she could work under anyone else. "When I was in trouble, I always felt that, in you, I had a personal friend to whom I could turn for protection and advice. . . . I can never cease to miss you . . . I think it is decidedly the worst thing that could have happened to the Red Cross."[59]

Conditions in the gulf region, such as the lack of an organized group of social welfare agencies, the wartime feelings of extreme patriotism, and the seemingly unending supply of volunteers, helped Hopkins attain a position of prominence within his chosen profession. Like the situation in New York in 1913, when he was a Democrat when Democrats were on the rise, and a social worker when there was mass unemployment, the time again was ripe for a man with Hopkins' talents. When the United States entered the war, the Red Cross increased its activities enormously to meet the needs at home and abroad. Division headquarters granted a good deal of autonomy to its regional offices, and Hopkins took the opportunity to build an effective, professionally-staffed agency. Harry Hopkins carefully nurtured associations with such people as Kingsbury and Leigh Carroll of the Red Cross.[60] He was determined not to let opportunity for professional advancement pass him by.

As part of his plan to establish himself in his profession, Hopkins joined with other social workers in June 1921 to form an association for the purpose of formulating professional social work standards. He helped draft a charter for the American Association of Social Workers (AASW) and was elected president in 1923. He tried to keep control of the association situated in the Northeast, particularly in New York City, ostensibly to ensure that it would have competent leadership. This, however, also can be interpreted as a demonstration of his continuing rejection of the rural Midwest as narrow-minded and backward. Nevertheless, the strong regional feelings of local committees overrode his proposal to concentrate authority in an executive committee controlled by a small group of eastern social work leaders. As president of the AASW, Hopkins declared that social workers were in the vanguard of the fight for social justice. He maintained that social progress came about as the immediate consequence of the humanitarian impulses and the scientific, professional techniques of the social worker. This was a clear echo of his Grinnell experience where his professors propounded the idea that social service was part of the "scientific spirit of the age."[61]

When Hopkins left the ARC, he again found himself looking for a job. Although he had a growing family to support, he seemed confident that his national reputation as a social worker would serve to employ him quickly. Ethel Hopkins recalled that when her husband heard that a position with a tuberculosis project in New York was open, his attitude was "if they need me they will call," and it took some urging on her part to get him to send a wire to apply for the position.[62] It is difficult to understand his reluctance because it seemed a job for which he was ideally suited. And he had access. His old friend and mentor, John Kingsbury, had left the Serbian Child Welfare Association of America, and had become director of the Milbank Fund,[63] a public health organization in New York City, newly committed to the old ideal of "emphasizing preventive work rather than simple charity." Kingsbury had been working on three concurrent health demonstrations—rural, small city, and large metropolis—to implement interest in public health. The larger purpose was to prevent tuberculosis. In this endeavor, he engaged the assistance of Bailey Burritt, director of the Association for Improving the Condition of the Poor (AICP), Homer Folks of the State Charities Aid Association (SCAA), and Dr. Donald Armstrong of the Community Health and Tuberculosis Demonstration in Framingham, Massachusetts (which provided the model).[64]

New York City was, not surprisingly, selected as the site of the large metropolis demonstration program. This Bellevue-Yorkville demonstration (officially begun in 1924) was jointly run by the Milbank Fund, the AICP and the SCAA in order to "apply the collective wisdom of a demonstration to complex metropolitan health problems that had previously defied solution."[65] One of the most important objectives of the project included the integration of health functions, both public and private, so as to ensure adequate health facilities for the city, with an emphasis on the prevention of tuberculosis, communicable children's diseases, and venereal diseases. The program's overriding principles included a dedication to the scientific method, cooperation between public and private agencies, and public (i.e., the municipal health department) responsibility for health work. For Hopkins, this would have been a very comfortable policy, given his background with the BCW and the ARC, where close cooperation between public and private organizations served as a trademark of his administrative style.[66]

In May 1922 AICP director Burritt offered Hopkins the job of heading up this demonstration project and in September Hopkins accepted. He was appointed assistant director of the AICP at $8,000 per year.[67] His salary was paid out of a special account of the New York Tuberculosis Association (NYTBA) and probably was supported by the Millbank Fund, which had traditionally maintained a close relationship with the AICP.[68] The AICP's Health Division was financed separately by the fund. Because of this Hopkins felt that he should be able to operate independently of Burritt's authority as head of the AICP. At the ARC, Hopkins had a great deal of autonomy; he was able to run his agency according to his own administrative style. In New York City, his old territory, he found it difficult to take orders from someone whose authority he did not accept. This situation caused considerable friction between the two divisions and the two men.

Robert Sherwood wrote that because Hopkins "was one who always chafed at ordinary, orderly administrative procedure, . . . he found himself so completely at home in the unconventional Roosevelt scheme of things." It was not so much Hopkins' unconventionality that made him feel so comfortable in the Roosevelt administration; it was more likely the position of power and influence that he had attained. Hopkins always had sought a power base with enough autonomy to act decisively. Nevertheless, if he felt constrained by the AICP chain of command, he managed to bury his resentment sufficiently to get on with his job. Because he was able to do this, much of his work in New York City during this period readied him for the myriad of administrative and political problems he later encountered in Washington.

One of the very valuable lessons that Hopkins learned from his experiences with relief organizations was that the successful public servant could amass a more useful currency than mere dollars. He learned that the economy of social service often was based on power. Sherwood noted "a distinct resemblance between the point of view of the welfare worker and that of the voluntary civil servant. Both were commercially unselfish, animated by public spirit and reconciled to careers uncomplicated by the profit motive. It was therefore not unnatural that both should strive to be paid off in the currency of increased authority and opportunity to extend influence."[69] Although Hopkins embroiled himself in this dispute with Burritt for reasons of power and authority, not for reasons of remuneration, he also was dedicated to the project's aim of wiping out tuberculosis.

One of the basic tenets of the social work profession held that illness was a prime cause of poverty. Hopkins had developed a keen interest in health issues through his prior work. His interest in tuberculosis could well have stemmed from the fact that his mother had contracted the disease in 1912.[70] Tuberculosis, then commonly known as consumption, was especially prevalent in poor areas and often was fatal. Hopkins had become familiar with the devastation the disease could inflict on a family when he administered widows' pensions in New York City. His work at the ARC further convinced him that the eradication or at least the control of this disease would go far in preventing much of the poverty that plagued rural as well as urban areas.[71]

Hopkins was assigned the duty of making a statistical analysis of disease in New York City, a task he eagerly accepted. He was delighted to be back in the city he loved. However, when he arrived to take charge, he was faced with yet another political tangle. The city's Bureau of Preventable Diseases was jockeying for a position of leadership in the field of disease prevention. Again he found himself in the midst of a turf war. Although the NYTBA had stepped into the fray and proposed that the AICP manage the program, a plan that called for cooperation between the city health commissioner and the AICP. In mid-1924, when the work on the Bellvue-Yorkville project was nearing completion, Dr. James Alexander Miller offered Hopkins the presidency of the NYTBA, and Hopkins tendered his resignation to the AICP. When Hopkins took over as executive director, the NYTBA had a surplus of $90,000. When he left it seven years later, it carried a deficit of $40,000. But everyone close to the association was delighted with Hopkins' work there. The association had grown enormously, had sold more of its famous Christmas seals than ever before, and, in early 1925, had absorbed the New York Heart Association (NYHA).[72]

Much of his work for the NYTBA had been focused on simplifying and uniting the many services for disease prevention. Hopkins was convinced that an agency created to prevent tuberculosis could easily direct its talents and energies toward preventing any other disease. He noted: "The machinery at any rate is already set up so that with a relatively small expense a new and specialized campaign can be developed within one organization."[73] The consolidation of the NYTBA and the NYHA, which resulted in the New York Tuberculosis and Health Association (NYTBHA), allowed the Heart Association to take advantage of much-needed educational, public relations, and informational services already in place at the Tuberculosis Association. As a result, a great deal of money was saved. Hopkins drove himself relentlessly during these years. He further expanded the scope of the TBA with the absorption of the Children's Welfare Federation, the Associated Out-Patient Clinic, and the Allied Dental Clinic. By 1930 the activities of the NYTBHA encompassed the areas of Manhattan, the Bronx, and Staten Island, serving a population of more than 3 million people.[74]

Hopkins' frenetic energy came at a price. Dr. Jacob A. Goldberg, secretary of NYTBA, described Hopkins as perpetually nervous and addicted to coffee and cigarettes. Goldberg said that Hopkins, always a careless dresser, often looked like "he had spent the previous night sleeping in a hayloft." So focused was Hopkins on the implementation of a project, he would never worry about its financing until later: "then he would scramble to get the money."[75] But in his mind this was justifiable. Illness, which came about as a result of an unfriendly and unhealthy environment, was merely another form of social injustice. Hopkins' critics pointed to his soon-to-be-characteristic free spending style, but this never bothered him. He cared little for the bottom line; his primary concern was human need. The money always came second, and it almost always did come. His lack of interest in money could well have stemmed from his always having worked for nonprofit agencies where the stock-in-trade was power and influence rather than profit; or from the tenets of the Ethical Culture Society; or from his mother's religious ethic. The mixture of altruism and ambition that was characteristic of Hopkins' personality later manifested itself in intense bursts of activity for extended periods; by 1934, it had also resulted in an ulcer.

By the mid-1920s, Hopkins had become a well-known figure in social work circles. In 1926 he spoke at the annual meeting of the National Conference of Social Work on the influence of social work on the public health movement in America. Hopkins always connected advancements in public health with social work rather than medicine. For him social justice became interlocked with public health. He declared that the "fields of social work and public health are inseparable" and that the "humanitarian impulses" of social workers had led to important social action in the field of public health. The NYTBA had effectively controlled disease and thus lessened the incidence of poverty. Hopkins believed that "every phase of public health work can be traced in part to the influence of private voluntary social groups demanding the attention of a passive public."[76]

Realizing that any adequate study of health conditions could not be confined by local jurisdictions, Hopkins typically began to think in larger and broader terms for his program.[77] For him, public health work drew attention to situations in the environment that affected the well-being of society: sanitation, plumbing, pure milk, health education, and especially health demonstration projects. The program's most important element, its scientific basis, became the model for other welfare agencies. This combination of science and humanitarianism, Hopkins believed, led to progress in the field of social welfare.[78]

Hopkins demonstrated the nature of his administrative style—a style he later perfected in Washington—in 1928. He and his colleague, former health commissioner for New York City, Dr. Haven Emerson, were walking past a work site on 42nd Street where men were drilling in the roadway. Dr. Emerson mentioned that these men were very susceptible to a disease called silicosis because of the silica dust that arose while they were drilling. Although Hopkins did not know what silicosis was, he immediately got as much information as he could about the disease and set out to remedy what he saw as the workers' needless suffering. He initiated a study of the incidence of the disease among city construction workers. As a result of this study, within one year a vacuum device was developed that successfully eliminated the dangerous dust. Furthermore, silicosis was designated as a compensable disease under workmen's compensation laws. Such was Hopkins' rather straightforward method of dealing with an immediate problem—find out as much as he could about it, formulate solutions, and select alternatives.[79] However, he also realized how important it was to balance competing interests in order to get the job done. Furthermore, he developed administrative policies that increased the efficiency of this staff. Hopkins relied on frequent and informal staff meetings because he especially valued cooperation and consensus among his workers.

When Hopkins was tapped by Governor Franklin Delano Roosevelt in 1931 to become executive director and later chairman of the Temporary Emergency Relief Agency (TERA), he brought to the job almost twenty years of experience in social welfare during which he had developed a distinctive style and a social philosophy that was a conglomeration of Populism, liberal progressivism, Social Gospel, and compassion for the underdog. He was contemptuous of bureaucracy, rejected the formalism of organization charts, and asserted that "effective administration was a mix of art and science, personality and skill, the expressive and the instrumental."[80]

Hopkins resigned from the NYTBHA on June 7, 1933. Linsley R. Williams, the president of the association, accepted his resignation with regret, and Vice President Homer Folks wrote a testimonial citing the association's enormous growth during the first six years of Hopkins' tenure: "Mr. Hopkins' intelligence, his industry, his initiative and balanced judgment made him a recognized force in the social work of the community."[81]

The social, economic, and political environment in Iowa, New York City, and the South certainly contributed to Hopkins' increasing influence within the social work profession. The economic depression and the strong progressive atmosphere in New York City when he worked for private charitable agencies, the increasing need for public pensions for poor mothers when he ran the BCW, the patriotism during the war years when he was building an agency for the Red Cross, and the prevailing emphasis on public health issues while he was with the New York Tuberculosis Association all combined to propel Hopkins to a position of prominence in 1931.

While Hopkins' career was booming, his personal life was deteriorating. When they returned to New York, Harry and Ethel had two sons: David, born in

New York City in 1914, and Robert, born in Atlanta in 1921. In 1920 an infant daughter died of whooping cough. By 1927 the marriage was showing signs of strain. Ethel, a woman of remarkable inner strength, relished her role as wife and mother. She also was ambitious for her husband and wanted very much to be part of his public life. She took a proud interest in his career and worked part-time so that she could earn enough to hire someone to care for the children. "I had this idea that I wanted to always be available to do things with him. . . . I wanted to be able to go places with him at night, to meetings and things and not be tied down."[82] She had married Harry in 1913 because they were very much in love, but each offered the other something more. For Ethel, Harry was her ticket to mainstream America, her entrée into the middle-class world she had always longed to join. For Harry, Ethel was to be a steadying influence. In 1913 she proudly acted as his guide to New York City's vibrant streets. She wanted to continue in this role; he wanted a silent partner and a mother for his children. Hopkins loved his family, but the larger world always would have the greater part of his attention. This devotion to his job developed into the fault line of their relationship.

One of the reasons Hopkins left the ARC was that his job involved too much travel. He realized that he needed to spend more time at home with his family. When they returned to New York, they first rented an apartment near Columbia University and then took a house on Sunnyside Drive in Ludlow, a little town just south of Yonkers, to be near John and Mabel Kingsbury. The Burritts also lived in the neighborhood. Although Hopkins had resisted the move to the suburbs (he was thoroughly urban by now), both he and Ethel were very glad to be back once more amongst their friends in New York. Within a year they were forced to move because the Yonkers house was in terrible disrepair. Again against Harry's wishes, they moved farther into the suburbs, this time near Donald and Eunice Armstrong. Here their third son, Stephen, was born in 1925.[83] The family lived in Sparta, a section of Scarborough, where architect and developer Frank Vanderlipp had remodeled some homes that had been badly neglected, perhaps due to the fact that they were very close to Sing Sing Prison. Although many wealthy people lived in Scarborough, Vanderlipp wanted to make these homes available to professionals like Hopkins, who did not make a great deal of money. The rent was scaled to what the family could afford. Vanderlipp also founded the very progressive Scarborough School where the Hopkinses placed sons David and Robert. Here the tuition also was scaled to the family's means.[84]

The Hopkins family seemed to be living an idyllic life. Summers were spent in Woodstock with the Kingsburys. Harry kept up a cheerful correspondence with his Grinnell classmates and with his family. But the image of happy middle-class family dissolved as trouble developed between Harry and Ethel.[85]

In 1926 Harry Hopkins met a young woman, Barbara Duncan, who worked for the New York Tuberculosis Association. She came from a very respectable upper-middle-class family in Port Huron, Michigan, and had attended the University of Michigan for two years before training as a nurse in New York City's Bellevue Hospital. Harry fell in love with her and saw her as often as he could.[86] Tensions within the Hopkins family understandably began to mount, although Ethel did not know about Harry's affair. Seeking escape from marital discord, Ethel took a trip to New Orleans in late 1927, ostensibly to visit friends. The separation did not help. In a letter to Harry she expressed both her anger and her sadness over the situation: "As far as I am personally concerned, prolonging my absence from home won't help me to solve my problems." But she worried that Harry did not want her to come home. "But if you think I should stay away longer I can do it by doing one of two things." She wrote, most uncharacteristically, she could either get a job and earn her own way or pursue a life of pleasure. "If I could use my powers in this direction it would be sufficiently interesting and diverting so that I would worry less and less about getting back to the children." She added that she could "develop a hard-boiled quality that is quite an asset in many ways and that I could never develop living with someone I love. . . . I want to be free. I'd like to come home to the children as I planned on November 21st. But if you are not ready to have me come I can make very definite plans along these lines and stay away for one month or even two months longer. This kind of life might make me very unfit to take up my duties at home again—but that is the chance we take and I don't think I do that kind of job particularly well any way."[87]

Ethel had always felt that her role as wife and mother was the most important in her life, and she took her duties very seriously. She read the latest volumes on child care and health; she was diligent in the care she gave her three children; she was proud of the support she gave to her husband's career. The tone and the content of this letter, so unlike Ethel, attests to the depth of the hurt that she must have felt at Harry's neglect—whether real or perceived. Harry's response to this letter, a brief telegram four days later, merely said that he was expecting her on the twenty-first. He made no reference to her threats or to her feelings. Hopkins consistently demonstrated great sympathy for the masses of people suffering from deprivation and expended enormous efforts in easing their pain, but he could not muster the same feeling for those closest to him.

Hopkins felt comfortable with the traditional gender roles within the family. His work with the BCW attested to this. Although Ethel, too, regarded her role with the family as proper and valuable, she did not want to be subsumed by her husband's career. The long hours and the time he spent away from his family irritated her; she no longer felt part of his life and they did not have the intimacy she longed for. On the other hand, her persistent demands for attention and inclusion may not have sat well with him during this busy and developmental time in his life.[88]

Their relationship did not improve over the next few years. In an attempt to address his problems, Hopkins underwent psychoanalysis with Dr. Frankwood E. Williams, a physician connected with the Milbank Fund who had been recommended by John Kingsbury. Essentially, Hopkins sought the doctor's help in getting over Barbara Duncan. Working with Dr. Williams seemed to make Hopkins more open and ready to discuss his problems but did not help the marriage. In order to put some distance between Harry and his marital problems, Kingsbury suggested that Hopkins take a trip to Europe with him; his daughter, Jean Kingsbury; and Katherine Lenroot to attend the first International Conference of Social Work in Paris in the summer of 1928. This trip was also to be a fact-finding trip to England to look into other social work methodologies. On the voyage over to Europe, Hopkins discussed his marriage with Kingsbury. Speaking openly about personal matters, especially his marital troubles, was extremely uncharacteristic for Hopkins. Dr. Williams' treatment seemed to make him more garrulous than usual. In Kingsbury's notes for his autobiography there is brief reference to what Hopkins told him on the SS *Amsterdam*. He mentioned Ethel's "domineering" personality, her intense needs, her "Jewishness," and the fact that he did not get along with her family as reasons for the separation. Kingsbury wrote that Hopkins told him that he had married Ethel because he felt sorry for the poor struggling Jewish girl and also to shock his Methodist family back in Iowa; his estrangement to Ethel had been caused by her Jewish relatives whom he did not like. Hopkins insisted that he was not interested in another woman. This last statement was patently untrue. He had been seeing Barbara Duncan for two years. It is also hard to believe that in 1913 Hopkins, fresh from Iowa, could feel anything like pity for Ethel when she was so actively involved in the social and political life of New York City. Hopkins, it is true, did not get along with Ethel's siblings, but since they were rarely around this should not have been too much of a problem. One can only conjecture that Hopkins was suffering from an extreme case of guilt over Barbara Duncan and needed to justify what he was doing in the eyes of his mentor, John Kingsbury. Still, his lack of honesty about his personal life did him little credit.

Harry and Ethel separated in September of 1929; she divorced him on May 11, 1931. Hopkins married Barbara Duncan one month later. He continued to support his sons and, until he died, gave half of his salary to Ethel. In 1964 Ethel, seemingly still unable to accept the fact that Harry had left her for another woman, remarked that the breakup of the marriage "had to do with a kind of environment and the kind of atmosphere [of] free and easy kind of . . . friendships and relationships. . . . We had a wonderful relationship . . . even though we were very different in many ways . . . we just grew apart." Harry's family took Ethel's side and for years his sister, Adah Hopkins Aime, would not speak to her brother because of the way he had treated Ethel.[89]

In 1925, when Hopkins jokingly described his family as typical of characters in Sinclair Lewis novels, he may have been revealing a resentment toward the very strong women in the Hopkins family—Anna, Adah, and Ethel.[90] In 1945 Sidney Hyman, a close friend of Harry Hopkins and Robert Sherwood's colleague, said Hopkins felt this dominating quality in Ethel. Today we might interpret it differently. Ethel was indeed a strong woman, a feminist who saw her role as wife and mother as both vital and demanding. Hopkins, ambitious, restless, and somewhat careless in his personal relationships, realized that he had "married a woman who took him by the hand and that he wanted to walk without a leadstring." He told John Kingsbury that Ethel did not give him enough rope.[91]

Although she was no longer part of Hopkins' public life, Ethel insisted on her place as the mother of his children. When tragedy struck the family in 1944 with the death of their youngest son, Stephen, in the Pacific campaign, Ethel wrote a controlled but angry letter to several newspapers that was printed in *Time* magazine. It reveals a great deal about her spirit:

> Notification has just come to me that Stephen, my youngest son, aged 18, a private first class in the United States Marine Corps, was killed in action. . . . I am writing this to you in order to call to your attention that Stephen, Robert and David are my three sons as well as the sons of Harry. L. Hopkins, confidential advisor to President Roosevelt. In all your news items and stories you either completely omit this fact or state it incorrectly. It has been my joy and privilege to bring up my three sons—to plan for their well-being and education, and I wish to be identified with them.[92]

Ethel explained her feelings to Harry in a letter: "I wouldn't hurt you for anything in the world, but when the heart breaking news came about Stephen I wanted to shout from the housetops, over and over again—my son Stephen was killed. I had to say it over and over again to believe it. I could not bear to be further removed from him by not being identified with him. It's terribly important to me to be his Mother at this time, just as important as when he was born."[93]

Despite their separation and divorce just two years before Hopkins gained national prominence, the strong and very positive influence Ethel had exerted on her husband contributed to his professional development. She was married to Harry during an extremely important phase of his life, and her insights into his character provide us with clues to his social philosophy. When they first met Harry was immediately drawn to her vitality as well as her exoticism. He also was attracted to her connection with important people. Hopkins had never been outside of Grinnell; Ethel had been on two trips to Europe with Katherine Mackay, had been active in the suffrage movement, and had access to prominent social workers through her association with Christodora House. Her intelligence, her energy, and especially her love and ambition for him did a great deal to further his career. Harry and Ethel corresponded frequently after 1931, mostly about the children, but there is no evidence that they ever saw each other again. Ethel eventually ran a theater arts workshop for children in Scarsdale, New York, raised their three sons, worked for the Red Cross during World War II, and became an accomplished artist. In 1949, three years after Hopkins' death, she remarried. Ethel Gross Hopkins Conant died in 1976 in Sydney, Australia, at the age of ninety.

The relationship between these two remarkable people marked a historical moment when the private clearly intruded into the public. During their courtship years, Ethel had acted as Harry's guide and as a mentor and she later nurtured her husband's ambition for position and power. Their divorce after 17 years of marriage released him from the restraints of family life and allowed him to pursue the very ambitions that had been brewing since 1912.

CHAPTER EIGHT

THE GREAT DEPRESSION AND WORK-RELIEF

[No one] taking federal funds . . . is going to be called a pauper while I am running this Federal Relief Administration.

We are going to meet this situation whatever it costs. We are going to take care of the victims of civilization. They are the first charges on our honor as a nation.

—Harry Hopkins, 1934

HARRY HOPKINS SEEMED TO BE AT THE PEAK OF HIS CAREER in the late 1920s. He ran a prestigious organization, had a national reputation as a social work administrator, and took an active role in shaping standards for his profession. He had worked his way through personal tragedy and, while relations with his family would always remain problematic, he had arranged his private life to suit his public pursuits. Yet he was merely on the threshold of a career about to skyrocket. The Great Depression set the stage for Hopkins to display the talents he had refined during the past fifteen years. The enormity of the disaster forced him to draw on his entire reserve of energy and imagination, yet he never transcended the bounds of "the American Way," remaining committed to democracy and capitalism. If he did not feel as suspicious of the poor as most Americans did, Hopkins still shared in the general attitude that government handouts without some rather strict rules would enfeeble recipients. The federal programs that Hopkins eventually set up in order to alleviate destitution may have seemed radical to the business elite, but, at least before 1936, they operated within a culturally conservative ideology, emphasizing self-reliance, personal industry, and the sanctity of the traditional American family. Like Roosevelt, Hopkins often spoke in defense of the newly destitute American worker, but his solutions to the economic disaster always fell well within the traditional format for public assistance. New Deal programs targeted overwhelmingly the previously-employed, newly-impoverished industrial worker.

When the Great Depression plunged New York State into economic chaos, Governor Franklin Roosevelt provided New York social workers with access to power. This activist group urged him to take action. By November of 1931, the unemployment rate was nearing 25 percent in some industrial cities. The governor undoubtedly faced a crisis situation. Roosevelt, according to historian Kenneth Davis, overcame his "conservative ideological aversion to providing state relief to individual persons" and declared that the state government was obliged to ensure the welfare of these people thrown into poverty because of circumstances beyond their control.[1] This notion of governmental responsibility certainly found common ground with Harry Hopkins, who had been in New York City struggling to secure diminishing private funds to support his work program. Hopkins recalled what it was like in New York City in 1929, stating that virtually millions of people had been thrown out of work: "Almost every time the clock ticked a man lost his job." Relief efforts for unemployed and destitute New Yorkers reflected not what was needed but merely what funds were available. For every man put to work, hundreds of others were relegated to the bread lines. Hopkins did not accept President Herbert Hoover's assertion that relief was a local problem and therefore a local responsibility. It quickly became apparent to Hopkins and to other social workers that their community no longer had the funds to relieve the destitution of the alarming number of unemployed workers. The Hoover administration, nevertheless, merely enjoined the people to rely on their proud national characteristic of "rugged individualism." However much the industrial worker wanted to be self-reliant, Hopkins and his colleagues knew that the economy simply would not allow it.[2]

The New York City social work community comprised a close-knit coterie that historian William Bremer called "a kind of interlocking welfare directorate," a hardworking and dedicated group of men and women who took the lead in establishing policies that not only would sustain the morale of the unemployed but would preserve the essence of democracy, capitalism, and self-reliance. Many became New Dealers: Edward Devine, Joanna Colcord, Gertrude Springer, and W. Frank Persons (late of the ARC) started out with the Charity Organization Society; Hopkins, John Kingsbury, and William Matthews began their careers at the AICP; Molly Dewson, an advisor to Franklin Roosevelt, had been the chapter president of the New York–based National Consumers' League; Porter Lee and Mary Simkhovitch were connected with the New York City School of Social Research; Mary Van Kleeck worked for the Russell Sage Foundation; Homer Folks was longtime secretary of the New York State Charities Aid Society; Jane Hoey helped form New York City's Welfare Council. In the midst of a massive nationwide economic depression, these largely middle-class, Protestant social workers were searching for a way to provide material assistance without engendering dependence or endangering the capitalistic system. They did not intend to upset the ship of state. Like Governor Roosevelt, they believed in politics by consensus rather than conflict or confrontation, and their common experience set the tone during the important New Deal years.[3]

Hopkins persisted in his belief that cyclical unemployment was not merely the fault of the individual nor the sole responsibility of private industry. If private charity could no longer meet the problem of destitution due to involuntary unemployment, it became the task of a democratic government to ensure the welfare of the people. When the economic catastrophe threw millions out of work, Hopkins' conviction only increased. But since not everyone agreed with him during the early years of the Great Depression, the practical social worker did what he could to alleviate the effects of unemployment within the confines of the private relief community. In 1930 he and colleague William Matthews, under the auspices of the AICP, raised $6 million from private contributions for a work-relief project, patently a clone of their 1915 project with the Bronx Zoo. In September of 1930 the AICP joined with the COS to establish an Emergency Work Bureau (EWB), headed by Stewart Prosser of Bankers Trust, to develop and run work-relief projects on city properties.[4] Hopkins, still director of the New York Tuberculosis and Health Association, gave what free time he could muster to help Matthews administer the project under the EWB. Supported by the park commissioners of Manhattan and the Bronx as well as Mayor James Walker, they put a total of 100,000 men to work in city parks. Every worker was paid the same wage, $5 a day. Although from 1930 to 1934 the EWB spent $30 million from private contributions on hundreds of projects, it was never enough. Social workers were well aware that the pay was very low, but it was the best that they could do. Matthews wrote that they looked on it as "something in lieu of unemployment insurance." The men could only work three days a week, or on alternate weeks; there were no means tests and no supervisory social workers. This combination of principles (which Hopkins would later use for the Civil Work Administration and in part for the Works Progress Administration), of course, was antithetical to every tenet of scientific philanthropy. But the crisis situation demanded new procedures. No one, least of all Hopkins, doubted that the unemployed wanted to work. When the inevitable criticism of the program's rather unconventional methods came pouring in from the conservative welfare establishment, Hopkins merely told them to "go to hell." Although he retained his acerbic personality, Hopkins soon learned that he would have to defend government jobs programs with more appealing rhetoric, stressing traditional American themes such as self-reliance and the Protestant work ethic. This was important both for the needy who were forced to accept the jobs and for those critics who lamented the imminent demise of the American capitalist system.[5]

During 1931 the problem of unemployment in New York City grew increasingly critical, and it was obvious that privately supported agencies could not handle the crisis. The long lines at the EWB discouraged even the most optimistic social worker. According to Matthews, the EWB represented the "largest single effort ever made to relieve by voluntary giving the distress caused by unemployment." But its money had simply run out because private contributions had all but dried up. By the time the EWB ceased functioning in 1933, it had spent millions in relief wages, starting well before the nation had taken any such steps to meet the problem. Its activities not only tested the validity of work-relief during a severe depression but also provided a body of experience for future relief projects.[6]

On the state level, however, Frances Perkins, Roosevelt's state industrial commissioner, indicated the direction that the governor preferred. Her 1930 Report of the Committee on the Stabilization of Industry for the Prevention of Unemployment stated that business and industry should do what they could to stabilize employment. This was the administration's first approach to the problem. Because unemployment represented an inevitable part of normal business cycles, she reported, "it behooves progressive managers of industry, to attempt a solution of the problem not only this year but every year, so that we can keep the flow of labor more evenly balanced and thus maintain the high purchasing power of as many workingmen consumers as possible." This policy, she argued, was merely consistent with sound business practices. "A man out of work is a drag upon his family, upon his community and upon industry itself, which might have kept him as a consumer if he had been working and, therefore, able to buy in normal volume. Unemployment, then, is not only harmful from a social point of view. It is wasteful and expensive from a business point of view."[7] Perkins insisted that industry could do a good deal to bring about stabilization of employment. Governor Roosevelt wholeheartedly agreed.[8]

Perkins and Roosevelt did consider other options, including work programs funded by the state. Both were aware of the earlier attempts undertaken in New York City during the depression in 1914-1915. Although they did not specifically refer to Hopkins' and Matthews' Bronx Zoo project, they noted that the current crisis reflected "just the same old unemployment that it was back in 1914." However, Perkins warned the governor that the problem was much more severe and widespread than it had been fifteen years ago and that new solutions had to be considered. She impressed him with the fact that "in an industrial system as complicated as ours, unemployment is just as much of an industrial hazard as accidents, and should therefore be insured in advance." No one, however, considered legislation on a federal level. Perkins, rather, was committed to meeting the problem through the cooperation of local government and industry.[9] This method, although it was meant to alleviate poverty connected with unemployment and at the same time to preserve industrial capitalism, proved largely ineffective. Hopkins, dedicated to employment as antidote to poverty, chary of the profit motives of American industry, and convinced that the government had to take the lead in relieving the distress caused by the Depression, had little of Perkins' confidence in the ability or desire of American industry to stabilize employment.[10]

Circumstances throughout the state reinforced Hopkins' position. Despite the lack of accurate statistics, all cities had reported that unemployment had reached unprecedented proportions. Perkins told Governor Roosevelt that because of the increasing intensity of the unemployment crisis, business and labor leaders alike, realizing that they could not take up the slack, hoped that some program of public works would be undertaken. New York, as the leading industrial state, had an especial need to maintain and develop the wage-earner market. With the support of labor and business, Perkins finally opted for public works projects as "the greatest source of hope for the future" and recommended the immediate institution of local public works along with public employment clearinghouses.[11]

In January 1931 newly reelected Governor Roosevelt suggested that the governors of the eastern industrial states meet for a three-day conference.[12] Roosevelt spoke at two of the sessions, declaring that the national economic emergency demanded new solutions for new problems. Deploring the "Polly-anna attitude" of the Hoover administration, Roosevelt called for experimental programs, a tactic that would endure throughout the New Deal years. "More and more, those who are the victims of dislocations and defects of our social and economic life," he declared, "are beginning to ask respectfully but insistently of us who are in positions of public responsibility why Government cannot and should not act to protect its citizens from disaster." The answer, according to

Governor Roosevelt, was that the government on all levels had to accept responsibility and act to protect the welfare of the people. He recognized the shortfall of private charities and local public agencies in the cities: "I am very confident that during the next few years State after State will realize, as we have begun to do in New York, that it is a definite responsibility for government itself to reach out for new solutions for new problems. In the long run, State and national planning is an essential to the future prosperity, happiness and the very existence of the American people."[13] At the time Roosevelt did not have any comprehensive or long-term plan to offer; but he did propose governmental action. The only question was one of method.

Two months later Roosevelt asked the state legislature to enact legislation to alleviate the distress of the unemployed in the state. The tone and the substance of his message became increasingly familiar to the American public:

> The serious unemployment situation which has stunned the Nation for the past year and a half has brought to our attention in a most vivid fashion the need for some sort of relief to protect those men and women who are willing to work but who through no fault of their own cannot find unemployment. This form of relief should not, of course, take the shape of a dole in any respect. The dole method of relief for unemployment is not only repugnant to all sound principles of social economics, but is contrary to every principle of American citizenship and of sound government. American labor seeks no charity, but only a chance to work for its living. The relief to which the workers of the State should be able to anticipate, when engulfed in a period of industrial depression, should be one of insurance, to which they themselves have in a large part contributed. Each industry itself likewise should bear a part of the premium for this insurance, and the State, in the interest of its own citizens, and to prevent a recurrence of the widespread hardship of these days, should at least supervise its operation."[14]

Many social workers, Hopkins included, realizing that this depression might not be as short-lived as they had believed or hoped, encouraged the governor to initiate state intervention to cope with the emergency. Consequently, Roosevelt called for immediate state aid to be given to the unemployed of New York. He declared that the purpose of the state is the protection and well-being of its citizens, that "the duty of the State towards the citizens is the duty of the servant to its master." Under authority granted to him by the Legislature in Extraordinary Session, the governor created the Temporary Emergency Relief Administration (TERA) in October 1931. The New York State Legislature appropriated $20 million for emergency relief of the unemployed and established an Emergency Work Bureau to be responsible for the administration of both direct and work-relief.[15] The TERA board (consisting of Jesse Straus, president of R. H. Macy department stores, John Sullivan, president of the New York State Federation of Labor, and attorney Philip J. Wickser), offered the job as executive director to Hopkins, who was then still head of the NYTBHA. Although he was not their first choice, and probably not even their second, Hopkins immediately accepted.[16] He was delighted finally to be in a government position where he felt he could do something substantive about the unemployment problem. Hopkins assumed his duties as executive director in October 1931, and the next August he took over Straus' position as president when the latter retired.[17]

Hopkins' most recent biographer, George McJimsey, accurately noted that, as head of the TERA, Hopkins called upon much of his past experience with the NYAICP, especially the early work-relief projects.[18] McJimsey emphasized Hopkins' administrative style, that is, his professional casework approach and his reliance on the supervisory role of the caseworker. While this aspect of Hopkins' methodology certainly influenced TERA policies, it was his commitment to the creation of jobs rather than direct relief as an effective antidote to economic depression that became the signature of his work in New York State and later in Washington.

Hopkins concentrated on creating a program that could set an example for other states. In directing TERA work-relief projects, Hopkins made sure that they were consonant with economic needs prevailing cultural attitudes. He insisted on socially useful projects that would not replace or duplicate normal municipal functions, that would not interfere with private industry, and that would pay wages in cash at the prevailing rate for the type of work performed. Because of limited funds, Hopkins had to require a means test for applicants and limit jobs to one person per household. While this last restriction essentially ensured that men got most of the jobs, there is no evidence that it was meant to disadvantage women. TERA regulations did prohibit discrimination on the basis of race, religion, or politics but made no mention of gender.[19] A statement prohibiting gender bias would not have occurred to most policy-makers in the 1930s. The TERA focused on unemployed industrial workers; issues as to women's proper place in American society or in the workforce did not enter into the debate.

Hopkins' administrative style had matured over the past eighteen years and embodied qualities that Governor Roosevelt needed and admired: unbounded energy and imagination, a can-do attitude, an easy acceptance of unorthodox procedures, and a dedication to getting relief efficiently and swiftly to those who needed it most.[20] Everyone on Hopkins' staff worked to his or her utmost capacity. In 1932 the board of the TERA published a statement that clearly reflected pride in what they had accomplished, sometimes at a high price. The members declared that the task assigned them by the State Legislature had "at times taxed our capacity." Yet they expressed enormous professional satisfaction in having taken part in "one of the greatest social and legal experiments ever undertaken" whereby provisions would be made for the citizens' well-being "without a tinge of beggary."[21] Attorney General of New York State John J. Bennett, Jr. stated that with the TERA, the Elizabethan Poor Law theories of the work test and less eligibility had finally and rightfully been set aside in favor of more modern theories of welfare provision. The work-relief component made it "revolutionary" because it assumed that those in need preferred work over cash and established the government's responsibility to ensure that the unemployed had access to jobs. Hopkins could not have agreed more with Bennett's description of the TERA as "the first enactment under which a State, as such, had accepted any liability for the support of its population, viewed not as wards but merely as men and women unable temporarily to accommodate themselves to the social scene, without at the same time placing such men and women in the position of recipients of a bounty or a dole [and] in such a manner as to preserve the self-respect of every beneficiary."[22]

The TERA might have been revolutionary, but it was not radical. It did not compete with private enterprise, and it did impose a means test in the social work tradition. Fifteen years earlier Hopkins had insisted that the unemployed wanted jobs, not charity. What was new now was his declaration that it was the ultimate responsibility of the government to provide those jobs. Furthermore, Hopkins applied this responsibility in a new way. The old poor-law tradition used the work test to weed out the lazy and therefore undeserving. Hopkins used work as an enticement—that is, as a carrot rather than a stick.

He realized, however, that even in the midst of a grave national emergency, most states still kept relief "as niggardly as possible in order to discourage people from seeking help."[23] This policy, the old poor-law tool of less eligibility, reflected the enduring perception that liberal relief policies merely encouraged dependency and created a permanent pauper class. Hopkins fought this attitude. For him, the nation's economic collapse had forced ordinary folks, good, hardworking people, to ask for public relief, and it was the duty of the government to alleviate their distress by ensuring, first, that they had the necessities of life to survive and, second, that those able to work had employment. Hopkins turned his attention to this army of unemployed workers, upstanding American citizens eager to work and unable to find jobs. For Hopkins this situation was deplorable. His relief programs were devised mainly to reach the men and women who, to his mind, had been betrayed by American industry.

Historians have pointed out that the policies initiated by Hopkins during the New Deal ended old poor law policies. However, it must be remembered that it was the Elizabethan Poor Law, created in 1601, that first established public responsibility for the poor. What Hopkins' programs during the New Deal did was change the emphasis from the stick to the carrot approach. The traditional theory (based on the conviction that deceitful paupers would willingly enjoy a life of idle dependency on the state and echoed in the British Poor Law Reform Act of 1834) insisted that the state make relief so distasteful and establish such arduous work in exchange for relief that only the most desperately needy would resort to public support. Hopkins, on the other hand, started with the assumption that the vast majority of those pushed into destitution by the Depression wanted nothing more than the opportunity to work. His programs established payments at subsistence level—not in the spirit of the Elizabethan work test, but in order to avoid competing with private business. While he recognized the need for work-relief—that is, work in exchange for relief payments to protect the dignity of the recipient—he preferred real work on useful public projects for wages based on the job and not on need. But his ultimate aim would always be a healthy, responsible capitalist system operating to the benefit of both employer and employee.

By 1932 industry had reached its lowest ebb, and it seemed that the people had reached the limit of their endurance. Banks were closing while local relief funds were drying up. The Hoover administration continued to minimize the situation by declaring that all the nation needed was a restoration of public confidence. Secretary of the Treasury Ogden L. Mills favored what Hopkins disparagingly called "the old Hamiltonian theory" of lending money to private corporations that presumably would use the funds to employ new workers. Hopkins could not agree with the administration's assumption that "so long as the top of the financial structure were taken care of with credit and subsidy, the foundation of our society, the millions of the population would receive bounteous prosperity as is percolated to them from the profits above."[24] Concerned for the economic security and the morale of those on the lowest rung of the economic ladder, he insisted that, with over 10 million American workers unemployed, people needed jobs more than industry needed credit. Not convinced that Hoover's trickle-down approach would help them, Hopkins began to formulate a plan for a combination of social insurance and government planning in the form of counter-cyclical public works to help the American worker attain full economic security.[25]

Hopkins always had believed in the American tradition of free enterprise, that government should stay out of the way of business. But he also was convinced that in many instances "predatory business" had refused to accept "responsibility along with privilege." Jacob Baker, Hopkins' lieutenant who later headed up the work-relief division of the Federal Emergency Relief

Administration (FERA), provided the Roosevelt administration with the needed statistics. In 1928 his charts showed that America's national wealth equaled at least $300 billion, equivalent to about $10,000 for each family. The national income that year was almost $90 billion, or $3,100 for each family. These figures clearly indicated that every American could have a decent standard of living. Baker emphasized that, despite the harrowing effects of the depression, the United States was still a wealthy nation enjoying a high per-capita income. The problem, of course, was that this income was neither evenly nor equitably distributed. Even before the stock market crash, while much of America basked in the Golden Glow of the 1920s, 50 percent of American families earned less than the minimum amount established as necessary for a healthy life.[26] These figures impressed Hopkins. As far as he was concerned, an increasingly acquisitive business community had forced the government to step in, to cross the "imaginary barrier between government and business." However, Hopkins' education, background, and social work had convinced him that, although some individual industrialists might be "predatory," the American system had to include capitalism. He was never radical enough to suggest otherwise. Nevertheless, he felt that the crisis demanded new solutions to national economic problems. For him there was only one answer: If private industry was unable to absorb the available workforce, then it was the government's duty to provide jobs. Furthermore, he felt that if local and state governments did not have the funds to provide these jobs, then the federal government must.[27]

Recognizing that relief administered in New York State was woefully inadequate, Hopkins wrote to Frank J. Taylor, commissioner of public welfare for New York City, outlining the shortcomings but also emphasizing the efficiency and courtesy with which the TERA had operated. Inadequate relief on the state level was caused only by lack of sufficient funds.[28] While Hopkins always insisted that the states participate in relief programs by providing the lion's share of the funding, he believed that the nation's economic problems existed outside of the environment of any particular community. Federally set standards for unemployment relief were absolutely essential. He stated, "[T]he surest way I know to have any relief for the unemployed deteriorating into the most wretched form of outdoor relief is to permit every local community to treat these people as they please." Federal responsibility also would convince the public that the unemployed were not at fault. For Hopkins this was crucial. He deplored what he perceived as a negative public attitude toward the unemployed as a permanent underclass. He wrote, with some cynicism, that the unemployed "are still people, and oddly enough, still citizens." In his opinion, a national commitment to alleviate unemployment by providing jobs would overcome this prejudice.[29]

The Hoover administration, however, would take no effective action. Senators Robert Wagner, Edward P. Costigan, and Robert La Follette did push a bill through Congress that provided $300 million to be loaned to the states for unemployment relief. Yet although this eased the plight of some, it was certainly no solution to the serious problem facing the nation. The Emergency Relief and Construction Act of 1932, which passed despite direct opposition from President Hoover, authorized the Reconstruction Finance Corporation (RFC) and provided it with $322 million to make loans (not grants) to the states for a federal public works program. The number of immediate and urgent applications from governors all across the nation demonstrated the enormity of the American workers' distress and the states' acute need for funds to meet the problem. Yet it was not nearly enough money. The Hoover administration, according to Hopkins, "still clung stubbornly to its harsh principles that relief of unemployment was a local responsibility, and that the government of the United States could give its distressed citizens nothing but information and advice." Despite its inadequacy, however, the RFC was the first indication that the federal government accepted any responsibility for mass and prolonged unemployment. Moreover, it provided an important stepping-stone for future programs.[30]

When Franklin Roosevelt was elected President of the United States in 1932, Hopkins' ambition for a government job on the federal level came to a rolling boil. He believed that only a federal relief program could save the country. He also thought he should run it. By 1933 Hopkins had had twenty years of experience in social work and welfare administration. He had refined many of the ideas he had formed under the tutelage of his Grinnell professors and had reinforced his commitment to preserving a democratic system of government that would ensure social justice for its citizens. Layered upon this rock-solid foundation was the social and political philosophy he had gradually fine-tuned from 1912 to 1933—that in a democracy, government, as the servant of the people, had the ultimate responsibility for their welfare. Hopkins' experience taught him that within the capitalistic system, American industry could not be expected to act outside of the profit motive; therefore, in times of depression, the federal government had to operate as mediator between competing interests. If he had patently eliminated any formal religious basis for his work, relying rather on a simple (Ethical Culturist) do-unto-others creed, a philosophy that would motivate much of his public service, he formed an almost religious commitment to the belief that the American worker always should be afforded the dignity of work at a living wage. He articulated these beliefs continuously throughout the Great Depression and never wavered in his uphill battle to guarantee help to those who needed it most.

Hopkins saw firsthand the extremely desperate situation of the unemployed in New York. People actually were starving to death. An article in the March 6, 1933, issue of *Better Times* (a social work journal) claimed that thirty-two people had died of starvation in hospitals in New York City, and this was just the tip of the iceberg; many more had died at home or in the streets. Many others suffered from malnutrition. During 1932 food consumption in America had fallen to a level of 6 million tons below that of 1929.[31] Another article in that same issue called for drastic action, including a comprehensive program of public works to re-create purchasing power and revitalize industry: "The great obstacles are the greed of the few who still enjoy an abundance of comforts, the timidity of the many who have never learned to think courageously . . . and the cowardice of those who occupy positions of leadership."[32] Hopkins was not the only one who saw the devastating effects of the Depression, but he was one of the few who not only had the courage to suggest some radical solutions but who would get the opportunity to put these solutions into practice. The economic disaster of the 1930s opened up opportunities for Hopkins to push his talents to the furthest extreme. During that decade a powerful president allowed Hopkins both the administrative leeway and the political support to realize his ambition for "bigger and better things." In 1933 Hopkins could hardly wait to jump into the First Hundred Days of the New Deal, into the midst of what he called "a series of bewildering pyrotechnical explosions."[33] These fireworks propelled him to a position of enormous power.

If Hopkins knew what to do with power and influence, he lacked savvy where his personal finances were concerned. If he was ambitions, it was not for a higher salary. In 1933, according to John Kingsbury, Jesse Straus offered Hopkins the enormous salary of $25,000 to come to work for his department store, Macy's. Hopkins turned him down, hoping against hope that the newly elected president and his old boss, Franklin D. Roosevelt, would offer him the job of organizing federal relief.[34] Governor Herbert Lehman wanted to keep Hopkins in New York State and offered him the job of industrial commissioner. Hopkins also gave that job serious consideration, but he wanted to be where the action was. He turned the governor down, saying, "I'd rather have a small job with the President of the United States than a big job with the Governor of New York or anyone else."[35] But Hopkins was not destined for a small job.

Soon after Franklin D. Roosevelt was inaugurated President of the United States in March 1933, he called his cabinet together to discuss ways to alleviate the nation's unemployment problem. Frances Perkins, Secretary of Labor, told the cabinet that large-scale public work programs took too long to initiate; therefore, she recommended direct relief. In light of the crisis situation, even conservatives such as secretary of state Cordell Hull agreed with the idea of direct relief. According to Perkins, Roosevelt did not consider this the dole, a remarkable fact in light of the strong bias against public relief in general and especially against federally administered relief.[36] Only the severity of the emergency could have advanced such a decision. It soon became apparent that the new administration in Washington was open to new ideas. This changing of the guard provided an important opportunity for those who had served in the TERA under Governor Roosevelt to air their opinion that the federal government finally had to step in to provide the necessary money and leadership to overcome what was clearly a national economic crisis.

It took Hopkins less than a week after Roosevelt's inauguration to go into action. With William Hodson, head of New York City's Welfare Council, he headed down to the capital. Secretary of labor Frances Perkins, Hopkins' colleague from New York, remembered that no one had actually invited them, "they just came." The two social workers met with her in the only place they could find room—"a hole under the stairs" at the Women's University Club— and they presented her with the plan they had devised for federal relief that included the appointment of a federal administrator in charge of both direct and work-relief programs. Neither made a bid for the job; they only wanted the president to take action—immediately. Perkins had already reviewed hundreds of such plans (2,000 were on her desk) but, "impressed by the exactness of their knowledge and the practicability of their plan," she agreed to take it to Roosevelt. The president quickly agreed to their strategy for a national relief agency headed by one federal relief administrator. Two months after Roosevelt's inauguration, Senators Costigan, La Follette, and Wagner, supported by the president, introduced the Federal Emergency Relief Bill to Congress. It passed both houses by May 12, 1933, with an initial appropriation of $500 million. Roosevelt immediately signed the act that would for the first time provide federal aid in the form of grants to the states to help them meet their relief needs.[37]

Hopkins had helped draft the work-relief bill, and he traveled to Washington often in the early spring of 1933, but he worried when he heard nothing from the president about who would run the show. Although he did not campaign for the position, Hopkins desperately wanted to be federal relief administrator. His dynamic style attracted Roosevelt, who would have been familiar with his record as TERA director. On May 19 the president called and offered the job to Hopkins. Within three days Hopkins resigned from the TERA and began his work as director of the Federal Emergency Relief Administration (FERA). According to Perkins, "it was as simple as that and the beginning of Hopkins' rise."[38]

At this point Franklin Roosevelt did not know Hopkins well. Even though Hopkins had headed up New York State relief for almost two years, the two had

had little direct contact. The day he appointed Hopkins as his federal relief administrator, the president sent a wire to his successor in Albany, Governor Lehman:

> Have just talked to Harry Hopkins and asked him to take over for a month or so administration of public relief measure. He has consented to come down and get work started. Due to situation in several states it was imperative that I get a man on the job immediately and have no one else available. Will talk it over with you when I see you next week. Very difficult to find a man fitted for this special work and felt Hopkins could get away for a month or two without interfering your state program.[39]

Clearly FDR did not appoint Hopkins because he felt he could do the best job. He knew that Hopkins could operate more than competently on a state wide level, and he knew that Hopkins' ideas about relief and work jibed with his own; but this telegram implied that the president believed that it would be only a temporary appointment.

In May 1933 Roosevelt called Hopkins to his office for a five-minute talk. The president told the Washington newcomer two things: Give immediate and adequate relief to the unemployed, and pay no attention to politics or politicians. Hopkins did just that. Thirty minutes later, seated at a makeshift desk in a hallway in the RFC Building, he began a program committed to action rather than debate, a program that eventually would put millions of people to work and establish new and more adequate standards of relief for those unable to work. Even more important, the FERA established the doctrine that adequate public relief was a right that citizens in need could expect to receive from their government.[40]

Late in 1933, Ida Tarbell, former muckraker and progressive reformer captured the spirit of the new administration in a newspaper article for the *New York Herald Tribune* headlined "We Gotta Do It." She described Hopkins' absolute dedication to overcoming the effects of the Depression and his attitude toward relief, quoting him as saying "[r]elief is no longer playing a lone hand, it is one of the great forces of the government marching with other forces to effect the recovery of our people." On May 22 the FERA assumed responsibility for 18 million people, representing 4 million families on public relief.[41]

Hopkins was well aware of the innovative nature of the FERA and knew that he would have to convince the American public that it was really not radical. To do this he used rhetoric that would appeal to most Americans. In his typical fashion Hopkins insisted that the unemployed were folks just like all of us. In a radio address he asked:

Who are these fellow-citizens? Are they tramps? Are they hoboes and ne'er-do-wells? Are they unemployables? Are they people who are no good and who are incompetent? Take a look at them, if you have not, and see who they are. There is hardly a person listening in who does not know of an intimate friend, people whom you have known all your life, fine hard-working, upstanding men and women who have gone overboard and been caught up in this relief structure of ours. They are carpenters, bricklayers, artisans, architects, engineers, clerks, stenographers, doctors, dentists, farmers, ministers; the whole crowd is caught in this thing, the finest people in America. That is who they are—or were before they lost their jobs.[42]

Hopkins reiterated this sentiment in his speeches and radio broadcasts throughout the Depression years. No longer would needy, unemployed industrial workers be considered outsiders. For Hopkins these people formed the backbone of a democratic nation and comprised a population eminently deserving of their government's help.

According to Corrington Gill, an economist and statistician who worked closely with Hopkins on the FERA, "the program was a step in uncharted territory." The FERA reveals much about the prevalent attitude toward the national relief program. A revolution was in the making, and not everyone was happy about it. When Hopkins invited Gill to join his staff, he warned him that if he accepted, he probably would be associated with a very unpopular man. Hopkins said: "One of the disagreeable things I will have to do will be to keep reminding the American public of the serious problem of unemployment and destitution and they won't want to hear it." Gill was not daunted and remembers that "daily association with [Hopkins] led me to the conviction that . . . the revolution in methods of caring for the unfortunate destitute that took place between 1933 and 1935 was most attributable to his energy, fearlessness, and breadth of vision."[43]

Despite the innovations that the FERA introduced, the most important being federal responsibility for needy citizens, the emergency was such that few states or local governments balked. Their need for federal funds was too great. And certainly Hopkins' energy in reiterating the need to preserve the self-esteem and independence of the American worker helped to ensure public acceptance of the program. Moreover, Hopkins had gained valuable experience in creating an agency from the ground up—he had done this as executive director of the New York City Board of Child Welfare and during his revamping the American Red Cross Home Relief Division during World War I. He also sharpened his administrative skills while he was expanding and fine-tuning the New York Tuberculosis and Health Association. The FERA job was perfect for Hopkins to demonstrate on a national level what he had learned.

Hopkins knew that his most substantive job was to remove as many people as he could from the relief rolls and place them in productive jobs. This effort, of course, reflected the prevailing public attitude. But until that was accomplished, his primary job was to provide relief for the destitute. It was became responsibility of the government, federal, state, and municipal, to ensure that every genuinely needy person in the United States received relief in order to survive.[44] Yet no one liked the dole. Hopkins' attitude remained consistent: "Give a man a dole and you save his body and destroy his spirit; give him a job and pay him an assured wage, and you save both the body and the spirit."[45] Almost immediately he added a work-relief component to his agency. In 1935, after the FERA had been folded into the WPA, Hopkins declared:

> For the benefit of those who have the idea that the F. E. R. A. existed only to encourage idleness, let me say that never at any time did I believe that relief alone was the answer to our problem. From the very first day I figured on a way to give jobs, and my greatest pride is that we soon had a work-relief program in operation that permitted 1,500,000 people to gain their relief through employ-ment. Useful employment too!

The dole was certainly cheaper, but for Hopkins it cost too much in terms of self-respect and pride. He declared that direct relief "tends inevitably toward the creation of a permanent pauper class, hopeless and helpless, and an increasing and crushing weight on the backs of the gainfully employed."[46] Still, work-relief was only one step removed from direct relief. Hopkins had not yet found a way to create a government job program that would duplicate but not interfere with private industry.

FERA had three main objectives: adequate relief, useful work for the able-bodied needy, and program diversification and flexibility. Wages for work-relief would be paid at a minimum level for similar work in the private sector, and relief workers would always be paid in cash. Projects would be selected based on low cost of materials and high labor absorption. Hopkins unremittingly insisted that the states, using their taxation and borrowing powers, do their fair share in providing for the needy. He believed that the logical sequence of responsibility was the county and then the state. Only if this proved inadequate should the federal government step in to help.[47]

For the president, as for Hopkins, the work program was the most important part of the FERA, for he believed it to be a "bridge by which people can pass from relief status to normal support."[48] Historians have questioned whether this bridge was as accessible for women as it was for men. Several months after the FERA got under way, Hopkins established a special division to provide work for women. This division's work projects included sewing rooms, canning centers, nursing, teaching, and other jobs that, in 1933, were considered to be specifically suited for women.[49] Every effort was made to find jobs for unemployed women who had been members of the workforce. Mothers with small children, however, were not considered unemployed; their job was to take care of their children and to raise healthy, honest citizens. If they were needy, female-headed families would get cash or in-kind relief either from state-run mothers' pension programs or from the FERA.[50]

Certainly for many needy women, especially those with young children, employment was not always the answer to their economic problems.[51] Popular assumptions about proper roles for men and women had a considerable effect on relief policies, but this was not primarily because of gender bias on the part of New Dealers. Hopkins' main concern was bringing about the nation's economic recovery in the shortest period of time and with limited funds. The scope and severity of the Great Depression dictated that the government jobs programs could support only one family member on its payroll; both men and women reformers in the 1930s agreed that the father/husband, as the traditional breadwinner, usually would get the job. Those suffering from acute deprivation during the Depression seemed to have only minimal concern with the rights of women. They were more interested in issues of social insurance and in the relative responsibility of the federal government and the business community to stabilize employment. The welfare of American workers and their families was foremost in the minds of the American public.

Roosevelt's federal relief administrator, however, was more concerned with "turf" issues than with gender issues. Roosevelt and Hopkins both felt strongly that the unemployed industrial worker, man or woman, should be the primary target for government assistance and that ultimate responsibility lay with the federal government to see that American workers and their families were helped. In his 1958 memoirs, Aubrey Williams, one of Hopkins' lieutenants, described a speech that Hopkins made in Detroit in June 1933 as "one of the historical statements, with respect to the entire undertaking of public relief during the Roosevelt Administration." In this speech Hopkins declared: "I am going to say that the federal government has a responsibility for the distribution of funds which are appropriated by Congress for the relief of the unemployed which it cannot delegate, in good conscience, to any other agency, but must itself assume the responsibility for their disbursement." This statement established the lines of authority and, according to Williams, "put the federal government into the battle of restoring economic health of the American working man in a fullfledged way." Hopkins made the important point that only government administration and control could rescue the needy from the indignity of private charity. According to Williams, "It is not too much to say that the entire social security program got its first great impetus from Hopkins' decision that day: that the federal government not only had a responsibility to provide funds but it had a responsibility to see that those funds were administered in a manner that would support the dignity and rights of the individual."[52]

In early June 1933 the FERA, with Hopkins at its helm, issued Regulation No. 1 stipulating that after August 1, federal emergency relief funds would be administered exclusively by public agencies. In addition, all individuals involved in the administration of federal relief had to be public officials. This regulation ended the fuzzy line between public and private agencies that had disturbed Hopkins since 1916 when New York City's subsidy system had caused such controversy. As the depression deepened between 1930 and 1933, local private agencies had found it necessary to turn to city and state governments for financial help. Many states followed the lead of Illinois and allowed federal funds granted to the state to be distributed to private agencies, reflecting a nationwide predilection for using established agencies to administer emergency relief funds rather than creating new administrative bodies. Josephine Brown, Hopkins' assistant in the FERA, observed that the effect of Regulation No. 1 "was to create consternation in the ranks of social workers and to start a process of reorganization wherever the subsidy system was in effect." Because local and state coffers were empty by this time, this regulation effectively eliminated all public subsidies to private agencies.[53]

Regulation No. 1 offended most social workers in the private sector. The Family Welfare Association of America, whose member agencies were largely affected, faced serious difficulties as a result of this new federal policy. Although some of the private agencies created a separate unemployment division that could then be absorbed by public authorities, others simply disappeared. The FERA regulation thus "established a principle and a precedent" that the government, not private citizens, had the primary responsibility for the administration of benefits to needy Americans. From 1933 on emergency relief administration was kept separate from local poor relief machinery and staffed solely with public employees. According to Brown, this revolutionized America's system of public relief, and it happened under Hopkins' leadership.[54]

Hopkins was adamant that everywhere only public officials administer public funds. The charities controversy from 1913 to 1916 probably influenced this policy. In addition, he wanted the FERA to see that the unemployed got relief, and he did not want "to develop a great social work organization throughout the United States." Brown worked very closely with Hopkins during these crucial years, and she noted that Hopkins realized that if he allowed public relief funds to be administered by established private agencies, canceling these privately administered programs once they became entrenched in the municipalities would be extremely difficult.[55] The economy would recover, and when the emergency ended and the FERA was no longer be needed, it would end. In 1933 no one was thinking in terms of permanency.

As a social worker Hopkins had held prominent positions in several private charitable agencies from 1912 to 1931. Why would he enact a regulation that essentially eliminated so many of his fellow social workers from center stage during the New Deal? There are two reasons: First, Hopkins knew that he could control federal administrators; second, he was looking for new solutions to old problems. In 1933 it seemed ultimately sensible to him to ensure that his programs were run by those he employed and those who were loyal to the administration. From the very beginning of his career, Hopkins had been a pragmatic social worker who willingly adopted innovative methods and new attitudes. If they proved adequate to the task at hand, he kept them; if not, he easily let them go. He had turned his back on the ruralism of the Midwest and on the religious sentiments of the settlement house. He left a marriage that seemed no longer suitable to his aspirations. In 1933 he rejected the methods of organized charity as outmoded and not appropriate for the new poor who deserved better from American society. In 1939, with the escalation of the war in Europe, Hopkins quickly changed his focus and turned his attention to foreign affairs at the expense of domestic economic problems. Always striving for what was bigger and better, always looking to the future rather than the past, Hopkins never lost his core of altruism, but he had little trouble moving on and moving up.

The FERA became the first step for Hopkins. The president had called for action, not debate, and he told Hopkins to get relief out fast. Hopkins knew that "people might starve to death while we were unwinding red tape in Washington." A master at getting money out quickly, he took administrative shortcuts, created innovative methods of disbursing relief, and raised the eyebrows of many a politician. He defended his program by saying "It is a wonder to me that we didn't blunder *more*. Almost overnight we were called on to feed fifteen million workless, hungry people, and with the problem further complicated by the necessity for speed, and the fact that we did not have a single chart to go by. It was almost as if the Aztecs had been asked suddenly to build an aeroplane." Hopkins felt fully confident that he was up to the task. Within sixty days the FERA had become "a machine that clicked."[56] But despite the efforts of FERA administrators, the number of needy Americans continued to increase.

By the autumn of 1933 it became increasingly clear to Hopkins and his colleagues Aubrey Williams and Jacob Baker that the FERA's work-relief program was not putting enough people to work. A special relief census revealed that 10 percent of Americans had been reduced to bare subsistence levels and stayed alive only because of public relief. Purchasing power had not increased enough to boost the economy of the nation. The large, top-heavy construction projects of what Hopkins referred to as Secretary of Interior Harold Ickes' "pinchpenny" Public Works Administration (PWA) had stalled in the planning stages. Overall, the outlook for the approaching winter seemed bleak. In October, while on a trip to Chicago and Kansas City, Hopkins began to formulate plans for a new work program. Aubrey Williams, a member of Hopkins' staff, probably came up with the original idea for the Civil Works Administration (CWA). He suggested to Hopkins that they should set up a work program in which the government itself acted as the contractor, employing architects, construction workers, and supervisors from the unemployment rolls. Although Hopkins was excited by the idea, he knew that they would have to ensure the support of organized labor before any such program could even be considered. And he knew that he would have to convince Roosevelt of organized labor's support. Williams enlisted the assistance of Dr. John Commons, a prominent labor economist from the University of Wisconsin, who fortuitously discovered that the leader of the American Federation of Labor (AFL) Samuel Gompers had recommended public work projects to employ workers during depressions.[57]

Discovering Gompers' endorsement of government work programs was crucial to Hopkins' plans to set up the CWA. In 1893, during a severe economic depression, Gompers had asked the New York City government to develop public works programs in order to alleviate hardships caused by unemployment, but was turned down by the Tammany mayor, Thomas Gilroy. When Gompers went to Albany and told Governor Roswell Flower that "labor wanted work, not soup houses," the governor merely recited the familiar litany that "[i]n America the people support the government [and] it is not the province of the government to support the people." Flower added: "Once recognized the principle that the government must supply public work for the unemployed, and there will be no end of official paternalism." Gompers and other labor leaders had been alarmed at the "radical rhetoric" that workers had adopted in response to the government's inaction and feared that the unemployed would take matters into their own hands. Consequently, they adopted two important resolutions when they met at the AFL convention in Chicago that December: "When the private employer cannot or will not give work the municipality, state, or nation must." And, further, that "it is the province, duty and in the power of our city, state and national governments to give immediate and adequate relief." Gompers insisted that American workers wanted work, not charity; but he also recognized that conditions were so serious that direct relief was urgently needed. He added an important concept, one that would be echoed in Hopkins' rhetoric forty years later: public work projects add to the economic health of the entire nation and to the wealth of all citizens.[58] The parallels between 1893 and 1933 could not be more clearly drawn for Hopkins. He felt that he now had enough ammunition to convince the president to back his innovative emergency plan for recovery: Any able-bodied unemployed person would be able to get real work at real jobs for regular wages.

On November 9, 1933, an executive order of the president created the experimental Civil Works Administration (CWA) under the authority of the National Industrial Relief Act (NIRA). Roosevelt appointed Hopkins director of the program and released $400 million of FERA money, channeled through the Public Works Administration (PWA), for the project. One week later Hopkins had a plan ready to present to the nation. By November 20 all work-reliefers were transferred to CWA rolls. Jobs, all of which were administered under force account (day labor), would fall between those undertaken as normal government activities and those long-term PWA projects administered by Harold Ickes. Hopkins had to walk a narrow path between private enterprise struggling to recover from the effects of the Depression and the large-scale public works projects, such as the PWA, that would greatly enhance the nation's wealth and economic health—in the long run. But, as Hopkins once angrily responded to an unfortunate staffer who told him that a project would help people in the long run, "people don't eat in the long run, they eat every day." Hopkins was sure his plan would work and called the CWA "the most heartening thing that has happened to those of us in relief work."[59]

The stated purpose of the CWA was "to provide regular work on public works at regular wages for unemployed persons able and willing to work."[60] Within four months Hopkins had put 4 million unemployed Americans, skilled and unskilled, to work. CWA jobs were paid at the prevailing rate fixed by local authorities, with the minimum set at thirty cents an hour for a maximum of thirty hours a week. Wherever possible, human labor would be used instead of machinery. Jobs would be allocated to women on the same basis as to men, and there would be no limitation of one job to a family as there was under FERA rules. Half of the workers were taken from the relief rolls and the other half from those unemployed persons who more than likely had been too proud to ask for relief. These jobs were to be socially useful public projects freed from the taint of work-relief; workers seeking employment were not subjected to any means test or intrusive supervision by social workers. Furthermore, CWA projects did not limit the amount of a worker's wage to the family's estimated budgetary deficiency, as did the FERA program. The CWA jobs program created public construction projects undertaken under normal conditions of employment and contract with standard rates of pay for jobs assigned according to the ability of the worker. Because hiring was done through employment agencies rather than social welfare agencies, these projects had nothing to do with emergency relief. The projects had to be ones that private industry would not undertake. Most important, they were judged primarily on their merits as labor absorbers. Again, as with the FERA, all state administrators of the CWA were sworn federal officials. For the duration of the CWA, eighty cents of every dollar spent went into the pockets of workers and twenty cents to buy materials. Because CWA workers were paid the prevailing wage for a normal job, these jobs allowed them to maintain their pride in earning an honest living. And government money respent by these workers would prime the pump of the national economy from the bottom up. By the time the CWA ended in the spring of 1934, over 200,000 worthwhile projects had been initiated, projects that Hopkins declared would be remembered for generations to come because they had "let loose a great economic and spiritual force."[61]

In November, just after the CWA got under way, Hopkins issued a directive calling on all his administrators to "pay particular attention that women are employed wherever possible." At the CWA conference, the Honorable Edith Nourse Rogers, a congresswoman from Massachusetts had asked Hopkins, "If you are going to employ women on these jobs, would it not be fair to set aside a certain sum for the women? There are many unemployed women with a number of dependents." Hopkins replied, "I don't think that is such a bad idea. We have got to go into this business of getting some jobs for women. It is our deliberate intention to work up projects upon which women can be used. We have been exploring that in the last few days and we think we already know of a substantial number."[62] Hopkins was indeed concerned that men were doing work that could be done by desperately needy women. Assisted by Ellen Woodward, his assistant administrator in charge of Women' Activities, he compiled a rather extensive list of suggested occupations particularly suited for women.[63] When Hopkins discovered that many women on relief did not have the qualifications for work within the scope of the CWA, he created the Civil Works Service (CWS) to employ women as administrators and support staff in relief agencies.[64] While women could be hired for any Civil Works project, many more women found jobs under the CWS. Still, women placed on CWA projects had to be certified by the U.S. reemployment offices and, unlike men, had to be on or eligible for relief in order to qualify for a CWS job. They fell under the same minimum wage and maximum hour regulations as men.[65] The success of the CWS in providing jobs for women had a decided impact on Hopkins. When he anticipated some sort of new work program after the CWA folded, he sent out a memo telling all the state directors of women's work that "[i]n the new program we expect that women will receive their full share of the jobs among those persons you are employing and it is highly desirable that this work be directed by some competent person on your staff."[66]

Hopkins made every effort to ensure that women participated in government jobs programs as clients and as administrators.[67] While his experience with widows' pensions in New York City influenced his policies toward needy women with dependent children—that is, enforced his idea that women should stay home and raise future citizens—the influence of his mother, his sister, and his first wife, who were all strong, competent women, along with the example of the prominent women social workers who had been his colleagues, also convinced him that women did indeed have a significant role to play in the public sphere, especially during the crisis years of the 1930s.[68]

For Hopkins, as for Roosevelt, the CWA had been merely a temporary, emergency measure and was never meant to be a permanent policy. In 1948 Robert Sherwood suggested that Roosevelt feared work-relief would become too embedded in American life and ordered its liquidation.[69] Biographer George McJimsey suggested it ended because President Roosevelt resisted the institutionalization of such a program; to do so would have been to admit the failure of his recovery program. And the president was optimistic in his belief that the depression would end with a business upturn in the spring.[70] However committed Hopkins was to the CWA model, he was practical enough to know that its radical nature would preclude its permanency. (In addition, he was very sensitive to the fact that he was using Harold Ickes' PWA money.) At the very first meeting of his staff, in November of 1934, Hopkins announced that this was only a temporary program. When asked what would happen when it shut down in four months, Hopkins responded, "No one need worry about what is going to happen three and four months hence. There is an immediate job to be done. You people have got to have faith in the Government, that the Government has a genuine interest in [the CWA]; it cannot make commitments, of course, any more than most of you can make commitment for your relief more than a month or two hence."[71] Hopkins typically was more concerned with addressing the current crisis rather than worrying about what would happen in the future. Moreover, he had faith in his government and in his boss.

Hopkins regarded the CWA as a means of providing a temporary form of employment assurance. It represented in its "broad outlines," he wrote, "a partial answer to the age-old problem of how America shall care for her unemployed." Even if it did prove to be unattainable, Hopkins realized that the CWA demonstrated to others who might be more cynical about people's willingness to work that "unemployed people want to work for what they get, and resent being asked to be a party to any subterfuge of a job as a means of getting relief, and for my part, I glory in their refusal and resentment of all such subterfuge."[72] A clear line was now drawn between work-relief and a government job program.

FERA work-relief as opposed to CWA projects highlighted this difference, and Hopkins was keenly aware of the important distinction drawn. Under the FERA, the jobs were given out as work-relief, that is, jobs were performed in exchange for relief payments. This was done in order to demonstrate the recipient's willingness to work for a relief payment and thus to establish his or her worthiness. Payment for work-relief was based on one's estimated need as determined by a social worker rather than the type of job done or the expertise of the worker. The benefit of work-relief was that it raised the morale of the unemployed worker forced by hard times to ask for help.[73] This element was extremely important to Hopkins and to the president, because it fit in so nicely with America's traditional work-ethic morality. Yet it still could not avoid completely the taint of public charity. In Hopkins' opinion work-relief, while far better than direct relief, was little more than an extension of the old poor-law work test, with no correlation between the worker's need or ability and the job; a social worker would determine a family's need and the "wage" would be set in accordance with that need. But Hopkins knew that the honest unemployed workers wanted real jobs for real wages, and the CWA, for a time, provided this.

In referring to the CWA in his book *Spending to Save*, Hopkins declared, "In the relief business where our raw material is misery and our finished product nothing more than amelioration, effectiveness has to be measured in less ambitions terms than success. That word applies better to marginal profit, cash or otherwise. Relief deals with human insolvency."[74] Hopkins assessed the CWA in noneconomic terms: "I know of no measuring stick by which we can give the gigantic dimensions of the benefits of CWA to the civil workers." He regarded it as eminently successful. Moreover, he judged it in terms of how many people it helped at that particular moment in time and what it did on a day-to-day basis, rather than what happened over the long term. He could not know its meaning for the future. There is no doubt that without the lessons of the CWA, the WPA would never have happened, and this, in itself, gives it enormous import.[75]

The CWA lasted less than five months but it was the largest employer of labor in American history up to 1933. Its more than 200,000 projects provided wages for millions of Americans over the hard winter of 1933-1934. It mobilized as many people during a two-month period as were "called to the colors" during World War I. Many severely criticized the CWA for its alleged slap-dash methods and its suspect administration, but Hopkins would give no quarter in his defense of his work program. He knew that the speed with which his program operated, although necessary, led to some blunders and to some waste. But, he said "we were not planning an expedition to dig up Egyptian mummies. . . . When a house is on fire, you don't call a conference, you put it out."[76] During its brief existence, the CWA brought hope to over 4 million Americans and their families.

The CWA was also enormously expensive. Early in January of 1934, Hopkins confided in Roosevelt that the program would be broke by February. This further convinced the president that the it had to end and he ordered Hopkins to begin the liquidating process. Despite Hopkins' heartfelt commitment to the ideals of government-supported jobs for the unemployed, which the CWA implemented, he orchestrated its demise. The CWA closed down April 1, 1934, and its projects were folded back into the FERA.[77]

Although the CWA's total expenditure reached almost $1 billion, in early spring of 1934 more than 11 million workers were still unemployed and on the relief rolls. Eighty percent of them were employable. For New Dealers this represented a deplorable waste of manpower. If the CWA was too radical, other methods had to be found to provide work for these people.

Hopkins was not happy with the way limited funds forced him to organize work-related assistance under the FERA. In mid-1934 a reporter asked him if he was satisfied with the program. He replied in his customary no-holds-barred fashion: "No, I hate it. We all hate it. We hate having to pry into the family affairs of millions of self-respecting people."[78] He deplored having to impose the humiliating means test. Yet, given the financial restrictions, he knew it was a necessary part of the program. He had learned this lesson as director of the New York City Bureau of Child Welfare, when lack of sufficient funds had forced him to use investigatory tactics to limit the number and amount of widows' pensions disbursed. But Hopkins was sure that there was a better way to provide help to the victims of the Depression. He felt that the government had to find an alternative that would preserve democracy, capitalism, and the independence of American workers.

The Progressive Era notion that the industrial system lay at the heart of the economic ills threatening the nation shaped Hopkins' early New Deal policies and programs. Industry, the site of both the cause and the cure for the Great Depression, became the focus for relief and recovery and jobs the cure-all for America's economic ailments. But how to offer work to the needy unemployed? Under the Federal Emergency Relief Administration, reliefers received jobs in exchange for needs-based relief payments to ensure that the American worker, almost always a husband and a father, could retain his dignity as the family breadwinner. Under the more radical Civil Works Administration, a real job (albeit a government one) for real wages replaced work-relief. Under this program, one did not have to be on relief to get a job, and the wage was based not on need but on the work performed. The issues that shaped relief policy during the First New Deal continued to define the debates over the relationship between relief and recovery that plagued the administration over the next several years. Only with the Works Progress Administration and the Social Security Act did America's current welfare system begin to take shape.

CHAPTER NINE

ECONOMIC AND SOCIAL SECURITY

Since most people live by work, the first objective in a program of economic security must be maximum employment.

—White House Report, 1935

EARLY IN 1934 HARRY HOPKINS BEGAN FORMULATING A NEW PROGRAM for the nation's unemployed. He emphasized the importance of work, not only as a relief measure but as an integral part of the national recovery effort. Direct relief was no curative for the individual or for the nation, he declared, and the government had to "stop pouring relief into an unfillable void." The unemployed needed the opportunity to work for wages and industry needed consumer dollars. He admitted that government jobs programs were expensive, but direct relief was "repugnant" and took an enormous toll on the nation's psyche. The cost of assuring workers a job became irrelevant when measured against the survival of American ideals.[1] Hopkins was convinced that a permanent, national program of employment assurance, working in concert with unemployment insurance, would lead to economic recovery for the nation, ensure real security for American families, and preserve the nation's democratic values. All he needed was the right occasion to talk it over with the president and he was sure he could convince him of the efficacy of his plan. Many months passed before he found this opportunity.

By the latter part of 1934, Roosevelt and Hopkins had begun to forge a close relationship. According to Frances Perkins, during these crucial years of the early New Deal, President Roosevelt increasingly regarded Hopkins as a man whose judgment he could trust, and she described "a temperamental sympathy" growing between the two men.[2] Therefore, it is not surprising that the president had noticed that Hopkins' health was beginning to decline. Roosevelt decided to send Hopkins to Europe—ostensibly to investigate how England, Italy, Germany, and Austria were dealing with the economic crisis, looking at their public housing and social insurance programs. But FDR also wanted Hopkins to relax a bit, to have a break from the arduous schedule he set for himself in Washington. The more Roosevelt came to rely on Hopkins' social instincts and enormous capacity for work, the more he worried about his physical condition.[3]

On the Fourth of July, Hopkins and his wife, Barbara, sailed to Europe, spending about six weeks overseas. During this time Hopkins showed only a vague interest in the European political situation, declaring only that it was "a sorry picture." People did seem worried about impending war, Hopkins told the American press, but a good portion of the newspapermen in Europe were much more interested in the economic situation in the United States. They seemed to think Roosevelt's New Deal was "the greatest show in the world."[4] The president's relief minister, by virtually ignoring the stirrings of war in Europe, demonstrated that he agreed with this assessment.

Hopkins was not generally impressed by the social programs he saw in Europe in 1934. By the end of his trip he concluded that the United States had to adopt a recovery program tailored to the country's specific situation. He declared that while the English system of relief was indeed impressive, it could not be "transplanted." The United States would develop its own program with two distinct policy branches—one ensuring the delivery of social insurance and the other assuring workers of a job. During a press conference in London, Hopkins announced that President Roosevelt would soon introduce a broad plan of social security to the American public, one that would encompass "all the rights of a civilized people," including a federally-guaranteed assurance of a job for all able-bodied workers.[5] In Hopkins' mind, unemployment relief had to be integrated into the president's plan for economic recovery. Thus recovery would trickle up from the increased buying power of the newly employed rather than trickle down from increased prices. To Hopkins, jobs and wages for the unemployed seemed the most effective way to preserve the traditional American values of independence and self-sufficiency and the most direct road to full economic health for the nation.[6]

Hopkins was not a political radical, and he avoided any overtly socialistic solutions to the problem of unemployment. When he was in Europe, John

Kingsbury sent him a letter urging him to meet with Beatrice and Sidney Webb (theorists of the Fabian Society) in London so that they could talk to him about what Kingsbury referred to as a "guiding principle." The Webbs, Kingsbury wrote, believed that unemployment was a permanent factor of industrial capitalism and could not be dealt with satisfactorily by social insurance schemes. Hopkins did agree with this in theory. He knew that the jobs programs of the FERA and the CWA provided important relief for destitute Americans. Kingsbury explained what the Webbs proposed: "In the end, abolition of private profit is an indispensable condition of complete social health and welfare [and] the capitalistic system must be abandoned, along with private profit-making."[7] However, while Hopkins was drifting to the left in his efforts to relieve the effects of unemployment, this "guiding principle" seemed inimical to his basic commitment to capitalism and to democracy. He had known John Kingsbury for twenty years and had worked closely with him for much of that time, but there is no indication that Hopkins took his old friend's advice to heart and sought out the Webbs. He did not ignore this advice out of ignorance. Hopkins had read everything that the Webbs had written and was familiar with their politics, but his attraction to socialism did not survive his early New York years.[8]

Upon his return from Europe in late August, Hopkins lunched with the president and, no doubt, hoped that he could talk with him about his ideas. Biographer Robert Sherwood pointed out that since Roosevelt had just returned from a 10,00-mile cruise on the USS *Houston* through the Panama Canal and then across the country by railway, he was eager to share the details of his adventure with his lunch guest; Hopkins probably did not get much of a chance to talk at all.[9] Therefore, when Eleanor Roosevelt invited Hopkins and his wife, Barbara, to Hyde Park over the Labor Day weekend, he leapt at the opportunity to talk to the president away from the pressures and distractions of Washington. This would be the perfect time for Hopkins to present his brainchild: a permanent federal employment program.[10] During the holiday weekend, Hopkins informed Roosevelt that he wanted to establish a Work Authority Corporation in each state. These corporations would put the able-bodied unemployed to work on self-liquidating projects at an estimated cost of approximately $5 billion per year. They would plan, develop, and administer these projects as well as make loans to cities. All employable persons getting public assistance, approximately 3.3 million people, would be taken from the relief rolls and put on job rolls. An additional 1 million unemployed and not on relief would also get jobs, bringing the total to 4.3 million. Those most in need of work would always be given preference.

In his 1987 biography of Hopkins, George McJimsey made an important distinction between Hopkins' approach and previous policies. Before 1935, New

Deal programs were meant to increase prices and thus bolster American business and agriculture. This, however, would cause increasing hardships for families on relief and already strapped for ready cash. Liberal New Dealers, especially Rex Tugwell, suggested instead that government policy should aim at expanding production and encouraging low prices. Hopkins agreed with this because it dovetailed nicely with his work-relief programs, but he was unable to convince the president to follow this liberal policy line.[11] Conservative business leaders still were looking for recovery from the top down, and in late 1934 FDR still seemed to be courting the business community. In addition, the anti-administration activities of the conservative Liberty League and the negative public reaction to a nationwide textile strike combined to put pressure on FDR to take the more conservative line. Despite the popularity of Father Coughlin, Huey Long, and Dr. Francis Townsend, despite what Robert McElvaine describes as the nation's leftward drift in 1934, the president resisted radicalism.[12] Roosevelt, however, still remained enthusiastic about Hopkins' work-relief programs, largely because of his aversion to direct relief.

The time was indeed ripe for some new thinking on social policy. By the latter part of 1934, after almost five years of depression, one in every seven American families received some sort of relief, usually direct relief averaging about $25 per month.[13] Few families could live for very long on this. With economic recovery still somewhere in the distant future, New Dealers knew that some other method had to be devised in order to ensure the survival of millions of Americans. The president realized that private enterprise could never consistently absorb the entire American workforce. Nor should it have to. He also knew that in order to prevent inevitable economic downturns from having a catastrophic effect on the nation, the federal government had to institute a coherent economic security program. Although at this point Roosevelt had a rather clear idea of what he wanted such a program to encompass—a contributory unemployment insurance, an old-age pension, a work program rather than relief, and health insurance—the very complicated details still needed to be worked out. But the president was adamant that, first and foremost, the program had to act as a stimulus to the economic recovery of the nation.

On September 23, 1934, FDR called Hopkins, member of the brain trust Raymond Moley, and Secretary of the Treasury Henry Morgenthau, Jr., to the White House to discuss the program that he was going to present to Congress. Hopkins believed that his job was to present the left-leaning argument, to balance what Moley would suggest. In the notes that he took on the meeting, he wrote: "[I] fussed as hard as I could for an economy of abundance in America rather than one of scarcity which had characterized the New Deal up to the present. Business has sold the President the notion that high prices in themselves will bring recovery."[14] Roosevelt's relief administrator believed that recovery would come through the employment of workers and filter up, that a healthy economy could come about only with increased consumerism, and that the wages of workers were the key to this. With newly acquired purchasing power, newly employed workers would rebuild America, priming the pump of the American economy just as effectively as Ickes' top-heavy projects. Roosevelt seemed amenable to the idea of employment assurance.

Hopkins hated the dole as much as Roosevelt. Social workers and policymakers alike had long agreed that direct relief had no lasting benefit and demeaned the recipient. Hopkins, however, did not agree with the moralistic precept that giving cash assistance weakened the moral fiber of the unemployed worker merely because he or she accepted something for nothing. It was the lack of gainful employment that dispirited the poor—that and the intrusion of "pantry snoopers" making needs assessments. Hopkins blamed the circumstances that forced a person onto public assistance rather than the individual. He was fully convinced that unemployed workers wanted the pride, satisfaction, and independence that working for an honest wage afforded them. Preachy admonishments against the pauperizing influences of the dole had little affect on Hopkins. Furthermore, while he understood the efficacy of preventive measures to ensure the economic security of American workers, he believed that job assurance would give workers the necessary leverage to control their own economic destiny. Nevertheless, providing jobs for the unemployed was an expensive business.

Lewis Douglas, FDR's director of the budget, opposed all forms of work-relief projects as costly and inflationary, but most of all because they fairly reeked of an unbalanced budget. Douglas had met with FDR in Hyde Park in late August, just before Hopkins arrived for his Labor Day visit. Unable to get the president to make a firm and uncompromising commitment to a balanced budget, including an end to all public works projects, Douglas resigned. He warned Roosevelt that the country would deteriorate into fascism, socialism, or communism—and surely economic disaster—if it continued along the path of public works and deficit spending. Faced with the defection of someone who had provided important ballast to the New Deal, FDR was both dismayed and angry.[15] The president, Hopkins, Morgenthau, and indeed most New Dealers did favor a balanced budget, but in the face of 18 million Americans foundering without jobs, the administration could not abandon its commitment to work-relief. However, with plans for long-term economic recovery on the table, it began to see a more extensive jobs program (instead of work *in exchange for* relief) as a preferable solution.

By November 1934, with the Democratic landslide in the congressional elections lending vigor to the administration, Hopkins knew that it was time to push for a much-expanded work program. The FERA was foundering and needed $250 million dollars more to meet its goal of employing 4 million idle workers. But Hopkins had to have something concrete to give to the president. He closeted himself in the Walker Johnson Building with his staff. "Boys," he told them, "this is our hour. We've got to get everything we want—a works program, social security, wages and hours, everything—now or never. Get your minds to work on developing a complete ticket to provide security for all the folks of this country up and down and across the board." Hopkins drove to Warm Springs on the day before Thanksgiving to present FDR a plan to extract some more money from the Reconstruction Finance Corporation, and he had high hopes that the president would react favorably.[16]

During the summer and autumn of 1934, plans were sputtering along for comprehensive economic security legislation, parallel to the ongoing debates about the efficacy of work-relief. In June FDR created a cabinet-level Committee for Economic Security (CES), consisting of Secretary of Labor Frances Perkins as chairman, Secretary of the Treasury Henry Morgenthau, Jr., Secretary of Agriculture Henry Wallace, Attorney General Homer Cummins, and Federal Relief Administrator Harry Hopkins. He charged them with the enormous task of designing comprehensive legislation that would provide social and economic security for the American citizen within the framework of industrial capitalism and the democratic system. According to Executive Order No. 6757, the CES "should devote its major attention [to] the protection of the individual against insecurity and distress" due to "the hazards and vicissitudes of modern life," including unemployment, accident, sickness, invalidity, old age, and premature death.[17] In his letter of transmittal to the committee, the president wrote that an economic security program "must have as its primary aim the assurance of an adequate income to each human being in childhood, youth, middle age, or old age—in sickness and in health."[18] Hopkins hoped to have a permanent government jobs program included in this broad array of cradle-to-grave economic safeguards for all Americans. Not everyone on the committee agreed. Frances Perkins may have been a visionary when she expressed the feeling that this would be not only impractical but essentially unattainable.[19]

Twelve years later Perkins wrote that it was difficult for most people to understand the "doubts and confusion" that accompanied the planning of "this great enterprise in 1934."[20] The administration was certainly picking its way over new ground, but any fears that the new policy would be radical were soon laid to rest. When Roosevelt appointed the CES, he declared: "Our task of reconstruction does not require the creation of new and strange values. It is rather the finding of the way once more to known, but to some degree forgotten, ideals and values. If the means and the details are in some instances new, the objectives are as permanent as human nature."[21] Hopkins also felt a strong affinity to such traditional values as democracy and the self-reliance of the American worker within the capitalist system. He had insisted that recovery had to incorporate "a policy of reconstruction in which the social order will be amended to include the right of people to work and an assurance of benefits for the workers that are not based on the whims of the individual but are grounded in social justice."[22] His use of such terms as "reconstruction" and "amended" were meant to legitimize the federal government's responsibility for the needy unemployed by grounding what seemed to be radical steps in the traditional past. Clearly on the same track as Roosevelt, Hopkins drew from the past to justify the new methods of the New Deal.[23] However, if Roosevelt and Hopkins had a meeting of the minds in their insistence that any plan to ensure the economic security of Americans also must preserve their traditions, Hopkins made no secret of his attachment to the somewhat radical idea of a permanent federal work corporation to cope with cyclical unemployment. Because of Hopkins' influence with the president, many thought that this was a definite possibility. Some even actively supported the idea.[24]

Unemployment relief, whatever form it might take, became central to Roosevelt's plan for economic security. "Fear and worry," the president declared, "based on unknown danger contribute to social unrest and economic demoralization. If, as our Constitution tells, our Federal Government was established among other things, 'to promote the general welfare,' it is our plain duty to provide for that security upon which welfare depends. I stand or fall by my refusal to accept as a necessary condition of our future, a permanent army of unemployed."[25] In September Hopkins had every reason to believe that public employment would be part of the proposed legislation.

Roosevelt wanted a draft of the economic security bill by December 15 and the completed bill on his desk by January, when the new Congress reconvened. This was not a great deal of time for such a mammoth undertaking. The CES had been delayed in getting started; both Perkins and Hopkins had been traveling, and the Committee did not get up to speed until September. Assisted by an Advisory Council on Economic Security and a Technical Board,[26] the CES debated old-age pensions, unemployment insurance, and aid to dependent children. Members also debated Hopkins' suggestion for a permanent federal jobs program.[27]

Edwin Witte, executive director of the CES, wrote Hopkins a letter in November 1934 calling his attention to two pages of an enclosed draft listing suggestions for the economic security legislation. These pages dealt with the unemployment problem and stated that because only "half of all unemployed persons can be brought under unemployment insurance laws [and] many will exhaust their benefits before they get back to work," there was "a distinct place for emergency work in a comprehensive long time security program." Witte concurred with Hopkins that unemployment insurance, "while a valuable first line of defense for the majority of our industrial workers, has distinct limitations."[28] Nevertheless, the committee's support of a permanent federal job assurance program was vague at best.

Just after the congressional elections, a two-day Conference on Social Security brought together several hundred people at Washington's Mayflower Hotel for the purpose of sharing information. John B. Andrews, Abraham Epstein, and Paul Douglas were among those who gave addresses. Harry Hopkins and Frances Perkins were the only CES members to take part in this national conference attended by representatives from almost every state. Hopkins addressed a luncheon session on child welfare chaired by Grace Abbott, Homer Folks, and Jane Hoey, and spoke as an advocate for the 18 million people on relief rolls, all of them competing for a limited number of jobs in private industry. Discussing in broad terms the pressing need for aid to fatherless families, unemployment benefits, and old-age pensions, he made no reference to government job programs.[29] Hopkins' deputy, Aubrey Williams, prepared a speech (delivered by an aide) that made oblique references to the necessity of work-relief in concert with unemployment insurance but also failed to emphasize the need for a permanent employment program.[30]

The CES Advisory Committee met a little over a week later, on November 22, to "suggest a point of view with reference to . . . public employment and assistance." Its informal report stated that because large numbers of people would not benefit from unemployment insurance, "public works and emergency work programs would be the most effective method of dealing with the problem of those without employment." The Advisory Committee stated that if "the program included only old age pensions and mothers' assistance, the needs of a great bulk of the families would be left to the present relief system, the evils of which are well recognized."[31] At this same time, Hopkins and his staff drew up the "Plan to Give Work to the Able-Bodied Needy Unemployed," which outlined ways to put people to work on government-sponsored projects. Work-relief—that is, work in exchange for cash assistance—was only "a stepping stone to the new Works Program [which would provide] full time work, assurance of earnings, and continuity of employment." It would not be merely an emergency measure but would ensure that heads of households remain breadwinners for their families.[32] The job assurance program would provide help for a large group of already unemployed workers (about 16.8 million) who would not be eligible for unemployment insurance benefits.[33]

In November, when Hopkins met with Roosevelt in Warm Springs, he reiterated his plan for employment assurance and added two measures: the use of marginal farmlands for displaced industrial workers and a low-income housing program. An article in the *New York Times* covering the meeting announced that the relief administrator spoiled the Thanksgiving dinners of many conservatives with his plan to spend as much as $9 billion to create a permanent civil works administration under what would be a "correlated government program" unifying recovery and relief activities. The article called this "revolutionary," involving "a considerable reorganization in America's present economy." Not only would the jobless be given government jobs, but they also would get livestock and tools for subsistence farming on marginal lands, a startling proposition for conservative minds. Hopkins' "bombshell" revelations that the unemployed had little hope of finding jobs in private industry, that unemployment insurance and old-age pensions were insufficient guards against economic insecurity, and that some "established practices" would have to be rearranged disconcerted a business community that was by this time convinced that it should "become the spearhead for the recovery drive."[34]

In early December journalist Delbert Clark added to the conservatives' nervousness over Hopkins' plan to relocate the jobless onto farms "to raise pigs, chickens, and lettuce and be independent." He dubbed it End Poverty in America after muckraker Upton Sinclair's EPIC (End Poverty in California) and knew that EPIA "was a word to make capitalists crawl under the bed." This "zag to the left," Clark wrote, included subsistence homesteads, rural rehabilitation, a public housing project, as well as an expansion of the FERA's work programs. The cost would be staggering—expenditures would increase by $1 billion a year. Clark noted that "the canny Relief Administrator [may be] asking for much more than he hopes to get as a means of obtaining much more than he otherwise would have received."[35] Certainly Hopkins could have been negotiating to ensure that his somewhat radical work assurance program would be absorbed within the more conservative security legislation.

On Christmas Eve Hopkins and Perkins presented Roosevelt with a draft of the economic security bill. The section on unemployment assurance began with the statement: "Since most people must live by work, the first objective in a program of economic security must be maximum employment." The CES recommended that during periods of depression and during normal times, able-bodied workers who could not find a job in private industry would be provided public employment. Government work projects, the committee suggested, should be planned in advance and coordinated with planned projects on the federal, state, and local levels. Work as an antidote to poverty caused by involuntary unemployment seemed vastly superior to relief. A program of rationally planned government projects was not meant to be merely an emergency measure, to be scrapped when the nation recovered; the Committee recommended the establishment of a permanent National Planning Board to administer the work assurance program.[36]

After a long session during which he reviewed each detail of the draft very carefully, FDR approved it. On January 15 the CES sent a report to the president outlining its final proposals for the bill. The first topic covered was employment assurance, called the "stimulation of private employment and the provision of public employment for those able-bodied workers whom industry cannot employ at a given time."[37] Throughout the negotiations, Roosevelt had insisted that the entire security program be enacted as a coordinated whole. Witte believed that this "omnibus nature of the social security bill" had a great deal to do with getting unemployment insurance passed. It was Hopkins who had convinced Roosevelt to make work assurance an integral part of the package. However, according to Witte, it was the budget director, Daniel W. Bell, Lewis Douglas' replacement, who persuaded Roosevelt to separate this from the economic security bill.[38]

The reason the president did not insist on including employment assurance in the economic security legislation might lie in the subtle differences between unemployment insurance and a permanent work assurance program. Both were responses to involuntary unemployment, and both sought to ameliorate any financial hardships that might follow the loss of a steady paycheck. Hopkins likened unemployment insurance payments under a govern- ment program to direct relief because money was collected with no work performed. The provision of a government-sponsored job, however, would conform to the socially accepted paradigm of work for wages. It would also bolster American industry, which could not possibly be responsible for full employment during economic downturns.[39] According to George McJimsey, both Hopkins and Tugwell thought that a comprehensive work program could take the place of unemployment insurance. Roosevelt, however, could see the value in both policies, and he saw them as complementary.[40] He and Secretary Perkins both had admitted that the fundamental purpose of unemployment insurance was to afford the unemployed worker protection for only a limited period of time. Without wavering in their commitment to a broad program of social insurance, they agreed that "when unemployment benefits are exhausted, relief, preferably in the form of work, must be provided on some means test basis." FDR still insisted on a clear line of demarcation between relief, even work-relief, and social insurance, fearing that long-term assistance would deteriorate into something like the English dole. Most American social policy makers deplored the system used by Great Britain that provided cash relief for the unemployed because they believed that this money was given too easily and for too long a time.[41] While Hopkins did not oppose the unemployment insurance proposed under the Economic Security Bill, a program that was intended to protect temporarily laid-off workers, he knew that most of those out of work for any extended period would become destitute very quickly. He also believed that American business could not turn a profit while supporting superfluous workers on the payroll, especially during times of depression. Furthermore, those workers who were already unemployed would not benefit from unemployment insurance as it was devised by the CES. Hopkins argued that "the alternative [to full employment by industry] is the extending of our unemployment insurance legislation and supplementing it with a broad program of public works in the fields most socially desirable as an established governmental activity not only to absorb but also to release the productive energies of persons who would otherwise be unemployed."[42] Hopkins' purpose was to make sure that the American worker and American industry were both protected. Secretary Perkins agreed with the end but not the means.

Frances Perkins had been concerned that the president would substitute a permanent program of government work for a program of unemployment insurance. The secretary considered this insurance absolutely essential for recovery and long-term economic security. When she and Hopkins met with FDR to discuss this issue, she addressed the issue of political expediency and argued that if this administration did not enact federally mandated unemployment insurance, "political confusion" would deter future administrations from such legislation. In other words, it was now or never. Hopkins continued to press his argument that while government-sponsored unemployment insurance unquestionably would help families for a certain length of time, only guaranteed employment could bolster a family's economy during a long depression. Unemployment insurance treated poverty as a symptom, he told the president, while the provision of jobs went to the root of the matter and eliminated the cause of poverty.[43]

The business at hand, however, was getting the economic security bill enacted. After one change in the financing of old-age insurance that delayed the bill, the president presented it to Congress on January 17, 1935. FDR strongly endorsed this proposed legislation and asked Congress to act quickly. Hearings in the House Ways and Means Committee began on January 21. In his opening statement to the committee, Edwin Witte made it very clear that the bill did not embrace all of the president's program for providing safeguards against the major misfortunes of modern life. What he called "the largest public works program that has ever been launched in any country is a companion measure to this bill." Employment assurance had been listed first in the CES report to the president, Witte declared, and had to be "regarded as an integral part of the program of economic security which the administration is presenting at this time."[44] Perkins testified to the necessity for the federal government to support a public works program to employ idle workers during "prolonged periods of depression" but emphasized compulsory unemployment insurance as the first line of defense against the loss of a job. Hopkins, during his rather short testimony on January 23, reiterated his commitment to employment assurance as part of the entire security program while supporting unemployment insurance. Cash benefits, he argued, would allow a worker suddenly thrown out of a job some time to look for another job.[45] However, Congress separated Hopkins' work program from the major legislation package. By the time Congress was debating the pros and cons of the economic security bill, Roosevelt had already announced his plans for a work-relief program ancillary to the bill. The House overwhelmingly passed what was now called the social security bill on April 19; two months later the Senate followed suit. On August 14, 1935, President Roosevelt signed the Social Security Act into law.[46] It contained no provision for employment assurance.

FDR still wanted to end the dole for the more than 2 million families on the relief rolls. Almost everyone in the administration recognized that cash assistance, although necessary in emergency situations, sapped the nation's morale and did not address the root causes of the economic problem. In his State of the Union Address on January 4, 1935, the president openly opposed direct government relief. He emphatically stated, "The Federal Government must and shall quit this business of relief. I am not willing that the vitality of our people be further sapped by the giving of cash, raking leaves or picking up papers in the public parks. We must preserve not only the bodies of the unemployed from destitution but also their self-respect, their self-reliance and courage and determination." But he also threw his support behind some kind of a work program, insisting that useful work had to be found for the able-bodied unemployed. This also would boost consumerism and get money circulating again. His plan called for a temporary government work program, and he requested the Congress to appropriate $4 billion to provide jobs for those 3.5 million already on relief. With the president's vigorous encouragement, Congress passed the Emergency Relief Appropriation Act, which gave Roosevelt a huge grant of legislative authority. However, Congress stipulated that no military projects were to be undertaken and that Senate approval would be necessary for any administrative position with a salary in excess of $5,000.[47]

Under this act, Roosevelt created the National Emergency Council on May 6, 1935. The following month he called Ickes, Hopkins, Morgenthau, and Frank Walker (the chairman of the National Emergency Council whose even temper and fair-mindedness would act, it was hoped, as a buffer between Hopkins and Ickes) to the White House to impress upon them the importance of the work program both for the economic health of the nation and the political health of the administration. The 1936 elections were not far off, and the president was reluctant to announce which one—Hopkins or Ickes—would head the new job program; both administrators had outspoken enemies in both houses of Congress.[48] Typical of the president's style, he combined recommendations from both Hopkins and Ickes in the design of the program. Roosevelt appointed Hopkins head of the Works Progress Division, originally the least important of the Council's three divisions. It was meant only to be an oversight, record-keeping, and informational body.[49] However, recognizing by this time that there was little chance of having his work program integrated into the Economic Security Bill, Hopkins used his influence with the president—along with his energy and aggressiveness—to turn the division into the Works Progress Administration (WPA), the dominant division that would provide government jobs for able-bodied workers on relief rolls. Doing so was possible because Roosevelt's Executive Order had stipulated that the Works Progress Division would have the responsibility of carrying out small projects. Hopkins, however, managed to have larger projects broken down so that they would fall under his division. By this time, the president was familiar with Hopkins' abilities and probably anticipated the possibility that his relief administrator would transform his division into the preeminent one. When FDR met with Hopkins, Ickes, and others to divide up the appropriation, he gave Hopkins the lion's share. FDR knew that the Hopkins' plan of getting money quickly into the pockets of newly employed workers was more effective than Ickes' top-heavy public works, especially when there were still so many unemployed. Ickes was furious.[50]

Hopkins, of course, had to contend with Ickes' temperament, and the secretary of the interior proved to be an irritating adversary. Roosevelt's military aide, Edwin "Pa" Watson, called him a "fuss-budget." Hopkins wrote in his diary that planning for the work program would have gone a lot smoother had Ickes cooperated, "but he is stubborn and righteous which is a hard combination." Dubbing Ickes the "Great Resigner," Hopkins complained that "[a]nytime anything doesn't go his way he threatens to resign." Still, FDR knew that he had to do something about the bickering between his two powerful and extremely valuable administrators. In an attempt to make peace, FDR proposed a three-week fishing trip aboard the USS *Houston*, inviting Hopkins, Ickes, and Pa Watson among the guests. The ploy seemed to work; by the end of the October 1935 voyage, Hopkins and Ickes managed to mend fences.[51]

There is no doubt that Hopkins' co-optation of the work program was a remarkable example of his "bullheadedness" and administrative deftness. But even more important to our understanding of the development of the American welfare state is the realization that the WPA was a compromise. Its conception as an alternative to a permanent program of government jobs marked an important signpost along the American way to welfare. It represented a fear of creeping socialism and a reluctance to extend federal intervention as well as an economizing impulse. Hopkins' growing political astuteness and his absolute loyalty to President Roosevelt impelled him to curb his leftist instincts and settle for the possible. Tilting at windmills became a luxury the relief administrator could no longer afford.

Over the course of seven years, the WPA generated over 3 million jobs each year, at a total cost of $10.7 billion. WPA workers hired under the force account method[52] could earn no more than an established monthly security wage which, while lower than what they could earn in private industry, was higher than relief. The hourly wages could be no less than the prevailing rate for private industry, but work hours would be limited to the number of hours necessary to meet an established security wage.[53] Thus these jobs would be in accord with both capital and labor. Neither President Roosevelt nor Hopkins wanted WPA jobs to compete with jobs in private industry. The government work program, after all, was supposed to be part of the comprehensive plan for the economic recovery of the nation. Responding to an article in the *New York Times* suggesting that a "public payroll psychology" would keep people from looking for jobs in the private sector, Hopkins angrily responded that that idea is "nonsense," that the real obstacle to full employment was the lack of jobs in private industry. Moreover, some workers felt that jobs in private industry lacked the security of a government job. Hopkins lashed out at the "anarchic irregularity and irresponsibility" of the American business community as responsible for this situation, for the destruction of hope among unemployed workers forced to accept government jobs. He threw out a challenge: "Guarantee steady jobs in private industry if you want enthusiastic workers. . . . Our intention is to help, not replace private industry."[54]

WPA jobs were not easy to get, and an unemployed worker had to meet strict requirements and possess an inordinate amount of persistence if he or she wanted to land a government job. One reason for the stringent restrictions on government jobs, of course, was to ensure that WPA jobs did not compete with private industry. There was another. Hopkins was sure that as soon as relief was raised to the level of a job, many more would apply—too many for the program to absorb. Therefore, in order to control this number, he limited each family to one government job. He also recommended instituting two poor-law policies: the means test and less eligibility. "By these two means, then," he declared, "the one requiring that people shall show that they face destitution, hunger, and eviction prior to receiving employment, and second, that the wage shall be less than what they can earn in private industry, it is believed that the number who are to be given aid could definitely be limited and controlled." These conservative policies tempered Hopkins' emerging radicalism. He defended such carryovers from the nineteenth century by claiming that professional social workers had developed a methodology "to apply financial tests to those who ask for aid which is at once effective and carries little in the way of stigma for those to whom it is applied. " Still, the WPA marked Hopkins' acceptance of the possible rather than the perfect.[55]

Hopkins continued to insist that the problem of unemployment would never be solved by emergency measures. A year after the Social Security Act was passed, he wrote: "While we have a problem of emergency proportions at the moment . . . we are faced for an indefinite number of years with a situation which will require a permanent plan that cannot be carried on as an emergency matter. We should face this frankly."[56] Hopkins advised extending unemployment insurance legislation and "supplementing it with a broad program of public works . . . as an established governmental activity."[57] Roosevelt disagreed, and out of loyalty to the president, Hopkins threw all of his considerable energies into the administration of the temporary WPA. In 1938 Hopkins presented to Roosevelt a report that listed the impressive array of the 158,000 projects undertaken by approximately 5 million WPA workers earning an average of $52 a month. While 80 percent of WPA funds were spent on construction projects, including roads, bridges, parks, playgrounds, air landing fields, and public buildings, there were also numerous non-construction jobs available. Sewing, educational, health, and clerical projects abounded; WPA workers provided disaster relief, did scientific research, restored historic shrines, and engaged in conservation programs. Hopkins emphasized both the social usefulness of these projects and the necessity of "salvaging labor that otherwise would waste in idleness."[58]

Despite the overwhelming number of unemployed men seeking relief, women formed a critical part of the army of unemployed in 1935.[59] Therefore, Hopkins, with the wholehearted support of Eleanor Roosevelt, established a Women's and Professional Division within the WPA. Ellen Woodward, appointed as assistant administrator in charge of the Women's Division, knew that unemployed women were just as eager to work as men and intended to include "[e]very able-bodied employable woman on relief who is the breadwinner for her family or who is dependent on her own efforts for a livelihood." Although the WPA Women's Division provided jobs distinctly in the women's sphere, with an emphasis on white-collar and professional employment, both Woodward and Eleanor Roosevelt worked to ensure that unemployed women got their fair share of the 3.5 million jobs planned under the WPA—and that they got equitable pay. According to Woodward, WPA administrators at all levels took women's work very seriously and made every attempt to see that women were given "equal consideration with men in the planning and in opportunities to work."[60] Nevertheless, it was an uphill battle due to the preference the administration gave to unemployed male heads-of-households, and women's jobs continued to be limited in scope.

WPA production-for-use programs were closely allied with the Women's and Professional Division. These projects either produced goods or preserved surplus food for distribution among those who were unable to buy such necessities. Hundreds of unemployed women gathered in over 10,000 sewing rooms across the country and produced huge quantities of much-needed garments. Additionally, WPA funds purchased textiles from private industry to stock these sewing rooms, giving a boost to the economy. Along these same lines, the WPA purchased surplus meat and fruit to be processed and redistributed to the needy, products that otherwise would have been wasted.[61]

Hopkins received a great deal of criticism when he developed the WPA Federal Arts Project, known as Federal One. This program had roots in FERA and CWA programs to help about thousands of unemployed artists, musicians, actors, and writers. Hopkins replied to the numerous critics who berated him for giving "boondoggling" jobs to people committed to the creative impulse: "Hell! They've got to eat just like other people." At a press conference, his defense of jobs for professionals and white-collar workers underlined this attitude:

> There is nothing the matter with [these types of jobs programs]. They are damn good projects—excellent projects. That goes for all the projects up there. You know some people make fun of people who speak a foreign language, and dumb people criticize something they do not understand, and that is what is going on up there—God damn it! Here are a lot of people broke and we are putting them to work making researches of one kind or another, running big recreational projects where the whole material costs 3%, and practically all the money goes for relief. As soon as you begin doing anything for the white collar people, there is a certain group of people who begin to throw bricks. I have no apologies to make. As a matter of fact, we have not done enough.[62]

For years the anti–New Deal press castigated Hopkins for his statement about "dumb" people.[63]

The Federal Arts Project, which accounted for about 2.5 percent of the WPA program, provided work for musicians under the directorship of Nikolai

Sokoloff. The Federal Theatre Project (FTP), under the direction of former Grinnellian Hallie Flanagan, brought live theater to about 1 million people each month in forty cities and twenty-two states. At its peak, the FTP gave about a hundred performances a day throughout the nation and provided work to unemployed actors, directors, playwrights, stagehands, and other theater people who had been forced onto the relief rolls—besides enriching the cultural life of Americans.[64] Holger Cahill directed the Federal Artists' Project, which provided work for thousands of unemployed muralists, easel painters, sculptors, and art teachers.[65] The main program of the Federal Writers' Project, under the leadership of Henry Alsberg, was the production of the American Guide Series, volumes that provided detailed information on various states.[66]

WPA projects touched upon just about every aspect of life in America. In 1937 Hopkins remarked about the WPA: "I don't suppose there has been anything like this done any place in the world."[67] When the work program began in August 1935, it represented for Hopkins "the beginning of a consistent, satisfactory, and well thought out solution to the most serious problem of the present economy." Not only did WPA wages provide an important boost to the economy, but they also prevented the unemployed from sinking into "a submissive, resigned acceptance of the dole."[68] For Hopkins the WPA was the most significant part of Roosevelt's New Deal.

The WPA represented an enormous amount of public spending on the part of the federal government.[69] It provided important purchasing power for the consumer by paying workers wages that private business could not or would not pay. In addition, the public expenditures for materials for public projects further stimulated the economy. This double-barreled effect removed the threat of destitution from millions of unemployed workers and increased the demand for goods produced by private industry, which, in turn, boosted private employment.[70] The WPA was indeed expensive but Hopkins, supported by economists Corrington Gill and John Kenneth Galbraith, was committed to the theory of deficit spending to finance relief and recovery during the Great Depression and aptly titled his (only) book *Spending to Save*.[71] This was not a popular concept. In a 1936 article called "What Price Recovery?" Hopkins made a direct appeal to the powerful American middle class in defense of his methods. These were the people who had gotten a disconcerting vision of "the doubt and insecurity which are normally the lot of the poor." Hopkins expressed the crux of his New Deal policies when he wrote that because of the Depression, "new ideas and new solutions to old problems seemed less alarming under such circumstances."[72]

In April 1938 Hopkins was called on to defend the WPA during the downturn in the economy that began in 1937 and reversed a gradual improvement. He took this opportunity to emphasize that the economy would always be fluctuating. "We are always expanding to a peak or contracting to a depression low." He repeated his mantra that there will always be a group of unemployed in an industrial society:

> Some unemployment will always be with us. For that reason we must plan a permanent security program. But I want to emphasize that we cannot stop with that. It is absolutely stupid for us to think that we cannot reduce unemployment to reasonable low levels. We have the initiative, ability, and brains to do it. We cannot, however, ignore our immediate responsibility to the unemployed merely because we believe we can reduce the problem. We must do both.

Hopkins envisioned a comprehensive security program for the nation that would ensure that each individual would accept it "as a matter of right—with no feeling of social inferiority. . . . The work program should be made an integral part of the federal economic security program." Hopkins' experience with the unemployed over the preceding five years had convinced him that a federally administered work program was the "democratic way" to solve the nation's inevitable unemployment problem because this policy increased both the morale of the individual and the stability of the nation's political and economic systems. In addition, Hopkins reiterated his continued belief that the government had to administer these programs on the federal level because the problem was national in scope and needed a consistent policy. While he stated that "[n]ational intervention to stimulate competition is the democratic method," Hopkins did not dismiss the importance of private industry acting according to the profit motive. Competition within a capitalist society and private investments were, for Hopkins, essential ingredients in permanent recovery

Hopkins' long commitment to democracy, capitalism, social service, and government responsibility for the welfare of citizens had in no way diminished over the years. In 1938 he echoed the aspirations of the New Deal: Any solution to

> the dislocations in our economic life . . . can only be achieved by the fullest cooperation between government, labor, agriculture and business. It can only be solved if profits to business genuine competition are encouraged; if labor is paid a fair wage; if the farmers attain a proper share in the national income; and if great masses of people who for any reason cannot obtain a minimum share in the national income are protected by an all inclusive program of social security.[73]

Harry Hopkins was neither an ideologue nor a radical. He merely believed implicitly in the power of work and in the government's responsibility to ensure that this work was available. Hopkins' social programs were designed primarily to address the problems caused by mass unemployment during the Great Depression and were meant to fit in with the culture of the 1930s. They were not intended to change society through social engineering. Like many New Dealers, Hopkins brought to the administration a set of principles and policies as well as the force of his personality. Over the years his personality tempered only slightly. His policies changed and he often adapted his programs to conform with the immediate situation, yet his principles remained the same. Basic to all of his relief work was his total commitment to making sure that Americans who needed help, for whatever reason, got it.

Hopkins spent billions of tax dollars to mitigate the ruinous effects of the Great Depression on American workers. He was never concerned with economizing. Putting men and women back to work was his primary concern, and he never for a moment doubted that the public's money was well spent. In 1938 the *New York Times* quoted him as saying:

> Perhaps many will think I am not the man to say what economy is—but I know what it is not. To permit idle men with their families to starve; to let our schools close; to let our city streets become a maze of holes; to see our land wash away and our homes go to rack is not economy.
>
> To use the wealth we have to put our idle people to work in the task of the internal development of our country and in the conservation of our natural resources is real economy. That is the heart of the work program.[74]

Hopkins admitted that work programs cost more than direct relief. They always had. But he pointed out that government jobs brought "material enrichments" to the community and added to the national wealth. In March of 1936 he asked: "What would America have to show today for the millions it has spent on relief if that relief had been in the form of a non-productive dole? Nothing except an army of disheartened, disillusioned, and resentful unemployed people nursing their sense of frustration and despair."[75]

The idealistic Hopkins had envisioned a permanent job assurance program as an important segment of America's welfare system. As he had demonstrated over and over, he could present government work programs as not only consistent with widely-accepted traditions but also as effective in solving unemployment problems for millions. He insisted that the opportunity to work was an inalienable right for all citizens and that government unemployment relief in the form of jobs should be part of any proposed social insurance package.[76] Yet between Hopkins' Hyde Park meeting with Roosevelt in early September 1934 and the following December, a period during which the CES had been debating all facets of the economic security program, the administration's policy makers turned a cold shoulder to a permanent and national job assurance program as part of the economic security bill. Unemployment insurance, old-age insurance, and aid to dependent children, on the other hand, did become permanent elements of the president's national plan. The elimination of the work assurance program had important ramifications for America during the next half century. Relief, including the provision of jobs, was relegated to a temporary sphere and expected to end as soon as business and the economy revived. Those afflicted by long-term unemployment, a population that Hopkins saw as inevitably growing, eventually might fall through the cracks in the safety net. To his great disappointment, Hopkins failed to convince the administration that cyclical unemployment would be a permanent malady of any industrial society and that unemployment insurance would not be sufficient to meet any future economic crisis.

The CES Advisory Committee shared the president's fear that the boundary between relief and social insurance would blur. The members did not want a government employment program to "deteriorate into forced labor" and become virtually indistinguishable from relief. This could happen, especially if the plan they adopted mirrored the work-relief (FERA) model, which restricted jobs to those on relief rolls and paid wages according to individual need rather than ability. The committee realized, however, that it was necessary to devise some form of work program. Therefore, the members recommended that candidates for employment be selected on the basis of ability rather than need and be paid according to work performed rather than an estimated budgetary deficiency. This proposed federal works corporation would provide diversified jobs paying adequate wages but also would involve enormous scope and expense.[77] This model, although clearly distinguishable from relief, was reminiscent of the somewhat radical, controversial, and expensive CWA. Thus it proved to be problematic for those who feared socialism creeping into the government as well as for those who wondered how the government was going to pay for such an ambitious program.

Both Roosevelt and Hopkins understood that long-term unemployment insurance had dangerous similarities to the English dole, a redistributive system that transferred money from those who earned it to those who, for various reasons, did not. As early as November 1933 the president believed that he was speaking for the majority of the people when he stated, "I have a feeling that the temper of the American people is not going to stand for the payment of insurance benefits over long periods of time to people who do not work." Unemployed American workers wanted the assurance of a job—any job, whether public or private—rather than the guarantee of extended unemployment insurance payments.[78] The CES agreed and in its report to the president in January 1935, it had recommended a job assurance program along with unemployment and old-age insurance, aid to fatherless children, and a public health program.[79]

Hopkins had consistently fought the idea that a comprehensive insurance program would eliminate completely the need for government employment. Yet government work programs, although in accordance with popular attitudes of the 1930s, were not included as part of the act that would form the basis of our welfare state. Instead, unemployment insurance became the mainstay of government efforts to provide economic security. At a 1955 ceremony in Washington, D.C., to celebrate the twentieth anniversary of the Social Security Act, Edwin Witte gave a clue as to why this happened. He recounted that in 1935 there had been real doubts that the economic security bill would ever get passed. The difficulties, he said, had to do with the continuing economic depression. "Because we were in the midst of a deep depression, the Administration and the Congress were very anxious to avoid placing too great burdens on business and also of adding to Government deficits."[80] Clearly the model that the Advisory Council recommended for a jobs program (the CWA model) came dangerously close to these pitfalls.

Hopkins biographer Searle Charles suggested that political reasons lay behind the fact that the Hopkins' work program failed. A federal work-relief corporation as a permanent part of its economic security program, with a price tag of $9 billion, terrified conservatives. In light of strong opposition from the Liberty League, the National Association of Manufacturers, and the United States Chambers of Commerce as well as banking and finance groups, presidential support for this measure was essential. Despite the boost given his administration by the off-year elections, FDR, according to Charles, capitulated to conservatism. This venture into job guarantees would tread dangerously close to socialism. Believing that the road to recovery lay in cooperation among labor, business, and government, the president opted for conciliation rather than confrontation.[81]

While these analyses help to clarify the situation in 1935, another explanation seems more likely. Hopkins' commitment to a work component in New Deal relief programs derived from his emphasis on preserving the capitalist system as well as the morale of the needy unemployed who had been forced to ask for assistance. Yet he had to ensure that government jobs programs did not undermine capitalism while trying to preserve it. Work-relief programs that duplicated wages, hours, and conditions of private businesses surely would have boosted the morale of the workers who found jobs through these agencies, but they also would have threatened private enterprise. The CWA, a popular program that was enormously successful in putting people to work quickly and with little taint of traditional relief, did just that and was scrapped within four months. Had the CWA followed more carefully "the American Way," likely it would have been extended. Because it came uncomfortably close to competing with private industry, Hopkins' plan for a permanent public works corporation was much too radical a step for the committee and for the president.[82]

If the Committee on Economic Security had difficulty in creating a work program that conformed to American traditions, it had less trouble devising a program to aid mothers with dependent children. It took for its model the various states' widows' pensions/mothers' aid programs that had been functioning since 1911, eventually in forty-five states. Like the state laws that permitted localities to provide funds for fatherless families, children, not the women who cared for them, were the targets for this aid. The CES used the same rhetoric so familiar during the debates early in the century over widows' pensions: "These are not primarily aids to mothers but defense measures for children. They are designed to release from the wage-earning role the person whose natural function is to give her children the physical and affectionate guardianship necessary not alone to keep them falling into social misfortune, but more affirmatively, to rear them into citizens capable of contributing to society."[83] Katherine Lenroot, who succeeded Grace Abbott as head of the Children's Bureau in 1934, reiterated the notion first emphasized in 1911 that unless a woman were highly skilled or a professional, "her contribution in the home was greater than her earnings outside the home."[84] Adherence to the principles that "the essential values of home life in the rearing of children and . . . no child should be separated from his family because of poverty alone" had endured intact from the Progressive Era to the New Deal.[85]

Hopkins had been actively involved in the hard-fought battle to pass the widows' pension law in New York State, and he therefore was familiar with the arguments and issues articulated on this subject. In a 1935 article he wrote for *Colliers* magazine, he brought up the subject of such pensions, calling them "enlightened care" for poor families:

> Widows' pensions in most states took on the character of a "right" and whether we like it or not these pensions gave to those families a type of security on the one hand and an independence in the community on the other that was not found in the great mass of people who received outdoor relief from the poor law authorities or from private charities. . . . There is a very nice distinction here and that is that it is quite possible in America to provide what amounts to pension benefits for the care of children that will in no wise separate people from the rest of the community and permit them to be raised in an atmosphere and under auspices which do not stigmatize them forever as a group set apart."[86]

Hopkins recognized full well that neither private agencies nor state programs could keep up with the demand for help during the Depression and regarded the recommendations of the CES as the first important acceptance of federal responsibility for these families. He hoped that such benefits would enable needy mothers to keep children home. Moreover, a federal program would allow them to retain "self-respect and dignity." This was exactly the hope he had for unemployed industrial workers. Yet he, like most members of the CES, the Advisory Committee, and the Technical Board, seemed more concerned with hammering out the very complicated plans for unemployment and old-age insurance than with aid to dependent children. An article in the *Baltimore Sun* in December of 1934 reported that Secretary Perkins had "brought back into the spotlight" measures that had been eclipsed by other issues deemed more important to unemployed industrial workers.[87]

Hopkins was especially concerned by the fact that so many fatherless children were on federal relief rolls when their families were also eligible for state-funded mothers' aid. Statistics compiled by the CES revealed that less than one-third of needy, fatherless families received state pensions (which were permissive rather than mandatory) and that the federal government was supporting the rest, largely through FERA relief payments. Thus the federal government was shouldering the major portion of the cost to support families— costs that should be absorbed by county or municipal agencies. The CES recognized that state mothers' aid provided for higher levels of relief than the FERA, but also knew that the funding necessary to absorb all the needy families simply was not available on the state level. It recommended, therefore, that federal grants-in-aid be paid to the states to strengthen the widows' pension programs, one federal dollar for every two dollars generated by the combined state and local funds available for mothers' pensions.[88]

At the National Conference on Economic Security held in Washington, D.C. on November 14, 1934, Grace Abbott chaired the roundtable discussion on child welfare as part of the committee's deliberations on how poor mothers with young children could avoid poor relief. In the eyes of the framers of our welfare system, work would not provide solutions for needy mothers whom society saw as necessary caregivers for their children. For these women, the insecurity of emergency relief would be replaced by the more adequate, less expensive, federally assisted and state-administered mothers' aid.[89] Arguments that used the pauperizing effects of public relief to defend work programs could not be used for mothers' pensions since, in 1934, most women (and especially mothers) still were assumed to be properly and permanently dependent upon a wage-earning male. The argument for mothers' pensions used in 1915 was echoed almost twenty years later: Poor, single mothers should remain at home doing the very important and appropriate job of properly raising their children.[90] The CES grouped these women with unemployables; mothers' aid was meant to do for the fatherless child what old-age pensions did for another group of unemployables—the aged.[91]

The participants of this roundtable discussion (Hopkins and many other veterans of the widows' pension debates included) reiterated the centrality of the family to any program of economic and social security. According to Homer Folks, an old warhorse from the Progressive Era, a federal program of security for children provided "a suitable opening wedge for the entire social security program." He related unemployment insurance and old-age insurance to the welfare of children, claiming that payments had to be geared to the number and ages of children in the family.[92]

Frances Perkins spoke of needy children and their mothers on the relief rolls as "the most important group in terms of the future welfare of our country."[93] Few involved in the debates would deny mothers' and children's needs or their right to assistance. Furthermore, all recognized the inadequacy of the state pensions. What bothered the members of the CES was that many women and children legally eligible for mothers' pensions were being cared for by emergency relief because the local programs had no money left. Although no one could agree as to the exact number of dependents and the exact amount given on the local level, all agreed that this mothers' aid was necessary. It helped ensure a wholesome home life for children and, moreover, prevented juvenile delinquency, health problems, and other social ills. The Depression had curtailed state aid to poor mothers, and many services for their children had been discontinued because of lack of funds.[94] The welfare of innocent children, the future citizens of America, had been seriously undermined.

It was clear that poor children and their mothers would get no immediate benefits from the other measures of the Social Security Bill, and there was little opposition to funding state programs that allowed mothers to remain at home and care for their children. Therefore, with the backing of the Children's Bureau, the CES recommendations to FDR included security for children. "We are strongly of the opinion that these families should be differentiated from the permanent dependents and unemployables, and we believe that the children's aid plan is the method which will best care for their needs."[95] Aid to Dependent Children, like old age-assistance, was not expected to be a permanent program. The framers assumed that need for both public assistance programs would decline as more and more families benefited from old-age pensions and unemployment insurance.[96] Hopkins, however, never was convinced that this would happen for dependent mothers and consistently advocated income maintenance for this population.

When the Social Security bill was submitted to Congress, it provided for the creation of a new agency, the Social Security Board, to assume administrative responsibilities for the insurance programs; the Children's Bureau was assigned responsibility for Maternal and Child Health, Crippled Children, and Child Welfare Services; and the FERA was to take charge of the Old Age Assistance (OAA) and Aid to Dependent Children (ADC) programs. However, during the seven months that the House and Senate deliberated, these assignments underwent important changes in standards, personnel, administration, and scope.[97]

Originally the CES had recommended that the FERA have responsibility for administering ADC and asked Hopkins' staff to submit a draft of the title pertaining to this section of the bill. In this draft, the FERA defined dependent children as "children under the age of sixteen in their own homes, in which there is no adult person, other than one needed to care for the child or children, who is able to work and provide the family with a reasonable subsistence compatible with decency and health." Hopkins sought to raise the standards of relief administration for needy families through an enlarged scope of federal aid for dependent children (as well as through an extended and permanent government work program.) This FERA draft for ADC did not stipulate that assistance should be based on the presence or absence of any particular family member; rather it should be based on the need of the entire family for a decent and healthy existence. It described broad eligibility requirements for all needy families with children under sixteen. However, before Congress passed the security bill, it added text to Title IV specifying reasons for dependency, additions that clearly placed it within the category of mothers' aid/widows' pensions programs. This was largely due to the influence of the Children's Bureau. ADC assistance thus was limited to children who had been "deprived of parental support or care by reason of the death, continued absence from home, a physical or mental incapacitation of a parent." This change came about as the result of a dispute between the FERA and the Children's Bureau over which body would administer ADC. Although the CES had recommended that the FERA have control of ADC, the Children's Bureau felt that this was its proper territory. But even more important, the Children's Bureau and the FERA had very different notions of what ADC should be. Hopkins' recommendations for ADC were much broader and not gender-specific whereas the Children's Bureau conceptualized a pension program that aided fatherless families; it relied on the same arguments used by advocates of mothers' pensions twenty years earlier. The CES included this interpretation in its final submission to the president but did not support the Children's Bureau campaign for administrative control of ADC. Its recommendation that FERA administer ADC was rejected by Congress, which delegated that task to the independent Social Security Board.[98]

Hopkins had developed his policies toward relief and recovery on the run. They evolved as a result of his experiences during the crisis years of the Depression, yet they also drew on his earlier social work career. He still believed that needy women with children deserved dignified access to public assistance. His design for ADC was based on state programs for widows' pension, but he had expanded and improved on the administration and spirit of that older model. He maintained his commitment to federal responsibility for efficiently and humanely administered public relief. But for Hopkins, a federal work program was the essential ingredient for the nation's economic recovery.

CHAPTER TEN

CONCLUSION

THE CULTURAL AND POLITICAL CURRENTS THAT SHAPED AMERICAN SOCIETY during the early decades of the twentieth century had a decided effect on the configuration of the American welfare system as it appeared in the 1930s. Social workers, politicians, and reformers carried those currents into the maelstrom of the Great Depression to influence New Deal policy. New York City took the lead in many of the movements that influenced the way Franklin Roosevelt's administration addressed problems arising out of economic crises during the Great Depression—the city's innovative approach to unemployment became a prototype for work-relief programs; the charities controversy conditioned much of the later policy surrounding public subsidies and child care; the city's widows' pension program laid the foundation for ADC. There were, of course, many social and political leaders from New York who brought their ideas and attitudes to Washington in 1933, including Frances Perkins, Homer Folks, and Jane Hoey. Harry Hopkins was unique among them because he seemed to combine all of the experiences that contributed to America's emergent welfare system. His proposed job assurance program was neither ameliorative nor preventive. Rather, it was meant to place economic agency in the hand of the worker because Roosevelt's federal relief administrator believed that relief did not improve status of the worker; only the security of an assured wage could do this.

Secretary of Labor Frances Perkins wrote Harry Hopkins a letter in 1940 when she thought (incorrectly, it turned out) that he was leaving the administration, recalling "that evening in March 1933 when you and I and Bill Hodson argued out the urgency of the relief situation and devised ways and means of bringing it to the attention of the President. . . . It was through your leadership the whole country, including the Government, discovered a new human area." Perkins praised Hopkins' creativity in constructing "a decent, reasonable relief system" that she predicted would give rise to real reforms in the future.[1] Despite the efforts of some of the nation's best leaders, this never happened.

Hopkins did not intend to construct a permanent relief system. He wanted to employ the temporarily unemployed. Moreover, for a time at least, Hopkins was successful in overcoming Americans' traditional aversion to direct, public relief. In 1933 the federal government, for the first time, accepted responsibility for the welfare of the people. This was innovative. Only the severity of the economic crisis allowed Hopkins' relief programs to be initiated. People were starving, and any program that would help them out of their misery, even the dole, would have their grateful support. Both Roosevelt and Hopkins believed that direct relief was inappropriate for most Americans. The able-bodied unemployed should be given the opportunity to earn wages that would provide security for the family and stimulate the economy through consumer spending. If all workers could be guaranteed a job, either through private enterprise or through government projects, the economic health of the nation would be assured.

Hopkins' work programs became the centerpiece of his plan for economic security. He first expressed this preference for work over relief in 1915 when he helped administer the Bronx Zoo project, which can be seen as a pilot program for New Deal work-relief. During the 1930s the government spent billions to provide jobs for America's idle workforce through the FERA, CWA, and WPA as well as through Harold Ickes' PWA. The WPA, the culmination of Roosevelt's program to get workers back on the job and to stimulate the economy, did provide work for millions. Although the program had its critics, it was enormously popular. The significance of the WPA to the story of the development of America's welfare system lies in the ideals that led to its creation and the compromises that it demanded.

Hopkins believed that the nature of America's economic system inevitably would lead to "reservoirs of unemployed knocking on the gates of our factories" because cyclical unemployment would become a permanent feature of the industrial system.[2] Thus it was up to the government to provide sufficient benefits for those unable to find employment in private industry. Those temporarily in need because of involuntary unemployment should no longer have to rely on private charity but should be provided for out of the national income.[3] Yet what Hopkins had hoped would become the third instrument of government relief policy never materialized. His proposed work program did not become a permanent part of the 1935 legislation. Loyalty to President Roosevelt as well as a practical turn of mind convinced Hopkins to accept the WPA as a compromise. At a time when most people believed that the nation was on its way to economic recovery, Hopkins could not have been surprised that the administration hesitated to take such a radical step. Government jobs had a socialistic tinge, might have competed unfairly with private business, and could have proven to be outrageously expensive. The 1935 Social Security Act thus led America on a different path to becoming a welfare state from what Hopkins had envisioned. Workers would be protected by federally mandated, time-limited, and state-administered unemployment insurance and, when they retired, by old-age insurance. There would be no government-assured job when unemployment insurance ran out. Means-tested public assistance would help those whose poverty did not result from unemployment due to the economic crisis, mainly mothers with dependent children and the elderly. Hopkins recognized that poor children probably comprised the largest single group of needy. Furthermore, while the Social Security measures might well be extended to many poor children, many others would remain beyond help. Those children would be reliant on ADC, whose benefits, Hopkins knew, were "far too meager in many states."[4]

In 1935 relief became a state-level responsibility. When the Social Security Act passed, Hopkins declared: "[W]e are going to quit Federal relief on November 1st." He called upon the states to assume responsibility for those unable to work, insisting that they had the resources. "There is no state in the Union that hasn't the power and wealth to take care of the unemployables if they want to. . . . And the Federal government isn't leaving them high and dry." However, Hopkins regarded federal monies for these programs and the federal mandate as a legitimizing element for this assistance, pointing out that the states received 50 percent of the cost of Old Age Assistance and one-third of the cost of ADC from the federal government.[5] Thus, according to Hopkins' plan, every family with an employable member would be supported by his or her earnings, and families with no employable member would be cared for by the state.[6]

Hopkins never gave up his commitment to a permanent program of countercyclical government projects to absorb unemployed industrial workers. For him unemployment was no longer just a temporary effect of the Great Depression. It would always be a pressing social problem, the result of technological advances, of normal business cycles, or of the market economy. The Social Security Act, Hopkins declared, is only the beginning; employment assurance must be added to public assistance and social insurance in order to complete the package. At the end of 1936, he wrote an article for the *New*

Republic in which he stated: "If it becomes evident that private enterprise cannot make the most efficient use of all available manpower and all available resources, people will look to public services as a means of supplementing private employment." The federal government, he wrote, should augment unemployment insurance with public works not only to employ idle workers but "also to release the productive energies of persons who would otherwise be unemployed." He insisted that if industry was unable to employ enough workers, then it must be prepared to pay its share of the cost of employing workers on public projects as well as the cost of unemployment insurance.[7] For years he had vigorously defended his program of government jobs for the able-bodied unemployed as the American way to welfare. Government work projects would stimulate the economy through public money, which would be spent for materials to support these projects and then respent by newly confident, wage-earning workers. Government jobs would prime the economic pump. And this, Hopkins declared, "is as American as corn on the cob."[8]

Hopkins knew what he was talking about, being from Iowa. The nature of the programs that he directed during the 1930s reflected much of his rural background and education as well as his early social work experiences. The commitment to public service, to democracy, and to capitalism that he took from his Grinnell experience never wavered. Neither did his belief that social justice was attainable. He rejected the formal religion of his mother and the religious impulse that had been so strong at Grinnell College and Christodora House for a more personal ethic. His moral standards simplified into a do-unto-others ideology and he discarded any notion that relief should be used as a lever for adjusting the behavior of its recipients. Practicality took root during Hopkins' early career when he realized that he needed a platform of power from which to implement his ideas. Throughout the New Deal years, he believed that prevention of poverty was just as important as amelioration, but that the security of a job paying a living wage was more important than either.

Hopkins' administration of work-relief and widows' pensions programs in New York City during the Progressive Era carried over into the New Deal with particular significance. Like many progressive reformers in the New Deal, he jockeyed for position within the Roosevelt administration in order to implement his policies and programs. However, unlike most, by 1935 Hopkins had an extremely close relationship with the president, which allowed him latitude and influence. Thus the programs he administered and the attitudes he imparted had an enormous impact on the nature of American social policy.

Harry Hopkins' ideal welfare state has never been realized. He clearly recognized the shortcomings of the Social Security Act of 1935. Yet although the act did not include a permanent job assurance or a national health program, programs he had campaigned for, it still established federal responsibility for the welfare of Americans. For this reason Hopkins felt the act was an important step along the American way to welfare.

A belief in the pauperizing effect of relief in any form and a tendency to judge relief recipients in moral instead of economic terms always has been an integral part of the national mind. This prevented America's welfare system from maturing into its complete form, with a work-assurance component.[9] Although Hopkins recognized this, he could not change it. Several months before his death in late January 1946, Harry Hopkins expressed his disdain of the paralyzing fear of doing harm by doing good. He challenged the fear that many of his critics expressed, the fear that if the government ensured its citizens of the opportunity to work, "it would destroy the incentive for hard work which is so characteristic of our American tradition." Hopkins did not believe in moralizing; he did not worry that people's character would be destroyed if they got old-age benefits or government jobs. In a democracy, the government had a responsibility to ensure the welfare of its citizens. He argued that "full employment must and can be attained within the framework of our traditional democratic processes" and that it was "a contradiction in terms" to fight for democracy abroad while admitting "that the system may not be able and certainly should not attempt to assure every man able and willing to work a right to an opportunity to secure the reasonable necessities of life that make up what we know as the American standard of living."[10]

By 1940, after seven years as Roosevelt's relief administrator, Hopkins had turned his attention almost completely to international affairs. The war in Europe distracted the president, and the manufacture of munitions began to have an effect on the economy. People were working again. World War II provided the nation with a public works project on a scale that not even Hopkins could have imagined. The worldwide attention Hopkins received as emissary to Winston Churchill and Joseph Stalin, as administrator of Lend Lease, and as the shadowy figure behind Roosevelt at the Big Three conferences subsumed his role as New Deal relief administrator. Yet not every one forgot his earlier efforts. Martha Gellhorn, one of the FERA's roving reporters, spoke of Hopkins' New Deal years: "That was his period of social conscience; he then switched and became the servant of the President, and that was his period of power diplomacy, and courtiership. He was much wittier and brighter in the second period and much nicer in the first period."[11] Not everyone would have agreed with this assessment.

Hopkins did not live long enough to write his memoirs. He is remembered only by what he did or did not do. Many hated him. In 1941 a journalist explained that "[n]o one could dispense $9,498,000,000 without making countless enemies."[12] He was often "crucified" in the press, usually from those who were opposed to his principles rather than his performance. Likened to a modern-day Rasputin, "a sinister puppeteer," he was described as "inscrutable," called the "Archangel of spending," criticized as both a "dreamer and a doer."[13] But many others admired him as the tenacious and irreverent New Dealer who marshaled the resources of the federal government to champion the rights of the lower one-third of the nation.[14] Charles Beard wrote that "Administrator, Harry L. Hopkins, has taken a realistic view of the appalling situation, has cast off all trivial clichés about the poor, and has acted with skill and promptness. With much justification, Mr. Hopkins may be called the most enlightened and realistic statesman in the whole administration at Washington, not excluding the President himself."[15]

In a congressional testimonial to Hopkins, one U.S. Representative remarked that his contribution to the nation will be remembered "long after those who have attacked him in recent years have been written off by their descendants as persons of unaccountable obtuseness."[16] This prediction did not materialize. Hopkins' programs have long been relegated to historical footnotes, remembered by most only as an ingredient of the New Deal alphabet soup. Nevertheless, Hopkins was proud of the work he did as a New Dealer and declared: "Now I get something of a thrill, I am perfectly frank to say, out of being engaged in an enterprise that belongs to the people. . . . [T]his is the toughest job that any Government has had to do, and we as servants and agents of that Government should be damn proud that we got a chance to work for this nation of ours."[17]

Hopkins never lost his compassion for the unfortunate despite the position of enormous power he attained, and he never lost his idealism despite the failures and political upheavals he experienced. In an address to the student body of Grinnell College given in 1939, Secretary of Commerce Hopkins declared,

> the government is going to treat people in ways we have never dreamed of before, and, therefore, the government should be good. With the world situation the way it is today, almost a mad house, with hate and fear sweeping the world; with this nation almost the last stronghold of Democracy; with the American people determined to maintain that Democracy, the kind of government that we have is extremely important, and it is the one thing in America that is important.

Hopkins believed that the uniqueness of America lay in the ability of the government to recognize its responsibility to provide for the welfare of those in need. Within a very short time he transferred those beliefs onto the world stage when he acted as Roosevelt's envoy to Churchill and Stalin and as Lend Lease administrator during World War II. He concluded his talk to the students by saying: "I have grown to have a tremendous affection and love for this country—the fields—the land—and the people. Nothing must happen to it, and those of us who get a chance, and many of us will because of the things this nation has done for us, should and will be motivated when the time comes to serve it well."[18] Although he battled with debilitating illness, Hopkins continued to serve his president and his country until his death in early 1946. He grew from his Iowa roots into a public servant and a patriot who dedicated his life to his country. His goal, however, a national income properly divided to give benefits to those people who had been dealt "deuces and threes," a guarantee of a regular income, a minimum standard of living, and the dignity of a job for every able-bodied worker remains an unfulfilled dream.[19]

"There is really nothing more to say—except why? But since why is so difficult to handle, one must take refuge in how."

Toni Morrison, *The Bluest Eye*

ABBREVIATIONS USED IN NOTES

ACSS   Archives of the Community Service Society
FDRL   Franklin Delano Roosevelt Library
GUSC   Georgetown University Special Collections
HBRC   Hazel Braugh Records Center, American Red Cross
HHP   Harry L. Hopkins Papers
HHPP   Harry L. Hopkins Personal Papers
JAKP   John Adams Kingsbury Papers
OGNY   Office of the Governor of New York
PPF   President's Personal Files
TMs   Typed manuscript

Notes

CHAPTER ONE

1. This incident occurred at University of Iowa when Hopkins announced Hallie Flanagan's appointment as head of the Federal Theatre Project. Flanagan, who attended Grinnell with Hopkins, declared that he "was never above a certain amount of hokum, and on that occasion he pulled a piece of business that would delight any stage manager." Joanne Bentley, *Hallie Flanagan: A Life in the American Theatre* (New York: Alfred A. Knopf, 1988), 192.

2. Harry L. Hopkins, "What Is the American Way?" July 16, 1938, 1, The Harry L. Hopkins Papers, Part IV, 1:52, Special Collections, Lauinger Library, Georgetown University, Washington, D.C. (Here after Hopkins IV, GUSC).

3. "Iowa's Harry Hopkins Seeks a New 'American Way,' He Wants a Place in the Sun for Those Who Can't Make a Living," *Press Digest,* March 3, 1937, Sec. 2, 4, 1-3, Hopkins I, 40:9, GUSC.

4. John Kingsbury, "Roosevelt and Hopkins, Personal Reminiscences," 4, John Adams Kingsbury Papers, Manuscript Division, Library of Congress, Washington, D. C. (Hereinafter JAKP), B81: Autobiography.

5. Memorial to Harry Hopkins written by John Steinbeck and read by Burgess Meredith, May 22, 1946, Hopkins I, 1:45, GUSC, and Grinnell College Archives, Burling Library, Grinnell College, Grinnell, Iowa. (Hereinafter Grinnell College Archives.)

6. Gwendolyn Mink, *The Wages of Motherhood: Inequality in the Welfare State 1917-1942* (Ithaca, N.Y.: Cornell University Press, 1995), viii.

7. Donald S. Howard, *The WPA and Federal Relief Policy* (New York: Russell Sage Foundation, 1943), 693.

8. The Progressive Era is loosely defined as 1900 to World War I.

9. *Proceedings,* "National Conference on Economic Security, November 14, 1934," RG 47, Box 4, National Archives. The National Conference was held at the Mayflower Hotel; the Round Table Conference on Child Welfare was chaired by Grace Abbott of the University of Chicago.

10. Robert Sherwood, *Roosevelt and Hopkins: An Intimate History* (New York: Harper & Bros., 1948), 14.

11. Ethel Gross Hopkins Conant, transcript of taped interview by Roger Daniels, August 17-October 26, 1964, 47, Oral History Archives, Powell Library, University of California at Los Angeles. (Hereinafter Conant Interview.) The tapes are available at UCLA's Powell Library; transcripts in author's possession.

12. Robert Sherwood to John Kingsbury, October 27, 1947; John Kingsbury to Donald S. Howard, February 26, 1956, JAKP, B11: Hopkins, Harry L.

13. Henry Adams, *Harry Hopkins* (New York: G. P. Putnam, 1977); Searle F. Charles, *Minister of Relief: Harry Hopkins and the Depression* (Syracuse, N.Y.: Syracuse University Press, 1963); Paul A. Kurzman, *Harry Hopkins and the New Deal* (Fairlawn, N.J.: R. E. Burdick, 1974); George McJimsey, *Harry Hopkins: Ally of the Poor, Defender of Democracy* (Cambridge, Mass.: Harvard University Press, 1987); Sherwood, *Roosevelt and Hopkins;* Matthew B. Wills, *Wartime Missions of Harry L. Hopkins* (Raleigh, N.C.: Pentland Press, 1996).

14. For example, James T. Patterson, *America's Struggle Against Poverty* (Cambridge, Mass.: Harvard University Press, 1986); James Leiby, *A History of Social Welfare and Social Work in the United States* (New York: Columbia University Press, 1978); Michael B. Katz, *Poverty and Policy in American History* (New York: Academic Press, 1983) and *In the Shadow of the Poorhouse: A Social History of Welfare in America* (New York: Basic Books, 1986); Alan Dawley, *Struggles for Justice: Responsibility and the Liberal State* (Cambridge, Mass.: Harvard University Press, 1991), 9; Edward Berkowitz and Kim McQuaid, *Creating the Welfare State: The Political Economy of 20th Century Reform* (Lawrence: University Press of Kansas, 1988); Theda Skocpol, *Protecting Soldiers and Mothers: The Political Origins of Social Policy in the United States* (Cambridge, Mass.: Belknap Press, 1992); Linda Gordon, *Pitied But Not Entitled: Single Mothers and the History of Welfare, 1890-1935* (New York: Macmillan, 1994); Mink; Martha Swain, *Ellen Woodward: New Advocate for Women* (Jackson: University Press of Mississippi, 1995); Molly Ladd-Taylor, *Mother-Work: Child Welfare and the State, 1890-1930* (Urbana: University of Illinois Press, 1994); Seth Koven and Sonya Michel, *Mothers of a New World: Maternalist Politics and the Origins of the Welfare State* (New York: Routledge, 1993); and Dorothy Brown and Elizabeth McKeown, *The Poor Belong to Us: Catholic Charities and American Welfare* (Cambridge, Mass.: Harvard University Press, 1998).

15. Donald S. Howard to John Kingsbury, January 13, 1956, JAKP, B11: Hopkins, Harry L.

CHAPTER TWO

1. Biographers have noted Harry Hopkins' kinship to Maine Democrat and newspaper publisher Marcellus Emery, who owned two newspapers during the Civil War (see McJimsey, 6.) Emery, a rabid Copperhead, was not Hopkins' grandfather, as some have reported, for Emery never did marry, but he probably was a relative of Hopkins' paternal grandmother, Mary Ann Emery Hopkins. In 1936 Harry Hopkins apparently made inquiries regarding Emery because he got a letter from Kenneth M. Sills, president of Bowdoin College in Brunswick, Maine, telling him that Marcellus Emery attended the college and graduated in 1853. An enclosed article stated that "he espoused the southern cause" and in 1868 was member of the Democratic National Committee from Maine. As a result of Hopkins' inquiries, a member of the WPA Writer's Project in Bangor collected some facts on this Hopkins ancestor. Emery, born 1830, acted as a private tutor for a family in Mississippi in 1855, where he probably got his pro-slavery ideas. He later became editor of two local newspapers, the *Bangor Daily Union* and the *Bangor Democrat.* In 1861 his pro-slavery sentiments resulted in a riot during which a mob broke into his offices, destroyed his press, and threatened him with hanging. Oddly enough, when Emery died in February of 1879, the obituaries in the local papers declared him to have been a learned man of superior intellect, an eloquent speaker, and a fine journalist. In the late 1860s, however, given Marcellus Emery's unpopular ideas, Mary Ann Emery might not have been too reluctant to leave town to

follow her husband to Iowa. Kenneth M. Sills to Harry Hopkins, August 26, 1936, with enclosures; Albert Abrahmson, Administrator, WPA, Maine, to Kathryn Godwin, September 11, 1936; Special Collections, Bowdoin College Library , Brunswick, Maine; Marcellus Emery Obituary, *Whig and Courier,* February 24, 1870; Genealogical note from Lewis Hopkins, in author's possession; Herbert W. Bathelder to Anna Pickett Hopkins (APH), May 8, 1929; J.W.C., "The Rear Seat," *Sioux City Journal,* April 6, 1930. The column features a piece written by Lewis Hopkins, son of Al Hopkins and brother of Harry Hopkins, recounting his father's story of his early life in Sioux City. In author's possession.

2. John Milton, *South Dakota, A Bicentennial History* (New York: Norton, 1977), 24-26; Herbert S. Schell, *History of South Dakota,* 3d ed. (Lincoln: University of Nebraska Press, 1975), 126-128.

3. Bathelder to APH, 1929; Charles J. Kimball to B. J. Petersen, undated; and B. J. Petersen to Harry Hopkins, January 1, 1937, in author's possession; Milton, 26.

4. See correspondence between David Aldona Hopkins (DAH) and Anna Pickett Hopkins (APH) and Ethel Gross Hopkins (EGH) and Harry Lloyd Hopkins (HLH), especially letters December 30, 1914; May 7, 1915; June 2, 1915; December 9, 1915, December 23, 1915; and June 15, 1916. These letters and correspondence cited below are in the author's possession and also in Hopkins II, GUSC.

5. 1915 Census (Card #786), Grinnell, Iowa; John R. Scott, "The Picketts of Lowville," unpublished typed manuscript (MS), in author's possession. Louis Hopkins was apparently a fine builder; one of his projects, the Austin-Whittier House, is now on the National Register of Historical Buildings, and houses the Clay County, South Dakota, Historical Society. Rome Miller to Harry Hopkins, January 24, 1937. In author's possession. Andrew's first wife and Anna Pickett's mother, Mary Ann McClaren, died in 1875.

6. Miller to HLH, January 24, 1937; DAH to EGH and HLH, March 11, 1915, August 22, 1914, January 22, 1915, June 15, 1916; APH to EGH and HLH, December 30, 1914, January 28, 1915, December 23, 1915, April 30, 1915, June 2, 1915 September 12, 1915; Emery Hopkins to EGH and HLH, May 7, 1915, October 10, 1915; Miller to HLH, January 24, 1937.

7. Halford E. Luccock, *Endless Line of Splendor* (Chicago: Advance for Christ and His Church, 1950), 55.

8. R. George Eli, *Social Holiness: John Wesley's Thinking on Christian Community and its Relationship to the Social Order* (New York: Peter Lang, 1993), 1-4; Bernard Semmel, *The Methodist Revolution* (New York: Basic Books, 1975), 1-5.

9. Semmel, 5; Ann Douglas, *The Feminization of American Culture* (New York: Doubleday, 1977), 22-30; A. Gregory Schneider, *The Way of the Cross Leads Home: The Domestication of American Methodism* (Bloomington: University of Indiana Press, 1993), 169-170.

10. A. G. Schneider, 169.

11. In 1920 Harry Hopkins returned to Grinnell for a visit with his family and, with rather careless cynicism, recorded the progress his three brothers had made thus far: "If Sinclair Lewis ever gets the complete history of the Hopkins family, he will make 'Main Street' look like ten cents. I wouldn't have missed it for the world—Rome engaged to a Follies girl who happens to be Catholic and divorced—the hero selling alcohol a shade or two inside the law. Lewis flat on his back [with a cold] practicing the 'honking art' and thoroughly disillusioned—and Emery, the 100% American selling baggage in a department store at $35 per. Rome smiles, plans matrimony and looks for bigger things—Lew smiles a little pathetically—changes the babies [*sic*] diaper and looks for a better [medical] practice from now on—Emery reads of heroes in the

American magazine—begets a healthy child,—and plans to make some money soon. All are broke—complain but little—have no alibis—are securely nailed to females who think they could have made a respectable living had they been wearing the trousers." Quoted in McJimsey, 38.

12.   Miller to HLH, January 24, 1937. Rome Miller was a contemporary of Al Hopkins and lived with the Hopkins' family when he had fallen on hard times in 1876. He married Sam Hayward's daughter at about the same time Al Hopkins and Anna Pickett were married. In this letter he told Harry Hopkins that he lent Al Hopkins $10,000 because of the "extreme kindness and consideration" the family extended to him in 1876 and also because Anna Pickett Hopkins and his wife were friends. This would have been an enormous figure in the late nineteenth century and one wonders if Rome Miller did not mean $1,000; he would have been in his eighties when he wrote the letter. There is no indication that Miller got any of his money back.

13.   APH to HLH, January 28, 1915, Hopkins II, 2:10, GUSC; McJimsey, 4-5; The *Minneapolis Morning Tribune,* January 13, 191_, 1 (date partially indecipherable). This article noted that Dad Hopkins was probably "the best known ten pin enthusiast in these United States of ours" and added that he had "bowled in every city of any size in the United States, with the exception of the Pacific Coast towns." The couple moved to Spokane, Washington, in 1925 where Al fulfilled a lifelong dream and opened his own bowling alley in the Davenport Hotel. When Dad Hopkins was very ill and obviously dying, his son Harry asked where he would like to be buried. He replied, "Any God-damned place but Grinnell." Despite this, he was buried right next to Anna in Hazelwood Cemetery in Grinnell; and Harry Hopkins is now buried there also. (Dr. James Halsted, untitled typed manuscript, chapter 2. Hereinafter Halsted MS.) Dr. Halsted had been married to Eleanor and Franklin Roosevelt's daughter, Anna, and later (in the mid-1970s) married Diana Hopkins Baxter, daughter of Harry Hopkins and Barbara Duncan. The two met while Halsted was researching a biography of Hopkins; the manuscript cited is a draft of that unpublished biography. Some of the manuscript is unpaginated; in author's possession. McJimsey noted that Hopkins' friends and fellow New Dealers Florence and Robert Kerr and Hallie Flanagan are buried nearby. The difficulties that Anna Hopkins faced during the early years of her marriage were indicated in a letter Harry Hopkins received in 1941 written to him by an old friend from Hastings, Nebraska, Mrs. R. J. Peterson (Marie Kinnau), "My Dear Mr. Hopkins: from Hastings—God bless you, Harry, in your good work and make you as good a man as your mother was in her place. She was not having an easy time with you five children, and your father's mother in the family, and a traveling man husband . . . but I never saw her cross, tho' worry did sometimes show on her face. I hope you know her Savior as intimately as she did." Hopkins responded warmly writing of his mother's "great and gallant spirit." HLH to Peterson, January 3, 1941, Hopkins I, 39:3, GUSC.

14.   Halsted MS, chapter 3, 26-27; Conant interview, 98, 115.

15.   Lewis Hopkins to HLH and EGH, May 7, 1915; APH to HLH and EGH, June 2, 1915, Hopkins II, GUSC. Al Hopkins hoped, apparently unsuccessfully, "to work up some enthusiasm for that business." APH to Harry and Ethel Hopkins, September 12, 1915, Hopkins II, GUSC.

16.   APH to EGH , December 23, 1915, Hopkins II, GUSC.

17.   DAH to HLH, August 22, 1914, Hopkins II, GUSC.

18.   DAH to EGH, January 22, 1915, Hopkins II, GUSC.

19.   See Sherwood, 6-8.

20.   APH to HLH and EGH, January 28, 1915, March 11, 1915, June 2, 1915; APH to Adah May Hopkins (AMH), March 11, 1915, Hopkins II, GUSC; Conant interview, 97.

21.   Conant interview, 100.

22. Harry Lloyd Hopkins, "Des Moines Speech," *Vital Speeches,* 1, no. 11 (March 15, 1939): 335.

23. John W. Schacht, "Four Men from Iowa," *The Palimpsest* 63 (1982): 4-5.

24. Robert M. Crunden, "George D. Herron in the 1890s: A New Frame of Reference for the Study of the Progressive Era," *Annals of Iowa* 42 (fall 1973): 83.

25. Grinnell College Timeline, 1996. Grinnell College; Henry H. Belfield, "One of the First Accounts," in *Grinnell College Blue Book, Sesquicentennial Issue* (Grinnell, Iowa: Grinnell College, 1996): 3-8. Belfield was a member of Iowa College class of 1858 while it was still located at Davenport. Quoted in Emery Stevens Bucks et al., eds., *The History of American Methodism* (New York: Abingdon Press, 1964), 332.

26. For a time Grinnell had been a stop on the Underground Railroad. The institution took the name of Iowa College; although it was commonly referred to as Grinnell, it did not formally adopt that name until 1909. See "Grinnell College Timeline" and John Shalte Nollen, *Grinnell College* (Iowa City: State Historical Society of Iowa, 1953). No faculty and no students went from Davenport to Grinnell. McJimsey, 8. Nollen, 100-104.

27. Aaron I. Abell, *The Urban Impact on American Protestantism* , vol. 54 (Cambridge, Mass.: Harvard University Press, 1943), 1-10.

28. Thomas M. Jacklin, "The Civic Awakening: Social Christianity and the Usable Past," *MidAmerica,* 64 (1982): 4.

29. Quoted in Crunden, 91.

30. William Deminoff, "From Grinnell to National Power," *Des Moines Register,* November 2, 1975. Kathryn Jagow, "Grinnellians and the New Deal," as quoted in Halsted MS, chapter 3, 32. Kathryn Jagow, a history student at Grinnell, wrote this paper in 1967.

31. McJimsey, 8-9; Deminoff; Charles Keserich, "The Political Odyssey of George D. Herron," *San Jose Studies* 3, no. 1 (1977): 79-94; Arthur Mann, ed., *The Progressive Era: Liberal Renaissance or Liberal Failure* (New York: Holt, Rinehart and Winston, 1963), 61-62; Nollen, 100; Crunden, 103.

32. Nollen, 102; "Herron Deposed from the Ministry," *The Grinnell Herald,* June 7, 1901, 2.

33. Nell Irvin Painter, *Standing at Armageddon: The United States, 1877-1919* (New York: W. W. Norton, 1987), xii, 138.

34. In the 1960s a student wrote that the scandal surrounding George Herron may have had a negative influence on the students, suggesting that "Grinnellians remember him as that man who ran away with the dean of women, rather than the man who began a lasting tradition of social concern at Grinnell." Jagow as quoted in Halsted MS, chapter 3, 33.

35. Nollen, 102.

36. *Grinnell and You* 20 (January 1934): 6-7, Grinnell College Archives, Burling Library, Grinnell College, Grinnell, Iowa.

37. *Iowa College Bulletin 1908-1909,* 23, Grinnell College Archives.

38. The Hopkins family remained in the house they rented at 1033 Elm Street, just across the street from the campus, until 1925 (except for a period of time when they lived a few blocks north). *Grinnell City Directory,* 1905, 1908, 1910, 1920, Grinnell College Archives.

39. Tuition amounted to $55 per year; room and board came to $3 to $5 a week, or about $150 a year. Tuition costs would have been hard for the Hopkins family to cover. Letters indicate that Anna's brother, John Pickett, who had moved to Manila around 1900 and established a successful harness and leather business there, helped pay for the children's educational expenses. When cars replaced horses, Pickett converted his

harness business into the hemp and rope business. Blayne Link (Harry Hopkins' niece) to author, June 3, 1990.

40. "The Hyde Prize Contest," *The Grinnell Herald,* June 7, 1901, 4.

41. Biographical Form, 1960, filled out by Adah May Hopkins Aime, Grinnell College Archives; Adah May Hopkins Transcript obtained from College Registrar; "College Commencement Exercises," *The Grinnell Herald,* June 16, 1905, 2. Seven years later, in 1912, Adah's mother, Anna, was diagnosed with tuberculosis.

42. *1911 Cyclone* (Grinnell College Yearbook); *1905 Cyclone,* Grinnell College Archives.

43. Nollen, 104.

44. *Scarlet and Black,* October 19, 1901, 3; *Scarlet and Black,* January 29, 1902, 2; *Scarlet and Black,* May 30, 1905, 1; The school newspaper, *Scarlet and Black,* reported the Debs speech in a very deprecatory article: "Grinnell's down-trodden laboring class was so busy working at from $2.00 to $5.00 a day that they didn't have time to stop to hear from Mr. Debs how miserable was their condition and as a result not a very large audience had gathered to welcome the candidate for president on the socialist ticket." Another article on the same page called Debs a fanatic and "the personification of radicalism." His appeal to the working class, his denunciation of wage slavery, and his call for "the social ownership of the modern machinery of production" mildly offended most of the Grinnell establishment, who nevertheless listened with polite attention. The article also reported that Debs made reference in this fifteen-minute speech to his supporter and fellow socialist whom the college and town had "crucified." *Scarlet and Black,* September 4, 1908, 1, Grinnell College Archives.

45. Lyman Abbott, author of *Christianity and Social Problems* (1898), edited the *Outlook,* a journal dedicated to the principles of the Social Gospel. Edward Steiner was a friend of Tolstoy; he stayed with him in 1903 while he was researching his book and admired his practice of working alongside his serfs on his own estate. Tolstoy believed that Christ wanted all to work together. Steiner died in 1956. See Sherwood, 18.

46. *1906 Cyclone,* 6-7, Grinnell College Archives. Edward Steiner, *From Alien to Citizen: The Story of My Life in America* (New York, Fleming H. Revell Company, 1914), 319.

47. Steiner would shock his students by opening his class with the remark, "You know, Jesus was a bastard." According to Florence Kerr, during World War I, he suffered abuse because of his German background and even had his house painted yellow. Jagow, as quoted in Halsted MS, chapter 3, 35.

48. Interviews with Grinnell College professors Brad Bateman and Joe Wall, October 1995. The *1906 Cyclone* lists Steiner's educational background as including study at "Gymnasia, Vienna, Pilsen, and Bohemia and at Universities of Vienna and Berlin," Grinnell College Archives.

49. *1906 Cyclone; Grinnell College Bulletin,* 1911-1912, 88, Grinnell College Archives.

50. *1906 Cyclone,* 6-7. See Steiner, *The Grinnell Herald,* September 14, 1909, 1; According to Grinnell Professor Brad Bateman, Steiner always traveled steerage, even when he could well afford a first-class ticket. He did this so that he could better document the immigrant experience.

51. "Address Before the Young Men's and Young women's Christian Association," *The Grinnell Herald,* June 17, 1904, 1.

52. Sherwood, 17; Nollen, 95-97. Jesse Macy retired in 1912, the year Hopkins graduated. Macy's protégé, John W. Gannaway (Grinnell, 1902), took over and taught political science at Grinnell until 1941.

53. Joan G. Zimmerman, "College Culture in the Midwest, 1890-1930" (Ph.D. diss., University of Virginia, 1978), 121-127, Grinnell College Archives.

54. Zimmerman, "College Culture in the Midwest," 121-127; Joan G. Zimmerman, "Daughters of Main Street: Culture and the Female Community at Grinnell 1884-

1917," in Mary Kelly, ed., *Woman's Being, Woman's Place: Female Identity and Vocation in American History* (Boston: G. K. Hall and Co., 1979), 154-167; *The Scarlet and Black,* September 14, 1901, describes how young women and young men first entering the college as freshmen are welcomed. The women were individually escorted by an "old girl" to a reception, tea, and piano recital in a hall decorated with flowers and pillowed sofas, while the men were welcomed by President Main in a much more serious talk expounding on the challenges they would meet at the college.

55. *Grinnell Herald,* June 17, 1904, 2; *Scarlet and Black,* June 13, 1905, 2; June 13, 1905, 2. In the college yearbook for 1904, Adah Hopkins' picture shows her to be an unsmiling and demure girl, with upswept hair, wearing what seemed to be the fashion for college girls of the day, a white blouse with a large black bow at the neck. Her fellow students recognized her charm as well as her contribution to the school. Below her picture reads:

> Shouldst thou, Adah divine
>
> Have on us a design,
>
> Our fond heart would not be resistant;
>
> But hope's course is run, hence thou hast become
>
> Our manager's able assistant.

Throughout the publication she is referred to as "Adah, the divine." 1904 *Cyclone,* 35, 141, Grinnell College Archives.

56. Zimmerman, "Daughters of Main Street," 156-159.

57. Zimmerman, "College Culture in the Midwest," 150-166.

58. See Susan Curtis, *A Consuming Faith: The Social Gospel and Modern American Culture* (Baltimore: Johns Hopkins University Press, 1991) for an enlightening discussion of women in the Social Gospel movement and the influence of novelist Elizabeth Stuart Phelps.

59. AMH to EGH and HLH, Spring 1915, Hopkins II, GUSC.

60. John Pickett, Anna's brother, who owned a very successful hemp factory in Manila, most likely helped the family with Adah's tuition at the University of Pennsylvania, as he had done before with the Grinnell tuition. There is no evidence that she received a scholarship from the university or any other source, and Al Hopkins could not have afforded the tuition.

61. The fact that Jane Addams and Ellen Gates Starr spoke to the students at Grinnell in 1897 may have provided some of the inspiration for this project. In 1899 two students of Iowa College saw a need for "recreation, entertainment and enrichment for the children of the area" and proposed a club to "furnish the boys an attractive substitute for the social gathering of the street corner and stimulate in them a more active interest in matters which will permanently benefit." The area in question, Happy Hollow in southwest Grinnell, was home to many of the workers in the Spaulding Buggy Company, the town's only industry other than agriculture, and the business had suffered setbacks because of the advent of the automobile. When the factory was forced to shut down, the workers felt the pinch. The Uncle Sam's Club was established originally to give the local boys moral direction and wholesome activities that would keep them off the streets. When the wife of a local doctor suggested that the girls were in just as much need of services and recreation to direct "their minds toward pure thoughts," they were included. The club's motto—"Mutual helpfulness and preparation for good citizenship"—reflected the settlement idea as expressed in Chicago, New York, and other cities struggling with the effects of immigration and industrialization. While Grinnell

did not have the same social problems as these urban centers, nevertheless these two students, E. F. Dennison and S. H. Crosby, saw a need to bring social services to their working-class families. The clubhouse was built on a lot donated by a wealthy resident and with community funds raised at several annual benefits. Students at the college worked regularly at the club, organizing sledding parties in the winter, Saturday-morning activities during the school year, reading groups, social hours, and training sessions. These activities brought as much to the college student, as they did to the youngsters who attended. Dorothy Pinder, "The Uncle Sam's Club," Grinnell College Archives; Pinder is now assistant editor of the local paper, *The Grinnell Herald Register.* Parts of this text has been used in her book *In Old Grinnell* (Grinnell: The Herald Register Publishing Company, 1995); *Grinnell Herald,* March 18, 1902; Additional information on the Uncle Sam's Club at Grinnell Historical Museum.

62.   *The First Annual Report of the Social Service League, 1912-1913.* Grinnell, Iowa: Grinnell Register Print, 1913, 4-7, 14-15, Grinnell Historical Society, Grinnell, Iowa.

63.   *The First Annual Report of the Social Service League, 1912-1913,* 3-7, 10-15.

64.   *The First Annual Report of the Social Service League, 1912-1913,* 10-11. Seeing a real connection between truancy and poverty, Adah Hopkins also served as truancy officer for the town.

65.   *The Second Annual Report of the Social Service League, 1913-1914.* Grinnell, Iowa: Grinnell Herald Print, 1914, 3, Grinnell Historical Society, Grinnell, Iowa.

66.   *The First Annual Report of the Social Service League, 1912-1913,* 4-7, 14-15.

67.   *The Second Annual Report of the Social Service League, 1913-1914,* 3-11.

68.   Charity Organization Society of New York City, *Eleventh Annual Report, 1892-1893,* 8.

69.   *The First Annual Report of the Social Service League, 1912-1913,* 15.

70.   *The First Annual Report of the Social Service League, 1912-1913,* 6; *The Second Annual Report of the Social Service League, 1913-1914,* 10-11.

71.   *The First Annual Report of the Social Service League, 1912-1913,* 9-13. *The Grinnell Herald,* April 22, 1913. It is interesting to note that the offices of the SSL, at 917 Broad Street, were just upstairs from Dad Hopkins' leather shop.

72.   *The Second Annual Report of the Social Service League, 1913-1914,* 5.

73.   Adah Hopkins to Social Service League, 1936, Grinnell Historical Archives. Garrett Wyckoff worked for Hopkins in the Gulf Division of the American Red Cross (ARC) Home Relief Division during World War I.

74.   *The First Annual Report of the Social Service League, 1912-1913,* 13, Grinnell Historical Society.

75.   *Grinnell College Bulletin, 1913-1914,* 94, Grinnell College Archives; *Grinnell Herald,* February 10, 1914, June 19, 1910. There is no mention in any of the family correspondence of her mother's health. While Adah was working in Pittsburgh, she met and married Frank Louis Aime, who was with the Royal Flying Corps of Toronto. *Pittsburgh Evening Sun,* December 12, 1918. Frank Aime later became an electrical engineer in New York and Adah sold insurance. *Fortune,* (July 1935): 60.

76.   Charles Roberts, interview with Florence Kerr, July 29, 1974, 3, Grinnell College Archives.

77.   *Grinnell College Bulletin,* 1908-1909, 152; *Grinnell College Bulletin,* 1909-1919, 136.

78.   Hopkins Academic Transcript, Grinnell College; *Grinnell College Bulletins,* 1908 to 1912; Lewis Hopkins' scrapbook, Grinnell College Archives.

79.   Hopkins' Transcript; *Grinnell College Bulletin,* 1911-1912, Grinnell College Archives.

80.   In 1880 Iowa ranked seventh in the number of native-born whites, twenty-seventh in number of "colored" population. Of the 16 percent foreign-born population in Iowa,

one-third of them came from English-speaking countries and most were Protestant. (Schacht, 4.)

81. Jesse Macy was a close friend of British historian and diplomat James Bryce who came to stay with Macy in Grinnell while he was writing a condensed version of *The American Commonwealth.*

82. Hopkins Transcript; *Grinnell College Bulletins* 1908 to 1912; Jagow as quoted in Halsted MS, chapter 3, 34.

83. See Swain for an excellent account of Woodward's career.

84. *Cyclone,* 1909-1913, Grinnell College Archives; Reminisces of Florence Stewart Kerr, Columbia University Oral History Research Office, Butler Library, Columbia University, New York, New York. Hereinafter CUOHRO. (This oral history is also in the Grinnell College Archives)

85. Quoted in *The Scarlet and Black,* June 12, 1912, 1, 3, Grinnell College Archives.

86. Quoted in Sherwood, 19-21.

87. Conant interview, 35.

88. Kerr remarked that "Steiner wasn't all that influential with Harry," that he was "vain," "complex," "overrated," and "certainly wasn't Harry's real spark plug." Florence Kerr to Jagow, 1967, as quoted in Halsted MS, chapter 3, 35-36.

89. Louis Hartson to Earl D. Strong, July 12, 1956, Grinnell College Archives. In 1956 Hartson wrote a letter to Grinnell professor Earl D. Strong, outlining how it was he and not Steiner (as some biographers, including Sherwood, had claimed) who got Hopkins the job at Christodora Settlement House in New York City and thus set him on the path to his social work career.

CHAPTER THREE

1. Hartson to Strong, July 12, 1956, Grinnell College Archives.

2. Sherwood, 22.

3. See Adams, Charles, Kurzman, McJimsey, and Sherwood.

4. Reminisces of Florence Stewart Kerr, CUOHRO, 63-64. Kerr remarked that after Hopkins' speech, "the Stock Market went up about a billion dollars that day."

5. McJimsey, 17.

6. Judith Trolander, *Professionalism and Social Change: From the Settlement House Movement to Neighborhood Centers, 1886 to the Present* (New York: Columbia University Press, 1987), 16-17.

7. Stanton Coit, a Protestant and leader of the Ethical Culture Society, settled in a largely Jewish neighborhood in New York City and sought to break down the barriers that might arise from an overemphasis on Christian religion. Trolander, *Professionalism and Social Change,* 7.

8. Jane Addams wrote about the diverse religious beliefs held by the residents at Hull House. "Jews, Roman Catholics, English Churchmen, Dissenters, and a few agnostics"—noting that because they could find no satisfactory form of worship that would express their religious fellowship, Sunday services were given up at Hull House. Yet her statement as to the motives underlying the settlement movement echoed the Social Gospelers' warning against individualistic religion: ". . . the good we secure for ourselves is precarious and uncertain, is floating in mid-air, until it is secured for all of us and incorporated into our common life." Jane Addams, *Twenty Years At Hull-House* (New York: The New American Library, 1961), 92-98, 307-308.

9. Ruth Hutchinson Crocker, *Social Work and Social Order: The Settlement Movement in Two Industrial Cities, 1889-1930* (Urbana: University of Illinois Press, 1992), 114.

10. See Walter Rauschenbusch, *Christianity and the Social Crisis* (New York: Macmillan, 1907) and *A Theology for the Social Gospel* (New York: Macmillan, 1917).

11. Harry P. Kraus, *The Settlement House Movement in New York City 1886-1914* (New York: Arno Press, 1980), 125. Kraus used Dr. Edward Steiner's unpublished manuscript, "Christodora, 1897-1940" in this book. See p. 109.

12. Allen F. Davis, *Spearheads for Reform: The Social Settlements and the Progressive Movement* (New York: Oxford University Press, 1967); Mina Carson, *Settlement Folk: Social Thought and the American Settlement Movement, 1885-1930* (Chicago: University of Chicago Press, 1990).

13. Davis, *Spearheads for Reform,* 15. In a note, Davis cites an article by Jon Gavit in which he calls Christodora House an exception to this.

14. Arthur C. Holden, *The Settlement Idea: A Vision of Social Justice* (New York: Arno Press, 1922), 136-137.

15. "Minutes," December 1, 1914, February 2, 1915, Christodora Collection, Christodora, Inc., New York City. The Christodora Collection has since been cataloged and is at Columbia University's Butler Library, Manuscripts Collection.

16. "Scrapbook, 1897," Christodora Collection.

17. Judith Weisenfeld, "'The More Abundant Life:' The Harlem Branch of the New York City Young Women's Christian Association, 1905-1945" (Ph.D. diss., Princeton University, 1992), 16.

18. Kraus, 108.

19. Edward A. Steiner, "Christodora, 1897-1940: Tribute to a Great Personality," 1940, chapter 1, "Up From the Cellar," MS, unpaginated, Christodora Collection. This short document was most likely a posthumous tribute to Christina Isobel McColl, who died December 10, 1939.

20. "Avenue B's Settlement Work," *New York Tribune,* undated. "Scrapbook, 1897," Christodora Collection.

21. Steiner, chapter 1, "Up from the Cellar." The effect of this environment indicated an early cultural division between the settlement workers and their guests. Steiner wrote that although the "hostesses were allergic to its odor, . . . it was ambrosia to those who were the guests at the reception."

22. Taking into account the makeup of the neighborhood, it can be assumed that the rest were predominately Irish Catholics and Germans.

23. Steiner, chapter 1, "Up From the Cellar." Although MacColl might have felt daunted at first by the behavior of working-class immigrant girls, it seems that she was referring especially to the Jews.

24. Steiner, chapter 1, "Up From the Cellar." The typing class was started because one young girl declared, "My mother would like to have me learn to play that thing you play on all day like a piano only it doesn't make any noises, it writes letters."

25. Steiner, chapter 2, "Hearts and Clubs."

26. "The Romance of the Social Settlement: The Story of the New Christodora House," undated, Christodora Collection.

27. "Minutes 1897-1904," October 5, 1897. Several months after the Young Women's Settlement was established, the name was changed to Christodora House. It was a unanimous decision. Steiner, chapter 3, "The Mothers' Club." See also Holden, 137.

28. From book of handwritten minutes, unpaginated, labeled "Property of the Secretary of the Young Women's Settlement, Minutes for 1897-1898-1899-1900-1902-1903-1904" (Hereinafter "Minutes 1897-1904"), October 5, 1897 and January 4, 1898, Christodora Collection.

29. The following were elected to the council at the annual meeting, April 4, 1899: Mrs. Margaret Sangster, Mr. Lescou, Mr. and Mrs. Howell, Mr. and Mrs. Gladding, Mrs. Taggart, Mrs. Fellow, Dr. North, Mrs. W. H. Maxwell, Mr. Hoyler, Mrs. Nelson. W. Smith, Mrs. Symmington, Miss Hoag, Miss Pierson, Dr. Josiah Strong, Mr. Coale, Miss Mabel Slade, Mrs. M. R. Greene. "Minutes 1897-1904," April 4, 1899; The Gladdings had contributed $1,000 the previous year for a larger house. "Minutes 1897-1904," January 24, 1898.

30. "Minutes 1897-1904," December 6, 1898.

31. "Minutes 1897-1904," December 3, 1901.

32. "Minutes 1897-1904," January 16, 1902.

33. "Minutes 1897-1904," October 3, 1899; "Young Women's Settlement," unidentified article, April 6, 1898. "Scrapbook, 1897," Christodora Collection; Josiah Strong, "The Problem of the City," in Paul H. Boase, ed., *The Rhetoric of Christian Socialism* (New York: Random House, 1969), 88-90.

34. In 1898 Christodora, responding to demands from the neighborhood boys, opened its doors to men.

35. "The Settlement Institute," *New York Tribune,* 1897, "Scrapbook, 1897," Christodora Collection.

36. S. Neisel, "The Value of Mothers' Clubs," *Christodora,* vol. 6, no. 11 (April 1907), Christodora Collection.

37. Sheila M. Rothman, *Woman's Proper Place: A History of the Changing Ideals and Practices, 1870 to the Present* (New York: Basic Books, 1978), xix, 114-117

38. Steiner, introduction, "The Immigrant Tide."

39. Steiner, chapter 6, "Religious Life and the Children's Hour."

40. Steiner, introduction, "The Immigrant Tide."

41. "Minutes 1897-1904," July 6, 1897.

42. "Report on Interview with Miss McColl of Christodora House," undated, unsigned, Christodora Collection.

43. Steiner, chapter 2, "Hearts and Clubs."

44. Strong, "The Problem of the City," 11, 88.

45. Susan Curtis, *A Consuming Faith: The Social Gospel in Modern American Culture* (Baltimore: Johns Hopkins University Press, 1991), 72-75; Josiah Strong, *The Next Great Awakening* (New York: Baker & Taylor, 1902), iv-v, 92-99.

46. Conant interview, 7.

47. Sherwood, 22.

48. Harry Hopkins, "Capital Punishment and Boys," *Survey Graphic* (April 25, 1914): 89.

49. HLH to EGH, February 21, 1913, Hopkins II, GUSC.

50. Now Kosice, Czechoslovakia.

51. Ethel Gross Hopkins Journal, in author's possession; EGH to Mr. John Dickson, managing editor, James T. White and Co., September 30, 1941; Conant interview, 47; author's telephone interview with Eugene Fodor, September 30, 1988. See Charles Loring Brace, *Hungary in 1851* (New York: Charles Scribner, 1852), 147, 415-418.

52. EGH Journal; Mary J. Shapiro *Gateway to Liberty* (New York: Vintage Books, 1986), 78.

53. According to the 1900 census for New York City, there was another Gross family from Hungary listed as living in their tenement, 356 E. Tenth Street. Gross is a common name, and they may have not been relatives at all. In the mid-eighteenth century, all Jews in Hungary were ordered to abandon their patronymics and adopt surnames. Those who could not afford to buy more elegant names were assigned mundane names such as Gross, meaning "tall."

54. Conant interview, 13.

55. Oddly enough, Ethel never filed for naturalization. She only claimed citizenship in 1913 after she married Harry Hopkins.

56. It is hard to believe that she was the only foreigner in the classroom, but this must have been her perception as a child.

57. EGH Journal.

58. EGH Journal; Conant interview, 13.

59. Report cards, SUNY, 1903, in author's possession.

60. This was before Christodora House had acquired Northover Camp in New Jersey.

61. Conant interview, 12-23. Ethel rejected the Judaism of her parents, although she never accepted the formal Protestantism practiced by most of her colleagues at the settlement.

62. EGH Journal.

63. EGH Journal. In author's interview with Eugene Fodor, he indicated that although there would have been anti-Semitism in Kaschau, the Gross family would have enjoyed a comfortable middle-class life there because of the glass factory they owned; Fodor suggested that the environment of the Lower East Side could have driven Celia to suicide. All of the records of Jewish families in Hungary were destroyed during the Holocaust.

64. Mary Ellin Barrett, *Irving Berlin: A Daughter's Memoir* (New York: Simon and Schuster, 1994), 20, 30, 85. Ellin Mackay, Katherine and Clarence Mackay's middle child, became a close friend of Ethel. Ellin later married Irving Berlin, who, much to the chagrin of her anti-Semitic father, was from Ethel's old neighborhood. Katherine Mackay Blake's second marriage produced four children but also ended in divorce in 1929 when Dr. Blake had an affair with (and later married) a nurse, Florence Drake, who was treating Katherine while she was recovering from cancer. It is interesting to note that Katherine converted to Catholicism in 1929. See Ellin Berlin, *Silver Platter* (Garden City, N.J.: Doubleday, 1957), 413-21.

65. Conant Interview, 1-35.

66. Felix Adler, *Atheism: A Lecture* (New York: Cooperative Printers Association, 1879), 19.

67. Felix Adler, *Life and Destiny* (New York: McClure, Philips and Co., 1903), 4. In 1907 the city passed a law that allowed Adler and his assistants to legally perform marriages. A 1909 article in the *New York Times* gently poked fun at a settlement house couple who had taken advantage of this law, announcing that they had been "Ethically Married," *New York Times,* November 1, 1909, VII, 1.

68. HLH to EG, February 24, 1913, Hopkins II, GUSC. Harry Hopkins' niece, Blayne Link, wrote that Ethel "was someone we did not talk about" because Blayne's mother, Hopkins' sister-in-law, was very prejudiced against Jews. Letter from Blayne Link to author, July 3, 1990.

69. EG to HLH March 3, 1913, Hopkins II, GUSC.

70. Harriot Stanton Blatch and Alma Lutz, *The Challenging Years* (New York: G. P. Putnam's Sons, 1940), 92-120.

71. HLH to EG, March 2, 1913, Hopkins II, GUSC.

72. There is no indication that he "lost" this job, that is, that he was fired. Head worker Christine MacColl helped him get a job with John Kingsbury at the AICP.

73. HLH to EG, April 14, 1913, Hopkins II, GUSC.

74. Conant interview, 99-100.

75. Conant interview, 113.

76. HLH to EG, March 28, 1913, Hopkins II, GUSC; Conant interview, 116-122.

77. Conant interview, 78, 130-131.

78. Arnold S. Rosenberg, "John Adams Kingsbury and the Struggle for Social Justice in New York, 1906-1918," (Ph.D. diss., New York University, 1968), 84, 123, 130;

Transcripts from John Kingsbury's journal, May 8-9, 1912, JAKP, B83: Reference Material Personal 1904-1926.

CHAPTER FOUR

1. Robert Bremner, *From the Depths: The Discovery of Poverty in the United States* (New York: New York University Press, 1956), 107; Franklin Roosevelt, *Looking Forward* (New York: John Day and Co., 1933), 22, 47.

2. William W. Bremer, *Depression Winter: New York City Social Workers and the New Deal* (Philadelphia: Temple University Press, 1984), 1.

3. Florence Stewart Kerr, CUOHRO, 3.

4. Lillian Brandt, *The Growth and Development of the AICP and the COS (A Preliminary and Exploratory Review)* (New York: Community Service Society of New York, 1942), 3.

5. Quoted in Brandt, 11.

6. Roy Lubove, *The Professional Altruist: The Emergence of Social Work as a Career 1880-1930* (Cambridge, Mass.: Harvard University Press, 1965), 3; Bremner, 69. See also Charles Loring Brace, *The Dangerous Classes of New York and Twenty Years' Work Among Them,* Montclair, N.J.: P. Smith, 1967, reprint of the 3rd ed., 1880.

7. Quoted in Brandt, 19.

8. Quoted in Brandt, 23.

9. Bremner, 15-27.

10. Brandt, 162-165.

11. New York Association for Improving the Condition of the Poor, *Fifty-Sixth Annual Report, 1898-1899,* 12, Archives of Community Service Society (ACSS), Manuscript Collections, Butler Library, Columbia University, New York City. In April 1939 the AICP and the COS merged to form the Community Service Society (CSS).

12. Daniel Nelson, *Unemployment Insurance: The American Experience* (Madison: University of Wisconsin, 1969), 5.

13. Robert Hunter, *Poverty* (New York: Macmillan, 1904), 3.

14. See remarks in *Proceedings of a Hearing on Unemployment,* January 29, 1914, 6-7, JAKP, A30: 13-2, re: belief that working at debased jobs was humiliating to workers. Therefore, idle workers should be given loans instead of jobs on make-work projects.

15. Isaac M. Rubinow, *Social Insurance with Special Reference to American Conditions* (New York: Henry Holt, 1913), 284-285.

16. "A Study of the Methods Employed by the A. I. C. P. to Secure Work for Unemployed Applicants," undated, probably 1908, 16: 7, ACSS.

17. AICP to State Engineer Mr. Fredrick Skane, April 6, 1908, ACSS, 16: 7.

18. "Statements and Resolutions by the Ethical-Social League," April 7, 1908, ACSS, 47: 321.

19. "Meeting, Sub-Committee for Unemployed," October 22, 1908, ACSS, 47: 321.

20. John A. Kingsbury, Address, November, 17, 1913, ACSS, 16: 1-6.

21. Sherwood, 23; McJimsey, 19. Kingsbury later raised Hopkins' "allowance" to $60 per month because of his impending marriage to Ethel Gross.

22. Brandt, 192-193; Association for Improving the Conditions of the Poor, *Seventieth Annual Report,* 1913, 13.

23. Sherwood, 23-24.

24. Conant interview, 71.

25. Harry Hopkins, "Report on Unemployment Department," undated, probably 1913/14, 8-18, ACSS, 47: 317.

26. See Edwin R. Lewinson, *John Purroy Mitchel: The Boy Mayor of New York* (New York: Astra Books, 1965), 88-147. Mitchel ran against Tammany candidate Edward E. McColl. According to Lewinson, Mitchel believed "that efficient government would serve the needs of the people so well that they would never again elect inefficient machine politics." Lewinson, 110.

27. John A. Kingsbury, "Progress lies in solving the problems . . . ," April 1914, 1-3, JAKP, A30:13-1, 4-6. The Municipal Lodging House (MLH) provided shelter for New York City's homeless population. Accommodating 800 men and women, "it is fitted with a perfect set of fumigating chambers, shower rooms, dining hall, examination rooms, and well-ventilated dormitories." By January of 1914 the MLH was registering about 2,000 people each night, twice the number it could accommodate. When all those who were physically fit were required to perform one hour's work, the population decreased.

28. This request for a survey shows how the AICP had changed its attitude toward the unemployed over the years. In 1873 the NYAICP had called unemployed workers demonstrating for public jobs " a vast hydra-headed class" ready to "strike at property and all we value most." The association referred to demonstrators as "whining . . . whimpering . . . loafing . . . lazy." In December 1873 New York City police clubbed thousands of unemployed workers who were in Thompkins Square agitating for public works. See Herbert Gutman, "The Failure of the Movement by the Unemployed for Public Works in 1873," *Political Science Quarterly* 70 (June 1965), 256.

29. Harry Hopkins, "A Detailed Plan of Organization and Administration of State Employment Agencies, as provided for by Chapter 184 of the Laws of 1914," Hopkins III, 6:2, GUSC.

30. Harry Hopkins, "Report on the Question of Unemployment in New York City," attached to "Annual Report," Employment Bureau, January 8, 1913, 2-4, ACSS, 47: 317.

31. Hopkins, "A Detailed Plan."

32. Hopkins, "Annual Report," Employment Bureau, January 8, 1913, 2-3, ACSS, 47: 317.

33. Harry Hopkins, "The chief difficulty at present . . . ," Hopkins III, 6:1, GUSC. (Handwritten on Equal Franchise stationery.)

34. Hopkins, "The chief difficulty."

35. From the AICP (probably Henry Bruere) to Mr. Charles Sprague Smith of the People's Institute, March 10, 1908, ACSS, 16: 317.

36. Hopkins, "A Detailed Plan."

37. Although his sister, Adah, did pursue a career and married relatively late, she nevertheless chose jobs in social work, well within the accepted female sphere.

38. *Proceedings of a Hearing on Unemployment*, 6-7, January 29, 1914, JAKP, A30: 13-2.

39. *Proceedings of a Hearing on Unemployment*, 9-10.

40. *Proceedings of a Hearing on Unemployment*, 22-23.

41. *Proceedings of a Hearing on Unemployment*, 32-33.

42. *Proceedings of a Hearing on Unemployment*, 25.

43. *Proceedings of a Hearing on Unemployment*, 28.

44. Leah Hannah Feder, *Unemployment Relief in Periods of Depression: A Study of Measures Adopted in Certain American Cities, 1857 Through 1922* (New York: Russell Sage, 1936), 289. In the 1890s the New York East Side Relief Committee planned work-relief for some neighborhoods under the direction of Josephine Shaw Lowell. Similar programs were undertaken in other cities, such as Boston, Philadelphia, and Hartford, during the depressions of 1915 and 1921. The AICP repeated its park program in 1921 and also began a subway employment program. See Philip Klein, *The*

Burden of Unemployment: A Study of Unemployment Relief Measures in Fifteen American Cities, 1921-22 (New York: Russell Sage Foundation, 1923); Samuel Rezneck two articles that describe earlier and less successful attempts at work-relief, "Distress, Relief, and Discontent in the United States During the Depression of 1873-1878," *Journal of Political Economy* (December 1950): 499-502, and "Unemployment, Unrest, and Relief in the United States During the Depression of 1893-1897," *Journal of Political Economy* (August 1953): 330-337.

45. William H. Matthews, "These Past Five Years," *Survey Midmonthly* (March 1938), unpaginated, ACSS, 47: 321.

46. During the six months the plan was operating, 668 men were offered jobs. The 1915 report states that of this number, 7 refused the work, 30 were no-shows; 90 quit; 23 were physically unable to work; 106 were fired; 396 worked and then left after finding regular work; 12 were working when the report was written. *AICP Yearbook 1915,* Director's Report, 28.

47. *AICP Yearbook 1915,* Director's Report, 12-13,

48. *AICP Yearbook 1915,* Director's Report, 27.

49. Hermann W. Merkel to AICP Executive Committee, June 15, 1915, ACSS, 47: 317.

50. Mayor's Conference on Unemployment, November 18, 1915, 2, ACSS, 47: 317.

51. Bailey Burritt to Mr. Hornaday of the New York Zoological Society, December 13, 1915, ACSS, 47: 317. The depression of 1915 led to two other efforts to provide work-relief projects for specific populations of the needy in New York City. The Crawford Shops, called "Old Men's Toy Shops," were established in 1916 along with a Sewing Bureau for elderly women. Both of these projects were attempts to give old people who were still able-bodied the chance to earn at least some of their living. "The How, What, and Why of A.I.C.P. Services" (undated), 10, ACSS, 14.

52. Feder, 289-290; William H. Matthews, *Adventures in Giving* (New York: Dodd, Mead & Company, 1939), 108-109. Matthews' exaggeration can be explained only by his enthusiasm for the project.

53. Matthews, "These Past Five Years."

54. Matthews, *Adventures in Giving,* 111-112.

CHAPTER FIVE

1. This chapter relies heavily on sources in two collections: The John Adams Kingsbury Papers at the Manuscripts Division, Library of Congress (JAKP) and the Tierney Collection, Special Collections, Lauinger Library, Georgetown University, Washington, D, C. (Hereinafter Tierney, GUSC). See also Dorothy Brown and Elizabeth McKeown, "Saving New York's Children," *U.S. Catholic Historian* (Summer, 1995): 77-95, and Brown and McKeown. For a comprehensive study of welfare in New York State, see David M. Schneider and Albert Deutsch, *The History of Public Welfare in New York State, 1867-1940* (Chicago: University of Chicago Press, 1941).

2. William Matthews to Dr. Jessica B. Peixotto, September 21, 1917, Hopkins III, 1:15, GUSC.

3. John Adams Kingsbury, "The Development of the Subsidy System of the City of New York," JAKP, A30: 13-3; Schneider and Deutsch, 62.

4. Charles H. Strong, "Report of Charles H. Strong to Governor Whitman," October 24, 1916, 10, Box 321, Tierney, GUSC, (Hereinafter The Strong Report).

5. The Strong Report, 78-81.

6. Of the 39, 18 were Protestant caring for 5,794 children, 17 were Catholic with 15,912 children, and 4 Jewish institutions cared for 3,691 children. The city paid $2,394,813.63 of the total cost ($3,906,963.47). JAKP, A16: Indictment.

7. The Strong Report, 4; Thomas Mulry, "The Government in Charity," 1912; James J. Higgins to Mayor Mitchel, June 2, 1916, Tierney, GUSC.

8. Many of the children in Catholic orphanages were not orphans at all but children whose families, for one reason or another, could not support them. Relatives would deposit a child with the nuns until their position improved enough for them to reclaim him or her.

9. John Kingsbury, "The Development of the Subsidy System of the City of New York," unpaginated, JAKP, A30: 13-3; Schneider and Deutsch, 60-65; William Hotchkiss, "Brief on Behalf of the Commissioner of Public Charities of the City of New York," Tierney, GUSC; Monsignor James J. Higgins to Edward J. Butler of the Catholic Home Bureau, April 27, 1914, JAKP, A18: Private Child-Caring Institutions, 1914-1917, A-J.

10. James J. Higgins, Letter, June 2, 1916, Tierney, GUSC.

11. Mulry, "The Government in Charity," 2-3, Tierney, GUSC.

12. Bird Coler, "The Red Paper of the City of New York," March 26, 1915, 4, 56, 58, Tierney, GUSC.

13. Paul L. Blakeley, S.J, "Catholic Charities and the Strong Commission," *America* 15 (May 6, 1916): 77-79, Tierney, GUSC.

14. *Nativity Mentor* 21 (August 1916), Tierney, GUSC.

15. Francis Hackett, "The Sacred Cow," *The New Republic* (June 3, 1916): 116-117

16. Donald A. Ritchie, "The Gary Committee: Businessmen, Progressives, and Unemployment in New York City, 1914-1915," *The New York Historical Society Quarterly* 57 (October 1973): 330-335. Ritchie pointed out that because of the economic dislocations caused by World War I, the city could not rely on financial assistance in the form of government loans. Bankers therefore supplied funds at 6 percent, to be paid out of taxes rather than long-term bond issues.

17. Quoted in Ritchie, 333.

18. John Purroy Mitchel, "Conditions on Child-Caring Institutions," 2, JAKP, A18: Private Child Caring Institutions, 1914-1915, K-R.

19. Mitchel.

20. "The Truth About the Attack on the Charitable Institutions: What Prendergast and Mitchel Did Against the Charitable Institutions," Tierney, GUSC; William H. Hotchkiss, "Brief on Behalf of the Commissioner of Public Charities of the City of New York," 1916, Tierney, GUSC.

21. JAKP, A37: 251 Political; JAKP, A1: AICP 1914-1916.

22. John Adams Kingsbury, "With Reference to Family Welfare . . . ," JAKP, A30: 13-3.

23. John A. Kingsbury to Father F. J. O'Hara of Catholic Charities of Brooklyn, June 16, 1914, Tierney, GUSC.

24. William Doherty contracted an eye ailment in the orphanage, which he blamed on unsanitary conditions there. Farrell suggested that because of this, Doherty should be disqualified. JAKP, A16: Indictment 1917.

25. JAKP, A18: Publicity 1914-1918; AWT to John Kingsbury , January 7, 1914, JAKP, A3a: William J. Doherty 1914-1917; "Charities Investigation," 5, Tierney, GUSC; "Municipal Welfare Work," Kingsbury Speech, probably mid-1917, JAKP, A30: 13-1; "A Study of the Results of Institutional Care," 4-5, Tierney, GUSC; Scrapbook, NY Charities Investigation, Tierney, GUSC; Hotchkiss "Brief on Behalf . . . ," 20-23, Tierney, GUSC; Moree Pamphlet, 16-18, Tierney, GUSC.

26. Hotchkiss, "Brief on Behalf . . . ," 6.

27. Thomas Mulry, "The Government in Charity," Tierney, GUSC; The Strong Report, 94. "Dr. Potter's Tears Halts Priests' Case," *New York Times,* July 26 1916, 6. This article

suggested that the stress of the Strong inquiry led to Mulry's death: "Leading Catholics have insisted that the attacks made upon the management of Catholic institutions in the Strong inquiry served to shorten Mr. Mulry's life."

28. The Strong Report, 85; Robert W. Hebberd, "The Charities Investigation: Its Inspiration," *America* 15 (May 13, 1916): 101-102.

29. Secretary to the Deputy Commissioner to Lester Roth, October 23, 1917. JAKP, A18: Private Child Caring Institutions 1914-1917, K-R; Hotchkiss, "Brief on Behalf . . . ," 16, Tierney, GUSC; "Report of Charles H. Strong to Governor Whitman," 5-6. Tierney, GUSC; Homer Folks denied that he convinced Whitman to appoint Strong as commissioner, claiming that he only had "informal conversation" with the governor during which Strong's name came up. Homer Folks, "The Strong Investigation and Certain Other Matters," *S.C.A.A. News* 3 (June 1916): 1, 4-5, 7. It is not clear from the documents whether the governor had created the commission before he received Kingsbury's report or not. However, given the time frame, it seems likely that he had.

30. William Doherty testified that he found "shocking, almost incredible conditions" and that "attention to health was inadequate and that the children were pale and weak." He reported filthy dormitories infested with vermin and lice and children overworked and sleeping on floors. *New York Times,* February 2, 1916, 20; *New York Times,* February 3, 1916, 20; *New York Times,* February 1, 1916, 8; *New York Times,* February 3, 1916, 20; *New York Times,* February 5, 1916, 9; *New York Times,* February 6, 1916, Section VII, 9.

31. Rev. William .B. Farrell, "A Public Scandal," February 18, 1916, passim, Tierney, GUSC.

32. Rev. William B. Farrell, "Priestbaiting in 1916," 5-10, Tierney, GUSC.

33. Kingsbury's Plaza Hotel Speech, March 25, 1916, 5; New York Charities Investigation Scrapbook, Tierney, GUSC. There are two documents of Kingsbury's Plaza Hotel speech. One in the Kingsbury Papers at the Library of Congress, Manuscript Division, is a press release of the entire written speech, entitled "Address Delivered by Hon. John A. Kingsbury Commissioner of Public charities at the Hotel Plaza." The second, found in the Tierney Collection, seems to be a transcription of the speech as it was actually given. From the few editorial comments inserted into the text, the transcriber was no friend of Kingsbury.

34. Folks, "The Strong Investigation," 5-6.

35. "Extraction of Minutes of March 14, 1916, Examination of Edward A. Moree," 6845, Tierney, GUSC; "Dismissal of Charges Against Respective Defendants of Wrongfully Obtaining Knowledge of Telephonic Messages, of Conspiracy in Perverting and Obstructing Justice, of Criminal Libel and Perjury," 3, JAKP, A16: Indictment 1917.

36. "Extraction of Minutes of March 14, 1916, Examination of Edward A. Moree," 6278, 6735, Tierney, GUSC; *Brooklyn Eagle,* March 23 1916, 1; "Catholic Charities and the Strong Commission," *America* 15 (May 6, 1916): 77. Even Homer Folks admitted that not all the headlines in the pamphlet were correct representations of conditions at institutions. Folks, "The Strong Investigation," 6.

37. Folks, "The Strong Investigation," 6-7.

38. Hotchkiss Deposition, JAKP, A16: Indictment 1917, 4-11; *Nativity Mentor* 21 (August 1916): 7. The New York City police also had been charged with illegally using wiretaps to listen in on conversations of the Allied Printing Trades Council to determine dates of planned strikes. *Brooklyn Eagle,* July 25, 1916, Tierney, GUSC.

39. *S.C.A.A. News* (June 16, 1916), Tierney, GUSC; *New York Times,* July 13, 1916, 17.

40. "Dismissal of Charges Against Respective Defendants," 1, 7-8, State Charities Aid Association Press Release, undated, JAKP, A16: Indictment 1917. Greenbaum declared that truth was a defense of libel, that no malicious intent was proved, and that,

in any case, criticism of public officials rarely could be deemed libel. Daniel Potter, who had been accused of trying to leave the state to avoid a subpoena, had died earlier, "removed by the hand of death from all earthly jurisdictions" according to Justice Greenbaum.

41. John A. Kingsbury to Harry Hopkins, May 24, 1916, Hopkins III, 1:14, GUSC.

42. The Strong Report, 31-32, 82-87, 97.

43. The Strong Report, 106

44. The Strong Report, 108-109.

45. The Strong Report, 112-113.

46. The Strong Report, 115.

47. "The Answer to the Strong Report," December 13, 1916, 1-2, 12, 22, 65-66, 78, 84, 90, 98-99, Box 321, Tierney, GUSC.

48. Mitchel, "Conditions in Child-Caring Institutions," JAKP, A18: Private Child-Caring Institutions, 1914-1915.

49. "Catholic Charities and the Strong Commission," 77-79.

50. Clipping *Survey* (April 8, 1916), JAKP, A11: State Board of Charities, A-K, 1914-1917.

51. "Memorandum of Suggested Division of Child-Placing in the Department of Public Charity," 1917, JAKP, A2: Children's Home Bureau, 1917 Prospectus; John Daniels, Director, "The New Children's Home Bureau, Special Report to the Advisor Committee, Meeting, November 23, 1916," 13-16, JAKP, A2: Children's Home Bureau, Advisory Board; William Doherty, "Brief Report of the Second Deputy Commissioner Concerning the Work of the Children's Home Bureau," 1-2, JAKP, A2: Children's Home Bureau Advisory Board 1916; "Resume of the Progress of the Work During the Four Month Period (July 1 to October 31, 1917)," JAKP, A2: Children's Home Bureau Advisory Board 1916.

52. William Matthews to Wilbur Phillips, Secretary of National Social Unit Organization, August 16, 1916, Hopkins III, 1:14, GUSC.

53. Conant interview, 51, 78.

54. Harvey Young, Jr., to Anne Kintner, Grinnell College Archivist, June 30 1989, Grinnell College Archives, 52 PY 81.

55. Harry Hopkins to Harvey Young, undated, probably 1916, Grinnell College Archives, 52 PY 81.

56. Harvey Young to his wife, July 27, 1916, Grinnell College Archives, 52 PY 81.

CHAPTER SIX

1. Walter Trattner, *From Poor Law to Welfare State: A History of Social Welfare in America,* 3rd Ed. (New York: The Free Press, 1984), 90.

2. Defined as those not from nuclear families or in institutions, foster care, or jail.

3. *Proceedings of the Conference on the Care of Dependent Children Held at Washington, D.C., January, 25, 1909* (Washington: Government Printing Office, Doc. No. 721.5400), 5.

4. *Proceedings of the Conference on the Care of Dependent Children,* 44, 91.

5. Grace Abbott, *The Child and the State: Vol. II, The Dependent and Delinquent Child* (New York: Greenwood Press, 1968, first published 1938), 231; "Report on Outdoor Relief," *Proceedings of the Conference of Charities 1877,* Boston: Williams & Co., 1877, 48-49, 51.

6. Josephine Shaw Lowell, quoted in *Proceedings of the National Conference of Charities and Correction 1888* (Boston: Geo. H. Ellis Press, 1888), 147. Lowell, the first woman appointed to the New York State Board of Charities (in 1876), formed the COS in 1882.

7. George M'Gonegal, "The Problem of Outdoor Relief," *Proceedings of the National Conference of Charities and Correction 1888,* 147.

8. Mrs. Louise Wolcott, "Treatment of Poor Widows with Dependent Children," *Proceedings of the National Conference of Charities and Correction.* Boston: Geo. H. Ellis Press, 1888, 137-138.

9. Mark Leff, "A Consensus for Reform: The Mothers' Pension Movement in the Progressive Era," *Social Service Review* 47 (September 1973): 402.

10. Frederic Almy, "Public Pensions to Widows: Experiences and Observations Which Lead Me to Oppose Such a Law," in Edna O. Bullock, *Selected Articles in Mothers' Pensions* (White Plains, N.Y.: H. W. Wilson and Co., 1950), 153-158.

11. Edward T. Devine, "Widows' Needs," *Survey* 32 (April 4, 1914): 27.

12. Edward Devine, "Pensions for Mothers," *American Labor Legislation Review* (June 1913), in Bullock, 176-81.

13. Devine, "Pensions for Mothers," 182-183.

14. Mary E. Richmond, "Motherhood and Pensions," *Survey* 22 (March 1, 1913), in Bullock, 62-64; Roy Lubove, *The Struggle for Social Security* (Cambridge, Mass.: Harvard University Press, 1968), 102.

15. Theda Skocpol, *Protecting Soldiers and Mothers: The Political Origins of Social Policy in the United States* (Cambridge, Mass.: Belknap Press, 1992), 426.

16. Richmond, "Motherhood and Pensions," in Bullock, 68. Richmond seemed oblivious to the lack of investigation in the case of Civil War pensioners.

17. "Wildfire Spread of 'Widows' Pensions'—Its Start—Its Meaning—And Its Cost," *Everybody's Magazine* (June 1915), in Bullock, 87.

18. The American Federation of Labor (AFL) and the American Association for Labor Legislation (AALL) endorsed widows' pensions but did not actively support the movement preferring instead legislative remedies. Leff, "Consensus for Reform," 407.

19. Leff, "Consensus for Reform," 402-407; Skocpol, *Protecting Soldiers and Mothers,* 427.

20. Skocpol, *Protecting Soldiers and Mothers,* 465.

21. According to Linda Gordon, this maternalist discourse implied and reinforced the subordination of poor women while at the same time carving out a space in the public sphere for reforming women. Many of these reformers saw day nurseries, an alternative that would allow some women to earn enough money to support their families or to supplement their pension, as merely undermining women's domestic role. Gordon, *Pitied But Not Entitled,* 23, 27, 55. See also Sonya Michel, "Limits of Maternalism," in Seth Koven and Sonya Michel, Mothers of a New World: Maternalist Politics and the Origins of the Welfare State (New York: Routledge, 1993), 227-280.

22. Miriam Cohen and Michael Hanagan, "The Politics of Gender and the Making of the Welfare State, 1900-1940," *Journal of Social History* (Spring 1991), 469.

23. Lubove, *Struggle for Social Security,* 102. See also Trattner, *From Poor Law to Welfare State,* 85.

24. Robert Bremner, "Origins of the COS," in Roy Lubove, ed., *Poverty and Social Welfare in the United States,* (New York: Holt, Rinehart and Winston, 1972), 39-40.

25. Untitled, *Survey* 32 (April 4, 1914): 2.

26. Cornelius N. Bliss, Jr., to Bailey Burritt, February 26, 1914, JAKP, A4: BCW M-Z. While the AICP and the COS eventually did merge, forming the Community Service Society, this did not happen until 1939. See Brandt.

27. Made up of three senators (Anthony J. Griffin, Henry W. Pollock and Ralph W. Thomas), five assemblymen (Frederick. S. Burr, Aaron J. Levy, who was elected chairman; Martin G. McCue, James W. Rozan, Thomas K. Smith) , and seven other interested parties appointed by the governor (Hannah B. Einstein, Sophie Irene Loeb, E. Frank Brewster, William Hard, John D. Lindsay, Ansley Wilcox). Robert Hebberd was hired as director of investigations.

28. State of New York, *Report of the New York State Commission on Relief for Widowed Mothers* (Albany, New York: J.B. Lyon Company, 1914), 1. The commission was formed June 1913 and the report was submitted to the New York state legislature March 27, 1914. Witnesses included Dr. Edward Devine, John Kingsbury, Homer Folks, Mary Richmond, Porter Lee, Mary Simkhowitch, Rabbi Stephen Wise, Mary Van Kleeck, Frank Persons, and Frank Bruno. See also *Survey* 32 (April 4, 1914): 1. Although somewhat radical, this statement of government responsibility for children was not unprecedented. At the 1898 National Conference of Charities and Correction, Hugh Fox quoted the New Jersey Constitution, which declared that "Government is instituted for the protection, security and benefit of the people." He added, "It is a wide departure from the Laissez Faire doctrine of the old economists." *Proceedings of the National Conference of Charities and Correction 1898,* 2.

29. State of New York, *Report,* 17-21. Witnesses included Dr. Edward Devine, John Kingsbury, Homer Folks, Mary Richmond, Porter Lee, Mary Simkhovitch, Rabbi Stephen Wise, Mary Van Kleeck, Frank Persons, and Frank Bruno. See also *Survey* 32 (April 4, 1914): 1.

30. State of New York, *Report,* 10, 17-20.

31. State of New York, *Report,* 15.

32. Elberfeld is a town in Germany near Dusseldorf.

33. *Proceedings of the Conference of Charities, 1877,* 47-48.

34. Frederic Almy, *Proceedings of the National Conference of Charities and Correction 1904,* 114-115.

35. She traveled to England, France, Germany, Denmark, Switzerland, and Scotland and made extensive investigations into "the effect of social insurance, workmen's compensation and other methods of relief in the special relation of widowed families with children." State of New York, *Report,* 187-191.

36. State of New York, *Report,* 192-196.

37. State of New York, *Report,* 10-13, 182.

38. State of New York, *Report,* 8.

39. Koven and Michel, *Mothers of a New World.* See introduction and Michel, "The Limits of Maternalism," 277-320. See also Linda Gordon, *Pitied But Not Entitled;* Ladd-Taylor; Mink.

40. Gordon, *Pitied But Not Entitled,* 55.

41. Michel, "Limits of Maternalism," 280.

42. *Proceedings of the New York State Conference of Charities and Correction 1914,* 127. Quoted in *New York State Commission Report,* 252.

43. State of New York, *Report,* 187-191.

44. Brandt, 195.

45. Correspondence between John Kingsbury and Ansley Wilcox (secretary of NYS Commission on the Relief of Widowed Mothers), November and December 1914, JAKP, A4: BCW M-Z.

46. John A. Kingsbury to Bailey Burritt, April 8, 1914. JAKP. A4: Board of Child Welfare 1914-1916 M-Z.

47. William Matthews to Fulton Cutting, November 22, 1913, ACSS, 36:177.

48. Letter from Bailey B. Burritt, General Director of AICP, to Edwin P. Maynard., November 8, 1915, Hopkins III, 1:14, GUSC.

49. "A Year's Work: Seventy-Fifth Annual Report of the New York Association for Improving the Condition of the Poor, For the Year Ending September 30, 1914," 13, ACSS, 36:177.

50. Thirty-seven of these forty-three families were Catholic.

51. "A Report to the Public of the Service Rendered by the New York Association for Improving the Condition of the Poor to 474 Widows with Dependent Children . . ." 1914, 7, JAKP, A4: Board of Child Welfare 1914-1916 M-Z; William H. Matthews, "Widows' Families: Pensioned and Otherwise," *Survey* 32 (June 6, 1914): 272; "A Year's Work: Seventy-First Annual Report of the New York Association for Improving the Condition of the Poor, For the Year Ending September 30, 1914," 13, Hopkins III, 1:14, GUSC. (Hereinafter AICP, Report 1914)

52. Brandt, 193.

53. AICP, Report 1914, 1-2.

54. AICP, Report 1914, 30.

55. AICP, Report 1914, 31.

56. AICP, Report 1914, 32. As early as 1889, the AICP declared its intention to use aid as a moral lever. See Francis S. Longworth, "Report of the General Agent," *Forty-Sixth Annual Report of the New York Association for Improving the Condition of the Poor* (New York, 1889), 24; AICP Report 1914, 32.

57. AICP, Report 1914, 4, 7.

58. William H. Matthews, *Proceedings of the Eighteenth New York State Conference of Charities 1917,* 257.

59. AICP, Report 1914, 4-5; see also Matthews, "Widowed Families," 271.

60. *Proceedings,* National Conference on Economic Security, Box 4, RG 47, National Archives.

61. AICP, Report 1914, 34.

62. Abbott, 229. The pensions paid to poor mothers, however, were never enough to keep them out of the workforce.

63. AICP, Report 1914, 35, 37.

64. Brandt, 197; "RESOLVED . . . ," JAKP A4: Bureau of Child Welfare M-Z.

65. Brandt, 196.

66. Letter from Bailey Burritt to Robert Hebberd, May 28, 1914, ACSS, 20:37-10.

67. Letter from Bailey Burritt to Editor of the *New York Times,* February 15, 1915, ACSS, 20:37-10.

68. William H. Matthews, *Adventures in Giving* (New York: Dodd, Mead and Company, 1939), 121.

69. Hannah B. Einstein, "Child Welfare Work and State Allowance for Widowed Mothers," address delivered to the State Federation of Women's Clubs, Rochester, New York, November 16, 1916, p. 1. See also *Notable American Women, 1607-1950,* 416.

70. Harry Hopkins, "The First Annual Report of the Board of Child Welfare of the City of New York, October 1, 1915 to October 1, 1916," 3-4, Hopkins III, 1:14, GUSC.

71. See BCW, "First Annual Report."

72. Hopkins' Résumé, November 15, 1915, Hopkins III, 1:14, GUSC; Matthews, *Adventures in Giving,* 121-122.

73. Christina Isobel MacColl to Edwin P. Maynard, November 6, 1915, Hopkins III, 1:14, GUSC.

74. Bailey B. Burritt to Edwin P. Maynard, November 8, 1915, Hopkins III, 1:14, GUSC.

75. Helen Ingram to E. P. Maynard, November 8, 1915, Hopkins III, 1:14, GUSC.

76. Brandt, 197.

77. Bailey Burritt to Harry Hopkins, November 11, 1915, Hopkins III, 1:14, GUSC.
78. "Work of the Board," undated, Hopkins III, 1:14, GUSC.
79. Bureau of Child Welfare, *Second Annual Report,* 4.
80. Conant interview, 42.
81. William Matthews to Harry Hopkins, October 5, 1916, Hopkins III, 1:14, GUSC.
82. Conant interview, 40.
83. BCW Staff to Harry Hopkins, March 2, 1917, Hopkins III, 1:14, GUSC.
84. Form letter, August 6, 1915, JAKP, A4: BCW 1914-1916 M-Z.
85. Henry W. Pollack to Sophie Irene Loeb, November 18, 1915, JAKP, A4: BCW 1914-1916.
86. John Purroy Mitchel to BCW, July 26, 1915, JAKP, A4: BCW M-Z.
87. Robert W. Hebberd to Sophie Irene Loeb, October 18, 1915, JAKP, A4: BCW 1914-1916 M-Z.
88. John A. Kingsbury to Mayor Mitchel, January 6, 1916, JAKP, A4: BCW 1914-1916 Widows' Pensions.
89. John A. Kingsbury to Mayor Mitchel, September 6, 1917, JAKP, A4: BCW. Kingsbury remarked in this letter that he bears no grudge against Loeb, nor against Father Farrell, indicating that the lines of demarcation in the charities controversy and the widow's pension movement had similarities; John A. Kingsbury, September 18, 1917, JAKP, A4: BCW. In this letter Kingsbury reminded Mitchel that they had "been through together these last four years." He attached a two-page diatribe against Loeb.
90. William Matthews to the managing editor of the *New York Times,* March 27, 1916; Bailey Burritt to Henry Bruere, April 3, 1916; William Matthews to John A. Kingsbury, November 27, 1916, JAKP, A4: BCW.
91. John A. Kingsbury to Mayor Mitchel, January 6, 1916, JAKP, A4: BCW; "Mayor Ignores Protest of Child Welfare Board," *Evening World,* January 14, 1916, 1.
92. See "Memorandum of Meeting of the Board of Child Welfare Held on March 2, 1916," and "Meeting of the Board of Child Welfare at Room 2, City Hall, on May 3, 1916," JAKP, A4: BCW.
93. Sophie Irene Loeb to William Prendergast, October 12, 1917, Hopkins III, 4:4, GUSC.
94. The BCW, established by the mayor on August 11, 1915, spent $464,772.50 in mothers' allowances to 1,605 widows with 4,915 children in the first six months. By 1921 it would spend $3,742,273.13 for 7,645 mothers with 24,538 children, and by 1925, when forty-four states had widows' pension laws, New York City appropriated $5 million dollars for this purpose. By 1921 wives of men with permanent disability were included and in 1924 deserted wives also included. William Doherty, "The Mothers' Allowance Movement in the U.S.," 5, 22, ACSS, 17:15.
95. Doherty, 5, 22.
96. "First Annual Report of the Board of Child Welfare of the City of New York, October 1, 1915 to October 1, 1916," 6, Hopkins III, 1:15, GUSC.
97. Harry Hopkins to Miss McKeever, October 19, 1917; Henry Bruere to Harry Hopkins, December 19, 1917; Harry Hopkins to Henry Bruere, undated, probably winter 1917, Hopkins III, 1:14, GUSC.
98. Nevertheless, because adequate housing was considered of the utmost importance for a normal family life, the BCW usually moved widows and their children into comfortable apartments.
99. "First Annual Report of the Board of Child Welfare," 8.
100. Conant interview, 131.
101. "The Report of the Board of Child Welfare 1917," 5-7, Hopkins III, 1:15, GUSC.
102. "Paying Pensions to Widowed Mothers," *New York Herald,* March, 18, 1917, Magazine Section, 5.

103. McJimsey, 22-23.
104. Harry L. Hopkins to John A. Kingsbury, April 20, 1917, JAKP, A37: Hopkins, Harry, L.
105. Conant interview, 71.
106. Rosalind Rosenberg, *Divided Lives: American Women in the Twentieth Century* (New York: Hill and Wang, 1972), 160, 262.
107. "Administrative Report of the Board of Child Welfare," 1917, Hopkins II, 4:5, GUSC.
108. Gordon, *Pitied But Not Entitled,* 3.
109. Ann Vandenpol, "Dependent Children, Child Custody, and the Mothers' Pensions: The Transformation of the State-Family Relations in the Early 20th Century," *Social Problems* 29, no. 3 (February, 1982): 221-235.
110. Lubove, *Struggle for Social Security,* 108.
111. "First Annual Report of the Board of Child Welfare," 10.
112. Barbara Nelson, "The Origins of the Two-Channel Welfare State: Workmen's Compensation and Mothers' Aid," in Linda Gordon, *Women, the State, and Welfare* (Madison: University of Wisconsin Press, 1990), 126.
113. Muriel N. and Ralph E. Pumphrey, "The Widows' Pension Movement, 1900-1930: Preventive Child-Saving or Social Control?", in William Trattner, ed. *Social Control or Social Welfare: Some Historical Reflections on "Regulating the Poor"* (Knoxville: University of Tennessee Press, 1983), 59; Theda Skocpol also makes this point in *Protecting Soldiers and Mothers,* 468.
114. Pumphrey and Pumphrey, 59.
115. Michel, "Limits of Maternalism," 299, 301.
116. Gordon, *Pitied But Not Entitled,* 38.
117. Pumphrey and Pumphrey, 60.
118. Ladd-Taylor, *Mother-Work,* 150.
119. *Proceedings of the New York State Commission on Relief of Widowed Mothers,* November 24, 1913, 10, 15.
120. Harry Hopkins, "To What Extent are Public and Private Agencies Supplementing Low Wages?" MS, undated, Hopkins III, 1:15, GUSC.
121. Rubinow, 9, 284.
122. Rubinow, 9.
123. Hopkins, "To What Extent," 11.
124. Hopkins, "To What Extent," 10.
125. Hopkins, "To What Extent," 3-6.
126. Hopkins, "To What Extent," 7.
127. Hopkins, "To What Extent," 7-8.
128. Hopkins, "To What Extent," 11-12.
129. Hopkins, "To What Extent," 2.
130. *Final Report of the Commission on Industrial Relations* (Washington, D.C.: GPO, 1916. Doc. No. 415, 64th Congress), 72.
131. Frederick Hoffman, "American Problems in Social Insurance," *Proceedings of the National Conference of Charities and Correction, 1914,* 350.
132. Conant interview, 131.
133. *Proceedings of the National Conference of Social Work, 1917,* 165.

CHAPTER SEVEN

1. "Child Welfare Secretary Resigns," *New York Times,* December 23, 1917, I, 9.
2. Quoted in Halsted MS, chapter 4, 73.

3. Kingsbury's expulsion from the BCW was likely the result of his feud with Sophie Irene Loeb rather than the effect of Tammany politics; his close relationship with Mayor Mitchel, who lost the election to the Hearst candidate, undercut his influence.

4. Matthews to Mr. Wilbur G. Phillips, August 16, 1916, in author's possession.

5. McJimsey, 23.

6. Emma O. Lundberg, *Public Aid to Mothers with Dependent Children* (Washington, D.C.: U.S. Department of Labor, Children's Bureau, 1928b), 3-11. "Defer Widows' Pensions," *New York Times,* August 4, 1915, 7.

7. Halsted MS, Chapter 8. Hopkins added, "my political beliefs . . . come from my father" (who was a Bryan Democrat) and "The first thing I can remember about politics is William Jennings Bryan having been in our house."

8. McJimsey, 23.

9. G. E. Scott to All Departments and Bureaus, June 28, 1918, Hopkins III, 1:4, GUSC.

10. W. Frank Persons to Emmet White, December 20, 1917, Hopkins III 1:4, GUSC.

11. Halsted MS, Chapter 4, 82.

12. Halsted MS, Chapter 4, 82-83. Ethel Gross Hopkins, probably reflecting her belief in woman's equality, also registered for the draft and was issued a draft card. She apparently did not agree with many of the women's organizations opposing the war. See Barbara J. Steinson, *American Women's Activism in World War I* (New York: Garland Publishing, 1982).

13. W. Frank Persons to Chairman of Local Board #135, July 11, 1918, Hopkins III, 1:4, GUSC.

14. Hopkins to Harvey Young, February 22, 1918. Harvey Young File, 52 PY 81, Grinnell College Archives. It is interesting to note that Hopkins clearly stated in this letter that this stay in the South was only temporary and that he hoped to see his friend in New York City "because of course we are going back." He had obviously severed his rural roots by this time.

15. Porter Lee, "The Task of Civilian War Relief—II," *Survey* (April 28, 1917): 90, found in JAKP, A12: State Charities Investigation.

16. "General Suggestions and Preliminary Outline of Program and Organization for the Permanent Peace Program of the American Red Cross, December 11, 1919," IX. American Red Cross Records, RG 200, 120:140.11, National Archives. (Hereinafter ARC.)

17. American Red Cross Civilian Relief, "General Suggestions and Preliminary Outline of Program and Organization for the Permanent Peace Program of the American Red Cross," December 11, 1918, IV, ARC, 120:140.11. The reliance on language to justify ARC programs was similar to that of the advocates of public aid to dependent mothers when they insisted on using the word "pension" to describe their program.

18. John Kingsbury to Mr. Howe, June 28, 1916, JAKP, A18: Publicity 1914-1917.

19. "Bureau of Civilian Relief," *Gulf Division Bulletin,* 1 (March 1, 1918): 1, Hazel Braugh Records Center, Falls Church, Va. (Hereinafter HBRC.)

20. Harry Hopkins, "Report of Bureau of Civilian Relief, June 30 to December 31, 1918," 3, Reel 24-4, "Certain Personal Correspondence," Harry Hopkins Personal Papers, FDRL, (Hereinafter HHPP.)

21. Halsted MS, Chapter 5, 92.

22. Leigh Carroll to Emmett W. White, January 16, 1918, Hopkins III 1:4, GUSC.

23. Halsted MS, Chapter 5, 86-91; Harry Hopkins, "Report of Bureau of Civilian Relief, June 30 to December 31, 1918," 23, Reel 24-4, "Certain Personal Correspondence," HHPP, FDRL.

24. Conant interview, 115.

25. Emmet White, "Report of the Bureau of Civilian Relief Gulf Division, American Red Cross for the Month of March, 1918," ARC, 14; Emmet White, "Report of the Bureau of Civilian Relief Gulf Division, American Red Cross for the Month of April, 1918," 94-95, ARC, 201:149.18. The New York School of Philanthropy, in cooperation with local agencies, offered training courses for Red Cross staff. The courses (made up largely of women) required attendance at classes for ten weeks, three days a week. Joanna C. Colcord, "Training for the Work of Civilian Relief," *Proceedings, National Conference of Social Work,* 1917, 143.

26. McJimsey, 24.

27. Reminisces of Jane Hoey, interview 2, CUOHRO; "Report of the Bureau of Civilian Relief Atlantic Division, American Red Cross for the Month of April, 1918," 76, ARC, 201:149.18.

28. Harry Hopkins, "Report of the Bureau of Civilian Relief Gulf Division, American Red Cross for the Month of June, 1918," ARC, 34-35; "Report of the Bureau of Civilian Relief Gulf Division, American Red Cross for the Month of March, 1918," ARC, 16; "Report of the Bureau of Civilian Relief Gulf Division, American Red Cross for the Month of September, 22, 1918," ARC, 201:149.18.

29. Harry Hopkins, "Report of the Bureau of Civilian Relief Gulf Division, American Red Cross for the Month of April, 1919," 85, ARC, 202:149.18. The fact that the child and the family served as the focus for this new methodology would have seemed especially relevant to Hopkins, given his background in family welfare and widows' pensions in New York City.

30. Harry Hopkins, "Report of the Bureau of Civilian Relief Gulf Division, American Red Cross for the Month of September, 1918," ARC, 21; "Report of the Bureau of Civilian Relief Gulf Division, American Red Cross for the Month of December, 1918," ARC, 201:149.18. The Red Cross was supported by private contributions. Additional funds came from the sale of Christmas Seals. Rhea Foster Dulles, *The American Red Cross: A History* (New York: Harper and Brothers, 1950), 90.

31. The American Red Cross war chest totaled $115 million by 1917 and more than doubled over the next year. By the end of the war the Red Cross had raised over $400 million. Of that amount, $48 million was allocated for Home Relief. The *Literary Digest* estimated that about 50 million persons made individual contributions. Dulles, 149-151.

32. W. J. Leppert to Harry Hopkins, January 29, 1919, ARC, 212: 149.01. By 1918 there were 3,864 local Red Cross chapters across the nation. Charles Hurd, *The Compact History of the American Red Cross* (New York: Hawthorne Books, 1959), 151.

33. McJimsey, 24. It may not have been that quickly or that extensive, but there is no doubt that Hopkins did much to improve social services in the South.

34. Conant interview, 127-129.

35. John F. McClymer, *War and Welfare: Social Engineering in America, 1890-1925* (Westport, Conn.: Greenwood Press, 1980), 163-167.

36. "Preliminary Report of Committee on the Future of Home Service," 1919, Hopkins III, 1:5, GUSC.

37. American Red Cross Civilian Relief, "General Suggestions and Preliminary Outline of Program and Organization for the Permanent Peace Program of the American Red Cross," December 11, 1918, IX-XVII, ARC, 120:140.11.

38. Harry Hopkins, "Report of the Bureau of Civilian Relief Gulf Division, American Red Cross for the Month of March, 1919," ARC, 57; Harry Hopkins, "Report of the Bureau of Civilian Relief Gulf Division, American Red Cross for the Month of August, 1919," 81-84, ARC, 202:149.18.

39. W. Frank Persons to Henry P. Davison, December 14, 1918, Hopkins III, 1:4, GUSC.

40. W. Frank Persons to Hopkins, December 28, 1918, Hopkins III, 1:3, GUSC.

41. William Matthews to Hopkins, December 20, 1918, Hopkins III, 1:3, GUSC.

42. Leigh Carroll to Chapter Chairmen, July 27, 1920, 1-2, Hopkins III, 1:6, GUSC.

43. McJimsey, 26-27.

44. Owen Lovejoy to Hopkins, December 16, 1921, Hopkins III, 1:7, GUSC.

45. Halsted MS, Chapter 5, 98.

46. Halsted MS, Chapter 5, 99-100.

47. William Doherty to Hopkins, April 27, 1920, Hopkins III 1:18, GUSC; John Kingsbury, MS Prospectus, Bk. IV, 40, JAKP, B81: Autobiography Draft. Kingsbury, headquartered in New York City, did some research work during this time for Albert G. Milbank, which resulted in the organization of the Milbank Memorial Fund, a philanthropic organization with activities in public health. In 1932 Kingsbury traveled to the Soviet Union to study medical practices there. This resulted in a book he wrote with Sir Arthur Newsholme, *Red Medicine: Socialized Health in Soviet Russia,* 1933, 40-41.

48. MS, in author's possession. Also Hopkins II, GUSC.

49. McJimsey, 26.

50. McJimsey, 25-26.

51. William Matthews to Hopkins, February 7, 1919, Hopkins II, GUSC.

52. Halsted MS, Chapter 5, 95.

53. Halsted MS, Chapter 3, 64.

54. Halsted MS, Chapter 3, 67.

55. "Preliminary Report of Committee on the Future of Home Service," 1919, Hopkins III, 1:5, GUSC.

56. See "Preliminary Report of Committee on the Future of Home Service," 1919, Hopkins III, 1:5, GUSC.

57. Jim Feiser to Hopkins, September 19, 1922, Hopkins III, 1:10, GUSC.

58. Hopkins to Leigh Carroll, undated, handwritten, Hopkins III, 1:10, GUSC.

59. Mrs. R. S. Butler to Hopkins, September 26, 1922. See, for example, Ruth C. Crenshaw to Hopkins, September 27, 1922; Katherine Hook to Hopkins, September 29, 1922; Mary C. Raymond to Hopkins, September 30, 1922, Hopkins III, 1:10, GUSC.

60. Halsted MS, Chapter 3, 92; McJimsey, 27.

61. McJimsey, 30-34. Hopkins' letters to his family from 1912 through the 1920s express a kindly but clear disdain for his hometown. See Hopkins' family correspondence, GUSC.

62. Conant interview, 53.

63. The Milbank Fund was established by Albert G. Milbank, chairman of the Borden Milk Company, to promote public health and had long been connected with the AICP.

64. Clyde V. Kiser, *The Milbank Memorial Fund: Its Leaders and Its Work 1905-1974* (New York: Milbank Memorial Fund, 1975), 24. Kingsbury had long been interested in public health work, especially fighting tuberculosis, which was known to be the chief cause of death worldwide and therefore closely associated with the causes of poverty. When the New York State Charities Aid Association had hired him to do anti-tuberculosis work in 1907, he and his staff mounted a statewide campaign; by 1917, New York City had the most advanced tuberculosis laws in the nation. Trattner, 129.

65. Kiser, 36.

66. Kiser, 37-38. See p. 40 for reference to Hopkins and Mayor Laguardia at the 1934 Annual Milbank Conference.

67. McJimsey, 29.

68. Halsted MS, Chapter 6, 105.

69. Sherwood, 26.

70. Halsted MS, Chapter 6, 110.
71. Halsted MS, Chapter 6, 108.
72. Harry L. Hopkins, "Consolidating Private Health Work Under One Banner," *The Nation's Health,* 9 (January, 1927): 2, Reprint, Hopkins File, American Lung Association Archives, New York City.
73. Hopkins, "Consolidating Private Health Work Under One Banner," 2.
74. "Mr. Harry Hopkins is Interviewed by Mr. Newcomb," March 1933, Harry Hopkins File, American Lung Association Archives.
75. Quoted in Sherwood, 29; Halsted MS, 113.
76. Harry L. Hopkins, "The Place of Social Work in Public Health," *Proceedings of the National Conference of Social Work 1926,* 222-227.
77. McJimsey, 30-34; Sherwood, 26-29; Halsted MS, 111
78. McJimsey, 33-34.
79. Sherwood, 28; Halsted MS, 112; McJimsey, 34.
80. Kurzman, 167-186
81. Homer Folks, "Testimonial to Harry Hopkins," June 7, 1933. 24:7, Harry Hopkins Papers, FDRL. (Hereinafter HHP.)
82. Conant interview, 34, 37.
83. Halsted MS, 116.
84. Conant interview, 159-162.
85. Halsted MS, Chapter 6, 119.
86. Halsted MS, Chapter 6, 122-133.
87. EGH to HLH, November 8, 1927, Hopkins II, GUSC.
88. See correspondence between Harry Hopkins and Ethel Gross Hopkins during the 1920s; Hopkins II, GUSC; and McJimsey, 37.
89. McJimsey, 35-43; Halsted MS, 128-133; John Kingsbury, "Autobiographical Notes," JAKP, B84: Reference Material; Conant interview, 109-110.
90. See Chapter 2, note 11.
91. Halsted MS, Chapter 6, 119-120.
92. *Time,* February 28, 1944, "People" Section.
93. EGH to HLH, February 15, 1944, Hopkins II, GUSC.

CHAPTER EIGHT

1. Kenneth Davis, *FDR: The New York Years, 1928-1933* (New York: Random House, 1994), 239.
2. Harry Hopkins, "I lived in New York in October of 1929 . . . ," 1-2, Hopkins I, 54:11, GUSC.
3. Bremer, *Depression Winter,* 2-10, 173-178.
4. Bonnie Fox Schwartz, *The Civil Works Administration, 1933-1934: The Business of Emergency Employment in the New Deal* (Princeton, N.J.: Princeton University Press, 1984), 14-16; Schneider and Deutsch, 299; Matthews, *Adventures in Giving,* 182-198; Barbara Blumberg, *The New Deal and the Unemployed: The View From New York City* (Lewisburg, Penn.: Bucknell University Press, 1979), 20-22.
5. Matthews, *Adventures in Giving,* viii, 182-186; McJimsey, 45.
6. Matthews, *Adventures in Giving,* 219.
7. Frances Perkins, "Report of the Committee on Stabilization of Industry," April 18, 1930; Press Release, Reel 177, Office of the Governor of New York, (hereinafter OGNY), FDRL .

8.   Frances Perkins, *The Roosevelt I Knew* (New York: Viking Press, 1946), 93.

9.   Perkins, *The Roosevelt I Knew,* 102-103.

10. "Unemployment Insurance Commission Holds First Meeting," May 29, 1931, Reel 68, OGNY, FDRL.

11. Frances Perkins, Press Release, March 27, 1930, Reel 177, OGNY, FDRL.

12. Attending were Joseph B. Ely of Massachusetts; Norman S. Case of Rhode Island; Wilbur L. Cross of Connecticut; Morgan F. Larson of New Jersey; Gifford Pinchot of Pennsylvania; George White of Ohio; William Tudor Gardiner of Maine; and John G. Winant of New Hampshire. Paul H. Douglas, an economist from the University of Chicago, organized the conference for Roosevelt. See Perkins, *The Roosevelt I Knew,* 104-105.

13. *Official Proceedings of the Twenty-Third Annual Conference of Governors,* June 1 and 2, 1931, 17, 24, Reel 68, OGNY, FDRL.

14. *Emergency Unemployment Relief Laws in the State of New York, 1931-1932* (Albany: Temporary Emergency Relief Administration and the Attorney General's Office, 1932), 18.

15. "Origin and History of the Commission," Reel 59, OGNY, FDRL.

16. Jesse Isidor Straus to Herbert Lehman, Lieutenant Governor of New York, October 7, 1931, Reel 173, OGNY, FDRL. William Hodson of the New York City Welfare Council was the board's first choice but was unable to leave his post. Straus indicated to Lieutenant Governor Lehman that the board had been "struggling for the last few days to find an executive director." Other candidates were not mentioned by name in the letter.

17. *Emergency Unemployment Relief Laws in the State of New York, 1931-1932,* 23-25; "Minutes of a Regular Meeting of TERA, March 22, 1932." Reel 173, OGNY, FDRL. Hopkins met Eleanor Roosevelt only after he had accepted the job as head of the TERA; she did not introduce him to her husband. In 1943 she wrote an angry letter to columnist Drew Pearson castigating him for misrepresenting her relationship with Hopkins. She states, ". . . I never heard of Mr. Hopkins until long after he had been working for my husband in New York State, so that whole paragraph on my having discovered him is untrue." Eleanor Roosevelt to Drew Pearson, August 14, 1943, Hopkins I, 19:1, GUSC.

18. McJimsey, 49.

19. Blumberg, 27; Chief Investigator to Miss Lena Parrott re: Charles H. Stone, December 9, 1932, Reel 173, OGNY, FDRL; "New York Unemployed Relief, Report for TERA, Nov. 1, 1931- June 1, 1932," Box 7, HHP, FDRL. The restrictions of one TERA job per family essentially meant that most of the jobs went to men.

20. See Davis, *The New York Years,* 239-242.

21. *Emergency Unemployment Relief Laws in the State of New York, 1931-1932,* 5.

22. *Emergency Unemployment Relief Laws in the State of New York, 1931-1932,* 7. The work test ensures that the type of work done in exchange for relief payments is so undesirable as to discourage paupers from choosing it over private employment. The term "less eligibility" refers to the stricture that relief payments must always be less than what one could earn from working in order to prevent unnecessary or extended dependency and to discourage all but the most destitute from applying for help.

23. When Hopkins went to Washington in 1933 to administer the Federal Emergency Relief Administration (FERA), he observed that he had "inherited a Relief Organization throughout the country which had changed little since the days of Queen Elizabeth I." Hopkins, "I lived in New York in October 1929. . . ," 4.

24. Harry Hopkins, *Spending to Save: The Complete Story of Relief* (New York: W. W. Norton, 1936), 58-62.

25. Harry Hopkins, *Spending to Save:,* 88.

26. MS, 49: Jacob Baker Memoranda, HHP, FDRL.

27. Hopkins, "What Is the American Way?" July 16, 1938, 4, Hopkins IV, 1:52, GUSC. Hopkins disliked Huey Long and could not ascribe to his Share Our Wealth scheme despite its grassroots appeal. See McJimsey, 92-93; and Sherwood, 77.

28. "Home Relief Efficiently Administered, but Inadequate, T. E. R. A. Finds," *Better Times,* 14 (March 6, 1933), 20.

29. MS, Hopkins I, 54:13, GUSC. Hopkins' support of local autonomy on the part of Red Cross chapters in the postwar reorganization phase can be attributed to the economic health of the era as compared with the crisis in the early 1930s, but his change of policy also denotes the development of his administrative talents.

30. Harry Hopkins, "I lived in New York in October of 1929 . . . ," 1-2; Corrington Gill, *Wasted Manpower: The Challenge of Unemployment* (New York: W. W. Norton, 1939), 148. Hopkins, *Spending to Save,* 91-95.

31. Herbert F. Powell, "People Still Starve to Death in New York City," *Better Times* 14 (March 6, 1933): 4-5, HHP, 7: FERA, FDRL.

32. The Reverend John A. Ryan, "Will the Depression Ever End?" *Better Times* 14 (March 6, 1933): 8-9, HHP, 7: FERA, FDRL.

33. Sherwood, 33-45; McJimsey, 52.

34. John Kingsbury, "Autobiographical Notes," 3, JAKP, B84: Reference Material.

35. Halsted MS, chapter 7, unpaginated.

36. Reminisces of Frances Perkins, *Reminiscences,* Social Security Project, vol. 4, Part 1, 469, CUOHRO.

37. Perkins, *The Roosevelt I Knew,* 183-185.

38. Perkins, *The Roosevelt I Knew,* 183-185; Perkins, *Reminiscences,* 472-479. FDR was also seriously considering William Hodson and Henry Morganthau for the position, but Hodson was needed by New York City's Welfare Council and unavailable for the appointment. Ironically, a year earlier Hodson had been Governor Roosevelt's first choice for executive director of the TERA, the position Hopkins got. Hodson turned it down because he felt that he could not leave his job at the Russell Sage Foundation for such a radical new state agency. See Sherwood, 32.

39. Telegram from Franklin D. Roosevelt to Governor Herbert H. Lehman, May 19, 1933, the President's Personal File (hereinafter PPF), 93, Folder: Lehman, Herbert H. 1933-1935, FDRL.

40. Harry Hopkins, MS, "They'd Rather Work," 1935, Hopkins I, 54:11 and 54:3, GUSC; Harry Hopkins, "When people talk about the mistakes . . . ," Reel 22, 1934, HHPP, FDRL.

41. Ida Tarbell, "We Gotta Do It," *New York Herald Tribune,* October, 27, 1933, 12, Hopkins I, 41:1, GUSC.

42. Harry Hopkins Radio Address, October 12, 1933, 7: Speeches, HHP, FDRL.

43. Gill, 152.

44. Harry Hopkins, "Fighting Destitution," *The Jeffersonian* (August 1933): 6-7, Hopkins I, 56:7, GUSC.

45. A dole is direct cash relief with no work requirements. Gill, 158; Bremer, 58; see 9: Speeches 1936, HHP, FDRL. The quote is from an address Hopkins made to United Neighborhood Houses, March 14, 1936.

46. Hopkins, "They'd Rather Work," 7.

47. Harry Hopkins, "Statement by Harry Hopkins, Federal Emergency Administrator," 1933, Hopkins I, 54:1, GUSC. Congress appropriated $500 million to the FERA in 1933 for grants to states, one federal dollar for every three dollars the states spent on relief.

48. Hopkins, "Fighting Destitution," 6.

49. "Report of the Federal Emergency Administration, May 22, 2933 to December 31, 1933," 83: CWA, John Carmody Papers, FDRL.

50. "Women's Division Activities," November 14, 1933, 23, FERA: Procedures Issuances, HHP, FDRL.

51. Recently scholars have challenged conventional modes of inquiry by looking at the welfare state through a gender lens, thus forcing a critical reexamination of previous histories. They describe a bifurcated welfare state originating in the New Deal that has turned out to be disadvantageous to women. Linda Gordon, in her recent work on the impact of the welfare state on single mothers, *Pitied But Not Entitled: Single Mothers and the History of Welfare 1890-1935,* asserts that the emphasis on unemployment relief during the Great Depression marginalized women and that, in particular, Hopkins' "disinterest" in providing work for women in his work-relief programs reflected overt discrimination.

52. Williams, "The New Deal: A Dead Battery," 1958, 33-35, 44: Speeches and Writings, Aubrey Williams Collection, FDRL.

53. Josephine Brown, *Public Relief, 1929-1939* (New York: Octagon Books, 1971, c. 1940), 184-186.

54. Brown, 188-190.

55. Brown, 301.

56. Hopkins, "When some people talk about the mistakes . . . ," 1-2, MS, Reel 22, HHPP, FDRL.

57. Charles, 46; McJimsey, 56-59; Sherwood refers to Gompers' 1898 "Day Labor Plan" as Hopkins' basis for overcoming labor's objection to work-relief. For more on Gompers' stance on public works see: "Work, Not Charity," *American Federationist* 1 (March 1894): 11-12; Donald L. McMurry, *Coxey's Army: A Study of the Industrial Army Movement of 1894* (Seattle: University of Washington Press, 1968, originally published 1929); *Proceedings of the American Federation of Labor,* 1893, 35; Louis Stark, "Labor on Relief and Insurance," *Survey* 65 (November 15, 1931): 186-187; "Employment Ideas Started by Labor Men," *Federation News* 33 (November 25, 1933): 8; Williams, "The New Deal: A Dead Battery," 76.

58. Stuart B. Kaufman and Peter J. Albert, *The Samuel Gompers Papers, Vol. 3, Unrest and Depression 1891-1894* (Chicago: University of Illinois Press, 1989), 365, 387.

59. "Report of the Federal Civil Works Administration, November 16, 1933 to December 31, 1933," 15-18, 2: CWA, HHP, FDRL; *Proceedings, Federal CWA General Meeting, November 15, 1933,* 5, 82: CWA Data, John Carmody Papers, FDRL. Hopkins quote was reported in "Secretary of Commerce Harry Lloyd Hopkins Speaks Before Iowa Legislature," *Des Moines Register* (February 24, 1939): 1.

60. "CWA Conference, General Meeting, November 15, 1933," 4, 2: CWA, HHP, FDRL.

61. These projects included parks and playgrounds, sanitation, highways, water supply, general public improvements, utilities, and sewer systems; Gill, 159, 162-166; Hopkins, *Spending to Save,* 110-114, 120-124; Civil Works Administration Conference, General Meeting, November 15, 1933, 12, Box 21, HHP, FDRL. Hopkins Press Conference, June 15, 1934, 5, Box 28, Folder Press Conferences 1934, HHP, FDRL. According to Hopkins wages ranged from forty-five cents an hour for unskilled jobs in the South to $45 a week for skilled labor in the North. Harry Hopkins, "Rehabilitation," draft for *Spending to Save,* Hopkins I, 54:14, GUSC, 11.

62. Hopkins added, "I can see that you don't belong to the Woman's Party or you would never suggest a specific allocation for women." CWA Conference, November 15, 1933, 27-28.

63. Memo from Hopkins to All State Civil Works Administrators, November 29, 1933, 23: FERA Procedural Issuances, HHP, FDRL.

64. "Report of the Federal Emergency Administration, May 22, 1933, to December 31, 1933," 17, box 83: CWA, John Carmody Papers, FDRL.

65. Memo from Hopkins to All State Administrators, December 5, 1933, 1-2, 23: FERA Procedural Issuances, HHP, FDRL

66. Memo from Hopkins to Directors of Women's Work in the States, May 14, 1934, 23: FERA Procedural Issuances, HHP, FDRL.

67. See Box 23: FERA Procedural Issuances, W1-W67, '33-'35, HHP, FDRL.

68. Susan Ware has shown how the extensive network that women fashioned for themselves during the early years of the twentieth century played a crucial role in the New Deal, which was never really "a strictly male affair." Women exerted significant political influence through the Children's Bureau and the Women's Bureau, and there is no doubt that Hopkins' programs "produced important if small steps for women workers." Susan Ware, *Beyond Suffrage: Women in the New Deal* (Cambridge, Mass.: Harvard University Press, 1981), 1-2, 89-110.

69. Sherwood, 56.

70. McJimsey, 60.

71. "CWA Conference, General Meeting, November 15, 1933," 24.

72. Harry Hopkins, MS, draft for *Today* article written two weeks after CWA was formed, "There were twenty-one million . . . ," December, 1933, 5-6, Hopkins I, 54:2, GUSC.

73. This was a holdover of the strong poor-law tradition in America that blamed poverty on moral degeneracy and laziness. The poor man should be forced to accept any sort of demeaning work in order to prove his industriousness and therefore establish his worthiness. Charity given in this spirit intended to reform the pauper and eliminate help to the degenerate who was satisfied to be a public burden. With major economic depressions at the end of the nineteenth century, a major attitudinal shift took place in the minds of many social reformers who now realized that industrialism, low wages, and job uncertainty caused poverty. But change was slow. The 1915 Bronx Zoo project run by Hopkins and Matthews had retained much of this "work test" notion; if any man refused to work, the agency denied him relief. Schwartz, *The Civil Works Administration,* 7-9; Harry Hopkins, MS, Draft, "Spending to Save, Rehabilitation," 6-7, Hopkins I, 54:14, GUSC.

74. Hopkins, *Spending to Save,* 125.

75. Hopkins Draft, "Rehabilitation," 18; Address by Harry Hopkins, April 9, 1934, Box 57, RG 69, National Archives.

76. MS, "Subject: Labor Relations," May 7, 1933, 1, John Carmody Papers, Box 82 Folder: Reminiscences CWA, FDRL; Lieut. Col. John C . H. Lee, "The Federal Civil Works Administration," 12, 49: CWA, HHP, FDRL. See also Reel 22, HHPP, FDRL.

77. Charles, 63; McJimsey, 62.

78. A. J. Cummings, "Meet America's Other Harold Lloyd," *Daily News Chronicle,* July 8, 1934, Hopkins III, 1:22, GUSC. Hopkins had been discussing Britain's unemployment insurance system and lack of work-relief policy. The writer apparently thought he had the same name of the famous actor and comedian, Harold Lloyd. In six years Hopkins' name would be as well known in England as in the United States.

CHAPTER NINE

1. Address by Harry Hopkins, April 9, 1934, 2-8, Box 57, RG 69, National Archives.

2. Perkins, *The Roosevelt I Knew,* 190-191.

3. Hopkins had been suffering from stomach problems for several months. Because his father had died five years earlier from cancer, he feared that he too had the disease. Yet his relentless work schedule led him to ignore the symptoms. Late in 1934 an X-ray revealed that he had a duodenal ulcer. Although Hopkins never again enjoyed good health, he kept up a grueling pace, traveled extensively, and maintained a rigorous schedule of meetings, conferences, and public appearances. Three years later, just months after his wife, Barbara, died of breast cancer, he did develop a malignant tumor of the stomach. The condition was complicated by the presence of a large ulcer in the cancer tumor that had invaded the lymph glands. On December 20, 1937, surgeons at the Mayo Clinic removed two-thirds of Hopkins' stomach and part of the duodenum as well as the cancerous lymph nodes. The severity of this procedure was hidden from the public, with the press reporting only that Hopkins had had an operation to remove an ulcer. The doctors informed him that he had a fifty-fifty chance that the cancer would recur; ever the optimist, Hopkins looked at this as good news. He recuperated for several months at Joseph Kennedy's home in Palm Beach and returned to his office in March of 1938. The cancer never did recur but Hopkins suffered from frequent bouts illness due to malnutrition. He died on January 29, 1946, from a long list of illnesses, including hemochromatosis, liver disease resulting from dozens of transfusions, anemia, and pulmonary edema. A rediagnosis in 1949 revealed adeno carcinoma, listed as grade II, metastatic and malignant. See Halsted MS, chapter 8; James A. Halsted, M.D., "Severe Malnutrition in a Public Servant of the World War II Era: The Medical History of Harry Hopkins," *Transactions of the American Clinical and Climatological Association,* 86 (1974), Reprint, Grinnell College Archives, 52 ph77ha; and Hopkins III, 6:4, GUSC.

4. Hopkins met with Benito Mussolini on July 25, and reported that he could not understand how Italy "could stand the racket." Il Duce was not the least interested in social programs and only wanted to know what Hitler was up to. Hopkins had to tell him that he had no idea because Hitler had broken his appointment for a meeting. MS, August 24, 1934, HHP, Box 28, FDRL.

5. *Daily News Chronicle,* July 18, 1934, Hopkins III, 6:22, GUSC; HLH to FDR, July 25, 1934, Hopkins II, 6:29, GUSC.

6. See Basil Rauch, *The History of the New Deal, 1933-1938* (New York: Creative Age Press, 1944), 156-159, for a discussion of this policy.

7. MS, HHP, 7: European Trip, 1934, FDRL.

8. Kingsbury, obviously upset by Hopkins' refusal to meet with the Webbs, noted (with some petulance) in his unpublished and unfinished autobiography that Hopkins "turned a deaf ear to my appeals to visit Sir Arthur [Newsholme] and the Webbs in Eng. notwithstanding fact that I made trip possible by $2000.00 grant from M. M. F. [Milbank Memorial Fund]." John Kingsbury, "Autobiographical Notes," JAKP, B84: Reference Material. Kingsbury had collaborated with Sir Arthur in writing *Red Medicine.* Conant interview, 132.

9. Sherwood, *Roosevelt and Hopkins,* 64. Sherwood noted that there are no records of this meeting.

10. "President's Remarks to the National Conference on Economic Security," Box 1: National Conference of Economic Security, RG 47, National Archives; "Speech, August 29, 1934," Box 28: Speeches 1934, HHP, FDRL; Quoted in Halsted MS, chapter 7; Harold L. Ickes, *The Secret Diary of Harold L. Ickes,* vol. 1, *The First Thousand Days, 1933-1936* (New York: Simon and Schuster, 1953), 194.

11. McJimsey, 74-75.

12. Robert S. McElvaine, *The Great Depression: America 1929-1941* (New York: Times Books, 1984), 248.

13. Arthur Schlesinger, Jr., *The Age of Roosevelt,* vol. 2, *The Coming of the New Deal* (New York: Houghton Mifflin, 1958), 294.

14. Handwritten notes, September 1934, Hopkins I, 54:10 GUSC.

15. Schlesinger, *The Coming of the New Deal,* 294.

16. Sherwood, *Roosevelt and Hopkins,* 65.

17. MS, "Final Report as of January 11, 1935," Box. 1, RG 47, National Archives.

18. Committee for Economic Security, "Final Report as of January 11, 1935," 9, RG 47, 1: Committee on Economic Security, National Archives.

19. Perkins, *The Roosevelt I Knew,* 282.

20. Perkins, *The Roosevelt I Knew,* 286.

21. Quoted in Frances Perkins, "The Task That Lies Ahead," November 14, 1934, HHP, 48: Economic and Social Security, FDRL.

22. Hopkins, "There were twenty-one million people . . ." 9, Hopkins I, 54:2, GUSC.

23. Frances Perkins also thought along the same lines. At the National Conference on Economic Security, November 14, 1934, she stated: "We, as a nation, are no longer content to ignore the rights of the individual and I believe that there is among us today a new concept of the old doctrines of liberty and equality, a new desire to make real the old ideal of brotherhood." See "Address of Miss Frances Perkins, Secretary of Labor," 3: Speeches B, RG 47, National Archives.

24. Jacob Baker, believing that people on relief wanted jobs, wrote that "The masses themselves will the direction" of the relief program. Jacob Baker, "The Range of Work Relief, " September 26, 1934. Box 7, RG 69, National Archives. See Edwin Witte, "Limitations and Value of Unemployment Insurance," November 1, 1934, 1, Mary Dewson Papers, 6: CES 1934, FDRL.

25. Helen Greenblatt to Mr. Witte, 5, Box 47, RG 47, National Archives. For over a year Harold Ickes' PWA had been creating valuable, long-term projects, but employment had never been Ickes' first priority.

26. The Technical Board was under the chairmanship of Arthur Altmeyer, second assistant secretary of labor; and "consisted of anyone in the government service who was known to have any special knowledge in any aspect of social security." The Advisory Committee on Economic Security was a huge group made up of nongovernmental experts appointed by President Roosevelt. It was chaired by Frank Graham, president of the University of North Carolina. Edwin Witte, "Twenty Years of Social Security," August 15, 1955, 5-7, Box 8, Mary Dewson Papers, FDRL.

27. "Preliminary Outline of the Work of the Staff of the CES," August 10, 1934, 1: Committee on Economic Security, RG 47, National Archives.

28. Edwin Witte to Harry Hopkins, November 13, 1934, and "Suggestions for a Long-Time and an Immediate Program for Economic Security," 7-8, Aubrey Williams Papers, 27: General Files 2, FDRL; Box 6: CES 1934, Mary Dewson Papers, FDRL; Edwin Witte, "Possible Approaches to the Problem of Economic Security," August 16, 1934, Box 48: Economic and Social Security, HHP, FDRL. See also "Informal Report of a Special Committee Advisory to the President's Committee on Economic Security," 2, Box 27: General Files 2, Aubrey Williams Papers, FDRL.

29. Edwin E. Witte, *The Development of the Social Security Act* (Madison: University of Wisconsin, 1962), 44; Witte, "Twenty Years of Social Security," 7; *Proceedings, National Conference on Economic Security November 11, 1934,* 105-107, Box 4, RG 47, National Archives. See also FERA, Folder: publicity, Box 57, RG 69, National Archives.

30. "Miss Greenblatt's Speech for Aubrey Williams," November 14, 1934 passim, Box 3, RG 47, National Archives. Edwin Witte had drawn up a list of questions re the economic security program dated November, 14, 1934, which indicated that Hopkins' employment assurance plan was still being debated. See "Some Questions Arising in Connection with the Suggested Program for Economic Security," Box 27, Aubrey Williams Papers, FDRL.

31. The committee also advised the federal government to grant money to state departments of public welfare on a permanent basis so that they could provide for the varying needs of the people. Further, it recommended that a permanent federal department of public welfare be established to coordinate all public assistance efforts. "Informal Report of a Special Committee Advisory to the President's Committee on Economic Security," November 22, 1934.

32. Memo, Harry Hopkins to President Franklin Roosevelt, August 23, 1935, "Genesis, History and Results of the Federal Relief Program 1935, the Work Relief Program," 2-6, RG69, National Archives.

33. "Informal Report of a Special Committee Advisory to the President's Committee on Economic Security," November 22, 1934.

34. Nonfederal programs would total $2 billion, federal programs $240 million, housing programs $1.5 billion, and nonliquidating projects $1.5 billion. "A Plan to Give Work to the Able-Bodied Needy Unemployed," November 1934, 1, Box 49, HHP, FDRL; "Work Relief Corporation to Spend 8 to 9 Billions, Hopkins Plan to End Dole," *New York Times,* November 29, 1934, Part 1, 1.

35. Upton Sinclair had proposed that California take over idle farms and put the jobless to work on them. Delbert Clark, "Flurry over Hopkins Finds His 'EPIA' at Work," *New York Times,* December 2, 1934, 1, Part 4.

36. "White House Statement Summarizing Report from the President's Committee on Economic Security (Excerpts)," January 17, 1935, PPF, 1935, 49-50.

37. "Report to the President of the Committee on Economic Security," January 15, 1935, 1-5, Box 3, Mary Dewson Papers, FDRL; Witte, 77; See also PPF, 1935, 49-50.

38. Witte, *Development of the Social Security Act,* 78-79.

39. Hopkins believed, however, that industry had to pay its fair share in taxes for this. "If industry cannot employ workers, it must be prepared to pay its share of the cost of unemployment insurance and the cost employing these same men on public projects." Harry Hopkins, "What Price Recovery?" *The New Republic* (December 1936), 12-13.

40. McJimsey, 76-78.

41. Frances Perkins, "The Task That Lies Ahead," November 14, 1934, HHP, 48: Economic and Social Security, FDRL; Perkins, *The Roosevelt I Knew,* 189.

42. Harry Hopkins, MS, "What Price Recovery?" Hopkins was convinced that there would be a permanent number of unemployed who would be dependent on government jobs for their subsistence. He believed that programs to deal with the needs of these people could be safely created within the capitalist system. See "Iowa's Harry Hopkins Seeks a New 'American Way,'" 2, Hopkins I, 40:9 GUSC.

43. Perkins, *The Roosevelt I Knew,* 188-189. Years later Winston Churchill would dub Hopkins "Lord Root of the Matter" for his uncanny ability to ferret out the essentials of a problem.

44. *Economic Security Act: Hearings Before the Committee on Ways and Means,* 74th Congress, 1st Session, January and February, 1935, 3-4, CIS Group 3, No. 74 H699-0.

45. *Economic Security Act: Hearings Before the Committee on Ways and Means,* 1935, 213-14, 181-182.

46. According to Witte, the term "social security" was not used until the House Ways and Means Committee substituted it for "economic security" in April 1935. See Witte, "Twenty Years of Social Security," 1955, 2.

47. *The Public Papers and Addresses of Franklin D. Roosevelt,* vol. 4, *The Court Disapproves,* (New York: Random House, 1938), 20. Hopkins helped Roosevelt draft this speech. See Kenneth S. Davis, *FDR: The New Deal Years, 1933-1937.* (New York: Random House, 1979), 464.

48. Arthur M. Schlesinger, Jr. *The Age of Roosevelt,* vol. 3, *The Politics of Upheaval.* (Boston: Houghton Mifflin, 1960), 344-46.

49. Davis, *FDR: The New Deal Years,* 309, 468-469. The other two divisions were the Division of Applications and Information headed by Frank C. Walker (who was replaced by Donald Richberg on the National Emergency Council) and the Works Allotment Division, headed by Harold Ickes. The ongoing feud between Hopkins and Ickes intensified after this.

50. New Deal relief was directed at productive individuals; unemployables did not fit into this free enterprise system and therefore were cut out of federal programs. Care for unemployables had always been considered the responsibility of the local agencies. Bremer, *Depression Winter,* 177; Donald S. Howard, 720; Rauch, 163-164; James T. Patterson, *The New Deal and the States: Federalism in Transition* (Princeton, N.J.: Princeton University Press, 1969), 75-78; Gill, 178-182. Arthur Schlesinger, Jr. noted that it took less than two weeks for the WPA to emerge as the dominant agency. Schlesinger, *The Politics of Upheaval,* 345.

51. Hopkins Diary, May 13, 1935; Hopkins I, Box 51, GUSC. See also Kenneth S. Davis, 569-570. Ickes' wife, Anna, had died recently ; soon after this trip, Hopkins discovered that his wife, Barbara, had breast cancer. She died October 7, 1937. He spent the evening of October 9 with Ickes, talking about his loss. Halsted MS, chapter 7, 51.

52. Using a force account method instead of a private contract, the WPA itself hired and paid the worker, bought the necessary supplies, and supervised the project. See Howard, 150-153.

53. Gill, 186.

54. Harry Hopkins, "People Want Steady Jobs," October 1936, MS, Draft for the *New York Times,* Sunday Magazine Section Article, 2-5, Hopkins I, 56:4, GUSC.

55. Although this means-testing ensured that WPA jobs would retain some of the stigmatizing aura of relief, as the Depression wore on, the unemployed increasingly regarded these government jobs as an entitlement. Harry Hopkins, "A Plan to Give Work to the Able-Bodied Needy Unemployed," November 1934, 2-4, Box 49, HHP, FDRL.

56. Harry Hopkins, MS, "There are as yet only a handful of men . . . ," May 2, 1936, 6, Hopkins I, 56:2, GUSC.

57. Hopkins, "What Price Recovery?" 12-13.

58. Harry Hopkins to "My dear Mr. President," June 30, 1938, Letter of Transmittal with Harry L. Hopkins, *Inventory: WPA, An Appraisal of the Results of the Works Progress Administration* (Washington, D.C.: Works Progress Administration, 1938), 7-8.

59. Hopkins estimated that there were about 225,000 women on FERA work-relief. MS, Press Conference, February 21, 1935, Box 29, HHP, FDRL.

60. "Address of Mrs. Ellen Woodward, Assistant Director, Works Progress Administration," September 10, 1935, 1-5, Box 9, Dewson Papers, FDRL. WPA projects hired women as musicians, nurses, musicians, researchers, seamstresses, domestic workers, canners, librarians, and so on.

61. Hopkins, *Inventory,* 57-58.

62. Sherwood, 57-61. See also MS, Hopkins' Press Conference April 4, 1935, 4, Box 29: Press Conferences 11/24/34-12/19/35, HHP, FDRL.

63. According to Sherwood, in 1944, the *Washington Post* referred to Hopkins as the man who thought that "the American people are too damned dumb," and the newspaper published an angry poem directed at him which ended "And we're telling you, by gum, We are not quite too damned dumb, Mr. Hopkins." See Sherwood, 61.

64. Hopkins, *Inventory,* 77.

65. Hopkins, *Inventory,* 81.

66. Hopkins, *Inventory,* 85.

67. Hopkins Speech, State Administrators' Conference, October 1937, 2, Box 26, HHP, FDRL.

68. "The Works Program," August 1935, 1, Box 49, HHP, FDRL.

69. At its height, the WPA spent approximately $585 million per month.

70. Gill, 218.

71. Gill maintained that "the fearful results of increased public debt have been grossly exaggerated." In his opinion, public spending stimulated business and, while it was no panacea, it did provide employment and helped the nation move toward economic recovery. Gill, 221-222; John Kenneth Galbraith wrote a detailed report to Roosevelt on long-range planned public works to offset unemployment which said in part: "The continued existence of unemployment as the central economic problem of the United States makes evident the need for planning a public works policy on a long-range basis. . . . The problem of unemployment is to be met in part through the construction of public works. But even if unemployment should cease to be a major problem, the need for a continuing program of public works construction would not disappear." Because economic depressions and the unemployment they caused were not self-correcting, he declared, permanent public work projects, capable of expanding and contracting with the economy, should be a necessary part of any corrective process. John Kenneth Galbraith, *The Economic Effects of the Federal Public Works Expenditures 1933-1938* (New York: Da Capo Press, 1975, orig. 1940), 1.

72. Harry Hopkins, Draft, "What Price Recovery?" Hopkins I, 46:5, GUSC.

73. Hopkins added that aid to dependent children should be expanded, that low housing should be built, and that an adequate public health program should be developed. He did not trust the states to carry out individual projects on their own, declaring that grants-in-aid to the states merely "constitutes an attack upon work and an endorsement of the dole. . . . [it] is a proposal to lower relief standards." Statement of Harry L. Hopkins, Work Progress Administrator Before Special Committee to Investigate Unemployment and Relief, Friday, April 8, 1938, 16-32, JAKP, B50.

74. Harry Hopkins, "Resurgent Democracy," October 8, 1938, JAKP, B50. See also Howard, 796-797.

75. Not everyone agreed that the WPA marched along the American Way. Martin Dies, chairman of the House Committee for the Investigation of Un-American Activities, announced in 1938 that he would request Congress to allocate $1 million to look into the activities of the WPA (and Ickes' PWA as well). The investigation aimed especially at Hopkins, in particular his perceived "communistic tendencies." The Dies Committee alleged that the WPA employed Communists on its projects, especially in Federal One, and that the WPA's Workers' Alliance of America was dominated by Communists. In 1943 Donald S. Howard pointed out the irony that the WPA, the program instituted "to prevent the development of subversive attitudes toward government," was investigated for un-American activities. Howard, 792-3.

76. Perkins, *The Roosevelt I Knew,* 283-284.

77. Report, "Special Committee on Employment and Relief, Advisory to the President's Committee on Economic Security," HHP, 48: Economic and Social Security, FDRL.

78. Kenneth S. Davis, *The New Deal Years,* 460; Untitled Speech, Baltimore, Maryland, November 27, 1933, Box 7: Speeches 1933 and Speeches 1935, HHP, FDRL.

79. "Report to the President of the Committee on Economic Security," Box 3: Social Security, Mary Dewson Pamphlet Collection, FDRL; "Final Report as of Jan. 11, 1935," 1: Committee on Economic Security, RG 47, National Archives.

80. Witte, "Twenty Years of Social Security," 12.

81. Charles, 95-101.

82. See William W. Bremer, "Along the 'American Way': The New Deal's Work Relief Programs for the Unemployed," 62 (November 3, 1975), 636-652, for an interesting discussion of the nature of work-relief.

83. Committee on Economic Security, "Security For Children," 68, Box 1: Lenroot, Katherine, RG 47, National Archives.

84. "Security for Children," 4. See also Grace Abbott, "Recent Trends in Mothers' Aid," *Social Service Review,* 8 (June, 1934), 191.

85. "Mothers' Aid," 1931, Children's Bureau Publication No. 220 (Department of Labor, 1933), 1, Box 47: Helen Greenblatt File, Business to C, RG 47, National Archives

86. Harry Hopkins, Untitled MS, Article for *Colliers,* November 1935, Hopkins I, 54:13, GUSC. The article essentially refuted Dr. Townsend's plan.

87. "Child Welfare to be Included in Social Plans," *Baltimore Sun,* December 23, 1934, Box 47: Child Welfare, RG 47, National Archives.

88. "Security for Children," 4, 69. See also Folks, "Spearheads for Social Security," Box 23: Security for Children, RG 47, National Archives.

89. "Child Welfare in the Economic Security Program," 3, Box 47: Carbon Copies Written Materials, RG 47, National Archives.

90. "Security for Children," 68.

91. Abbott, "Recent Trends in Mothers' Aid," 193; "Memorandum by Miss Grace Abbott on Mothers' Pensions," July 18, 1934 Box 47: Child Welfare, RG 47, National Archives.

92. *Proceedings, National Conference on Economic Security,* November 14, 1934, 11, Box 4, RG 47, National Archives. Very few men attended the session.

93. "Radio Address, Miss Perkins, N. E. A. Program, Saturday, December 22, 1934," 47: Helen Greenblatt File, Business to C, RG 47, National Archives.

94. "Security for Children," 14; Katherine Lenroot, "Security for Children: Relationship of Special Measures for Children to a General Security Program," 4, Box 1, RG 47, National Archives.

95. Committee on Economic Security, "Summary of Major Recommendations," 13-14, Box 1, RG 47, National Archives.

96. Harvard Stikoff, *Fifty Years Later: The New Deal Reevaluated* (Philadelphia: Temple University Press, 1985), 90-91. Gwendolyn Mink also claimed that the expectation was that ADC would be phased out when social insurance finally prevented future dependent motherhood. However, only for middle-class women did this become a reality; poor women continued to rely on public assistance. Mink, 126, 134-135, 175. Due to the population explosion in the 1950s, the continued escalation of poverty in the United States, and the decline in the number of nuclear families, the number of families dependent on ADC (later AFDC) support increased enormously. See Josephine Brown, 303.

97. Josephine Brown, 306-308.

98.   Josephine Brown, 308-312; see Kriste Lindenmeyer, "*A Right To Childhood" : The U.S. Children's Bureau and Child Welfare, 1912-1946,* (Urbana: University of Illinois Press, 1997).

CHAPTER TEN

1.   Frances Perkins to Harry Hopkins, August 26, 1940. HHP, 94: Frances Perkins, FDRL.
2.   Harry Hopkins, Speech, May 15, 1937, 4. HHP, 9: Speeches 1937, FDRL.
3.   Harry Hopkins, Speech, May 15, 1937, 5. HHP, 9: Speeches 1937, FDRL.
4.   Harry Hopkins, "Address of Harry L. Hopkins, WPA Administrator," May 19, 1937, Box 9: Speeches 1937, HHP, FDRL.
5.   "Press Conference, August 8, 1935," 6, and "Press Conference October 31, 1935," 5, Box 29: Press Conferences 11/2/34-12/19/35, HHP, FDRL. Federal funding, however, failed to lift from ADC the ancient stigma of public outdoor relief, what we now call "welfare," and recipients, once considered outside of the workforce and now castigated for failing to work, are regarded with suspicion. As Joel Handler correctly observed, American welfare policy "stlll lies within the shadow of the sturdy beggar." Joel F. Handler, *The Poverty of Welfare Reform* (New Haven, Conn.: Yale University Press, 1995), 5.
6.   Harry Hopkins, Radio Address, "Works Relief Program," 6, Box 9: Speeches 1933-1936, HHP, FDRL.
7.   Harry Hopkins, "What Price Recovery?" 9-13. David K. Niles, editor of the *New Republic,* wrote Hopkins that the article might be "too much Marxist which might 'Tugwell' us later." This in reference to the liberal politics of Rexford Tugwell; Richard Wilson, "Harry Hopkins Field Marshall of the New Deal," 1, 14, undated, Hopkins I, 40:9, GUSC. Wilson wrote that with the establishment of the WPA, Hopkins began to speak of a permanent class of the unemployed "who might forever be in need of public assistance."
8.   Harry L. Hopkins, "What is the American Way?" July 16, 1938, 1, Hopkins IV, 1:52, GUSC.
9.   See Handler, chapter 2, "The Past is Prologue." A rare exception to this was New York State Solicitor General Henry Epstein who called the WPA a "strange interlude" and expressed his belief in intelligently administered relief. "Work projects should not overshadow the relief aspect, lest it give an illusion of permanence and 'security' which are not present. . . . Direct relief . . . is nothing to recoil from. It is a necessary social mechanism in a government of democratic principle." Henry Epstein to Franklin Roosevelt, November 26, 1935, Box 500: Epstein, Henry, PPF, FDRL.
10.   Harry Hopkins, "Address to Field Representatives of the WPA," 12, Box 9: Speeches 1933-1935, HHP, FDRL; "Address of Harry L. Hopkins, September 6, 1945," Hopkins IV, 1:43, GUSC.
11.   Martha Gellhorn Oral History, February 1980, 6-7, Eleanor Roosevelt Oral History Project, Box 2, FDRL. This division between Hopkins' two careers, one domestic and one international, is supported by Hopkins' daughter, Diana Hopkins Halsted, who said that when Hopkins got interested in the war, Eleanor Roosevelt thought that he had abandoned the needy. "Something happened between her and Harry that really tore her up and sent her packing off to New York." Diana Hopkins Halsted Oral History, 1979, 8, Eleanor Roosevelt Oral History Project, Box 2, FDRL.
12.   Marquis W. Childs, "The President's Best Friend," *The Saturday Evening Post,* 19 April 1941, 128.

13. Bill Costello, CBS Broadcast, July 3, 1945. Hopkins I, 46:10, GUSC; Walter Trohan, "White House Harry Hopkins—A Modern Rasputin," *Chicago Sunday Tribune,* August 9, 1943, Graphic Section, 1.

14. New York City public planner Robert Moses called Hopkins "as friendly and generous as an Indian rajah on a toot in Paris." Quoted in Searle F. Charles, "Harry L. Hopkins: New Deal Administrator, 1933-1938," Ph.D. Dissertation, University of Illinois, 1953.

15. Charles Beard, "Behind the New Deal," *Saturday Review* 23 (December 22, 1934), Box 57, FERA Records, RG 69, National Archives.

16. "Remarks of the Hon. Thomas C. Hennings, Jr., August 28, 1940. *Congressional Record,* August 30, 1940, 17258-17259.

17. "Text of address by Mr. Harry L. Hopkins, luncheon of the Catholic Charities, Hotel Commodore, New York City, May 4, 1935," 16, Box 9: Speeches 1933-1936, HHP, FDRL. By 1935 Hopkins had gotten smarter about his public; he crossed out the word "damn" in the written speech.

18. Secretary Harry L. Hopkins' Grinnell College Chapel Speech, Wed. Feb. 22, 1939, Box 12, HHP, FDRL.

19. Harry L. Hopkins, "Address, December 28, 1935," 12, 9: Speeches 1933-1935, HHP, FDRL.

.

Sources

The following archival collections were used in this book:

Manuscript Collection, Columbia University, New York, N.Y.:
Archives of Community Service Society (ACSS).
Christodora Settlement House Papers.

Columbia University Oral History Research Office, Social Security Project, Columbia
University, New York, N.Y. Reminisces of:
Arthur Altmeyer.
Paul Appleby.
Frank Bane.
Henry Bruere.
Homer Folks.
Jerome N. Frank.
Jane Hoey.
Florence Kerr.
Frances Perkins.

Franklin Delano Roosevelt Library (FDRL), Hyde Park, N.Y.:
Aubrey Williams Collection.
Eleanor Roosevelt Oral History Project.
Eleanor Roosevelt Papers.
Frances Perkins Papers.
Franklin Delano Roosevelt Papers.
Harry L. Hopkins Papers.
Harry L. Hopkins Personal Papers.
Henry Morganthau, Jr., Papers.
Mary Dewson Papers.
Office of the Governor of New York
President's Personal Files.
Robert E. Sherwood Papers.

Special Collections, Lauinger Library, Georgetown University (GUSC), Washington, D.C.:
Harry L. Hopkins Papers. Parts I, II, III, and IV.
Richard Tierney, S.J. Papers.
Senator Robert F. Wagner Papers.

Grinnell College Archives, Burling Library, Grinnell, Iowa. (Arranged by subject.):
Adah May Hopkins.
Edward Steiner.
George Herron.

Grinnell College.
Harry Lloyd Hopkins.
John Sholte Nollen.

Grinnell Historical Society, Grinnell, Iowa:
Grinnell Social Service League Collection.

National Archives, Washington, D.C.:
Children's Bureau RG 102.
Commission on Industrial Relations.
Social Security Administration RG 47.
WPA RG 69.

Manuscript Division, Library of Congress, Washington, D.C.:
John Adams Kingsbury Papers.

New York State Archives, Albany, N.Y.:
Transcripts of Hearings, 1913-1914, Commission on Relief for Widowed Mothers.

Lehman Social Work Library, Columbia University, New York, N.Y.:
Proceedings of the Conference of Charities, 1877.
Proceedings of the National Conference of Charities and Correction, 1888, 1898, 1904, 1914, and 1915.
Proceedings of the National Conference of Social Work, 1917.

Bibliography

Abbott, Grace. *The Child and the State*, Vol. 2, *The Dependent and Delinquent Child*. Chicago: University of Chicago Press, 1938.

Abbott, Grace. "Recent Trends in Mothers' Aid," *Social Service Review* 8 (June 1934): 191.

Abell, Aaron I. *The Urban Impact on American Protestantism*. Cambridge, Mass.: Harvard University Press, 1943.

Abramovitz, Mimi. *Regulating the Lives of Women: Social Welfare Policy from Colonial Times to the Present*. Boston: South End, 1988.

Adams, Henry. *Harry Hopkins*. New York: G. P. Putnam, 1977.

Addams, Jane. *Philanthropy and Social Progress*. New York: Crowell, 1893.

Addams, Jane. *Twenty Years at Hull-House*. New York: Macmillan, 1910.

Adler, Felix. Atheism: A Lecture. New York: Cooperative Printers Association, 1879.

Adler, Felix. *Life and Destiny*. New York: McClure, Philips and Co., 1903.

Almy, Frederic. "Public Pensions to Widows: Experiences and Observations Which Lead Me to Oppose Such a Law," in Edna O. Bullock, *Selected Articles in Mothers' Pensions*. Debaters' Handbook Series. White Plains, N.Y.: H.W. Wilson and Co,1950.

Atherton, John, ed. *Christian Social Ethics: A Reader*. Cleveland: Pilgrim Press, 1994.

Axinn, June, and Herman Levin. *Social Welfare: A History of America's Response to Need*. New York: Hill and Wang, 1975.

Badger, Anthony J. *The New Deal: The Depression Years, 1933-1939*. New York: Hill and Wang, 1989.

Bane, Mary Jo, and David T. Ellwood. *Welfare Realities: From Rhetoric to Reform*. Cambridge, Mass.: Harvard University Press, 1994.

Barrett, Mary Ellin. *Irving Berlin: A Daughter's Memoir*. New York: Simon and Schuster, 1994.

Bellush, John. "Old and New Left: Reappraisals of the New Deal and the Roosevelt Presidency." *Presidential Studies Quarterly* 9 (Summer 1979): 243-266.

Bentley, Joanne. *Hallie Flanagan: A Life in the American Theatre*. New York: Alfred A. Knopf, 1988.

Berkowitz, Edward, and Kim McQuaid. "Businessmen and Bureaucrats: The Evolution of the American Social Welfare System." *Journal of Economic History* 38 (March 1978): 120-142.

Berkowitz, Edward, and Kim McQuaid. *Creating the Welfare State: The Political Economy of 20th Century Reform*. Laurence, Kans.: University Press of Kansas, 1992.

Berlin, Ellin Mackay. *The Best of Families*. Garden City, N.J.: Doubleday, 1970.

Berlin, Ellin Mackay. *Silver Platter*. Garden City, N.J.: Doubleday, 1957.

Bernstein, Irving. *A Caring Society: The New Deal, the Worker, and the Great Depression*. Boston: Houghton Mifflin, 1985.

Bernstein, Michael A. *The Great Depression: Delayed Recovery and Economic Changes in America 1929-39*. New York: Cambridge University Press, 1987.

Betts, Lillian W. *The Leaven in a Great City*. New York: Dodd, Mead, 1902.

Blatch, Harriot Stanton, and Alma Lutz. *The Challenging Years*. New York: G. P. Putnam's Sons, 1940.

Blumberg, Barbara. *The New Deal and the Unemployed: The View from New York City*. Lewisburg, Penn.: Bucknell University Press, 1979.

Boase, Paul H., ed. *The Rhetoric of Christian Socialism*. New York: Random House, 1969.

Bolin, Winifred D. Wandersee. "The Economics of Middle-Income Family Life: Working Women During the Great Depression." *Journal of American History* 65 (June 1978): 60-74.

Boris, Eileen. *Home to Work: Motherhood and the Politics of Industrial Homework in the United States*. New York: Cambridge University Press, 1994.

Boyer, Paul. *Urban Masses and Moral Order in America, 1820-1920*. Cambridge, Mass.: Harvard University Press, 1978.

Brace, Charles Loring. *The Dangerous Classes of New York and Twenty Years Work Among Them*. Montclair, N.J.: P. Smith, 1967, reprint of the 3rd ed., 1880.

Brace, Charles Loring. *Hungary in 1851*. New York: Charles Scribner, 1852.

Brandt, Lillian. *The Growth and Development of the AICP and the COS (A Preliminary and Exploratory Review)*. New York: Community Service Society of New York, 1942.

Breckenridge, Sophinisba. *Public Welfare Administration in the United States: Select Documents*. Chicago: University of Chicago Press, 1927.

Bremer, William W. "Along the American Way: The New Deal's Work Relief Programs for the Unemployed." *Journal of American History* 62 (November 3, 1975): 636-652.

Bremer, William W. *Depression Winter: New York Social Workers and the New Deal*. Philadelphia: Temple University Press, 1984.

Bremner, Robert H. *From the Depths: The Discovery of Poverty in the United States*. New York: New York University Press, 1956.

Brinkley, Alan. *Voices of Protest: Huey Long, Father Coughlin and the Great Depression*. New York: Alfred A. Knopf, 1982.

Brogan, Dennis. *The Era of Franklin D. Roosevelt: A Chronicle of the New Deal*. New Haven, Conn.: Yale University Press, 1952.

Brown, Dorothy. *Setting a Course: American Women in the 1920s*. Boston: Twayne, 1987.

Brown, Dorothy, and Elizabeth McKeown. *The Poor Belong to Us: Catholic Charities and American Welfare*. Cambridge, Mass.: Harvard University Press, 1998.

Brown, Dorothy, and Elizabeth McKeown. "Saving New York's Children." *U.S. Catholic Historian* (Summer 1995): 77-95.

Brown, Josephine. *Public Relief, 1929-1939*. New York: Octagon Books, 1971. Originally published 1940.

Bruere, Robert W. "The Good Samaritan, Inc." *Harper's Monthly* 120 (May 1910): 833.

Bruno, Frank. *Trends in Social Work as Reflected in the Proceedings of the National Conference of Social Work: 1874-1956*. New York: Columbia University Press, 1948.

Bucks, Emery Stevens, et al., eds. *The History of American Methodism*. New York: Abingdon Press, 1964.

Bullock, Edna O. *Selected Articles in Mothers' Pensions*. Debaters' Handbook Series. White Plains, N.Y.: H. W. Wilson Co., 1950.

Burns, Eveline M. *Toward Social Security*. New York: Whittlesey House, 1936.

Burns, James McGregor. *Roosevelt: The Lion and the Fox*. New York: Harcourt, Brace, 1956.

Campbell, Helen. "Certain Convictions as to Poverty." *Arena* 1 (1890): 101-113.

Campbell, Rita Ricardo. *Social Security: Promise and Reality*. Stanford, Calif.: Hoover Institution Press, 1977.

Carson, Mina. *Settlement Folk: Social Thought and the American Settlement Movement 1885-1930*. Chicago: University of Chicago Press, 1990.

Carter, John Franklin. *The New Dealers*. New York: Simon and Schuster, 1934.

Carter, Paul Allen. *The Decline and Revival of the Social Gospel: Social and Political Liberalism in American Protestant Churches, 1920-1940*. Ithaca, N.Y.: Cornell University Press, 1954.

Chambers, Clarke. *Seedtime of Reform: American Social Service and Social Action, 1918-1933*. Minneapolis: University of Minnesota Press, 1967.

Charles, Searle F. "Harry L. Hopkins: New Deal Administrator, 1933-1938." Ph.D. diss., University of Illinois, 1953.

Charles, Searle F. *Minister of Relief: Harry Hopkins and the Depression*. Syracuse, N.Y.: Syracuse University Press, 1963.

Chenery, William. "Unemployment at Washington." *Survey* 37 (1921): 47.

Childs, Marquis W. "The President's Best Friend." *The Saturday Evening Post* 19 (April 1941): 128.

Clark, John Maurice. *Economics of Planning Public Works*. Reprints of Economic Classics. New York: Augustus M. Kelley, 1965. Originally published 1935.

Classon, Charles C. "The Unemployed in American Cities." *Quarterly Journal of Economics* 8 (January 1894): 168-217.

Cloward, Richard A., and Frances Fox Piven. *The Politics of Turmoil: Essays on Poverty, Race and the Urban Crisis*. New York: Pantheon Books, 1974.

Cohen, Miriam and Michael Hanagan, "The Politics of Gender and the Making of the Welfare State, 1900-1940." *Journal of Social History* (Spring 1991): 469-484.

Colcord, Joanna. *Broken Homes: A Study of Family Desertion and Its Social Treatment*. New York: Russell Sage Foundation, 1919.

Colcord, Joanna. *Community Planning in Unemployment Emergencies*. New York: Russell Sage Foundation, 1930.

Coman, Katharine. "Social Insurance, Pensions, and Poor Relief." *Survey* 32 (May 9, 1914): 187-188.

Commission on Industrial Relations. *Final Report*. Doc. no. 415, 64th Congress. Washington, D.C.: GPO, 1916.

Conkin, Paul K. *The New Deal*. London: Routledge and Kegan Paul, 1967.

Conway, Jill K. "Jane Addams: An American Heroine." *Daedalus* 93 (1964): 761-780.

Crocker, Ruth Hutchinson. *Social Work and Social Order: The Settlement Movement in Two Industrial Cities, 1889-1930*. Urbana: University of Illinois Press, 1992.

Crunden, Robert M. "George D. Herron in the 1890s: A New Framework of Reference for the Study of the Progressive Era." *Annals of Iowa* 42 (fall 1973): 83-113.

Cummings, A.J. "Meet America's Other Harold Lloyd." *Daily News Chronicle*, July 8, 1934, Hopkins III, 1:22, GUSC.

Curtis, Susan. *A Consuming Faith: The Social Gospel and Modern American Culture*. New Studies in American Intellectual and Cultural History. Baltimore: Johns Hopkins University Press, 1991.

Daniel, Anne J. "The Wreck of the Home." *Charities* 14 (April 1, 1905): 624-628.

Davis, Allen F. "Social Workers and the Progressive Party." *The American Historical Review* 69 (April 1964): 671-688.

Davis, Allen F. *Spearheads for Reform: The Social Settlements and the Progressive Movement*. New York: Oxford University Press, 1967.

Davis, Kenneth S. *FDR: The New Deal Years 1933-1937, A History*. New York: Random House, 1979.

Davis, Kenneth S. *FDR: The New York Years, 1928-1933*. New York: Random House, 1994.

Dawley, Alan. *Struggles for Justice: Responsibility and the Liberal State*. Cambridge, Mass.: Harvard University Press, 1991.

Degler, Carl. *At Odds: Women and the Family in America from the Revolution to the Present.* New York: Oxford University Press, 1980.

Deminoff, William. "From Grinnell to National Power." *Des Moines Register,* November 2, 1975, section C: 1.

Demhoff, G. William. *The Power Elite and the State: How Policy Is Made in America.* New York: Aldine de Gruyter, 1990.

Derber, Milton, and Edwin Young, eds. *Labor and the New Deal.* Madison: University of Wisconsin Press, 1961.

Devine, Edward T. *Misery and Its Causes.* New York: Macmillan, 1920.

Devine, Edward T. "Pensions for Mothers," in Edna O. Bullock, *Selected Articles in Mothers' Pensions.* Debaters' Handbook Series. White Plains, N.Y.: H.W. Wilson and Co; 1950.

Devine, Edward T. *The Principles of Relief.* New York: Macmillan, 1904.

Devine, Edward T. "The Shiftless and Floating Population." *Annals of the Academy of Political and Social Science* (September 1897): 149-164.

Devine, Edward T. "Widows' Needs." *Survey* 32 (April 4, 1914): 27.

Dieterich, H. R. "Radical on Campus: Professor Herron at Iowa College." *Annals of Iowa* 37, no. 6 (1964): 401-415.

Dorn, Jacob Henry. *Washington Gladden: Prophet of the Social Gospel.* Columbus: Ohio State University Press, 1967.

Douglas, Ann. *The Feminization of American Culture.* New York: Doubleday, 1977.

Dubofsky, Melvyn. "Success and Failure of Socialism in New York City, 1900-1918: A Case Study." *Labor History* 9 (Fall 1968): 361-375.

Duffus, Robert L. *Lillian Wald: Neighbor and Crusader.* New York: Macmillan, 1938.

Dulles, Rhea Foster. *The American Red Cross: A History.* New York: Harper & Brothers, 1950.

Ehrenreich, Barbara, and Frances Fox Piven. "The Feminization of Poverty: When the Family Wage System Breaks Down." *Dissent* 31 (Spring 1984): 162-170.

Ehrenreich, John H. *The Altruistic Imagination: A History of Social Work and Social Policy in the United States.* Ithaca, New York: Cornell University Press, 1985.

Einaudi, Mario. *The Roosevelt Revolution.* New York: Harcourt, Brace, 1959.

Eli, R. George. *Social Holiness: John Wesley's Thinking on Christian Community and Its Relationship to the Social Order.* New York: Peter Lang, 1993.

Ely, Richard T. "Pauperism in the United States." *North American Review* 152 (April 1891): 395-409.

Ewen, Elizabeth. *Immigrant Women in the Land of Dollars: Life and Culture on the Lower East Side, 1890-1925.* New York: Monthly Review Press, 1985.

Ezekial, Mordecai. *Jobs for All Through Industrial Expansion.* New York: Alfred A. Knopf, 1939.

Feder, Hannah Leah. *Unemployment Relief in Periods of Depression: A Study of Measures Adopted in Certain American Cities, 1857 through 1922.* New York: Russell Sage Foundation, 1936.

Fitzpatrick, Ellen. *Endless Crusade: Women Social Scientists and Progressive Reform.* New York: Oxford University Press, 1990.

Fraser, Steve, and Gary Gerstel. *The Rise and Fall of the New Deal Order, 1930-1980.* Princeton, N.J.: Princeton University Press, 1989.

Freidel, Frank. *Franklin D. Roosevelt: Launching the New Deal.* Boston: Little, Brown, 1973.

Freidel, Frank. *Franklin D. Roosevelt: Rendezvous with Destiny.* Boston: Little, Brown, 1990.

Frisch, Michael. "Political Culture in the Progressive Period." *Political Science Quarterly* 97 (summer 1982): 295.

Fusfield, Daniel. *The Economic Thought of Franklin D. Roosevelt and the Origins of the New Deal.* New York: Columbia University Press, 1956.

Galbraith, John Kenneth. *The Economic Effects of the Federal Public Works Expenditures 1933-1938.* New York: Da Capo Press, 1975. Originally published 1940.

Garfinkel, Irwin, and Sara S. McLanahan. *Single Mothers and Their Children: A New American Dilemma.* Washington, D.C.: The Urban Institute, 1986.

Gerstel, Naomi, and Harriet E. Gross. *Families and Work: Towards a Reconceptualization.* Philadelphia: Temple University Press, 1987.

Gettleman, Marvin E. "Philanthropy and Social Control in Late-Nineteenth-Century America: Some Hypotheses and Data on the Rise of Social Work." *Societas* 5 (winter 1975): 49-59.

Gibbons, Cardinal. "Wealth and Its Obligations." *North American Review* 152 (April 1891): 385-394.

Gilder, George. *Wealth and Poverty.* New York: Basic Books, 1981.

Gill, Corrington. *Wasted Manpower: The Challenge of Unemployment.* New York: W. W. Norton, 1939.

Gilman, Charlotte Perkins. "Paid Motherhood." *The Independent* 62 (January 10, 1907): 321-324.

Gilman, Charlotte Perkins. "Pensions for Mothers and Widows." *Forerunner* 5 (1914): 7-8.

Gladden, Washington. *Reflections.* New York: Houghton Mifflin, 1909.

Goldfield, Michael. "Worker Insurgency, Radical Organization, and New Deal Labor Legislation." *American Political Science Review* 83, no. 4 (December 1989): 1257-1282.

Goldman, Eric. *Rendezvous with Destiny: A History of Modern American Reform.* New York: Random House, 1953.

Goodwin, Joanne. "An American Experiment in Paid Motherhood: The Implementation of Mothers' Pensions in Early Twentieth Century Chicago." *Gender and History* 4, no. 3 (autumn 1992): 323-342.

Goodwyn, Lawrence. *The Populist Moment: A Short History of the Agrarian Revolt in America.* New York: Oxford University Press, 1978.

Gordon, Linda. "Black and White Visions of Welfare: Women's Welfare Activism, 1890-1945." *Journal of American History* 78 (September 1991): 559-590.

Gordon, Linda. *Heroes of Their Own Lives: The Politics and History of Family Violence, Boston 1880-1960.* New York: Viking, 1988.

Gordon, Linda. *Pitied But Not Entitled: Single Mothers and the History of Welfare 1890-1935.* New York: Macmillan, 1994.

Gordon, Linda. "Social Insurance and Public Assistance: The Influence of Gender on Welfare." *American Historical Review* (February 1992): 19-54.

Gordon, Linda, ed. *Women, the State, and Welfare.* Madison: University of Wisconsin Press, 1990.

Gorrell, Donald K. *The Age of Social Responsibility: The Social Gospel in the Progressive Era 1900-1920.* Macon, Ga.: Mercer University Press, 1988.

Gould, Lewis L. *The Progressive Era.* Syracuse, New York: Syracuse University Press, 1974.

Graham, Otis. *An Encore for Reform: The Old Progressives and the New Deal.* New York: Oxford University Press, 1967.

Grantham, Dewey W., Jr. "The Progressive Era and the Reform Tradition." *MidAmerica* 46 (1964): 227-251.

Grinnell College. *Blue Book, Sesquicentennial Issue.* Grinnell, Iowa: Grinnell College, 1996.

Gronman, Carol, and Mary Beth Norton. *"To Toil the Livelong Day:" America's Women at Work, 1780-1980.* Ithaca, New York: Cornell University Press, 1987.

Gutman, Herbert G. "The Failure of the Movement by the Unemployed for Public Works in 1873." *Political Science Quarterly* 70 (June 1965): 254-272.

Hackett, Francis. "The Sacred Cow." *The New Republic* (June 3, 1916): 116-117.

Handler, Joel F., and Yeheskel Hasenfeld. *The Moral Construction of Poverty: Welfare Reform in America*. Newberry Park, Calif.: Sage, 1991.

Handler, Joel F. *The Poverty of Welfare Reform*. New Haven, Conn.: Yale University Press, 1995.

Handy, Robert T., ed. *The Social Gospel in America*. New York: Oxford University Press, 1966.

Hard, William. "The Moral Necessity of 'State Funds to Children.'" *Survey* 29 (March 1, 1913): 769-773.

Harrington, Michael. *The Other America: The Discovery of Poverty in the United States*. New York: Macmillan, 1962.

Hays, Samuel P. *The Response to Industrialism: 1885-1914*. Chicago: University of Chicago Press, 1957.

Herron, George. *Between Caesar and Jesus*. New York: T. Y. Crowell and Co., 1899.

Hicks, John. *The Populist Revolt: A History of the Farmers' Alliance and the People's Party*. Ann Arbor: University of Michigan Press, 1931.

Hilgard, Ernest R. "From the Social Gospel to the Psychology of Social Issues: A Reminiscence." *Journal of Social Issues* 42 (spring 1986): 107-110.

Hofstadter, Richard. *The Age of Reform: From Bryan to FDR*. New York: Vintage Books, 1955.

Hofstadter, Richard. *The Progressive Movement: 1900-1915*. Edgewood Cliffs, N.J.: Prentice-Hall, 1963.

Hofstadter, Richard. *Social Darwinism in American Thought 1860-1915*. Boston: Beacon Press, 1959.

Holden, Arthur C. *The Settlement Idea: A Vision of Social Justice*. New York: Arno Press, 1922.

Hollander, John. *Abolition of Poverty*. New York: Houghton Mifflin, 1914.

Hopkins, C. Howard. *The Rise of the Social Gospel in American Protestantism, 1865-1915*. New Haven, Conn.: Yale University Press, 1940.

Hopkins, Harry L. "Capital Punishment for Boys." *Survey Graphic* (April 25, 1914).

Hopkins, Harry L. "Consolidating Private Health Work Under One Banner." *The Nation's Health* 9 (January, 1927): 2, Reprint, Hopkins File, American Lung Association Archives, New York City.

Hopkins, Harry L. "Des Moines Speech." *Vital Speeches of the Day* 1, no. 11 (March 15, 1939): 335.

Hopkins, Harry L. "F. E. R. A." *Congressional Digest* 14 (January 1935): 16.

Hopkins, Harry L. . "Fighting Destitution." *Jeffersonian* (August 1933): 6-7.

Hopkins, Harry L. "Giving 16 Million People a New Chance." *Today* (June 30, 1934): 6-7.

Hopkins, Harry L. *Inventory: WPA, An Appraisal of the Results of the Works Progress Administration*. Washington, D.C.: Works Progress Administration, 1938.

Hopkins, Harry L. "Social Planning for the Future." *Social Service Review* 59 (September 1985): 506-517. Reprint.

Hopkins, Harry. *Spending to Save: The Complete Story of Relief*. New York: W. W. Norton, 1936.

Hopkins, Harry L. "The War on Distress." *Today* (December 16, 1933): 8-9, 23.

Howard, Donald S. *The WPA and Relief Policy*. New York: Da Capo Press, 1943.

Hudson, Winthrop Still, ed. *Walter Rauschenbusch: Selected Writings*. Sources of American Spirituality. New York: Paulist Press, 1984.

Huggins, Nathan. *Protestants Against Poverty: Boston Charities 1870-1900*. Westport, Conn.: Greenwood, 1971.

Hughes, Charles Evans, and C. F. Murphy. "The Metamorphosis of Progressivism." *New York History* 46 (January 1965): 25-40.

Humphreys, Jane. "Women: Scapegoats and Safety Valves in the Great Depression." *The Review of Radical Political Economics* 8 (spring 1976): 107.

Hunter, Robert. *Poverty*. New York: Macmillan, 1904.

Hurd, Charles. *A Compact History of the American Red Cross*. New York: Hawthorne Books, Inc., 1959.

Ickes, Harold L. "My Twelve Years with F.D.R." *Saturday Evening Post* (June 5, 1948): 15-18, 78-84.

Ickes, Harold L. *The Secret Diary of Harold L. Ickes*. Vol. 1, *The First Thousand Days, 1933-1936*. Vol. 2, *The Inside Struggle, 1936-1939*. Vol. 3, *The Lowering Clouds, 1939-1941*. New York: Simon and Schuster, 1953-1954.

Jacklin, Thomas M. "The Civic Awakening: Social Christianity and the Usable Past." *MidAmerica* 64, no. 2 (1982): 3-18

Jeffries, John W. "The "New" New Deal: FDR and American Liberalism, 1937-1945." *Political Science Quarterly* 105 (3 1990): 397-418.

Johnson, Hugh S. *The Blue Eagle, From Egg to Earth*. Garden City, N.Y.: Doubleday, Doran and Company, 1935.

Karl, Barry. *The Uneasy State: The U. S. From 1915-1945*. Chicago: University of Chicago Press, 1983.

Katz, Michael. *In the Shadow of the Poorhouse: A Social History of Welfare in America*. New York: Basic Books, 1986.

Katz, Michael. *Poverty and Policy in American History*. New York: Academic Press, 1983.

Katz, Michael. *The Undeserving Poor*. New York: Pantheon, 1989.

Kaufman, Stuart, and Peter J. Albert. *The Samuel Gompers Papers,* Vol. 3. *Unrest and Depression 1891-94*. Chicago: University of Illinois Press, 1989.

Kelley, Florence. "I Go to Work." *Survey* 58 (June 1, 1927): 271-277.

Kennedy, Albert J., ed. *Settlement Goals for the Next Third of a Century*. Boston: National Federation of Settlements, 1926.

Kennedy, David M. "Overview: The Progressive Era." *Historian* 37 (1975): 453-468.

Kerber, Linda. "Separate Spheres, Female Worlds, Women's Place: The Rhetoric of Women's History." *Journal of American History* 75 (June 1988): 9-39.

Kerber, Linda. *Women's America: Refocusing the Past*. New York: Oxford University Press, 1991.

Kerber, Linda, Alice Kessler-Harris, and Kathryn Kish Sklar, eds. *U.S. History as Women's History: New Feminist Essays*. Chapel Hill: University of North Carolina Press, 1995.

Kerber, Linda, et al., eds. *Transforming U. S. History: New Feminist Essays*. Chapel Hill: University of North Carolina Press, 1995.

Keserich, Charles. "The Political Odyssey of George D. Herron." *San Jose Studies* 3, no. 1 (1 1977): 79-94.

Kessler-Harris, Alice. *Out to Work: A History of Wage-Earning Women in the United States*. New York: Oxford University Press, 1982.

Kessler-Harris, Alice. *Women Have Always Worked*. New York: Feminist Press, 1981.

Kidd, Stuart. "Redefining the New Deal: Some Thoughts on the Political and Cultural Perspectives of Revisionism." *Journal of American Studies* 22 (1988): 389-415.

Kirkendall, Richard S. "The New Deal as Watershed: The Recent Literature." *Journal of American History* 54 (March 1968): 839-852.

Kirschner, Don. "The Ambiguous Legacy: Social Justice in the Progressive Era." *Historical Reflections* 2 (Summer 1975): 69-88.

Kirschner, Don. *The Paradox of Professionalism: Reform and Public Service in Urban America*. New York: Greenwood Press, 1986.

Kiser, Clyde V. *The Milbank Memorial Fund: Its Leaders and Its Work 1905-1974*. New York: Milbank Memorial Fund, 1975.

Klein, Philip. *The Burden of Unemployment: A Study of Unemployment Relief Measures in Fifteen American Cities, 1921-22*. New York: Russell Sage Foundation, 1923.

Koven, Seth, and Sonya Michel. "Gender and the Origins of the Welfare State." *Radical History Review* 43 (Winter 1989): 112-120.

Koven, Seth, and Sonya Michel. *Mothers of a New World: Maternalist Politics and the Origins of the Welfare State*. New York: Routledge, 1993.

Kraus, Harry P. *The Settlement House Movement in New York City 1886-1914*. New York: Arno Press, 1980.

Kunzel, Regina G. "The Professionalization of Benevolence: Evangelicals and Social Workers in the Florence Crittendon Homes, 1915-1945." *Journal of Social History* 22 (Fall 1988): 21-43.

Kurzman, Paul A. *Harry Hopkins and the New Deal*. Fairlawn, N.J., New Jersey: R. E. Burdick, 1974.

Ladd-Taylor, Molly. *Mother-Work: Women, Child Welfare, and the State, 1890-1930*. Urbana: University of Illinois Press, 1994.

Lash, Joseph. *Dealers and Dreamers: A New Look at the New Deal*. New York: Doubleday, 1988.

Leff, Mark. "A Consensus for Reform: The Mothers' Pension Movement in the Progressive Era." *Social Service Review* 47 (September 1973): 397-417.

Leff, Mark. "Taxing the 'Forgotten Man': The Politics of Social Security Finance in the New Deal." *Journal of American History* 70 (1983): 359-381.

Leiby, James. *A History of Social Welfare and Social Work in the United States*. New York: Columbia University Press, 1978.

Lerner, Gerda. *The Majority Finds its Past: Placing Women in History*. New York: Oxford University Press, 1979.

Lester, Richard A. "Emergency Employment in Theory and Practice." *Journal of Radical Economy* 42 (August 1934): 466-491.

Leuchtenburg, William E. *Franklin D. Roosevelt and the New Deal, 1932-1940*. New York: Harper & Row, 1963.

Levine, Daniel. *Jane Addams and the Liberal Tradition*. Madison: University of Wisconsin Press, 1971.

Levine, Daniel. *Poverty and Society: The Growth of the American Welfare State in International Comparison*. New Brunswick, N.J.: Rutgers University Press, 1988.

Lewinson, Edwin R. *John Purroy Mitchel: The Boy Mayor of New York*. New York: Astra Books, 1965.

Lindenmeyer, Kriste. *"A Right to Childhood": The U.S. Children's Bureau and Child Welfare, 1912-1946* (Urbana: University of Illinois Press, 1997).

Lindsay, Samuel McCune. "Next Steps in Social Insurance in the United States." *American Labor Legislation Review* 9 (1919): 111.

Link, Arthur. *Woodrow Wilson and the Progressive Era 1910-1917*. New York: Harper & Row, 1954.

Link, Arthur, and Richard L. McCormick. *Progressivism*. New York: Harper & Row, 1983.

Lloyd, Gary A. *Charities, Settlements and Social Work: An Inquiry into Philosophy and Method 1890-1915*. New Orleans: School of Social Work, Tulane University, 1971.

Locke, Benita. "Mothers' Pensions: The Latest Capitalist Trap." *The Woman Rebel* 1 (March 1914): 4-5.

Loeb, Sophie Irene. "Johnny Doe, His Mother and the State." *Harper's Weekly* 58 (January 13, 1914): 24.

Lotta, Maurice. "The Battleground for the Social Gospel in American Protestantism." *Church History* 5 (September 1936): 256-270.

Lubove, Roy. *The Professional Altruist: The Emergence of Social Work as a Career, 1880-1930*. Cambridge, Mass.: Harvard University Press, 1965.

Lubove, Roy. *The Progressive and the Slums: Tenement Reform in New York City, 1890-1917*. Pittsburgh: University of Pittsburgh Press, 1962.

Lubove, Roy. *The Struggle for Social Security*. Cambridge, Mass.: Harvard University Press, 1968.

Lubove, Roy. "The Welfare Industry: Social Work and the Life of the Poor." *Nation* (May 23, 1966): 609.

Lubove, Roy, ed. *Poverty and Social Welfare in the United States*. New York: Holt, Rinehart and Winston, 1972.

Luccock, Halford E. *Endless Line of Splendor*. Chicago: Advance for Christ and His Church, 1950.

Luker, Ralph. *The Social Gospel in Black and White: American Racial Reform*. Studies in Religion. Chapel Hill: University of North Carolina Press, 1991.

Lundberg, Emma O. "Aid to Mothers with Dependent Children." *American Academy of Political and Social Science Annals* 98 (November 1921): 97-98.

Lundberg, Emma O. "Progress of Mothers' Aid Administration." *Social Service Review* 2 (September 1928a): 435-458.

Lundberg, Emma O., and Katharine F. Lenroot. *Illegitimacy as a Child-Welfare Problem*. Washington, D.C.: U.S. Children's Bureau Publication No. 66, 1920.

Mann, Arthur, ed. *The Progressive Era: Liberal Renaissance or Liberal Failure?* New York: Holt, Rinehart, and Winston, 1963.

Mann, Arthur, ed. *The Progressive Era: Major Issues of Interpretation*. Hinsdale, Ill.: Dryden Press, 1975.

Matthews, William H. *Adventures in Giving*. New York: Dodd, Mead, & Company, 1939.

Matthews, William H. "Breaking the Poverty Circle." *Survey* 52 (April 15, 1924): 96-98.

Matthews, William H. *When Fathers Drop Out*. New York: New York Association for Improving the Conditions of the Poor, 1924.

Matthews, William H. "Widows' Families: Pensioned and Otherwise." *Survey* 32 (June 6, 1914): 270-275.

May, Henry F. *Protestant Churches and Industrial America*. New York: Harper, 1949.

May, Martha. "The 'Problem of Duty': The Regulation of Male Breadwinning and Desertion in the Progressive Era." *Social Service Review* 62, no. 1 (March 1988): 40-60.

McBride, Paul. *Culture Clash: Immigrants and Reformers 1880-1920*. San Francisco: R and E Research Associates, 1975.

McCarthy, Michael P. "Urban Optimism and Reform Thought in the Progressive Era." *The Historian* 51 (February 1989): 239-262.

McClymer, John. *War and Welfare: Social Engineering in America 1890-1925*. Westport, Conn.: Greenwood Press, 1980.

McElvaine, Robert S. *The Great Depression: America 1929-1941*. New York: N.Y. Times Books, 1984.

McJimsey, George. *Harry Hopkins: Ally of the Poor, Defender of Democracy*. Cambridge, Mass.: Harvard University Press, 1987.

McKinley, Charles, and Robert W. Frase. *Launching Social Security: A Capture and Record Account*. Madison: University of Wisconsin Press, 1970.

McMurray, Donald L. *Coxey's Army: A Study of the Industrial Army Movement of 1894*. Seattle: University of Washington, 1968. Originally published 1929.

Meyer, Donald B. *The Protestant Search for Political Realism, 1919-1941*. Berkeley: University of California Press, 1960.

Michel, Sonya. "Limits of Maternalism," in Seth Koven and Sonya Michel. *Mothers of a New World: Maternalist Politics and the Origins of the Welfare State*. New York: Routledge, 1993.

Michel, Sonya. "Womanly Duties: Maternalist Policies and the Origins of the Welfare State in France, Germany, Great Britain, and the United States: 1880-1920." *American Historical Review* 95 (October 1990): 1076-1108.

Milkman, Ruth. "Women's Work and Economic Crises: Some Lessons of the Great Depression." *Review of Radical Political Economy* 8 (spring, 1976): 75-77.

Milkman, Ruth, ed. *Women, Work, and Protest: A Century of Women's Labor History*. New York: Routledge, 1985.

Miller, Dorothy. *Women and Social Welfare: A Feminist Analysis*. New York: Praeger, 1990.

Milton, John. *South Dakota: A Bicentennial History*. New York: W. W. Norton, 1977.

Mink, Gwendolyn. *The Wages of Motherhood: Maternalist Social Policy and Women's Inequality in the Welfare State, 1917-1942*. Ithaca: Cornell University Press, 1995.

Miringoff, Marc L., and Dandra Opdycke. *American Social Welfare Policy: Reassessment and Reform*. Englewood Cliffs, N. J.: Prentice-Hall, 1986.

Moynihan, Daniel Patrick, ed. *On Understanding Poverty: Perspectives From the Social Sciences*. New York: Basic Books, 1968.

Muller, Dorothea R. "The Social Philosophy of Josiah Strong: Social Christianity and American Progressivism." *Church History* 28 (1959): 183-201.

Muncy, Robin. *Creating a Female Dominion in American Reform: 1890-1935*. New York: Oxford University Press, 1991.

Neibuhr, H. Richard. *The Kingdom of God in America*. New York: Harper & Row Torchbook, 1937.

Nelson, Barbara. "The Origins of the Two-Channel Welfare State: Workmen's Compensation and Mothers' Aid," in Linda Gordon. *Women, the State, and Welfare*. Madison: University of Wisconsin Press, 1990.

Nelson, Daniel. *Unemployment Insurance: The American Experience*. Madison: University of Wisconsin Press, 1969.

Nollen, John Shalte. *Grinnell College*. Iowa City: State Historical Society of Iowa, 1953

Nugent, Walter K. *The Tolerant Populists: Kansas Populism and Nativism*. Chicago: University of Chicago Press, 1963.

O'Neill, William L. *The Progressive Years: America Comes of Age*. New York: Harper Row, 1975.

Orloff, Anna Shola. *The Politics of Pensions; A Comparative Analysis of Britain, Canada and the United States*. Madison: University of Wisconsin Press, 1993.

Pacey, Lorene, ed. *Readings in the Development of Settlement Work*. New York: Association Press, 1950.

Painter, Nell Irvin. *Standing at Armageddon: The United States, 1877-1919*. New York: W. W. Norton, 1987.

Patterson, James T. *America's Struggle Against Poverty*. Cambridge, Mass.: Harvard University Press, 1986.

Patterson, James T. *The New Deal and the States: Federalism in Transition*. Princeton, N.J.: Princeton University Press, 1969.

Pearce, Diane. "The Feminization of Poverty: Women, Work, and Welfare." *Urban and Social Change Review* (1978): 28-35.

Peattie, Lisa, and Martin Rein. *Women's Claims: A Study in Political Economy*. New York: Oxford University Press, 1983.

Pells, Richard H. *Radical Visions and American Dreams: Culture and Social thought in the Depression Years*. New York: Harper Torchbooks, 1974. Originally published 1973.

Perkins, Frances. *The Roosevelt I Knew*. New York: Viking Press, 1946.

Pinchot, Amos. *History of the Progressive Party*. New York: New York University Press, 1959.

Pinder, Dorothy. *In Old Grinnell*. Grinnell, Iowa: The Herald Register Publishing Company, 1995.

Piven, Frances Fox, and Richard Cloward. *Poor People's Movements*. New York: Random House, 1977.

Polacheck, Hilda Scott. *I Came a Stranger: The Story of a Hull House Girl*. Chicago: University of Chicago Press, 1991.

Polakow, Valerie. *Lives on the Edge: Single Mothers and Their Children in the Other America*. Chicago: University of Chicago Press, 1993.

Pollack, Norman. *The Just Polity: Populism, Law, and Human Welfare*. Chicago: University of Chicago Press, 1987.

Pollack, Norman. *The Populist Response to Industrial America*. Cambridge, Mass.: Harvard University Press, 1962.

Pollack, Norman, ed. *The Populist Mind*. New York: The Bobbs-Merrill Company, Inc., 1967.

Proceedings of the Conference on the Care of Dependent Children, 1909. Washington, D.C.: GPO, 1909.

Pumphrey, Muriel W., and Ralph E. Pumphrey. "The Widows' Pension Movement 1900-1930: Preventive Child-Saving or Social Control?" In Walter I. Trattner, ed., *Social Welfare of Social Control? Some Historical Reflections on "Regulating the Poor."* Knoxville: University of Tennessee Press, 1983.

Pumphrey, Ralph E., and Muriel Pumphrey, eds. *The Heritage of American Social Work: Readings in Its Philosophical and Institutional Development*. New York: Columbia University Press, 1961.

Quadagno, Jill. "Race, Class, and Gender in the U. S. Welfare State." *American Sociological Review* 55, no. 1 (1990): 11-28.

Rader, Frank. "Harry L. Hopkins: The Ambitious Crusader: An Historical Analysis of the Major Influences on His Career." *Annals of Iowa* 44 (2 1977): 83-102.

Rauch, Basil. *History of the New Deal*. New York: Creative Age Press, 1944.

Rauschenbusch, Walter. *Christianity and the Social Crisis*. New York: Macmillan, 1907.

Rauschenbusch, Walter. *A Theology for the Social Gospel*. New York: Macmillan, 1917.

Resek, Carl. *The Progressives*. New York: Bobbs-Merrill Company, 1967.

Rezneck, Samuel. "Distress, Relief, and Discontent in the United States During the Depression of 1873-1878." *Journal of Political Economy* (August 1950): 499-502.

Rezneck, Samuel. "Unemployment, Unrest, and Relief in the United States During the Depression of 1893-1897." *Journal of Political Economy* (August 1953): 330-337.

Richmond, Mary A. "Motherhood and Pensions." *Survey* 29 (March 1, 1913), in Edna O. Bullock, *Selected Articles in Mothers' Pensions*. Debaters Handbook Series. White Plains, N.Y.: H. W. Wilson and Co., 1950, 58-72.

Richmond, Mary E. *Friendly Visiting Among the Poor*. New York: Macmillan, 1899.

Richmond, Mary E. *Social Diagnosis*. New York: Russell Sage Foundation, 1917.

Riis, Jacob. *How the Other Half Lives*. New York: Charles Scribner's Sons, 1890.

Riis, Jacob. "Special Needs of the Poor in New York City." *Forum* 14 (1892): 492-502.

Ritchie, Donald A. "The Gary Committee: Businessmen, Progressives, and Unemployment in New York, 1914-1915." *The New York Historical Quarterly* 57 (October 1973): 330-335.

Robinson, Edgar E. *The Roosevelt Leadership, 1933-1945*. Philadelphia: J. B. Lippincott, 1955.

Rochefort, David A. *American Social Welfare Policy: Dynamics of Formulation and Change*. Boulder, Colo.: Westview Press, 1986.

Rochefort, David A. "Progressives and Social Control Perspectives on Social Welfare." *Social Service Review* 55 (December 1951): 568-592.

Rogers, Harrell R. *Poor Women, Poor Families: The Economic Plight of America's Female-Headed Households.* Armonk, New York: M. E. Sharpe, 1986.

Romasco, Albert. *The Politics of Recovery: Roosevelt's New Deal.* New York: Oxford University Press, 1983.

Romasco, Albert. *The Poverty of Abundance.* New York: Oxford University Press, 1965.

Roosevelt, Franklin. *Looking Forward.* New York: John Day and Co., 1933.

Rose, Nance E. *Put to Work: Relief Programs in the Great Depression.* New York: Monthly Review Press, 1994.

Rose, Nancy E. "Work Relief in the 1930s and the Origins of the Social Security Act." *Social Service Review* 63 (1989): 63-91.

Rosenberg, Arnold S. "John Adams Kingsbury and the Struggle for social Justice in New York, 1906-1918" (Ph.D. diss., New York University, 1968.

Rosenberg, Rosalind. *Beyond Separate Spheres: Intellectual Roots of Modern Feminism.* New Haven, Conn.: Yale University Press, 1982.

Rosenberg, Rosalind. *Divided Lives: American Women in the Twentieth Century.* New York: Hill and Wang, 1972.

Rosenman, Samuel L., ed. The Public Papers and Addresses of Franklin D. Roosevelt. Vol. 1, *The Genesis of the New Deal, 1928-1932.* Vol. 2, *The Year of Crisis, 1933.* Vol 3, *The Advance of Recovery and Reform.* Vol. 4, *The Court Disapproves.* New York, Random House, 1938.

Rothenberg, Paula S. *Race, Class, and Gender in the United States.* New York: St. Martin's Press, 1992.

Rothman, Sheila M. *Woman's Proper Place: A History of the Changing Ideals and Practices, 1870 to the Present.* New York: Basic Books, 1978.

Rousmaniere, John P. "Cultural Hybrid in the Slums: the College Woman and the Settlement House 1889-1894." *American Quarterly* 22 (Spring 1970): 45-66.

Rubinow, Isaac M. *Social Insurance with Special Reference to American Conditions.* New York: Henry Holt, 1913.

Saludos, Theodore, and John D. Hicks. *Twentieth Century Populism: Agricultural Discontent in the Middle West, 1900-1939.* Lincoln: University of Nebraska Press, 1951.

Sambor, Harold A. "Theodore Dreiser, *The Delineator Magazine*, and Dependent Children: A Background Note on the Calling of the 1909 White House Conference." *Social Service Review* 32 (March 1958): 33-40.

Sarri, Rosemary. "Federal Policy Changes and the Feminization of Poverty." *Child Welfare* 64 (May/June 1985): 235-247.

Schacht, John N. "Four Men From Iowa." *The Palimpset* 63, no. 1 (1982): 4-11, 30-31.

Scharf, Lois. *To Work or to Wed: Female Employment, Feminism and the Great Depression.* Westport, Conn.: Greenwood Press, 1980.

Schell, Herbert S. *History of South Dakota.* Lincoln: University of Nebraska Press, 1975.

Schlesinger, Arthur, Jr. *The Age of Roosevelt.* Vol. 1, *The Crisis of the Old Order.* Vol. 2, *The Coming of the New Deal.* Vol. 3, *The Politics of Upheaval.* Boston: Houghton Mifflin, 1958-1960.

Schneider, A. Gregory. *The Way of the Cross Leads Home: The Domestication of American Methodism.* Bloomington: University of Indiana Press, 1993.

Schneider, David M., and Albert Deutsch. *The History of Public Welfare in New York State, 1867-1941.* Chicago: University of Chicago Press, 1941.

Schram, Sanford F. *Words of Welfare: The Poverty of Social Science and the Social Science of Poverty.* Minneapolis: University of Minnesota Press, 1995.

Schwartz, Bonnie Fox. *The Civil Works Administration, 1933-1934: the Business of Emergency Employment in the New Deal*. Princeton, N.J.: Princeton University Press, 1984.

Schwartz, Bonnie Fox. "New Deal Work Relief and Organized Labor: CWA and AFL Building Trades." *Labor History* 17, no. 1 (1976): 38-57.

Scott, Anne Firor. *Natural Allies: Women's Associations in American History*. Urbana: University of Illinois Press, 1991.

Scott, Anne Firor. "On Seeing and Not Seeing: A Case of Historical Invisibility." *Journal of American History* 71 (June 1984): 7-21.

Scott, Joan Wallach. "Gender: A Useful Category of Historical Analysis." *American Historical Review* 91 (December 1986): 1053-1075.

Scott, Joan Wallach. *Gender and the Politics of History*. New York: Columbia University Press, 1988.

Semmel, Bernard. The Methodist Revolution. New York: Basic Books, 1975.

Shapiro, Mary J. *Gateway to Liberty*. New York: Vintage Books, 1986.

Sharistanian, Janet, ed. *Gender, Ideology and Action: Historical Perspectives on Women's Public Lives*. Westport, Conn.: Greenwood Press, 1986.

Shaw, Albert. "Relief Measures in American Cities." *Review of Reviews* 9 (January 1894): 29-37.

Sherrick, Rebecca. "Private Visions, Public Lives: The Hull House Women in the Progressive Era." Ph. D. diss. Northwestern University, 1980.

Sherrick, Rebecca. "Their Fathers' Daughters: The Autobiographies of Jane Addams and Florence Kelley." *American Studies* 27 (spring 1986): 39-53.

Sherwood, Robert E. *Roosevelt and Hopkins: An Intimate History*. New York: Harper & Brothers, 1948.

Sidel, Ruth. *On Her Own: Growing Up in the Shadow of the American Dream*. New York: Viking Press, 1990.

Sidel, Ruth. *Women and Children Last: The Plight of Poor Women in Affluent America*. New York: Viking Press, 1986.

Simkhovitch, Mary. *The Settlement Primer*. Boston: Federation of Settlements, 1936.

Sitkoff, Harvard. *Fifty Years Later: The New Deal Reevaluated*. Philadelphia: Temple University Press, 1985.

Sitkoff, Harvard. *A New Deal for Blacks: The Emergence of Civil Rights as a National Issue, The Depression Decade*. New York: Oxford University Press, 1978.

Sitkoff, Harvard. *Fifty Years Later: The New Deal Reevaluated*. Philadelphia: Temple University Press, 1985.

Sklar, Kathryn Kish. "Hull House in the 1890s: A Community of Women Reformers." *Signs* 10 (Summer 1985): 657-677.

Skocpol, Theda. "America's First Social Security System: The Expansion of Benefits for Civil War Veterans." *Political Science Quarterly* 108 (Spring 1993): 60-91.

Skocpol, Theda. "Political Responses to Capitalist Crises: Neo-Marxist Theories and the Case of the New Deal." *Politics and Society* 10 (1980): 155.

Skocpol, Theda. *Protecting Soldiers and Mothers: The Political Origins of Social Policy in the United States*. Cambridge, Mass.: Belknap Press, 1992.

Skocpol, Theda. *States and Social Revolution*. New York: Cambridge University Press, 1979.

Skocpol, Theda, and Edwin Armenta. "States and Social Policy." *Annual Review of Sociology* 12 (1986):

Smith, Eve. "The Failure of the Destitute Mothers Bill: The Use of Political Power in Social Welfare." *Journal of Sociology and Social Welfare* 14, no. 2 (June 1987): 63-87.

Smith, Timothy L. *Revivalism and Social Reform in Mid-Nineteenth-Century America*. Nashville, Tenn.: Abingdon, 1957.

Smith-Rosenberg, Carroll. *Disorderly Conduct: Visions of Gender in Victorian America*. New York: Alfred A. Knopf, 1985.

Sproat, John. *The Best Men: Liberal Reformers in the Gilded Age*. New York: Oxford University Press, 1968.

Stadum, Beverly. *Poor Women and Their Families: Hard Working Charity Cases 1900-1930*. Albany: State University of New York Press, 1992.

Stark, Louis. "Labor on Relief and Insurance." *Survey* 65 (November 15, 1931): 186-187.

State of New York. *Report of the New York State Commission on relief for Widowed Mothers*. Albany, New York: J. B. Lyon Company, 1914.

Steiner, Edward A. *From Alien to Citizen: The Story of My Life in America*. New York: Fleming H. Revell Company, 1914.

Steiner, Edward A. "Christodora, 1897-1940: Tribute to a Great Personality." 1940, MS, unpaginated, Christodora Collection.

Steinson, Barbara J. *American Women's Activism in World War I*. New York: Garland Publishing, 1982.

Strong, Josiah. *The Next Great Awakening*. 8th ed. New York: Baker & Taylor, 1902.

Strong, Josiah. *Our Country*. New York: American Home Missionary Society, 1885.

Strong, Josiah. "The Problem of the City," in Paul H, Boase, ed. *The Rhetoric of Christian Socialism*. New York: Random House, 1969.

Swain, Martha. *Ellen Woodward: New Deal Advocate for Women*. Jackson: University of Mississippi Press, 1995.

Thelan, David P. *The New Citizen: The Origins of Progressivism in Wisconsin: 1885-1900*. Columbia: University of Missouri Press, 1972.

Tilly, Louise A., and Patricia Gurin. *Women, Politics, and Change*. New York: Russell Sage Foundation, 1990.

Tilly, Louise, and Joan Scott. *Women, Work, and Family*. New York: Holt, Reinhart and Winston, 1978.

Tobin, Eugene M. *Organize or Perish: America's Independent Progressives*. Westport, Conn.: Greenwood Press, 1987.

Tobin, Eugene M., and Michael H. Ebner, eds. *The Age of Urban Reform: A New Perspective on the Progressive Era*. Port Washington, NY: Kennikat Press, 1977.

Trattner, Walter. *From Poor Law to Welfare State: A history of Social Welfare in America*. 3rd ed. New York: The Free Press, 1984.

Trattner, Walter. "Theodore Roosevelt, Social Workers and the Election of 1912: A Note." *MidAmerica* 51, no. 1 (1968): 64-69.

Trohan, Walter, "White House Harry Hopkins--A Modern Rasputin," *Chicago Sunday Tribune*, August 9, 1943, Graphic Section, 1.

Trolander, Judith. *Professionalism and Social Change: From the Settlement House Movement to Neighborhood Centers, 1886 to the Present*. New York: Columbia University Press, 1987.

Trolander, Judith. "Response of Settlements to the Great Depression." *Social Work* 18, no. 5 (1973): 92-102.

Trolander, Judith. *Settlement Houses and the Great Depression*. Detroit: Wayne State University Press, 1975.

Tugwell, Rexford. *The Democratic Roosevelt*. New York: Doubleday, 1957.

Tugwell, Rexford. "The New Deal: The Progressive Tradition." *Western Political Quarterly* (1950): 390-427.

Vandenpol, Ann. "Dependent Children, Child Custody, and the Mothers' Pensions: The Transformation of the State-Family Relations in the Early 20th Century." *Social Problems* 29, no. 3 (February 1982): 221-235.

Vital Speeches of the Day. Vol. 1, no. 11 (March 15, 1939) New York: The City News Publishing Company, 1937-1975.

Wade, Louise C. "The Heritage From Chicago's Early Settlement Houses." *Journal of the Illinois Historical Society* 60 (1967): 411-141.

Walby, Sylvia. *Patriarchy at Work: Patriarchal and Capitalist Relations in Employment*. Minneapolis: University of Minnesota Press, 1986.

Wald, Lillian D. *The House on Henry Street*. New York: Dover Publications, 1915.

Walkowitz, Daniel J. "The Making of a Feminine Professional Identity: Social Workers in the 1920s." *American Historical Review* 95 (October 1990): 1051-1075

Walling, William. "What the People of the East Side Do." *University Settlement Studies* 1 (1903): 79-85.

Wandersee, Winifred. *Women, Work, and Family Values, 1920-1940*. Cambridge, Mass.: Harvard University Press, 1981.

Ware, Susan. *Beyond Suffrage: Women in the New Deal*. Cambridge, Mass.: Harvard University Press, 1981.

Ware, Susan. *Holding Their Own: American Women in 1930*. Boston: Twayne, 1982.

Ware, Susan. *Partner and I: Molly Dewson, Feminism and New Deal Politics*. New Haven, Conn.: Yale University Press, 1987.

Warner, Amos G. *American Charities*. New York: Crowell, 1894.

Weibe, Robert H. *Businessmen and Reform: A Study of the Progressive Movement*. Cambridge, Mass.: Harvard University Press, 1962.

Weir, Margaret, Anna Shola Orloff, and Theda Skocpol. *The Politics of Social Policy in the United States*. Princeton, N.J.: Princeton University Press, 1988.

Weisenfeld, Judith. "The More Abundant Life: The Harlem Branch of the New York City Young Women's Christian Association, 1905-1945." Ph. D. diss., Princeton University, 1992.

Welter, Barbara. "The Cult of True Womanhood 1820-1860." *American Quarterly* 18 (summer 1966): 151-174.

Welter, Barbara. *The Woman Question in American History*. Hinsdale, Ill.: The Dryden Press, 1973.

Wesser, Robert F. *A Response to Progressivism: The Democratic Party and New York Politics, 1902-1918*. New York: New York University Press, 1986.

Wetherford, Doris. *Foreign and Female*. New York: Shocken Books, 1986.

White, George Cary. "Social Settlements and Immigrant Neighbors." *Social Services Review* 33 (March 1959): 55-66.

White, Ronald C. *Liberty and Justice for All: Racial Reform and the Social Gospel (1877-1925)*. The Rauschenbusch Lectures. San Francisco: Harper & Row, 1990.

White, Ronald C., Jr., and C. Howard Hopkins. *The Social Gospel: Religion and Reform in Changing America*. Philadelphia: Temple University Press, 1976.

Williams, Edward Ainsworth. *Federal Aid for Relief*. New York: Columbia University Press, 1939.

Wills, Matthew B. *Wartime Missions of Harry L. Hopkins*. Raleigh, N.C.: Pentland Press, 1996.

Wilson, Joan Hoff. *Herbert Hoover: Forgotten Progressive*. Boston: Little, Brown, 1975.

Witte, Edwin E. *The Development of the Social Security Act*. Madison: University of Wisconsin Press, 1962.

Woloch, Nancy. *Women and the American Experience*. New York: Alfred A. Knopf, 1984.

Woods, Robert A. *The Poor in Great Cities*. New York: Arno Press, 1971. Originally published 1895.

Woods, Robert A. ed. *The City Wilderness: A Settlement Study be Residents and Associates of the South End House*, New York: Garrett Press, 1970. Originally published 1898.

Woods, Robert A., and Albert J. Kennedy. *Handbook of Settlements.* New York: Charity Publications Committee, 1911.

Wunderlin, Clarence E., Jr. *Visions of a New Industrial Order: Social Science and Labor Theory in America's Progressive Era.* New York: Columbia University Press, 1992.

Yellowitz, Irwin. *Labor and the Progressive Movement in New York State, 1897-1915.* Ithaca, N.Y.: Cornell University Press, 1965.

Zimmerman, Joan G. "College Culture in the Midwest, 1890-1930." Ph.D. diss., University of Virginia, 1978.

Zimmerman, Joan G. "Daughters of Main Street: Culture and the Female Community at Grinnell 1884-1917," in Mary Kelly, ed., *Woman's Being, Woman's Place: Female Identity and Vocation in American History.* Boston: G. K. Hall and Co., 1979.

Zinn, Howard, ed. *New Deal Thought.* New York: Bobbs-Merrill Company, 1966.

Zopf, Paul E. *American Women in Poverty.* New York: Greenwood Press, 1989.

Newspapers cited:

Brooklyn Eagle
Daily News Chronicle
Des Moines Register
Grinnell Herald
Grinnell Herald Register
Minneapolis Morning Tribune
New York Herald Tribune
New York Times
New York Tribune
Pittsburgh Evening Sun
Sioux City Journal
Washington Post

Index